ON LIVING LIFE WELL

Echoes of the Words of the Buddha
from the Theravāda Tradition

Edited by

John Ross Carter

Onalaska, WA, USA

PARIYATTI PRESS
an imprint of
Pariyatti Publishing
867 Larmon Road, Onalaska, WA 98570
www.pariyatti.org

ISBN: 978-1-928706-89-2 (Print)
ISBN: 978-1-928706-90-8 (Ebook)

Library of Congress Control Number: 2010938226

For

L.P.N. Perera

G.D. Wijayawardhana

Godwin Samararatna

Venerable Dhammarakkhita

Venerable Dhammavihāri

Venerable Paññāsīha Mahānāyaka

Who have walked in the footsteps of the Buddha
in Sri Lanka and who have gone on before.

PREFACE

For nearly four decades Colgate University has recognized the lasting educational value of extending the intellectual horizons of undergraduates by physically shifting the perspectives on those horizons through Study Abroad Programs, with a full semester of living and studying in another country, and Extended Courses, which have as a component a month's study tour in another country culminating in a course conducted on campus. Uniformly, students have celebrated the quality of their learning experiences in these programs, but one of the limitations discerned has been the difficulty of sharing more widely key aspects of those learning experiences. This volume is an attempt to do just that: to disseminate more widely through publication almost all of the talks given to students at Colgate and in Sri Lanka that formed an important dimension of three study tours, entered in Colgate catalogues as "Living in the Buddhist Heritage in Sri Lanka." The publication of talks provided by leading Japanese scholars[1] to American undergraduates, resulting from a successful study tour program in Japan, forms a companion piece to this volume.

Students, in almost all cases, completed a full semester course on the Theravāda Buddhist tradition with special reference to Sri Lanka before participating in this study tour. A few augmented this course with another taught in University Studies: Core Cultures—Sri Lanka, an interdisciplinary introduction to the country and culture of Sri Lanka. Both courses were offered by the editor, who served as program director. The first phase of the study tour was in the capital city of Colombo. The first scheduled activity upon arrival in Sri Lanka was a visit to a Buddhist temple

[1] *The Religious Heritage of Japan: Foundations for cross-cultural understanding in a religiously plural world,* edited by John Ross Carter, Portland, Oregon: Book East, 1999.

(*pansala*) to meet with distinguished monks (*bhikkhus*) and to observe the sincerity of expression apparent in talks and the piety demonstrated in worship. Visits were also made to the Kelaniya temple, on one occasion for a magnificent *perahera,* and also to the Temple of the Tooth (Dalada Maligawa), in Kandy. On one of the study tours, the students had the remarkable opportunity to "show compassion," (*karuṇākaranavā*) by climbing Śrī Pāda, participating in the exchange of memorized chants, while taking full advantage of visiting other pilgrimage sites. On each occasion trips were arranged for unhurried visits to what is known as "The Cultural Triangle": Anurādhapura, Mihintalē, with a visit to the Aukana Buddha image on the way to Polonnaruva, and stops at Sigiriyagala, Dambulla, and Aluvihāra, before arriving for the next phase of the study tour in Kandy. Complementing talks given to the students in Kandy were outings to the Botanical Gardens, to meditation sessions at Nilambe, to Gadaladeniya, Lankatillake, and Ambekke, to Watārama near Polgahawela, to an elephant orphanage in Pinnewala, to the Malwatte Chapter House for an *upasampadā* ceremony, and to the Asgiriya Chapter House, both chapters of the Siam Nikāya. After visiting a tea factory and a night in Nuwara Eliya, the students went on to Kataragama before arriving in Yala. The remaining few days were spent along the southwest coast in serious seminar presentations (8:00 a.m. – 12:00 noon) and serene sun bathing (thereafter) before returning to Colombo for delightful farewell parties.

Two different presentations were required of the students: one, a project report, and the other a more sustained seminar presentation. Both were drawn from their on-campus course work but developed differently during the study tour. The project report was begun on-campus and refined on-site in Sri Lanka. The seminar paper was the culmination of course work, conversation with the distinguished speakers in Sri Lanka, and reflection sustained over approximately five months. Examples of projects presented after dinner the evening before visiting the sites or observing the ceremonies were: "Anurādhapura," "On statues of the Buddha," "the Jetavana Stūpa," "On the Bodhi Tree," "Mihintalē," "Polonnaruva," "Gal Vihāra," "Poya," "*Pūja*: flowers, light, incense, sound," "the *Pirit* ceremony." Examples of seminar papers offered in focused seminar sessions were: "The Role of the *Saṅgha* in the Life of the Laity," "*Anattā* as a Religious Concept," "*Dukkha* as a Religious Concept," "The Significance of the Other," "On Dealing with Unanswered Questions," "The Buddha and the Christ," "Meditation and Prayer," "Why Aspire to Live the Religious Life?" "Where Does Transcendence Begin?" "What Does It Mean To Be Truly Human?" "In What Sense Are the Four Noble Truths True?" "Perfecting the Inner Self of a Social Being," among others.

It was not possible to have all speakers review all of their talks before this volume reached its final form. The original form of presentations has been maintained except for inserting the English plural "s" onto Pali, Sanskrit and Sinhala words rather than presenting the plural forms in those languages. Some editorial recasting was done to avoid repetitions and colloquialisms common in oral presentations and to establish some consistency for a published format: revising references from "the other day," or "yesterday," and the like, to "in the chapter entitled," or "in the talk by." Every effort was made to keep the questions and responses, a significant contribution of this volume, in the form and sequence in which the exchanges actually occurred.

Our scholars, academics and members of the *Saṅgha* have introduced us to a profound religious view that forms foundations for a way of life, manifested also in impressive religious practices and in Sri Lanka.

John Ross Carter

Hamilton, New York

ACKNOWLEDGMENTS

For a program that has given rise to remarkable educational experiences of young men and women, such as is reflected in the pages that follow, a special word of thanks is due first to those fifty or so young men and women, undergraduates of Colgate University, who, on three separate occasions, seriously pursued course work on campus and engaged in study-tours in Sri Lanka with intellectual keenness and interpersonal courtesy. Their faithfulness to their subject and to the program director will remain one of the most enduring memories to be carried into the future.

One expresses appreciation and also admiration for the colleagues who prepared and gave the talks presented here. In many cases they managed to do this at considerable inconvenience: in one case a colleague came down from Kandy to Colombo to speak with the students in response to a change in his schedule requiring that he be out of the country on the date originally set for his contribution. Noteworthy throughout, from contributions by academics, from representatives of the *Saṅgha,* from socially engaged institutions, and from our U.S. Ambassadors, a quality of authenticity rings true.

Behind the scenes of such programs there were very many men and women of Sri Lanka who contributed mightily to the success experienced. Particularly do the students and the editor remain indebted to Ms. Beeta Hegodagedeera and Ms. Malani Kadinappulige who traveled with us, introduced us to subtle dimensions of Buddhist piety and insight, both at Colgate where they served for a time as Coresident Supervisors of Chapel House and during the study-tours in Sri Lanka. Mr. Prasad Wijeweera (Alpine Toys Limited) worked patiently on the scene to corroborate

9

and reconfirm schedules and commitments established through airmail correspondence: talks, accommodations, transportation. His daughter, Nalini, was helpful to the students during a trip to the Cultural Triangle. Professor A.B. Dissanayake not only spoke to the group on three occasions but also traveled with us to share his truly wide-ranging knowledge about the great historical sites in the Cultural Triangle.

It was not possible to include all presentations in this volume. We are grateful to Professor J.B. Dissanayake who gave a brief talk to the students on Sinhala Buddhist culture. We were warmly received by the Vice-chancellors of Jayawardhenepura University and Kelaniya University. Professor Richard Gombrich very kindly came down from Oxford to Heathrow Airport to lead an engaging orientation session, during a layover, about perspectives on Buddhist thought and Buddhist practices in Sri Lanka. Some of our distinguished contributors spoke with the students both at Colgate and in Sri Lanka: Mahinda Palihawadana, G.D. Wijayawardhana, W.S. Karunatillake, Godwin Samanaratna and Lily de Silva. Learned *bhikkhus* signaled the importance of our venture. Venerables Piyatissa, Kemananda, and Ginaratana of the New York Buddhist Vihāra, offered *pirit* for us, with Dr. and Mrs. B. Sirisena at JFK airport upon our departures, and Venerable Gnanissara Nayaka Thera and others received us at the Gangaramaya Temple, Colombo, for a *pinkama*, an enhancing act of *pirit* chanting and other religious observances, upon our arrival. In the background, steadily supportive over many years, has been Mr. Albert Edirisinghe, sometime Royal Nepalese Consul General in Sri Lanka, and now Venerable Ganegama Devamitta. We note, too, Professor J.D. Dheerasekera, internationally known scholar of the *Vinaya,* who too has become a "son of the Buddha." We have been warmly received by Venerables Dhammarakkhita of Vidyalankara Pirivena, Paññāsīha Mahānāyaka Thera of the Mahāragāma Bhikkhu Training Center, Amanasiri and Dhammasara of Parama Dhamma Cetiya, Mt. Lavinia, and Pollamurē Sorata Thera at Gätembē.

We are grateful for the assistance provided by the United States Educational Foundation: Tissa Jayatilake, Executive Director at the time, and Duncan MacInnes and Bill Maurer, serving as Directors of the U.S. Information Service in Sri Lanka, and Mrs. Mary Jo Furgal, Colombo American Center Director. Facilities were made available for us in Colombo where some of the talks by professors, and those by our Ambassadors at the time, were given to the students.

M. Mazzahim Mohideen, then Director of Administration of Marga Institute, helped to arrange our visits there as did, initially, Paul Bischof, director of Lanka Jathika Sarvodaya Sangamaya (Inc.), for our visits to Sarvodaya. Myrtle Perera and the late Bogoda Premaratna contributed significantly to a roundtable discussion during one of our visits to Marga Institute.

Many families in Colombo opened their homes to the students for several days: Mr. and Mrs. Albert Edirisinghe, Mr. and Mrs. M. Samarakoon, Mr. and Mrs. D.L. Liyanasuria, Mr. and Mrs. Mithra Wetimuny, Mr. and Mrs. Gamini Edirisinghe, Mr. and Mrs. Alfred Edirisinghe, Mr. and Mrs. Susantha Karunaratne, Mr. Nalin de Silva, Mrs. Daya Nanayakkara, and Mr. and Mrs. Prasad Wijeweera. Mangala Samarakoon was particularly helpful in organizing these homestays. Christ Tomasides, a Colgate Alumnus in Sri Lanka at the time, and his wife received one of the student groups for a magnificent reception. The hospitality so evident on this occasion will be long remembered.

The preparation of this volume has gone through several stages over a number of years. As it is not difficult to imagine, the transcriptions from tape recordings of Sinhala Buddhist scholars speaking with a beautiful, but non-American, English accent, making frequent references to canonical Pali texts and utilizing Pali and Sanskrit vocabulary, and in some cases referring to Sinhala texts and words, necessitated that I undertake those transcriptions. Sandra, my wife, who has long known most of our lecturers, offered two initial transcriptions, and Mary Elizabeth, our daughter, who accompanied the undergraduates on one of the study-tours, provided a first transcription of one lecture. It was after I had acquired a dictation machine, start-stop pedal and earphones, that I finished a completely transcribed collection of the talks. Justin Henry, a former Colgate student who had at the time not visited Sri Lanka but now is conducting graduate studies in Theravāda, Sinhala and Tamil subjects, in the United

States and Sri Lanka, spent part of a summer going through the collection offering some helpful suggestions. Subsequently, after another editorial review was completed, Clara Lantz, the Administrative Assistant to the Director of Chapel House and of the Fund for the Study of the Great Religions, read through parts of the manuscript and provided constructive suggestions. Not being astute in the arts of word-processing systems, of fonts and diacritics, of WordPerfect with personalized "hot keys" and a personally improvised MSWord system of diacritics, I was led by Jeff Glenn into the distinct advantages of MSWord and the Unicode Times Ext Roman font, which enabled digital revision and electronic transmission of the final copy with its diacritics.

Now, after periodic disruptions over several years due to other academic research and year-round administrative duties, it has been my pleasant opportunity, in preparing this presentation of the talks for publication, to learn afresh from these scholars right alongside some American undergraduates. Errors that might remain in the text would be, of course, mine.

Without the cheerful participation of all of these persons mentioned here and the important financial support from the Fund for the Study of the Great Religions of Colgate University, the study-tours in Sri Lanka would not have been possible and this collection of talks would not have been recorded, preserved, transcribed, edited, and now made available as "On Living Life Well: Echoes of the Words of the Buddha from the Theravāda Tradition."

TABLE OF CONTENTS

INTRODUCTION

WHAT MUST I DO TO LIVE LIFE WELL?

John Ross Carter

We tend quickly to realize, when once we take the time to reflect thoroughly upon our day-to-day decisions and activities, that there is very little in our experiences in getting on in life that is inevitable. And so it has been for most of us who have participated in what we are coming to see is our global religious history. Just as we too become engaged in living our lives today—considering alternatives, discerning ramifications, gauging possible consequences and making decisions—so it has been for men and women of all ages who have had the good fortune, indeed in some cases the luxury, to seize an opportunity to evaluate their motives for action and to find wherein their behavior has been consistent with the persons they were discovering themselves in the process of becoming, while expressing responsibility to the community in which they were living and also to their posterity. Things change, persons in all divisions and disciplines in our universities agree. Religious traditions are no different. They have changed over the centuries in different cultures under different circumstances because men and women living at the time became engaged in differing degrees and in different ways with those traditions. Persons have made their contributions, have failed to rise to the level of their capability, or have soared to magnificent heights of human aspirations, have carelessly forgotten themes and insights, or have methodically set about to preserve the heritage that was and is theirs. In the study of the foundations for a quality of life that indicate what it might be like to become genuinely human, one does not lose sight, even for a moment, of the persons who are seeking for, or indicating the presence of, that quality of life. It is in learning of the thinking and responses of those persons that a student can perceive a dynamic interplay of self-evaluation in light of their received religious heritage and their focused aspirations in attempting to become more aligned with the insight of their religious heritage. Life would hardly be attractive were there to be no guidelines or pointers for how one might live life well. In the book of Acts of the Christian New Testament (Acts 16:30) the question is raised by a jailor to Paul and Silas: "Sirs, what must I do to be saved?" Christian writers have made much of this question, presenting it as the core, most profoundly consequential, question one could conceivably ask of oneself and about one's soteriological status. But there is an entirely comparable question, one that is even more comprehensively applicable to more men and women around the globe living within differing world views in different centuries: "What must I do to live life well?"

The jailor's question is surely profoundly personal and weighty and, depending upon one's orientation to questions related to salvation, of both individual and cosmic significance. But the other question with its use of the adverb "well" is poignantly unrestricted by individuality on the one hand and notions of the next life on the other. What does one do with the adverb? Of course one could ground the lexical meaning of the word solely on social norms and mores, that is, one who lives life well is one who is well received by persons with whom one lives. But the adverb is more dynamic than this. It presses the frame of reference beyond the local, and the individual and above the routine and customary, to the degree that the existential depths of the question become aligned with an awareness of the significance of life itself.

Our religious traditions speak to this question, "What must I do to live life well?", in different yet complementary ways. The Buddhist tradition was the world's first great religious movement that reached beyond cultural, linguistic, geographical boundaries and limitations, and it has continued impressively to do so today. The Buddhist tradition has achieved this distinction because men and women realized that by participating in this religious tradition they were able to discover how one might set about to live life well. And they did not want to hoard this wisdom but to share it freely as it had been shared with them. This tradition today is multifaceted in its considerable variety in languages, in scriptures, in rituals, in doctrinal formulations, in temple architecture, and in modes of lay and monastic involvement. Yet in all of these various strands, a focal point enabling one to begin to formulate a response to this question, "What must I do to live life well?", is the image of the Buddha, however appropriated over the centuries and in the life of one person from day to day.

Today, a person can pick up a book on "Buddhism" and painstakingly amass a great deal of information—there are a great number of books out there. One can draw general time lines for texts and thinkers. One can chart doctrinal developments, diverging and complementary views held by monks and laity, contrasting emphases presented by different sects in different countries; one can learn a good deal and control a great deal of information. But one will not gain an *understanding* of Buddhists, of persons, of those without whom what has rather recently come to be called "Buddhism" would not have been there in the first place, if one does not begin to consider what Buddhists have affirmed about living life well.

One of the oldest continuing movements within the complex and variegated Buddhist tradition, as it developed in and through Asia, is called the Theravāda, the way or position or school (*vāda*) of the elders, the seniors in the monastic order (*thera*). Although this school was well established centuries before the introduction of facets of the Buddhist tradition into Tibet and over a millennium prior to the introduction of a recognizably distinct school of Zen in Japan, many persons, if not most, in North America tend to take the Dalai Lama as *the* "spokesperson for Buddhism," and tend to equate Japanese Buddhism with Zen. Of course the Tibetan and Zen forms of the Buddhist heritage are impressive, but there is far more to the sweep and depth of the Buddhist cumulative tradition than represented by these two manifestations. There are many millions more men and women who are adherents of the Theravāda than of the Tibetan and Zen forms combined.

However, it is difficult to say that the Theravāda represents "pristine Buddhism," as some affirmed several decades ago, and a few might claim today. The Theravāda too has undergone change and development over the centuries and in the different cultural settings into which this tradition and the men and women who appropriated it moved, particularly early through India and subsequently into Sri Lanka (Ceylon), into Myanmar (Burma), Thailand (Siam), to some degree Cambodia and Laos and elsewhere in Southeast Asia, and more recently around the world. Although Theravāda Buddhists have spoken and continue to speak in many languages and dialects in these different settings, they have come to endorse for very nearly two thousand years canonical texts, in what was handed down orally for several centuries and has come to be called *Pāli*, which originally meant what was inscribed in rows as in writing, and now refers to the language of these texts. Today the Theravāda Buddhist tradition is based on the Pali texts. And to the degree that men and women who are Theravāda Buddhists have been enabled to find continuity in the way those texts communicate what has been held (revealed?) to be the teaching of the Buddha with their own aspirations to live life well, to the extent that these men and women have become enabled to find community with others focusing on a center of value disclosed in those texts, and to the depth that they have been led to the point of rediscovering salvific truth through those texts, those texts themselves are held as scripture.

The historical matrix of the Theravāda in interplay among distinctive cultures is fascinating, particularly regarding India, Sri Lanka, Myanmar and Thailand. Buddhist missionaries from India brought the supportive basis for righteous living (*Dhamma*) to Sri Lanka, and from this resplendent isle like-minded persons brought this truth to Myanmar and on to Thailand. During subsequent centuries, when historical circumstances in Sri Lanka required, Buddhist monks from Myanmar and Thailand revived the tradition in Sri Lanka, not without leaving traces there of this historical interplay.

An uninformed person might discard the Theravāda as being something like "navel gazing," sarcastically framing an interpretation of this religious tradition as exerting a drag on development toward what some call "modernization," as offering little that provides perspectives for engaging social, economic, and political issues. But activities launched and led by Buddhist men and women in Myanmar demonstrate quite the opposite: U Nu (1907–1995) served as the first Prime Minister of Myanmar and his secretary, U Thant (1909–1974), was appointed Ambassador to the United Nations, later becoming the third Secretary General of this important international organization. Aung San Suu Kyi (1945–), a contemporary proponent for democratic rule in her country, received the Nobel Peace Prize in 1991 and, in 2008, received an honorary Doctor of Letters degree (D. Litt.) *in absentia* from Colgate University. There are many more leading Buddhists in Myanmar who have been active in socio-economic and political issues. Television news reports have recently made clear the significant influence of the Buddhist monastic order (*saṅgha*) in taking to the streets in demonstrations.

In Thailand, Sulak Sivaraksa (1933–) has been a leader in what is called "Engaged Buddhism" both in Thailand and beyond. Also of particular note is Venerable Buddhadasa (1906–1993), one of the leading Buddhist interpreters of Buddhist thought and practice not at all limited to Thailand. And the examples could go on and on.

Turning to Sri Lanka, the focus of this volume, we see both the antiquity of the Theravāda in this culture and country, its development, and its relevance today. The Sinhala people represent overwhelmingly the largest ethnic group in Sri Lanka and of this group Buddhists comprise the overwhelming majority. The language spoken by these Sinhala people is called Sinhala. Again and again in the chapters that follow, we will learn how frequently, with ease and without affectation, our Sinhala Buddhist speakers draw upon their religious heritage to communicate the bases for their responses to life. Their doing so does not represent a peculiarly recent innovation among Sri Lankan Buddhists. At the Peace Conference held in San Francisco in 1951, J.R. Jayawardene, a Prime Minister of Sri Lanka, spoke to the issue of whether to hold Japan to war reparations. He chose to quote a verse from one of the key scriptures of the Theravāda tradition, which can be translated as follows:

Not by enmity are enmities quelled,
Whatever the occasion here.
By the absence of enmity are they quelled.
This is an ancient truth.[2]

In the pages that follow, laypersons will offer their interpretations of the relevance of Theravāda thought to personal composure and constructive communal living. Members of the monastic order too will indicate their awareness of the symbiotic relationship between the lay and monastic communities contributing, ideally, to social well-being. Within one volume we will learn the fundamental Theravāda Buddhist teachings, find their relevance to psychological well-being, learn how they form the basis for ethics, discern how they reflect the role of women, note lay religious practices, catch a glimpse of the centrality of meditation, listen to monks who speak from within the Buddhist monastic experience, understand important dimensions of the historical development of the Theravāda tradition in Sri Lanka, its patterns of formation and a way in which it can respond constructively to our global human foibles. And all of this is presented by internationally known Sinhala Theravāda Buddhists.

A person seeking to "get a handle on Buddhism," looking for the "doctrinal formulations of Buddhism," might say that the presentations in this volume are repetitious; the same formulae are represented by the several scholars. But a close reading by one seeking to understand Buddhists will find the significance of what our scholars have done with these central

---

[2] Jayawardene caught the point of this verse and his stating it clearly has not been forgotten by leading members of the Japanese government in their special relationship with Sri Lanka. No doubt Jayawardene was fully aware of the old commentary on this passage which reads "One who reviles the reviler, one who strikes back at the striker, is not able to pacify hatred with hatred. On the contrary, one [thereby] creates more hatred still. Thus, at no time whatever are enmities calmed through enmity—they only increase [thereby]." And the commentary continues, "Enmities are extinguished and pacified and they cease to be, by means of the absence of enmity, by the [clear] water of patience . . . and loving-kindness . . . and also by proper attentiveness." *The Dhammapada: A New English Translation with the Pali Text and the First English Translation of the Commentary's Explanation of the Verses with Notes Translated from Sinhala Sources and Critical Textual Comments*, by John Ross Carter and Mahinda Palihawadana, New York: Oxford University Press, 1988, v. 5, pp. 13, 95-96.

Buddhist affirmations. The former approach would be as though one surveyed a number of paintings and would note only how frequently the colors red and blue are utilized over and over again without noticing the way these colors and others are blended to present different perspectives. Strands of a common matrix are being drawn upon in this book to present magnificently variegated and complementary views of creative responses to the human predicament.

In order to catch this interplay of a living religious tradition springing forth ever afresh in the contemporary responses of Sinhala Buddhist men and women in Sri Lanka, we have to gain grounding in the basic world view sustained in that tradition and forming foundations for a way of life today. Six premier academics and one *bhikkhu*, a member of the monastic community, who was himself formerly an esteemed professor, will lead us into our consideration of these foundations. These internationally known scholars demonstrate the seriousness of living, the importance of our intentions in acting (*kamma*) in our life context, which is marked by three characteristics (*tilakkhaṇa*): being impermanent (*anicca*), awry (*dukkha*), and insubstantial (*anattā*). Recognizing the pervasiveness of a causal sequence explaining how all things have come to be and how they might become altered, refreshingly, soteriologically, our teachers present the relevance of salvific truth to living life well as communicated in the Four Noble Truths. This leads a person to find the uplifting quality of virtuous living, of awareness, of the liberating freedom available to all men and women.

These ideas relate in every case to the formation of a wholesome mind and of a moral person, neither of which requires isolation but can be openly expressed in one's ethical living and commitment to others. By considering wherein persons might sense that they have lived inadequately, one learns wherein their values truly lie. Once the foundations for a way of life that enables one to live life well are set out, we turn to a consideration of what Buddhists do, how beliefs help set the context for practice and how practice continues because of its supportive efficacy.

In the third section of this volume, we turn to consider particularly the case of the Buddhist tradition in Sri Lanka with succinct presentations about the formation of Sinhala Buddhist self-understanding, and of our own human foibles and detrimental propensities. And we learn of a rich literary heritage discussed by one of the great scholars of Sinhala literature.

In the Appendices, we sit at the feet of *bhikkhus*, as it were, to learn of the energy and vision related to a monastic training center and of the committed life of an extraordinary monk-counselor. Sri Lanka is on the move; it boasts one of the most vibrant intellectual centers devoted to development studies (Marga) anywhere in the world, and at the same time it has nurtured a quiet, well-run internationally known center that enables people to give the gift of labor in uplifting others (Sarvodaya). Our introductory survey closes with two former United States Ambassadors speaking candidly about Sri Lanka, its accomplishments and its challenges, which, of course, immediately involve the lives of men and women who are Buddhists.

These are not "armchair lectures," quietly hammered out in isolation by pedantic authors interested in narrow academic pursuits and peculiar problems, isolated in ivory towers. These talks were given, offered, by Sinhala Buddhists, men and women, monks and laypersons, to American undergraduate students in a live face-to-face situation. The questions and responses that appear in this book give evidence to the seriousness of the give-and-take of ideas, their importance in helping one to come to understand another and to gain a deeper understanding of oneself, which is part of what is required in one's attempt to live life well.

I

FOUNDATIONS FOR A WAY OF LIFE

Theravāda Buddhists have long affirmed that the way one chooses to live one's life and the intentions with which one acts are of enormous consequence. Carefully formulating those choices and thoroughly reflecting upon those intentions can enable one to become aware not only about oneself, but also of one's relation with others and of one's responses to the world-at-large as it has come to be. The Theravāda tradition provides foundational perspective and constructive guidance for men and women who seek more than species-living by living freely and wisely, by being genuinely human. For centuries men and women in Sri Lanka have found that there is a way to live a life entirely meaningful.

CHAPTER I

OUR ACTIONS (*KAMMA*)

G.D. Wijayawardhana

The late Professor G.D. Wijayawardhana, former holder of the most prestigious chair in Sinhala literature, at the University of Colombo, leads us into our consideration of what one must do to live life well. One begins by carefully considering one's actions, being keenly aware of one's intention and conscious of likely consequences. We learn that action, when understood this way, refers to "volitional acts of moral significance which find expression in thought, speech, and physical deeds . . . ." With this insight into the significance of action, the talks begin.

The matter of *kamma* is very central in Buddhist thought. Most readers will have read something in English on this subject. I want to address this topic more from the point of view of a practicing Buddhist. So the considerations might not be so philosophical, but they represent the point of view of an ordinary Buddhist.

The word *kamma* is the Pali form, but we in Sri Lanka are more accustomed to the Sanskrit form, *karma*, since we have a tendency to use the Sanskrit forms in our Sinhala texts. For our purposes, the two forms are identical in meaning. The word *karma* means "action." Since action can be of so many kinds, the word would have many meanings. For example, *karma* could mean an occupation that a person is pursuing. It could be any social function or duty, even religious duties, expected of a person. In the *Pali Text Society's Pali-English Dictionary*,[3] there is a very long entry on *kamma* with numerous meanings offered for the word.

In this chapter we will not be so concerned with all the different meanings, but will concentrate on its more technical meaning of moral action which would bring on some effect (P. *vipāka*) either beneficial or nonbeneficial, either now or in a future birth. It would be best to leave the word *karma* untranslated, keeping in mind the technical sense in which we are using it.

The concept of *karma* is not confined to Buddhism alone. It was part and parcel of the religious traditions in the Buddha's day and also remains an important concept in the religious traditions of India today. Brahmanism and the Sanskrit *Upaniṣads*, Jainism, even the Sikh religion all share with Buddhism the concept of *karma* as moral action leading to results in one's present life or future lives. So *karma* was part of the common tradition which Buddhism acquired from the religious milieu of the time. Although *karma*, as it is understood in Buddhism today, is basically similar to the idea in other traditions, there are differences in the way it is presented. This makes the Buddhist understanding of *karma* unique.

Any moral action could be *karma*, but there is another aspect to it. It should be *volitional*—it should be an act done with definite intention. It is not ordinary action that one does, like driving a car down to the city. Such activity is a *karma*, but such activity has no question of morality involved. Similarly, if one accidentally treads upon a beetle and kills it, although technically an action, it does not come within the sphere of *karma* as we are considering it because the action was not the result of volition. *Karma* is a moralistic action that is volitional and is committed with a definite intention in mind.

There is a basic division in the notion of *karma*. *Karma* could be morally desirable, and as such it is called, in Pali, *kusala kamma*, "wholesome *kamma*," and includes all action

---

[3] *The Pali Text Society's Pali-English Dictionary*, edited by T.W. Rhys Davids and William Stede, London: Published for the Pali Text Society by Luzac & Company, Ltd., 1966.

that is conducive to beneficial or wholesome results. And there is *akusala kamma*, actions that are undesirable, not wholesome, and will lead to undesirable consequences. For example, an act of harming a person or slandering a person would be *akusala kamma*, an action leading to an undesirable effect. Whereas listening to the preaching of *dhamma* or looking after your elders or giving alms would be *kusala kamma*.

There is another category that is called *avyākata kamma*, meaning action that is not explained, action that is not defined. In this category are those actions that are neither wholesome nor unwholesome, neither moral nor immoral. Although the Buddha in his teachings presented this category of *kamma* for our consideration, at the moment it really does not matter.

Cetanā is a Pali term for this volition that prompts *kamma*. *Cetanā* can be translated as "one's will" or "one's desire." Actually the Buddha has placed so much emphasis on this *cetanā* which stands behind *karma* that he has gone to the extent of saying, "I call *cetanā karma*," which means that fundamentally it is the volition behind it that would make an act good or bad.

For an act of *kamma* to be complete it should have volition behind it. If we consider killing, the texts give several prerequisites that should be completed for an act of killing to be an act of *karma*. One has to know that what is being killed is a sentient being. Then one has to make a definite effort to kill from one's own volition. And the texts continue the elaboration.

Kamma could be performed in various ways. There could be physical *kamma*, that is, an action of killing or stealing and so forth. These are bodily actions and are called *kāya kamma*, physical volitional action. Looking after one's aged parents would be a *kāya kusala kamma*. Killing an animal, say, would be a *kāya akusala kamma*. There are actions performed through words, verbal actions, called *vacī kamma*. For example, when a monk is preaching he is performing an act of *vacī kamma*. If one is stating a falsehood with the intention of harming or slandering someone, one is performing a *vacī kamma* that is *akusala*. The next process, the third, is mental *kamma*, *mano kamma*, an action completed by the mind. An example would be meditation, *bhāvanā*, a wholesome act of *mano kamma*. An action that is confined to the mind and does not involve the body or speech remains an action, *kamma*. What motivates *karma*? Three things: greed or craving (*lobha*), hate or animosity (*dosa*), delusion or lack of proper understanding (*moha*). These are the three motivating factors for *akusala kamma*.

Kamma means, therefore, volitional acts of moral significance which find expression in thought, speech, and physical deeds, and which are either desirable or undesirable, and which give results either immediately or in some stage of your cycle of existence. According to one's *karma,* it is said, a person fares in this cycle of existence, born as a being in a fortunate existence as in a heavenly world, or in an unfortunate existence in a state of suffering as in a life of an animal, or born as an intelligent or unintelligent being. Having a sickly disposition and the like are determined because of one's past *karma* at conception and even more so at the moment of one's death when one is leaving this life. Sometimes a person who has given himself to a life of unwholesome deeds, if he has committed some wholesome act in his lifetime and he can recall it and it appears in his mental processes at the time of his passing away, it is said that such would be conducive to his being born in a comfortable state. What really matters most is what enters your mental processes at the time of passing away.

Buddhism holds that the very continuance of one's existence in the cycle of birth, death and rebirth, which goes on for innumerable years, is due to *karma*. Individuals, including the Buddha himself before he was born in his last birth, have to go through many rebirths in the cycle of *saṃsāra*. So long as one's karmic force remains active, is not stopped by higher attainments or the realization of Nibbāna, one continues in various stages of samsaric existence.

Karma would affect you in many ways. It can even modify character in this world, this very life itself. Whatever you do could help to modify your character in this life without having to await a next life. Or *karma* could, of course, lead to results in another existence. There are certain actions the fruits of which are experienced in this existence, in this very life itself (*diṭṭhe-dhamma-vedaniya*). There are numerous instances in stories in the texts where people experience the fruits of their good or bad actions in that very existence without waiting for their fruitions in a future life. An act of *dāna*, an act of giving, which you perform while you yourself are in grave need, when you yourself are hungry and in need of food—but you have the magnanimity to give food to the Buddha or to an Arahant—sometimes that kind of action with the thought of sacrifice, and the sincere feeling that you have, could produce results in this very life, and thus might modify your future career. So even though you are destined to be a particular kind of person by the karmic force from your past birth, some wholesome act that you have performed in this life could change the whole course of events and then lead you to a better existence, a better disposition, a better character.

There are other *karmas* that would give fruition only in your next existence or not at all, that is, not further along in the samsaric process. There is a third kind of action which could produce an effect any time during your existence in *saṃsāra*. One cannot anticipate exactly when it would arise to lead one to a worse or better state. There is a fourth category which is sometimes cancelled out. Although you have accumulated consequences of previous actions, there are other extraneous factors which intervene in the course of your life that do not bear any fruition but simply are cancelled out at a certain stage of your existence because of the force of other actions that you have performed.

There is a very interesting example in the story of Aṅgulimāla, mentioned in Buddhist texts, which is very well known in the Theravāda Buddhist tradition. Aṅgulimāla was a highwayman who killed so many people that he even lost count of the number. Being a very bright pupil, as a child he had gone to study under a certain teacher, who became aware that Aṅgulimāla would surpass him some day. He became jealous of his pupil's performance and thought of a ruse to get him killed. So he said to his pupil that the benefits of his learning would not arise unless he killed a thousand people. The teacher thought that in the course of attempting to kill that many people Agulimāla would himself get killed. Goaded by this vicious thought, Aṅgulimāla began and continued killing people. He killed more than a thousand. However, because of the latent karmic force that destined him someday to meet the Buddha, to listen to his teaching and to become an Arahant in that very life, it so happened that while killing people, he came within the Buddha's vision and the Buddha decided to pay him a visit. The Buddha preached *dhamma* to him and Agulimāla became an Arahant and realized Nibbāna. Thus he brought an end to his existence in this life cycle.

Although it is a very serious action to kill a living being, for Aṅgulimāla, even though he had killed thousands of human beings, the whole karmic process of killing did not take effect because of his previous karmic energy. He was able to realize Nibbāna and thus this activity of killing was cancelled out and had no further unwholesome effect on him. There is, then, this body of *karma* which, due to various extraneous factors that influence it, could just exhaust itself without giving any kind of fruition. With regard to these categories, therefore, an act either has to bear fruition in the period specified or not at all.

Karma also has intensity. Some *karma* is very strong and would certainly lead to good or bad results. These are called *garuka*, "heavy," *karma*, either good or bad. Such action has more potential to bear fruit at a certain stage. For example, an act of killing one's mother or father is a very serious *karma* which will definitely yield serious consequences in the next birth. It might not necessarily yield detrimental consequences in one's present life. One might be happy to inherit one's father's property by killing him. But certainly, in one's next birth one is going to pay for it. The consequences of these heavy *karma*s one cannot escape.

There are other *karma*s which one has been practicing over a long period of time. Going to the temple, listening to *baṇa* preaching, paying homage to the Buddha, and doing this over a long period of time so that it becomes one's second nature—this kind of *karma* also has its special specificity in bearing fruition. For example, a person on his deathbed has a tendency to bring into the mental faculties this *karma* that he or she has been practicing over long years and this will be conducive to his or her being born in a better state in his or her next birth. The action of practicing a particular set of *karma*, whether wholesome or unwholesome, over a long period of time so that it becomes second nature, has a very strong force of its own.

There is another kind of *karma* which one performs nearer the moment of death, which would stick in one's mind, which would recur in one's mind, which one would find hard to forget. That kind of action would also have a special effect as a contributing factor in determining one's future existence, because there is a likelihood of remembering it at the moment that one is leaving this world. So a wholesome *karma* on this occasion would certainly lead to a conception and birth in a favorable state.

Once again, there could be so many actions, *karmas*, that do not belong specifically to any of these categories but one simply acts and at some point or other there is the fruition. So, we believe that our life in *saṃsāra*, whether we are to be born an endless number of times in *saṃsāra*, or whether our samsaric existence which is, of course, suffering is going to be terminated soon, or whether we are being born in a favorable existence, all this is conditioned by our karmic energy or the way we have acted in this life and in previous existences.

This brings us to a very central problem in this whole view of *karma* which has been raised time and again and discussed through and through. That is whether *karma* in Buddhism is a fatalistic force, whether one can escape from it. If you have done good or bad deeds in the past, will retribution follow in any case? Do we have any control over it? Is there no personal effect that one can exert upon it? Whether one likes it or not, regardless of how one might strive to act against it, is it going to lead one to what one is destined for— in short is this whole idea of *karma* a fatalistic phenomenon from which one has no escape?

This was a question to which people have applied their minds in almost all religions of India. Most of the religions during the Buddha's time had something or other to say about this problem. For example, Jainism holds that *karma* is more or less an inevitable force that one must expiate at some stage. So if one is to escape the evils of *karma* one would have to undergo some mortification so that expiation is achieved. Without that the process would go on. The only escape was by means of undergoing rigorous penance because the *karma* has to yield its effect one way or other. In order to escape its effect in a future birth the only thing one could do would have to be voluntary, to subject yourself to intense self-mortification. Therefore through one's own conscious will one tries to get past some of these bad effects. Jainism preaches that the consequences of *karma* are inevitable; you will have it one way or the other. Of course they say that expiation is possible by means of voluntary self-mortification which would lead to some kind of escape, but it is really the hard way.

On the other hand, the Ājīvakas, another ascetic sect existent at that time, strictly believed that *karma* has its consequences, whether one likes it or not. And the only way to recover from its effects is to go through endless life cycles in *saṃsāra* and suffer for one's *karma* so that eventually the effects of all these *karmas* will be exhausted, and only then will one be able to find some kind of relief. There is expiration here through nearly endless cycles of life in *saṃsāra*. Perhaps one might refrain from accumulating bad *karma*, but for what you have accumulated there is no solution other than going through the consequences in innumerable existences of life.

Of course the Buddha's view was quite different. He recognizes that *karma* is a force, that *karma* would certainly have the tendency that gives some result, bad or good. But the Buddha does not say that it is invariably so. There are many other factors that could influence the course of this fruition, which could lessen the force of *karma,* or which could totally destroy this karmic force. For example, in terms of intensity *karmas* differ. So an intense *karma* would supersede whatever lesser *karmas* one may have committed. Now, if at the time of birth one recollects an intense *karma* of a heavy nature that one has committed, it would override some minor *karma* which one has accumulated in previous existences. That would have precedence over others. And apart from everything, in one's final birth, as in the case of Agulimāla, if one happens to reach the state of Arahant, whatever previous *karma* one has accumulated would be cancelled, that is, will not come to fruition. The Buddha, in a similar way, mentioned several forces that would act as either a supportive factor or an obstructive factor to whatever *karma* one has committed, so that the effect of a particular *karma* becomes intensified or totally cancelled.

CHAPTER II

THE THREE CHARACTERISTICS (*TILAKKHAṆA*)

Mahinda Palihawadana

Professor Mahinda Palihawadana, distinguished Professor of Sanskrit emeritus of the University of Sri Jayewardenepura (formerly Vidyodaya University), demonstrates dimensions of the Buddha's brilliant teaching effectiveness in helping one to understand the context in which one perceives, considers, and responds in speech, thought, and deeds. The starting point is to free the mind from preoccupying projections so that one can see things as they really are in the process of becoming: impermanent, awry, and insubstantial.

In this chapter, we turn to a subject frequently discussed in the Theravāda tradition: *tilakkhaṇa*, "the three [*ti*] characteristics [*lakkhaṇa*]." The word refers to the three aspects of phenomena which are invariably found in all phenomena with one exception —Nibbāna. *Tilakkhaṇa*, then, are the three characteristics of everything else.

In the literature of the Theravāda tradition, one often finds phrasing such as "the three" this and "the four" that and "the five" that, and so forth. In a sense this obscures the dynamic nature of the Buddha's teaching because, if one has the "threes" and "fours" and "fives," then one has sort of fixed categories. But I think that the strength of the Buddha's teaching was something rather different. First, then, I would like to address that and consider the salient feature of the Buddha's teachings as I see it. Or, I might say, what would be an appropriate way to introduce the teachings of the Buddha? What would be a single word, for example, that might tell us something about the Buddha, the religious teacher?

The Buddha was one who never took anything for granted. When we think of his life, of the way he was brought up and the way he reacted to the immediate environment, the way he refused to just go along with what generally were the current opinions—all of that tells us something very important about the Buddha. He was one who took a good hard look at whatever was given, even at the religious teachings advanced by the experts of the time.

The religious teachings that were current in India in and around Kapilavāstu, where he lived, were broadly of two kinds, as we can see from the Pali literature. One notion, regarded as an essential teaching and as the bedrock of the religous life, was that of a permanent self—an unchanging entity that remains constant through life and then at death also remains to take on a new birth—an unchangeable component in the human personality, or as Rune Johansson put it, "something with which we identify ourselves, which we take seriously, attach ourselves to, remember and build upon." Johansson, who has written a very nice book on the dynamic psychology of early Buddhism,[4] says it would seem that the doctrine of a self prevalent at the time of the Buddha, and criticized by him, was a combination of several conflicting ideas based on typical human ambition. The real self must be a permanent, undying essence and must have characteristics like perfection, happiness, and unrestricted power. Since everyday reality evidently does not correspond to this ambition, man is forced to assume a hidden agent within which he is as pure, eternal, and powerful as he wants to be. This is one teaching which took for granted a certain unchanging self.

The other teaching denied this. Death is the end. The first teaching is generally called "the eternalist teaching," or *sassatavāda*. There are many shades of this teaching, but for our purposes I am focusing on only one kind of this eternalist

---

[4] See Rune E. A. Johansson, *The Dynamic Psychology of Early Buddhism*, "Scandinavian Institute of Asian Studies Monograph Series," No. 37, London: Curzon Press, 1985 (new impression of the work first published in 1979).

teaching (*sassatavāda*). The other teaching, the one that says that death is the end and there is nothing more is called *ucchedavāda*. *Sassata*, in Pali, means "eternal," *uccheda* is "cutting off or breaking off, destruction," and *vāda* means "theory or teaching."

The Buddha, when he was faced with this kind of teaching, either the one or the other, questioned those teachings. Now why did he question them? He could not accept the notion of permanence, so he questioned the eternalist position. He, as a teacher, was more than anything else a creative critic of the notions that his audience assumed. Naturally his listeners already had many preconceptions and assumptions regarding the subject of discussion or about the person they came to hear. The general approach of the Buddha was to begin with these preconceived ideas assumed by his audience and then question them. After an exposition he would ask the audience, "What do you think?" Because one of his main concerns was to disabuse the minds of his audience, to make those minds active and ready to question anything, it is better to say that he could not accept the notion of permanence (*niccatā*), rather than to say that he tried to inculcate the teaching of impermanence (*anicca*). It is more important from the Buddha's point of view to remove the notion of permanence that people had rather than to introduce another notion of impermanence. This is the opposite of the procedure that one finds generally adopted in the Pali literature. In the literature we are told that the Buddha taught the three characteristics. That is something positive—he taught something. But what I am saying is that first he demolishes what was being taught. So it is reasonable to assume that the notion of the three characteristics is a distillation stemming from the Buddha's critique of the notions of permanence and their logical consequences. One of his main concerns was to disabuse the preconceptions and preoccupations in the minds of his audience.

While the Buddha was living it appears that he set about his task chiefly as a critic of the prevailing notions, ideas, and concepts. But once he disappeared, after his death, evidently there must have been a lot of thinking and the disciples sat down and composed a body of doctrines. In this body of their doctrines we have the notion of "the three this" and "the four that" and "the five that"—the three characteristics, the four noble truths, the five hindrances, the six bases of perception, the seven factors of enlightenment, the eightfold path, the nine transcendent *dhamma*s, and so forth and so on. This habit of introducing the teaching by numbers is very common, it is almost a characteristic feature of Theravāda. This can be a bit misleading. It all came about, as I suggested, because after the death of the Buddha the necessity was felt of giving a definite shape to the teaching.

It seems somewhat cruel to go to a teaching which was very timely and which sought to address the minds of people having their own difficulties, and to remove those difficulties from those minds—to make everything clear. As a matter of fact, what was important at the early stage of the Buddha's teaching was to make the mind *free* of the various notions with which it was preoccupied. But latterly, almost the very opposite of that procedure takes place.

The first characteristic is *anicca*. The word *nicca* means "permanent." In Pali, "*a-*" means the opposite, so *anicca* means "impermanent." The second characteristic is *dukkha*, which means "sorrow, suffering." The third is *anattā*. Here, also, is "*a(n)-*" plus *atta*. *Atta* is the word for "self." *Anattā* is the opposite of *atta* and means "no self." In introducing the teachings, people would say that *Buddhadhamma* teaches that all phenomena are characterized by these three characteristics. There is no permanence; there is always *dukkha*, sorrow, an ever-present factor; and there is no permanent self. That is the meaning of "the three characteristics."

We will turn to some translations of passages in the Pali literature in which these ideas are expressed. In fact, these passages are found throughout the canon. Although the three characteristics are presented as (1) *anicca*, (2) *dukkha,* and (3) *anattā*, in order of importance, perhaps the third is more important than the other two. As we will see, these three are all interconnected. The argument usually follows from (1) to (2) and from (2) to (3). In the *Saṃyuttanikāya* occurs this passage: "All is impermanent. What is the 'all' that is impermanent? The eye is impermanent, forms are impermanent, eye-consciousness is impermanent"—eye contact, that is, contact with the eye—"whatever is felt as pleasant, painful, or neither painful nor pleasant, born of eye-contact is impermanent." The same formula continues. This formulaic structure is characteristic of sayings found in the Pali canon. There are good reasons for this, of course, because these texts were meant to be learned by heart. The written word was not common. One tended to hear and to remember. So the more repetitions there were, the easier it was to remember. That explains the rather repetitive nature of the Pali texts. So it is with the ear and with all the six sense organs, including the nose, the tongue, the whole body, and finally the mind.

This passage tells us the things to which the description "impermanent" can be applied. This is very significant. What, in fact, do we have here in this passage? All that you see, all that you hear, all that you touch, all that you can smell, taste with your tongue, and all that you can think with the mind, all are impermanent. In some passages, the Buddha asked the question, "What is all (*sabba*)?" And he answered: what you can see with your eye, what you can hear with your ear, smell with your nose, and so on. Why is that important? Once you say "all that," the entire world is included, the phenomenal world, the world that can be perceived with your senses, and also all that upon which you can think. So, if you have something abstract, of which you can make concepts, even that is included because the mind is included. Sometimes the Buddha says, "this is the world." Replying to the question "What is the world?" the Buddha said "what you can perceive with your senses and what you can think with your mind." That is to say, he is not speaking of a world that is not perceived. It is the world to which you react, with which you are interacting with your senses. In other words, there is no world which you do not see, or you do not perceive such a world in any other way. Persons aware of what is going on in modern physics might find that to be a remarkably interesting statement, one that was made twenty-five centuries ago. As the Buddha goes step by step you see the argument being employed, the reason that is behind the idea—that all this is *anicca*, impermanent.

We might ask, "Is this really true?" Is what you see with the eye impermanent? Well, of course, you know that, if we look at an organism, a living thing, and you look at it again three years later, it will have changed a lot. But if you see it between two moments, you might not see the change. But since it does change over long periods of time, obviously then it changes all the time. By simple perception you can deduce the fact that there is change always.

Then it is argued that what is impermanent is suffering. If things are changing all the time, then that cannot be something that gives us happiness. And if there is suffering, sorrow, then the Buddha says there cannot be "self." Let's examine this argument. It is often said that if the body were the ego, then the body would not become ill. And one could say about the body, "may my body become such." What does it mean to say that a thing is "self" if you do not have control over it? If you have control over it surely you would not like the body to fall ill. The fact of illness is one argument that is often adduced. This same procedure is taken for perception, for feeling, for impressions, and for everything. That is to say, if your perceptions constitute the self then you should be able to say "I will have this kind of perception." But perception differs in terms of what is presented to it, what it sees—you may see something pleasant, something unpleasant. You cannot help it. You do not have control over it. Perception cannot be self. The body cannot be self. In this way, all possibilities are examined and in every possibility are found the two factors of impermanence, changeability (*anicca*), and also of suffering (*dukkha*).

What we really posses can be changed according to our wishes. But we, as Johansson puts it, have only impersonal processes and what is impersonal cannot be possessed. And there is no possessor. If you cannot possess, then there is no point of talking about a possessor. If you take the human personality and examine its various component elements, you cannot speak of any thing permanent, anything that can be called the possessor.

One canonical passage presents a discourse on the characteristic of "no self." Again we have the repetitions. The passage begins, "*Bhikkhus*, material form is not self." Then there follows six things that are separately taken up and discussed. The first is material form (*rūpa*). Generally *rūpa* is understood to be the physical body. That is not self. If material form were self this material form would not lead to affliction. If it is self, you would not want it to lead to misery. If you could say, "Let my material form be thus," this would mean that you could really dictate to it. But you do not have that control over it. And since you do not have control over it, it is pointless to call it self. In fact, material form leads to affliction.

The second is "feeling" (*vedanā*). You see an object. First of all you have an impression. And immediately after the impression, you have some reaction to it, maybe biological, which is instantaneous—either pleasant sensation or unpleasant. That is *vedanā*—that first reaction. About that you can say the same thing. You cannot dictate to it, you cannot have it the way you like. It will give a particular sensation, whether pleasant or not. You cannot help it. You have no power over it.

The next is perception (*saññā*). Now, you saw something and there was a pleasant or unpleasant sensation, and then you recognize it and you call it something: it is a piece of chalk. That stage at which the mind gives a name is *saññā*, when the mind has perceived something and has put it into its register. The same thing can be said about that: there is no control over it. You cannot give it any other name than the name that it has.

Next, formations (*saṅkhāra*) are not self. What are these? First we had the material, in this case the eye. The eye sees and then there is a sensation, and then a naming, and then there are the *saṅkhāra*, often translated "formations." That is one of the most difficult notions or conceptions in the Theravāda tradition.

Next is *viññāna*, normally translated "consciousness." This, again, is a controversial term. Actually, these four—*vedanā*, *saññā, viññāna, saṅkhāra*—are all psychological, or they belong to the inner world, whereas *rūpa* is physical. The four constitute the various aspects of inner experience; it's all mind. Now *viññāna* is a general term for all that is mental. But also it is a specific term for the first impression.

Once you have all these three—(1) first impression, (2) the first emotive reaction, the liking and the disliking, the pleasant and the unpleasant, (3) the recognition, you put it into the conceptual frame—all other mental phenomena would be *saṅkhāra.* What are those? When we examine our inner life, we will find that perceiving, feeling, and conceptualizing—not everything, though that is a lot—we also react, we have "gut reactions." You see something and you either want to smash it or you want to capture it. There are strong emotions. There is a will to do something about it; you either want to accept it or you want to reject it. Those dynamic volitive, emotive contents of the mind are called *saṅkhāra.*

Rune Johansson, to whom I have referred, has, following a thorough study, come to some remarkable and illuminating conclusions. Although there are some things in his book with which I do not agree, by and large his discussions of the psychological terms in the early period of the Buddhist tradition are very helpful. He calls them "activities." But there is no doubt that this means all the unconscious reactions—*saṅkhāra.* They have power, they have strength. Those, too, are not self. Why? When you see a thing, can you say what your powerful inner reaction to it will be? It does not mean that everything will evoke a powerful response. Unfortunately powerful reactions are evoked and sometimes at the most embarrassing times. One can speak of a propensity for violence.[5] Suddenly, in wars and in massive public reactions to events, revolutions in the world, you find people behaving in unpredictable ways. Where does all of this come from, the power that is brought out at such times? Each one of us has that power somewhere stored, as it were. Each one of us is a kind of volcano. That volcanic power inside is also *saṅkhāra. Saṅkhāra* are there and we cannot control them. Therefore they do not constitute "self." The "self" one must be able to control.

The Buddha asks, "How do you conceive this *bhikkhus,* is material form permanent or impermanent?" Now, when such questions are put the expected answer is, "impermanent." The next question is, "Is what is impermanent pleasant or unpleasant?" "Unpleasant," the answer comes. "Is it fitting to regard what is impermanent, unpleasant, subject to change as 'this is mine, this is what I am, this is my self?'" The answer is "No."

---

[5] I will turn again to some of these powerful reactions when I speak later of a propensity for violence.

I come now to a splendid passage, in a sort of verse form. This is supposed to be an utterance that the Buddha made a few weeks after the great change that happened to him beneath the bodhi tree. Such utterances are called *udāna*. There is the observation, "This world is anguished, being exposed to contact." "Contact" here means all these things: there is an object that is perceived, there is a pleasant or unpleasant reaction, and it is recognized and that it draws out all these other inner reactions to it. That is contact, and the consequences of contact. So, being exposed to contact the world is anguished. Because we are in relationship trouble always arises. So sorrow is something that you cannot avoid. The very fact of sorrow, although quite simple, might be rather difficult to discern in a country like the United States where things are comparatively easy. The time comes, in spite of all the good things that one has, when one is insecure, alone, the inevitability of suffering becomes clear even in the midst of affluence. For other people elsewhere suffering is a fact of daily experience. "Even what the world calls 'self' is ill," that is, it is something that gives suffering. Think of anything—the fact is ever other than that which is considered. That is to say, that thing is not as you conceive it. It is different. That is, you never see reality as it is. Our perception is always defective. That again is very much in tune with what recent physicists speak of, is it not; that reality is never to be experienced. For the moment that you experience it, it changes. There also is the truth of impermanence, of change.

CHAPTER III

ON "DEPENDENT ORIGINATION" (*PAṬICCASAMUPPĀDA*) WITH SPECIAL REFERENCE TO "CLINGING" (*UPĀDĀNA*)

Mahinda Palihawadana

Professor Palihawadana continues to remind us of the Buddha's inquiring mind, how he found different views, current during his lifetime, insufficient to answer the predicament of human life. Part of the answer that he found which explained what was occurring around him was Dependent Origination; whatever there is in life is more adequately understood in the context of cause and effect. Once this is understood, one can begin to put an end to embracing craving, not whimsically, of course, but through continually observing the causal process developing in and around us, and with patience to allow the creative transformation to arise of itself.

In this chapter, I would like to turn our attention to *paṭiccasamuppāda* or "Dependent Origination" and try to probe this somewhat, having in mind a few questions. For example, why did the Buddha proclaim such a notion? Why was it necessary? What is its broad thrust? Finally, what are its implications? First, we should think of the intellectual and spiritual environment that prevailed during the time of the Buddha in the sixth or fifth century before Christ. The exact date of the Buddha, as you probably know, is a matter of some controversy. The recent tendency of Western scholars is to bring it down as closely as possible to the time of the famous emperor

Aśoka of India. It is almost certain that it could not have been very much later than the fifth century.

At this time, what were the kinds of things people were talking about, discussing, religiously? That is an important question when we try to understand why the Buddha spoke about Dependent Origination. What we know of this period, apart from the Buddhist sources, we gain from the Hindu and the Jaina sources. From the Hindu sources we learn of the *Upaniṣads* and the thinkers who are mentioned in the *Upaniṣads*. From the Jaina tradition, whose founder was a senior contemporary of the Buddha, there is a massive literature. But from the Buddhist sources themselves we gather that there were scores of other religious teachers. It was in fact quite a remarkable period in the intellectual and religious history of India. There was a tremendous religious ferment on the one hand and, on the other, society was extraordinarily tolerant of all these diverse religious views.

The *Upaniṣads* teach many things, but the predominant Upanishadic teaching is the teaching of *Ātman* and *Brahman*, or *Ātman-Brahman*; ultimately they are not two concepts. More important is *Brahman*. The Upanishadic thinkers or philosophers who were religious men, who were for the most part Brahmins, as a caste, were the custodians of the religious tradition of India, even up until today. In the 5th century B.C. and even a thousand years earlier, the Brahmins were an exclusive class practicing their religion and imparting it to others, a religion mostly ritually oriented.

At about this time, about the sixth or seventh century B.C.—exact dates are impossible during this period in Indian history—something new was taking place among the Brahmins, either as an internal development or by way of assimilation of other religious ideas that must have prevailed among the indigenous people of India. The Brahmins belonged to the racial stock known as the Aryans, whose forefathers came to India from the Northwest, perhaps through the Kabul valley to the Punjab, and who produced the Vedic literature. But in India there was, at the time the Aryans came, what has been called the Indus valley civilization with many cities. It may be that at this time the Indus valley civilization was decaying and crumbling and, as an organized civilization, might even have crumbled at the time. But still they had some kind of religious tradition of which we have remnants in India even today, notably Śiva worship. Śiva is the great God of India. We do not know what other religious views or philosophies these people professed. But they were not the only source from which the Aryans could have borrowed religious ideas. There must have been other indigenous people with a long history of their own religious development.

From these various non-Aryan sources, influences seem to have been streaming toward the Brahminical elite. As a result, we find about the sixth or perhaps even the seventh century before Christ a kind of new thinking among the Aryans in which the practice of ritual in the original Vedic religion apparently was losing an associated deep-seated numinous feeling. Excessive ritualism seems to have arisen but not without some criticism. One form that such criticism took was the absorption of ideas from non-Aryan sources. It may be because of that kind of absorption that a new emphasis on this idea of *Brahman* arose. The main thrust of this is that the Aryans were looking for certain answers to basic questions related to their own lives. From whence have we come? What is our source? What happens after death? One does not find a trace of this kind of thing in the early Vedic literature. But now these become all important questions and the solution reflected in the *Upaniṣads* is found in the idea of *Brahman*, the world soul, and *Ātman,* the individual soul. Actually they are not two; the individual soul is only the microscopic reflection of the world soul, and this, whether what is in the human being is considered a self or some irreducible element, is the same as *Brahman*. If one knows *Ātman*, one knows *Brahman*. And the main fact about *Ātman-Brahman* is that it is eternal, it is unchanging, and it is consciousness, the source of consciousness, and the source of bliss. The idea of an unchanging self was one of the main current ideas during the time of the Buddha.

There were other ideas, of course. In the old Brahmin scriptures we also find the idea of a personal Brahmā, a creator god, sometimes called Puruṣa or Prajāpati in the Vedic scriptures. In Buddhist sources, this creator god, known as Brahmā, made the world with all its multifarious organic beings and inorganic matter.

On the scene also, as we can see from Buddhist texts themselves, and partly from the *Upaniṣads*, was the Sāṃkhya philosophy. In Sāṃkhya the basic teaching is of two final elements: primordial matter and innumerable souls or selves. Primordial matter evolves, and in the course of evolution there arises the visible manifest world, the world of matter. The body, senses, even the mind of a human being comes from that primordial matter. But there is more to a human being. There is also a soul, a self, called *puruṣa*. So you have this idea of primordial matter and spirit. As many human beings as there are, so many souls there are. Whereas in *Ātman-Brahman*, a teaching of non-duality, it is all one, Sāṃkhya is a teaching of duality; dual in the sense that there is a stark distinction between matter and spirit, but also multiple in the sense that there are innumerable souls. Their teaching was of the inevitable evolution of primordial matter, which evolves on its own without any interference by any external agent. The spirit is not subject to this.

Also on the scene were materialists for whom, just like any other materialism, the mind is a product of matter, as the body is, but a kind of refined matter. Death is the end. The idea of another world, a world beyond this life, is a falsehood. The most predominant expression of this sort of materialism reflected in the Buddhist texts is the notion that after death there is nothing, therefore life must be lived fully and enjoyably during the brief period in which we live. There is no point to religious concerns.

Another important idea I would like to mention is a kind of deterministic philosophy that everything is determined by something like fate or past actions. Nothing can be done, all things are preordained. And further, there is nothing we can do to change our spiritual condition. So, attempting to live a religious life is a waste of time. These were some of the ideas in the intellectual and spiritual environment in the Buddha's time. There definitely were more ideas on the scene. Jainism would be important to consider, but we must move on.

We are familiar with the basic themes in the story of the Buddha, how he set out at the age of 29 from a palace, having seen a few weeks earlier what are called the four signs: an old man, a sick man, a dead man, and a monk. It is best not to take this literally, but, rather, symbolically. Surely there is no way that he could not have known of old age, sickness, and death prior to encountering these sights. The story's message is that at this time, in this stage of his life, he saw those facts, those facts which he already knew very well, in a different light. All the biographical literature says that it was, as it were, the opening of a new eye. Although there is a great deal of legendary and mythological material dealing with the life of the Buddha, if you sift through it you find a human being. Some accounts might represent the Buddha as being eighteen feet tall, but if you read the discourses, *suttas*, carefully there are clear indications to the contrary; rather, that he, being of ordinary physical size, was not even recognized, in one instance, by one of his own monks. The stories are best understood in a symbolic sense.

Definitely, his was an inquiring mind, and he was not satisfied with any of the explanations for what he saw around him. That was why he set out on his own journey to find out in his own way the answer to the predicament of human life.

We know that for six years he looked for an answer, and when he came up with an answer, one of the major aspects of that answer was this teaching of Dependent Origination. He said, "He who sees *paṭiccasamuppāda* [Dependent Origination], sees me" which shows how important the teaching of *paṭiccasamuppāda* is in the Buddha's teaching. As you know, *paṭiccasamuppāda* is a teaching of cause and effect, a teaching of causality. There is, apart from a formula of *paṭiccasamuppāda* in twelve lengths (*nidānas*), a general teaching of causality in the Buddhist teachings. You find a special mention of it in the Mahāyāna texts when you read a writer who is conversant with the northern variety, the Mahāyāna, like Th. Stcherbatsky, a famous Russian author, who speaks of a general theory of causation and a special theory of causation. Personally I do not like the word "theory" here because, from my other readings of Buddhist texts, I get the sense that "theory" was an anathema to the Buddha. But we ascribe all these things to him—I think that is the price a great religious personality has to pay for being what he was, an influential person about whom others thought and said various things after his death.

The general theory, or the general idea or application, has to be understood first. The general idea is expressed in phrases like this: "this being, that happens." If "A" then "B," something like that, you see. The key phrase is "when this is there, that takes place," (in Pali, *imasmiṃ sati idaṃ hoti*) and put negatively it is, in effect, if there is no "A" then there is no "B." So both the positive and the negative are mentioned. That is interesting because to know whether two things are related causally, you should also know whether in the absence of what appears as the cause, if the effect is also absent, then you can be all the more certain that the two are causally related. So, that in brief is the general idea.

It had wide implications: whatever exists in life, in the environment, in society, it is reasonable to try to understand it as a matter of cause and effect. Whether it is the weather, or the transport system, or litter on the road, there are always causes for what you find. The Buddha was looking at the human predicament from this point of view. That is, he was asking the question—following a Pali expression which is different from the idiom in English—"When what is there, is there sorrow?" that is the question. The Buddha was, right from the beginning, aware of the compelling idea that there is a great deal of suffering in the world. He was interested in knowing why there is suffering and what could be done, or is there a way out, an exit (P. *nissaraṇa*). When he asked the question, "When what is there, is there suffering?" or as we would put it, "What's the cause of suffering?" by that kind of reasonable inquiry (P. *yoniso-manasikāra*: literally, "applying the mind from source"), which the Buddha recommends for everybody, he sought answers. After his own reasonable inquiry, which was directed at finding the causes of suffering, he found a string of causes each leading to the other. And it is this string of causes that we call the teaching of Dependent Origination.

The formulaic structure of Dependent Origination might look like twelve things, one following the other, as if those twelve can be separated from one another because they are numbered one, two, and so on, up to twelve. The general tendency of anybody studying this might be to regard them as a sort of sequential arrangement, and that, for example, number one is literally, "not knowing, ignorance," (*avijjā*). And then there is the next one, *saṅkhāra*. One might, of course, then say that *avijjā* creates *saṅkhāra* and then *avijjā* goes and there is *saṅkhāra*, and *saṅkhāra* creates *viññāna* and so forth. Now if you look at it that way—that the first causes the second and then the second causes the third and so on—that is totally wrong. It is not the way it was understood in the teaching. In fact, there is a very interesting statement about the general theory in the Buddhist books, both in the Theravāda and the Sanskritic non-Theravāda sources. It goes like this: "Not one from one or many from one but many from many" which means that it is not the case that A creates B and A vanishes, B is there and B creates C and B vanishes. It is not to be understood in a temporal sequence. Actually you cannot explain B as just arising from A. A is not the only cause of B. That is what is meant by "not one from one." And you cannot say that B and C have come from B, C and D, i.e., "not many from one." The truth is that many come from many, maybe A B C D come from or give X Y Z. In this way, according to the general teaching of Buddhist causality, everything gets related in the end; the entire universe is related. And if you look at it very, very finely you cannot do a thing without disturbing everything else or without affecting everything else. Of course we know that nowadays, with all that human civilization has gone through, with the terrific ecological disasters on the horizon or already here, we know that it is many from many—all lines are related.

But then, although that is the case, it is also true that there may be one which is more of a cause than the others. For example, for a plant you need the seed, you need air, you need light, you might need manure—all that goes to make the plant. So these things also have other byproducts—many from many—but there is also a special relationship between the seed and the plant. Without that seed there cannot be the plant. It is in that sense that we have to understand *paṭiccasamuppāda*. That is, for *saṅkhāra*, the special cause is *avijjā*, and so on.

It is difficult to translate the Pali words in the formulation of *paṭiccasamuppāda* in a way that would readily make some sense, because it is a rather difficult thing to understand. For example, take the case of *avijjā*, a common meaning is "not knowing, ignorance." But there are all kinds of ignorance. You and I do not know everything but probably that kind of ignorance has nothing to do with our spiritual predicament. There are hundreds of things that we do not know which do not go into our spiritual problem, into our sorrows, into the loneliness that we suffer, and so on. So *avijjā* must mean something other than just ordinary ignorance. That is why I gave the other word also. Normally, etymologically, you have to translate the word as "ignorance," but it is ignorance of a different kind.

If you look at your own mind, if you close your eyes and try to look inward, you will find that you cannot locate hundreds of things that are there which you can at other times see and feel. You all know that we are capable of great anger, violence, but we do not see it now in us. We are all very civil, polite, to each other. But we cannot see that seed of anger which erupts when the circumstances favor. Can you see it right now? You can't. Therefore we are ingorant about ourselves, our own inner characteristics. We have also, as you know, the great idea of the unconscious, which epoch-making psychologists unraveled— Freud, Jung, and others. But the Buddha was equally aware of the unconscious. There is no doubt about it. I think *avijjā* is that kind of ignorance: we are not aware of certain things that happen to us, how we assimilate them, how we take in those events, what traces they leave in us. It all happens unawares. For instance, if you get into a fit of anger with your friend, or parent, or sibling, you are not aware at the moment that it leaves a trace. I think that is the ignorance that is meant when you say *avijjā* brings *saṅkhāra* because *saṅkhāras* are generally mental forces, things that have collected in us from our lifelong experience, and, who knows, perhaps, from other lives.

The Dependent Origination teaching has been understood by Buddhists, both in the Theravāda and in the Mahāyāna, as consisting of three areas (*trikhandha*). That is, it spreads over three lives. Links 1 and 2 belong to one life, from 3-10, the next life, and 11-12 have been taken to refer to the life beyond. Therefore the structure of the formula is closely related to the idea of rebirth. *Avijjā* and *saṅkhāra* are the prenatal forces which lie unconsciously in our own mind and which affect us, which color our view of action, our attitudes, our thoughts, of every thing that we do. We do not see them, but they are there in our minds. What the Buddha is saying is that they do not end with physical death. They continue and carry on into another life to create the potential for consciousness in a new fetus, and that is *viññāna*. Ordinarily it means consciousness, but in this context it means the potential for consciousness which has come from the mental/psychic energies of the previous life.

Next comes what is normally taken as "name and form" or "mental and physical" constituents (*nāma-rupa*), referring to the development of mental and physical constituents in a newborn child. And then, following on that, come "six sense faculties" (*salāyatana*). As a result of the development of mental and physical constituents, there is the further diversification into the six sense faculties. There is a kind of biology in this: sight, hearing, smell, taste, skin sensation and mind—those are the sense organs and the sense faculties.

And then comes "contact" (*phassa*), but in this context it means the experience by contact of senses with the world or contact of the mind with other senses. As a result of that comes feeling (*vedanā*). You experience something, you see an object and then you know it is that object and immediately along with that seeing you have some feeling about it. There must be either a pleasant feeling, or an unpleasant feeling, or there is a trace of feeling which is so weak that you cannot call it pleasant or unpleasant, but still it is there. With that feeling there is the desire to have that pleasant feeling or the desire not to have that unpleasant feeling and that is the eighth stage, "craving" (*tanhā*).

Following that comes "grasping" or "clinging" (*upādāna*). It is a problematic word and a word worth delving into. It cannot mean just grasping. It must have a finer meaning, something psychologically determinant. I think it means the deep cravings that we have—you want the pleasant thing and you do not want the unpleasant things. Even the not-wanting is a form of wanting and is also classed under "craving" (*tanhā*). We accept these things. We embrace these things. We embrace our cravings. Sometimes we like to dislike. We so strongly dislike a person we

say "I hate him" and say it with conviction and relish. So there is
this acceptance. I think it is that acceptance, the fact of embracing
this and therefore collecting it in ourselves, "taking to oneself,"
which is the meaning of *upādāna*.

As a result there is "becoming" (*bhāva*). Now that, again,
is a pregnant word. It has a very dynamic sense. It means the
continuing unconscious buildup of these psychic forces. It is
said that when you accept your cravings you are building up
the ego. But you do it unconsciously. The whole thing happens
unconsciously. And we are all involved in this "I want to
become"—you are studying in order to get a degree. Our whole
life is a process of becoming. We want to be more than what we
are. There is never a respite. In the world of today, we cannot
even sit down to look. We do not have that space to look at
ourselves, just for the fun of it, to see what's happening. So that
is becoming, the continuous buildup of the psychological forces
involved with the idea of "I am" and "I will be."

Of course this continues, in the Buddhist teaching, as a
thing that rises and falls. It's not that the same feeling exists now
and at the next moment and at the next moment and so on, but it
is a continuing process. That is why the Buddha has always said
that everything is impermanent, *anicca*. In a teaching which says
that everything, except, perhaps, Nibbāna, is *anicca* you can't
think of becoming as something that ends at the end of this life,
at death. The becoming must therefore be a continuing of series
of the psychic forces being born and dying. And therefore, in
Buddhist teaching, even death is regarded as two things: the
conventional death, but also, philosophically speaking, there is
the recurrent death which happens at every moment in the sense
that things change.

The Buddha did not go so much into this question, but
later scholars found that you cannot have *anicca* in the true
sense of the word if you will grant anything as being permanent.
Therefore everything must be changing every instant. Though
there is a pattern in the change and the change is always the result
of cause and effect, you know you have change and the result is
not so different from what existed previously. So there is not such
a radical departure from moment to moment, but a kind of flow.

In that sense, of course, there is death even now. There is also physical death, the conventional death.

Then, after death, because of the presence of all these psychic forces, there is birth. Therefore *bhāva* and *saṅkhāra* are more or less the same. Just as *saṅkhāras* produce a new life so *bhāva*, being also a series of *saṅkhāras*, produces a new life, a new "birth" (*jāti*, "rebirth"). Then, because of birth there is naturally growth, there is decay, there is death, there is suffering. In this way the Buddha understood how suffering is caused.

In a sense these twelve factors are always here; they are not divisible. There is ignorance in us. The *saṅkhāra* are active in us. There is consciousness, but in this particular context, although it refers to consciousness at birth, which is the essential factor for a successive life according to the Buddhist teaching, mere physical conception does not guarantee a life. It is held that consciousness must get coupled with that physical life. In that sense, there is a special meaning in the word *viññāna* in this context: there is consciousness which is unconscious, that is, the psychic, mental faculty which is still largely unconscious or slightly conscious. Our intellect operates on a very superficial level in. All of these, in a sense, are involved together right now. In that sense we should not take them as sequential, as one leading to another and advancing.

In the general teaching I said that the positive as well as the negative holds good. If you say A causes B, you have to understand also that when A is not there B is not there. That realization was very important to the Buddha because he said if there is no suffering then there will be a cessation of birth. And if there is a cessation of birth there has to be a cessation of becoming, and so on. For a real change to happen in the whole chain there has to be a cessation of ignorance or unawareness. Therefore he found the answer that the secret to transformation was to cut this, to sever this link that is unawareness. If there is awareness then there cannot be unawareness and then there cannot be the creation of mental forces and so on, and the whole thing. Therefore, a crucial element in the whole religious life is that there should not be this acceptance of craving. There is no way to simply throw it away. You do not have that control over yourself. But you can still snap this link by being aware, which does not mean that in an instant, if you are aware, everything will vanish. But as a matter of fact it may be that if you are *really* aware everything *will* vanish. However, the problem is, when we are structured as we are, when our psychic constitution is what it is, it is not possible to have a total awareness of this whole multilayered consciousness. That is very difficult.

The point is, and the Buddha has many times said, you do not have control over yourself. You are not the master (*issara*) of yourself. There is then, in Dependent Origination, this explanation of how this all happens and there is the idea that we do not have total control.

If we do not have control of ourselves, are we not therefore bound up in determinism, which was one of the positions available to the Buddha? This is a very important question. In fact some Buddhist scholars have been saying that there is no such thing as free will, one among them being Walpola Rahula. He says, with everything conditioned like this, how do we have free will? The problem is if we do not have the freedom to be aware, we are finished. Then we would be back with one who says nothing can be done. As a matter of fact, when one of the Buddha's followers asked, "Why do you say that?" he pointed to a park, somewhere near, and said "Look at that park. If you want to go to that park, can't you?" Of course he could. So it *is* possible to do good. If it is not, the religious life is impossible. So we have this problem then, why does he say that? On the one hand there is *paṭiccasamuppāda*, cause and effect, and therefore, because of this long history of having been subjected to this process, our not being able straightaway to get out of this. That is the meaning of saying we are not in control.

But it does not mean that we cannot make a beginning. There are two things, the Buddha says, that can change your outlook. One is the call of another, an enlightened person, a Buddha, a Christ, someone. Or there is the reasonable inquiry. Now in the case of the Buddha there was no one who could awaken him. He said it was his own reasonable inquiry which opened his eye of Dhamma. When that call of another or that reasonable inquiry takes place, it makes a little dent, a little space is created which makes you feel interested in doing something about yourself. It is not normal to be interested in changing yourself. It is the normal thing to run along with the current. I would not want to be dogmatic about it. Maybe the normal thing is also to inquire. The question therefore is when a situation arises are we committed to just doing nothing?

When you see a park with beautiful trees, is there something in you that commits you to just one course of action—either you have to go into it or you do not have to go into it, or you cannot go into it? Of course this is a very complex situation although it looks so simple. It may be that you are pressed for time, you have to go to class and you cannot stop to admire the trees; there may be a compelling factor. But there is always an option. You could do one or the other. I think therefore that there is in every instance a choice; at least a choice between doing it and not doing it. And maybe the predispositions, *saṅkhāras*, compel you, but even if you are compelled you may be doing it with a bit of regret, "Ah, I should have gone." And that regret may work. It may open your eyes. So the Buddha's teaching cannot be taken as a teaching of the fatalistic determinism of *paṭiccasamuppāda*. No, certainly it is not. The Buddha said on many occasions that if you are tied to the world and its allurements and this is inevitable, and if, as he said to one man, the only way to get out of it is to shut your eyes then the religious life is impossible.

Followers of the Jain sect, somewhat misrepresented in the Buddhist books, come to the Buddha and the Buddha asks "What does your teacher say?" Then someone says that "*avijjā* is *kamma* and we are bound by its effects. Therefore you must not do *kamma*—that is the only way to stop it." And the Buddha replies, therefore, that there is no religious life. Since he was teaching a religious life, it goes without saying that he was taking for granted that it is possible to take initiative.

Important in all of this is this embracing frame of mind, a sense of accumulating it, willingly giving in to it—*upādāna*. Now what are the *upādānas*? What forms are the *upādānas*? There are many kinds. First there is the acceptance and the willing grasp of the pleasures of the senses (*kāma*). Then there is the willing grasp of opinions, ideas, ideologies (*diṭṭhi*). There is also the willing grasp of ritualism (*sīlabattha*). And also there is the willing grasp of the notion of "I," the ego notion.

I am quite interested in the way we willingly grasp ideas, opinion, perhaps most suitably referred to in modern times as ideologies, embrace them, and go. And we say, "That's the truth." And Buddhist books always speak of people who say "This is the truth. Everything else is all wrong." There are so many ascetics and religious teachers who say this. The Buddha said that even his teachings are like a boat to cross from here to the other side, not to be carried on your heads after you have finished crossing the river. In that context he says, just as previously you rejected or you gave up things that are not in accord with Dhamma, so you must also relinquish *ideas* about the Dhamma. Some people think you must relinquish the Dhamma. I do not think that is the meaning. You can neither grasp Dhamma nor relinquish it. But ideas about the Dhamma, your ideology, saying "I'm a Buddhist," "this is what Buddhists say," everything else is false and so on for the others—that is *upādāna*. And that the Buddha certainly did not recommend.

I would like to close this chapter with the question, "What can you do?" Is there free will? The Buddha showed that we have to operate within the given laws of nature. We can understand the situation and observe what causes produce what effects. In doing so we will see that there are certain areas of freedom. We can do certain things and suffer their ill effects. An example is smoking. I can smoke, so of course I do not have the liberty of not getting cancer. We can also avoid doing such things and, without any other exertion on our part, benefit by the good effects that nature affords for such behavior.

When we observe the mental sphere, we can see that certain kinds of attitudes, emotions, expressions and such things will produce certain effects. We can see what emotions produce what effects, either directly on ourselves or secondarily by the reactions they provoke in others immediately or in course of time; sometimes the reaction does not occur immediately. Sometimes a person remembers what was done and there is a grudge that has its way many years later. The observation of the situation itself will induce certain effects on our behavior.

What we would wish to happen may or may not happen, or may happen in the course of time without our being aware of it. But we are definitely not tied down to one and only one pattern of action. We may choose to observe or not to observe. But once we have done one of these, i.e., once we have either observed or not observed, we have no freedom to annul its consequences. Our choice in the first place may have been due to our own background or conditioning. To that extent one might say that even seeming liberty is not a true liberty. The freedom available is that the conditioning is never so complete as to shut out our making use of the exits provided. The Buddha always said there is an exit (nissāraṇa). What the Buddha seems to deny is the fatalistic view that there is at no time any exit provided.

Therefore the view that we have no control, often expressed in the Buddha's statements, should also be taken into account. We often wish things to be different from what they are, but things do not become otherwise just because we want them to become different. We do not have that kind of control over any of the five khandhas. But if we observe how things happen, how we cannot change them by mere wish, and then decide to try the Buddha's advice to continue observing, we may learn a patience which we did not have before and allow for nature a space we would otherwise not have allowed. The Buddha seems to be saying that such space is precious. The nature of things is such that in that space catalysis takes place. The picture that emerges from this, too, is neither total control nor total bondage.

CHAPTER IV

THE FOUR NOBLE TRUTHS

Mahinda Palihawadana

*Professor Palihawadana, building upon the insight of Dependent Origination, introduces what is perhaps the most popular formulation of the Buddha's teachings, the Four Noble Truths, noting how they "in summary, proclaim first of all the existential predicament as known by experience." But Professor Palihawadana reminds us, again, not to cling to this formulation, to this doctrine, but to see how it can help one begin to move toward the goal. At the close of this talk, we have our first **Questions** raised by students and **Responses** by Professor Palihawadana.*

One of the characteristic features of the Buddhist enterprise is that it originated basically as a human enterprise. In other words, it has no external point of reference; that is to say that man himself has to work out his liberation and set about the tasks that make him a better human being. So the Buddhist enterprise sets out from the existential fact of human discontent. It is only through the depths of the human personality that early Buddhism taught that solutions to human problems are discoverable. What was necessary from the Buddha's point of view was that one should have a clear understanding of this existential predicament. To understand a matter as it exactly is; that is of paramount importance.

We find in the later books that refer to the period after the Buddha's enlightenment, that well-grounded thinking or reasonable thinking (*yoniso manasikāra*). For this, you have to be free of prejudices both for and against activities of fears and confusions, or, as you might say, you have to face the problem impartially in a tranquil and unemotional frame of mind. When we read the texts recording the early days of the life of the Buddha, just before his enlightenment, we find the Buddha setting about his tasks in this frame of mind, that is, with well-grounded thinking. He sought an explanation of man and the world. What explanation of man and the world did the Buddha find?

We have discussed the three characteristics (*tilakkhaṇa*) in Chapter II as one way of explaining the world, that is to say, they describes the features that are essentially found in any phenomenal occurrence. The four truths seem to be another characterization of life of a similar nature. Now it dawned on the Buddha that suffering existed as long as certain conditions existed. And it did not exist when those conditions disappeared. This was true of everything. Take anything and you will find that there are certain conditions upon which its presence is contingent and upon whose disappearance its absence is contingent, that is, the absence of that thing also depends upon certain conditions, the disappearance of those conditions which made it in the first place possible. This was the Buddha's famous causal principle of *paṭiccasamuppāda*, which is sometimes translated as "dependent origination," sometimes as "conditioned genesis." It is really not strictly a theory of causality because, in the case of causality, one might argue that the cause goes into the effect. Of course this is highly debatable. There are all kinds of arguments about this theorizing. But in the case of the Buddhist's *paṭiccasamuppāda*, it sets out the conditions upon whose presence something comes into being. It does not follow that the condition itself moves into the effect.

Basically this can be stated in this way: A being there, B arises. That is the first formulation. In some of the discourses pertaining to the period immediately after enlightenment, you have this statement:

> At the end of the seven days, he emerged from
> that concentration and in the first watch of the
> night his mind was occupied with dependent

arising in forward order thus: that comes to be
when there is this [which I translated as A being
there, B arises]. That arises with the arising of
this.

Then he goes on to particular things: with ignorance as
condition the *saṅkhāras* (formations) come into being, and so on.
So we have this general principle of conditioned arising.

In the famous first discourse of the Buddha, called the
"Discourse on the Setting in Motion the Wheel of Dhamma" (*Dha
mmacakkappavatanasutta*),[6] we have this statement, "there is this
noble truth of suffering." And he goes on to list the constitutents:
birth is suffering, old age is suffering, sickness is suffering, death
is suffering, and then all the attendant phenomena of sorrow,
lamentation, grief and despair. That is all *dukkha,* suffering.

Additionally, association with the loathed, that is to say,
meeting someone whom you do not like, that is suffering.
Dissociation from the loved, that is, to lose those you love, not to
be in their company—that is suffering. Not to get what you want,
that is suffering. In short, the five categories affected by clinging
are suffering. What does that mean?

The five categories (*khandha*) we have noted in Chapter
II: form (*rūpa*) sensation or feeling (*vedanā*), perception, really
the image (*saññā*), dynamic internal states, will, strong emotions
(*saṅkhāra*); and consciousness, also impressions, the first thing
in the mental act (*viññāna*). Actually the mental act begins
with the body (*rūpa*) and proceeds. These are called the five
categories affected by clinging. That is, their normal existence
is one thing, but when you cling to any one of them, then desire
arises. You have experienced something and there is a particular
perception and you want that perception again and again, then it
is that category affected by clinging. There is a distinction made

---

[6] This famous discourse is found in *The Vinaya Piṭakam*, edited for the Pali
Text Society by Hermann Oldenberg, London: Luzac & Company, Ltd., 1964,
I, 10 ff., with an English translation in *The Book of the Discipline*, translated by
I. B. Horner, London: Luzac & Company Ltd., 1962, IV, 13 ff. It is also found
in *Samyutta-nikāya*, edited for the Pali Text Society by M. Leon Feer, London:
Luzac & Company, Ltd., 1960, V, 420 ff., with an English translation in *The
Book of the Kindred Sayings*, translated by F. L. Woodward, London: Luzac &
Company, Ltd., 1956, V, 356 ff.

between these *khandhas.* Once the identification with them—
clinging—takes place, then we speak of *upādāna,* which means
"clinging." The Pali texts speak of the five *khandhas* that, when
they become the subject of clinging, are the source of suffering.
So the mere fact of having a body is not what is emphasized
here but the fact that the body is the source of clinging and
identification: it is my body and therefore I must at any cost
safeguard it against everything else. So, by the first formulation,
that is "A being there B arises," it follows that these factors being
there sorrow arises. That is the first noble truth.

Then we get the second. There is this noble truth of the
origin of suffering. It is craving which produces renewal of being.
Craving is the thirst of the body and the mind which produces
this renewal of being. This is commonly understood as rebirth.
But also it means the continuity from moment to moment. In a
sense if in every moment we realize we are born afresh, I suppose
our life would be of a completely different order. We never look
at things afresh. We are unable to do that. Why? Because the
past comes along; and the next moment is always affected by
the previous moment. We see a man or a woman and all kinds of
memories arise in our mind. These intervene between the object
and us. So we never see afresh every moment. This carrying
over of the past to the present and into the future is also renewal
of being, which is rebirth. Actually, the word used is the same:
punabhāva. Bhāva is "being" and *puna* is "again." One way
craving (*taṅha*) is described is as leading to this becoming again.
What produces this re-becoming is craving, or the thirst of the
body and the mind. That is what produces renewal of being. That
is the origin of suffering.

Craving is threefold: craving for sensual desires, craving for
being and craving for non-being. You want to *be,* and sometimes
you want *not* to be. There are various technical meanings attached
to this, but the words by themselves are being (*bhāva*) and non-
being (*vibhāva*). So there is this threefold craving. And that is
what produces suffering. Therefore, the fact that there is craving
and that craving produces suffering is the second truth: the noble
truth of the origin of suffering. If you think of the dependent
origination formula, it is the positive formulation that applies:

suffering (A) arises when craving (B) is there, that is, suffering arises when craving is there.

Then there is a third truth: the noble truth of the cessation of suffering. Here there is the negative application of the dependent origination formula: when A is not there, B does not arise. That is, when craving is not there, there is the cessation (*nirodha*). So we call it the truth (*sacca*) of cessation (*nirodha*), the truth of cessation (*nirodhasacca*), the cessation of suffering. This word *nirodha* is also used to indicate the state of mind which is completely free of content. Does that make sense to you: mind free of content?

You have heard of meditation. When you read descriptions of meditation you find that the description moves from a state of mind that has lots of thoughts gradually to a state of mind in which the thought content is less and less. And finally you find that there is no content at all. This is obviously possible. You find this not only in Buddhist literature but also in the *Upaniṣads*. The *Upaniṣads* speak of the state when the mind is asleep, inactive, and not even dreaming, so that there is no knowable content of mind at that time. The *Upaniṣads* describe that state of mind as the state of deepest sleep—when there is no activity of mind at all, when the mind is not dreaming—as a state almost identical with the highest. It's interesting to know that in the Buddhist books the Arahant is said to be not in sleep, not dreaming.

Both traditions seem to say that in the highest state of experience, the mind is free of content; content meaning, sensation or feeling (*vedanā*), perception, (*saññā*), dynamic internal states, will, strong emotions (*saṅkhāra*) and all that. That is also *nirodha*, to be free of content. In fact, there is a special category of meditative experience (*saññāvedayitanirodha*) and when all of that is absent, it is in cessation. That is the highest form of meditation that is described in the books. There is the truth of the noble cessation of suffering. It is the truth of reaching the highest meditative experience, in a sense. But there are also overtones of meaning which are rather difficult to discuss at this stage. If the mind is free of content, it is a fresh mind. At every given moment it is a fresh mind in the sense that it is not generating content. It seems that the experience of Nibbāna is also similar.

I said that this, as a way of working it out, was a negative form of the formulation of *paṭiccasamuppāda*, when A is not there B does not arise.

Then there is the fourth truth: the noble truth of the way leading to the cessation of suffering. You can say that this is the positive formulation: when the way exists the cessation of suffering arises. The way is described as the noble eightfold path. The first step of the path is right view, perhaps better expressed as right understanding. The second step is called right thought, which is more likely translation than right intention. The remaining steps are right speech, right action, right livelihood, right effort, right mindfulness, and right concentration. These constitute the eightfold path. You will hear often that this is the Buddhist way of life. You find reference to this in all of Buddhist literature of all the schools. Similarly the four noble truths are mentioned in all the schools, Mahāyāna as well as Theravāda. They definitely must be a very old formulation.

The noble eightfold path also falls into three categories that will help us to understand another important and popular classification. If you take the first and second ones, right understanding and right thought, these two form what is called "wisdom," "insight" (*paññā*). So when you speak of insight, it can, in this formulation, be regarded as right understanding and right thought.

The next three are, right speech, right action and right livelihood. What is the common denominator for all three: speech, action, and livelihood? Those are, to speak rightly and to do rightly and to live rightly. Those things are connected with the ordering of one's daily life. You do certain things and you choose not to do certain things. That is what is called virtue (*sīla*) or, perhaps, if you think of the meanings attached to it, as in the famous *Visuddhimagga*, you find it is the same thing as "order,"—having order in your life. In any case, virtue is the common translation for *sīla*. So you have the first two, constituting insight or wisdom (*paññā*), and the second three constituting "virtue or "order" (*sīla*). Why is *sīla* order? Because if you are disorderly, there is no *sīla*. So under that would come things like your table manners, your manner of dress, and acceptability so far as they are intelligent and necessary, not overdoing such things and of course this might develop into a form of clinging behavior.

The final three are right effort, right mindfulness, and right concentration. What is the common denominator? If you look at the last two, right mindfulness and right concentration, of course, you see the application of mind. And in the idea of effort itself is the idea of application. So we have those three constituting "concentration" (*samādhi*), which could also be translated "integration," in the sense of "bringing together."

So we have these three: virtue or order (*sīla*) concentration or integration (*samādhi*) and wisdom or insight (*paññā*). I am giving two translations; the second are my preferences.

Why are these three given in this order and not in another, i.e., in *paññā*, *sīla*, and *samādhi*, rather than the other order of *sīla*, *samādhi*, and *paññā*? It might have been a consequence of agreeing with the order of the eightfold path. This is a common characterization of the constituents of the religious life: *sīla*, *samādhi*, and *paññā*. I think obviously they are in that order because *sīla*, the first, concerns the most elementary things, the easiest things to do to set your life in order, your external life. *Samādhi*, the meditational things, are also possible. But *paññā*, one cannot dictate to that. You have to wait until it comes; though it is right view and right intention, it only happens when something else happens. I will have to describe that in another chapter.

We have the eightfold path and also the four truths. These things flow into one another. The four truths, in summary, proclaim first of all the existential predicament as known by experience. Suffering—the first truth. The second is the discovering of its cause, following the positive formulation of this *paṭiccasamuppāda* principle. The third shows a state in which the first, the existential predicament of *dukkha*, is absent. And this is known by the negative formulation, when the conditioning factors of a situation are absent, that situation is absent. Then, in the fourth, we are introduced to a way to help this state to arise, which was explained by the positive formulation, that is, when *sīla, samādhi,* and *paññā* are present cessation (*nirodha*) of *dukkha,* takes place.

The notion of the path, which is very important in Theravāda, and which is also referred to in other traditions of the Buddhist enterprise, is very strongly challenged by one school. The Mādhyamika, a school called a philosophical school because it produced very profound philosophical texts, is a school which speaks of emptiness (Skt. *śūnyatā*). The school of Nāgārjuna, regarded as the greatest exponent of this position, challenged all of these categories. They didn't really negate these categories—the four noble truths, eightfold path, the way, and all that—but they said these are only little aids to get you moving. Do not take them as the last thing, do not cling to them. All these notions, all the categories, belong to what they called, true but only conventionally true (Skt. *vyāvahārika*). It is like a piece of paper that has no value in itself, like a dollar—you can take it to the shop and get your breakfast cereals with it. It is only a convention. The little piece of money has little value, but still it is useful, a necessary convention. So similarly, these things, the way and all that, are conventional truths. Ultimate truth (Skt. *paramārthasatya*) has nothing to do with these things. Why? Because it is not concerned with thought. That is the moment of mind when thought is itself absent. But these concepts and formulations are all forms of thought.

Questions and Responses

Mahinda Palihawadana: Do you really agree that life is sorrow? You have a lot of enjoyment in life, don't you? When I was young I enjoyed life. The formula supplies a kind of skeleton to help us think, but we can depart from it if we think it is wrong. It is for you yourself to criticize it. The Buddha has always encouraged his listeners (sāvakas), to question not only what he said but also the way he lived. He says that if the way I live is objectionable then there is no meaning in what I say. So keep a critical eye on what I do. All Buddhists are welcome to think afresh, to question.

Our question is "Is life really sorrow?" You seem to agree and I am a little surprised about it. I know why you agree, but I want you to say that.

Student: There is enjoyment in life, but enjoyment ends and there is sorrow in that. So life is suffering because enjoyment ends.

MP: Happiness (*sukha*) is considered in the Buddhist tradition. This *sukha* is the opposite of *dukkha*. But this is basically, unalterably, and inevitably transient. This is a fact, and when you realize that, you have a different approach to the idea of sorrow. Even sorrow itself loses force when you know its real nature.

Q: Then you can have moments of happiness, like a sound wave; moments of happiness and then sorrow at its loss.

MP: I would rather not put it that way because that would give regularity, but you do not see that regularity. Suffering is much more underlying, since everything phenomenal is transient. It is true that suffering is also transient if you take the facts of suffering, the moments of suffering, times of suffering. But as a truth, it is of a different order. You will find that the other's suffering is also present so that there is no moment when you can be free of suffering because there is always suffering somewhere in the world.

Now we found that to be so in Sri Lanka when our troubles started. I was perfectly easy at home. I was cloistered. We had food. The situation was alright for me. I knew that there was no harm for me. But I was suffering all the time. I suffered, endlessly. I have been thinking about the truth of suffering. The other's suffering is also my suffering. I cannot help it. Even if I wanted it to be otherwise I couldn't help it.

Q: Does a Buddhist give any thought to what ordained that this whole scheme should be so? In other words, you have this cycle of rebirth and this journey to Nibbāna; does a Buddhist give any thought to what set up a whole scheme like this? Or does it simply exist?

MP: Are you asking me whether the Buddha set this up or not? I think Theravāda takes it for granted, that it has been there all the time. The Mahāyāna, as you know, speaks of the Buddha's use of similes, that there was a strategy on his part (Skt. *upāyakauśalya*) to get the people to come into the house of Dharma. So, this may have been part of that. This might be one possible way to explain it. It is also there in the literature, from the beginning.

Q: When you talk about the path as being conventional, is that the same with various rituals? Would you say that the aim, then, of ritual is to get to a point where one can abolish the need for ritual?

MP: Yes, because the need for ritual is one of the first things that is supposed to go away, to vanish from you, when you realize the addiction to ritual. By the way, the notion of journey to Nibbāna is a questionable notion because Nibbāna is an instant. It's like turning a coin. There is no time. A journey needs time. There is time taken in this journey, but that time is just wasted because ultimately it is only at the last point that you get to the other shore. You see, you have a lake and you walk round and round the lake and finally you find that you just step into the water. Being on the shore, at one point or another point, you cannot call it progress. The real difference is when you jump into the water. So, in one sense it doesn't make sense to speak of the journey to Nibbāna.

Q: Do Buddhists believe that eventually from happiness there arises sorrow?

MP: Yes. That is a fact, is it not? I mean happiness always ends in sorrow.

Q: But why can't you take a moment of happiness, just take happiness for that moment?

MP: Yes, the Buddhists speak of that but the only happiness that is real is the happiness of Nibbāna. There are other happinesses like the happiness of being in heaven—nowadays Buddhists are not taking heaven and hell in the older sense, that is, hell is where suffering is, and it may be right here, and heaven is where the absence of suffering is, and it may be right here. Those kinds of happiness, like the happiness of having money and being able to buy what you want, being able not to suffer from cold when it is cold, are somewhat illusory now; we could raise the window and the cold increases, and so forth. So, all kinds of happiness are dependent upon condition. Such is not unconditional. I think that you have to grant that. Don't you think so?

Q: Well, then, where does this sorrow idea come in?

MP: That's it! Even happiness is conditional and not unalterable. It is not unconditional. Sorrow in this sense means you get disillusioned with what is supposed to be not sorrow. And to realize that is the truth of suffering. There is a difference between suffering and the truth of suffering. Suffering is a physical thing which you experience at times and don't experience at other times. The truth of suffering is to understand that happiness itself is conditional. It brings disillusionment.

CHAPTER V

VIRTUE, CONCENTRATION, AND INSIGHT (*SĪLA, SAMĀDHI, PAÑÑĀ*)—*I*

Mahinda Palihawadana

In the first of two talks on this subject, Professor Palihawadana focuses on the religious life as these three key notions are involved in one's rightly orienting purposeful action. Virtue, he suggests, is rooted in orderliness, which is ideally seen in completely following the precepts, both those for the laity and those for the monks, although not an easy thing to do. The refreshingly live context of these talks immediately arises with the first question about the government and the religious life of men and women in Sri Lanka.

O ccasionally some confusion arises due to the fact that we are dealing with Theravāda, which, in a sense, encapsulates early, canonical Buddhism and, in addition, has elements of later development. If you speak purely of early Buddhism, the Buddhism that is reflected in the canon, especially in the *Sutta Piṭaka*, it contains a simpler form of religiousness. But Theravāda contains also what you have in the commentaries to these texts, which represent later developments that on occasion might seem to conflict with early Buddhism. We should remember that there is a distinction between what is found in the early texts and what is found in the purely Theravāda texts.

The presentation of virtue (*sīla*), concentration (*samādhi*), and *insight or wisdom* (*paññā*) in this chapter will follow the specifically Theravāda interpretation, particularly as presented in the *Visuddhimagga* by Buddhaghosa, which was required reading in a Theravāda education in the olden days. Buddhaghosa was a famous scholar monk who wrote commentaries on most of the important early texts of the canonical collection or "baskets" (*piṭakas*). We will for the most part rely on the scheme that Buddhaghosa presented.

This Theravāda, as found in the *Visuddhimagga*, categorizes the function or the purpose of the religious life as virtue or moral conduct, concentration, and insight or wisdom (*sīla*, *samādhi*, and *paññā*). So to be virtuous, to develop concentration and to attain insight would be, according to this scheme, the purpose of the religious life. But there is a more popular version of this: to practice the habit of giving (*dāna*), to be virtuous (*sīla*) and to develop insight (*bhāvanā*). Most Buddhist monks today would use in their sermons the scheme of *dāna*, *sīla*, and *bhāvanā* more often than *sīla*, *samādhi*, and *paññā*. Their threefold division is retained. The purposes are indicated as three. *Samādhi* and *paññā* are collapsed into *bhāvanā*. So one has really *sīla*, *samādhi*, *paññā* plus *dāna*. *Dāna* is a new category, or rather it is a case of the implicit being made explicit. This is significant because the practice of giving (*dāna*) sustains the institutional religion by means of the assistance this practice provides in various forms of giving: money, food and all such things.

Although in this chapter we will be focusing on the religious life in terms of *sīla*, *samādhi*, and *paññā*, the division of *dāna*, *sīla*, and *bhāvanā* is very important and will be considered by Professor Wijayawardhana in his chapter "Buddhist Beliefs and Practices." As he probably will point out, there are two kinds of *dāna*: actual gifts in kind (*āmisadāna*), and the gift which is the following of certain principles (*paṭipattidāna*). They are also called giving gifts in kind with reverence (*āmisapūja*) and reverence rendered by following certain principles (*paṭipattipūja*). *Pūja* is a very important notion and means offering gifts in a reverential gesture. So there is the activity of giving gifts in kind (*āmisapūja*) and the gift which is the following of certain principles (*paṭipattipūja*), that is, something much more internal; you might say the external *pūja* and the internal *pūja*. In this context, one's following a certain moral conduct, respecting certain principles, amounts to an act of reverence (*pūja*) to the Buddha, Dhamma, and Saṅgha. That is the internal act of reverence or paying homage (*pūja*). Following from a review of these things it would appear that the Theravāda absorbed many kinds of popular religious practice. These forms of *pūja* are, probably, later than the time of the Buddha. Many of them seem to have little relation to earlier religious views. Some, in holding the idea that Buddhism is a philosophy or a way of life or a meditational religion, might see this as a contradiction. Is this not a discrepancy to have so much ritual and ritualistic practices? Our discussion will touch upon this problem, whether or not there is a discrepancy.

We can ask the question whether there has been any theoretical basis for such absorption of popular religious practices. Was it done in some haphazard way or was it a principled form of absorption of popular religious practices? The theoretical basis of the teaching of *kamma* is purposeful actions—not just any action—that strengthen either greed (*lobha*), hate (*dosa*), and ignorance (*moha*), which are called the "roots of the unwholesome" (*akusalamūla*), or they strengthen the "roots of the wholesome" (*kusalamūla*), that is the opposite of greed (*alobha*), the opposite of hate (*adosa*), and the opposite of ignorance (*amoha*). The addition of the "*a*" negates the meaning of the word. So, purposeful actions strengthen either one set or the other set. These Pali words mean "greed" (*lobha*), "hate" or "ill-will" (*dosa*), and "ignorance" (*moha*). *Moha* could also mean "delusion," or "confusion," "unawareness" (*moha*). I, personally, think that it means "unawareness." The mere fact that we are not aware of our own unconscious mind constitutes ignorance. That is the basic ignorance. Then there is the absence of those things: the absence of greed, craving, the absence of hate or ill-will, and the absence of unawareness, the presence of awareness.

I would stress that it is purposeful action that strengthens one set or the other. To give with a real charitable intention thus strengthens the wholesome root (*kusalamūla*) of the absence of greed—not just to give, but to give with this real charitable intention. Similarly, to entertain genuine feelings of kindness strengthens the second one, the absence of hate. To exercise awareness of our mind strengthens the absence of unawareness. Thus, for example, to be aware of impermanence when offering flowers is not just the act of offering flowers but to be aware of the fact that the flowers are a symbol for impermanence, because it is easy to see that the flower fades within a few hours. Such awareness of impermanence in the act of offering flowers is a meditative act, although it is a slight act, and it strengthens awareness. So the many simple religious acts were explained in this way as strengthening one's "wholesome deed" (*kusalakamma*).

The *sine qua non* of the wholesome deed, the most necessary thing, was the genuineness of the accompanying act. Why is this so? Because *kamma*, almost by definition, is "intention." There is a famous statement by the Buddha which we hear often repeated by Buddhist monks when they preach (*baṇa*): "O *bhikkhus*, I say that *kamma* is intention (*cetanā*)." When in the external act of giving the mind is also free from greed, then it is a wholesome (*kusala*) act. It strengthens the absence of greed (*alobha*). It was regarded as making some purification of mind. Thus you see that the whole gamut of religious acts is regarded as purifying the mind, ridding or reducing the content of *lobha*, *dosa*, and *moha*. That was the theoretical basis for these acts.

In this way, giving (*dāna*) ties up with meditation (*bhāvanā*) because as you give you also reflect. When you offer flowers, you reflect on impermanence. So, every religious act done in the temple is theoretically explained as a meditative act. That is the basic difference between *pūja* in Buddhism and *pūja* in Hinduism. Externally, they are all very similar. You will find *pūja* in any Hindu temple. You will find similar—not identical—*pūjas* in a Buddhist temple. Yet the theoretical explanation differs. There is not such a theoretical explanation in the Hindu case.

Virtue, basically moral conduct (*sīla*), is also of this kind. It amounts to orderliness, and I think it began as orderliness and developed into a more formal tenet. *Sīla* is often described negatively, as the avoidance of something, avoidance of various forms of wrong or disorderly conduct. In our considerations of "The Four Noble Truths," we found that *sīla* constitutes three of the eight limbs of the eightfold path: that was "right speech," "right action," and "right livelihood."

What is right speech? Right speech is abstinence from malicious speech, false speech, harsh speech, frivolous or senseless speech. To abstain from them is the negative way to describe it, but of course the content of this is positive. To abstain from them is right speech, which comes under *sīla*.

Similarly, right action is also defined as abstinence from killing, stealing—the word used is not "stealing," but "taking what is not given"—and sexual misconduct.

The next limb, right livelihood, is described as the avoidance of harmful occupations, which involve killing, deception, or which bring physical, moral, and economic harm to others. For example, soldiering—you can't be a member of the army if you are following right livelihood. This is something that would never be stressed by Buddhists. There is a kind of tacit silence, a conspiracy of silence, on this important debate. It is never stressed that a Buddhist cannot be a soldier because society cannot function without hypocrisy. I have never heard it said in Sri Lanka that if you are a Buddhist you cannot be a soldier. I do not think you can even join the police. So the manufacture of arms, which condemns the entire world today, is absolutely un-Buddhistic, and Buddhist countries also engage in this. So also are the sale of liquor, charging excessive interest, especially in some countries where there are other forms of usury, and also prophesying and soothsaying—so astrology is also out. But astrology is a very important element in Sri Lankan culture. So, you see, there are obvious contradictions. The Buddha has stated that the stars have nothing to do with one's life. But still, even Buddhist monks practice astrology. All that goes under "wrong livelihood" and avoidance of that kind of livelihood is "right livelihood." And that comes under *sīla*. So you see that while *sīla* has many formal aspects of conduct, there are also hints in it of what was the thrust of the original message.

These three—right speech, right action, and right livelihood—constitute *sīla* for lay people. Occasionally the question is asked whether the Buddha had a message for the lay people. Of course he had. There are a number of discourses (*suttas*), in the Pali canon that particularly address lay people. I do not think the Buddha spoke, or addressed himself, to one particular group, although since he founded the Saṅgha most of what he said seems to be more appropriate for the Saṅgha. That was because he was interested in having a nucleus of people who would change the world, and for practical reasons he realized that not everyone could join such a nucleus. So looking at the teachings, one gets the impression that they are addressed almost exclusively to the Saṅgha. But, of course, that is not so. The message to the Saṅgha is really the message to the world because he hoped through the Saṅgha to bring about a new quality of life. What we have described is the *sīla* for the lay people.

We have said that *sīla* is basically similar to *dāna*. We can elaborate on this point. With *sīla* also, it is abstinence which involves a positive wholesome intention that counts. *Sīla* is such intention manifested in speech and action. So, although it is negatively described, it can, when stated positively, be said that the observance of the five, or the eight, or the ten precepts is *sīla*.

The five precepts (*pañca-sīla*, which gets simplified in its Sinhala form as *pan-sīl*), in brief, are: (1) I take upon myself the precept of abstaining from the taking of life; (2) I take upon myself the precept of abstaining from taking what is not given, that is, from theft; (3) I take upon myself the precept of abstaining from sexual misconduct; (4) I take upon myself the precept of abstaining from lying, falsehood; (5) I take upon myself the precept of abstaining from intoxicants, which includes not only liquor but obviously also what we now call drugs—anything that makes the mind lose its natural quality. So it could even be, by implication, getting intoxicated is an idea, although it is never explained that way. But it should be, because the purpose is that the mind should function naturally without being excited one way or the other. These are the five precepts that every Buddhist is expected to follow.

It is quite a lot if you can, for example, abstain from killing and stealing. I suppose we would never have had racial riots in Sri Lanka. You can't kill, so the major act stops. You can't loot, so the second activity ceases. You have no business to meddle with another person's legitimate property. Those are the two major acts in such riots: killing and the destruction of property. I had always thought that these precepts were only a formality. But now I realize just how important they are. If only Buddhists could follow those five, it would make an enormous difference to society. But they are hard.

The five precepts are to be observed every day. But, on specified days of the month, the devout observe what is called the eight precepts (P. *aṭṭhaṅgasīla*; Sinhala: *aṭa-sīl*). The eight precepts embody the first five with one little difference, namely that the third precept, dealing with sexual misconduct, is here changed into total chastity. This is, for the layman, for the day specified for retreat. The specified days follow the lunar calendar: the eighth, the fifteenth, the twenty-second, and the twenty-ninth: the first quarter of the moon, the full moon, the third quarter and the new moon.

Even prior to the days of the Buddha, these four days were days of religious observance. They were called *uposatha* days. It is a Hindu word, originally, in Sanskrit *upavasatha*, meaning "living near," that is, living near the gods. The idea in the Hindu tradition was that on those days the people observed religious rites. In that tradition to do so meant to offer sacrifices, to give oblations, to the gods and therefore the gods would come down to attend, living near the humans. So it was a day when the gods and the people were living near each other. By the time of the Buddha, the word *upavasatha* had become a common word meaning "the religious day." So the Buddhists, and the Jains also, took the term but they had their own observances.

In the early days, the observance was simply for the Buddhists physically to purify themselves, to dress in clean white clothes, and lead a meditative life of retreat. This has come down from that time onwards but now, in addition to the observance of the eight precepts and the meditative life, various kinds of *pūja* are performed on these days. So the temple is a hive of activity on these days, which are called in Sinhala *poya* days. Before the coming of the British, these four days were holidays. On those days, people would not work in their normal occupations, but go to the temples.

In 1965, the government reintroduced this scheme. Rather than having Sunday as the holiday the *poya* days were made the holidays. But the trouble with this in following the lunar calendar is that you do not get 52 holidays for the year: sometimes it is 53 sometimes it is 54, because the lunar month is 29 days. Sometimes, then, the holiday would fall on a Tuesday and the next on a Monday. There were all kinds of practical inconveniences and finally the scheme had to be abandoned and now we have reverted to the seven-day week.

On the *poya* days the eight precepts are observed. There is a little change in the meaning of the third precept. Whereas sexual misconduct refers to adultery, in the classification of eight precepts it means chastity or sexual abstention altogether. The fourth precept and the fifth precept are similar. The sixth precept is fasting, which means that one eats only in the morning and fasts through the afternoon. The seventh is avoidance of all kinds of enjoyments: song, dance, and music. The eighth is avoidance of all kinds of personal adornment: you do not wear flowers, apply scents, unguents, or ornaments on those days.

There is another set of percepts called the ten precepts (*dasa-sīla*). This is not generally observed by most lay people. It is a kind of more complex commitment. The young monks, novices, are expected to follow not the complete code of *vinaya* rules for the *bhikkhus*, but rather these ten precepts (*dasa-sīla*). So it is a much simpler code for them in their first few years of training. The ten are the eight we have considered plus two others. The ninth precept is avoidance of the use of luxurious furniture: no bed or luxurious seats and so forth. The tenth is money: silver and gold. One who observes the ten precepts is not expected to handle money. Those ten constitute the precepts for the young monk, *bhikkhu*.[7]

---

[7] Often documentary films representing formal activities of *bhikkhus* turn out to be somewhat deceptive. Documentaries are false by nature because a documentary is a selective presentation. Looking only at the ordination rites you will get the feeling that life is utterly regimented because such film presents shots of certain, specific incidents of the life of the monk. But what happens *after* the ordination is much more important than the ritual of ordination. Seeing the regimen, the monks walking in single file, you get the feeling that these monks are programmed—they are programmed, every one of us is programmed—but these monks cannot be

Also there are women often mistakenly called *bhikkhunīs*, which is the word for nuns. However, these women are like the novice monks and observe the ten precepts (*dasa-sīla*). The more complex rules and precepts that apply to those who have undergone the higher ordination (the *upasampadā*), do not apply to these lay sisters, sometimes also called "ten-precept mother" (Sinhala: *dasasīlmāṇiyō).* These women observe these ten precepts for life. They wear a special dress, a saffron robe like the monks. In appearance they are like monks, but they observe a much more simple order of rules.

Higher ordination (*upasampadā*) is not for the women. It was in the past, but the institutional lineage of *bhikkhunīs* (*bhikkhunīsāsana*) died out many centuries ago and it has not been able to be revived because the *bhikkhus* resisted. It is said that they exist in other countries, perhaps in China, but not in other Theravāda countries and certainly not in Sri Lanka.

The *sīla* for the *bhikkhus*, those who have taken the higher ordination, is much more elaborate and much more difficult. There is supposed to be some two-hundred-odd rules which they are to follow. They have to observe a special ceremony every fifteenth day. It is called *pāṭimokkha*. It is a kind of confession. They assemble on an *uposatha* or *poya* day and there is a rigid formulary according to which the whole meeting is conducted. If one has transgressed any of the rules, one has to confess it in the presence of the other monks. So in this way, an attempt is made to keep the observance of the *vinaya* pure.

This whole elaborate conduct (*sīla*) of the monk is summed up under four headings. It is called the fourfold purity (*caturparisuddhi*). The first is the restraint of observing the monastic code. The second is the restraint of the senses. The third is restraint of the way of living; therefore a monk should not get

programmed so easily. They are very boisterous and very rebellious. The young monks are often a problem for the older monks, which is not the impression that you get from the documentaries. One would have thought, from such films, that the monks are *very* obedient and that they would *never* transgress the teacher's word. They do worship their teachers, but after the worship they do the plotting. This is natural human nature. In any group you will find that. Remember, too, that in such films things are orchestrated. The monks know that they are being filmed and they are extra obedient.

into professions that are not in keeping with being a monk. In this sense the only thing open to a monk is teaching and, perhaps, attendance on the sick. Fourth is restraint in the utilization of requisites (*paccaya*). These requisites are supposed to be four: (1) robes, that is, clothing, (2) alms, that is food, (3) dwellings and (4) medicine. What is the point in speaking of restraint in the utilization of these requisites? The monk must realize that these are not for indulgence—your clothes, your food, your dwellings, and your medicine—but merely for one's maintenance, the minimum needed for health and the minimum to avoid inordinate discomfort.

The Buddha in his very first discourse said that he wants his way to be a middle way, to avoid extremes. Of course, looked at from today's point of view even this middle way appears to be an extreme because we have, over the centuries as humankind has undergone so-called development, increased our facilities and luxuries. I suppose this should be interpreted rather particularly, i.e., looked at from today's point of view we know what is luxury and what is not luxury. But what is not luxury today might have looked like luxury two hundred years ago. I think the point behind this is that we do not indulge in these things to the extent that others will be deprived.

In our next chapter, we will turn to the other two factors of *samādhi* and *paññā*.

Questions and Responses

Q: To what extent are the religious ways of the Buddhists incorporated into the government and to what extent does the government play a role in the religious life of Sri Lankan people?

MP: Since Buddhists are approximately 70% of the population, from around 1920 or so there was a strong cry on the part of the Buddhists for restoration of lost rights, and since it was becoming a very easy rallying cry, even during colonial days, governments have always been sensitive to Buddhist demands. In 1956, there was a strong agitation for making

Buddhism the state religion, but in spite of many pressures the government resisted going that far. The first independent constitution of Sri Lanka does not have any reference to Buddhism. But the next two revisions of the constitution contain a clause which says that Buddhism, as the religion of the majority, will be accorded its due place while the rights of all other religions will also be recognized. So the government is, by constitution, pledged to safeguard not only Buddhist places of worship but also those of other religious institutions. In point of fact, this policy has been more or less followed. I would not say that there has been any great discrimination against others. If there appear to be so, it was mostly in agitations and in the fact that when troubles start, the government, whatever the constitution says, would be a little more frightened to step in where Buddhists were strongly agitating for something. They might not have done the same thing regarding others. So there has been a little bit of bias.

Recently a government came into power saying they would create a *dharmiṣṭa* society, which means a society established on righteousness. But *dharmiṣṭa* is a word which is equally applicable to any religion. So I would not say that the Christians would object to the idea of creating a righteous society. Everyone accepted this. Unfortunately, during the tenure of that government, a lot that is *adharmiṣṭa*, the riots and other such things, which of course cannot be controlled by a slogan, occurred. The government came into power with this slogan, to create a righteous (*dharmiṣṭa*) society.

CHAPTER VI

VIRTUE, CONCENTRATION, AND INSIGHT
(*SĪLA, SAMĀDHI, PAÑÑĀ*)—II (CONTINUED)

Mahinda Palihawadana

Turning now to concentration (samādhi) and insight (paññā), Professor Palihawadana turns to the great Theravāda commentary, The Visuddhimagga, and its consideration of concentration, together with the development of tranquility and the different trances. In this concentration, we learn "the mind becomes supple, pliant, lustrous, firm, joyful and happy and the physical processes of the body, relaxed. The mind is composed, undistracted, integrated . . . ." And this leads to salvific insight, "then comes the real breakthrough." as Palihawadana puts it.

In our previous chapter, I spoke about the religious enterprise as divided threefold into a division of *dāna, sīla,* and *bhāvanā,* and also in a triple division of *sīla, samādhi,* and *paññā,* which is found more frequently in the books. In preaching, the monks would more often refer to *dāna, sīla,* and *bhāvanā.* There is fundamentally no difference between these two sets because this *dāna* can be subsumed under any of these things, especially under *sīla,* or even *paññā,* because what mattered was not merely the act of giving but the thought of it, so that it was really a case of the implicit being made explicit, when one makes *dāna* a separate category. As for *sīla* and *bhāvanā, sīla* is common to both, and *bhāvanā* is *samādhi* and *paññā,* because *bhāvanā* covers both tranquility meditation (*samātha-bhāvanā*) and insight meditation (*vipassanā-bhāvanā*), while tranquility meditation (*samātha-bhāvanā*) is *samādhi* and insight meditation (*vipassanā-bhāvanā*) is *paññā*. So, basically there is no distinction between the two threefold formulas.

I will proceed with the triple division of the religious enterprise as *sīla*, *samādhi*, and *paññā*. *Sīla* is to lead a virtuous life. *Samādhi* is to develop concentration of mind. And *paññā* is to develop insight. We have mentioned *sīla* previously. With regard to *samādhi*, we turn to the *Visuddhimagga*, a kind of textbook for Theravāda,[8] and there *samādhi* is defined as "the state by virtue of which consciousness and its concomitants or its contents remain evenly and rightly on a single object undistracted and unscattered." So we see from this that *samādhi* was visualized as a state of undisturbed, unscattered, composed and concentrated mind.

Samādhi would be the state in which five factors are not permitted to operate. These five are called the hindrances (*nivaraṇa*). If these five factors do not operate, then the mind is in a state of *samādhi*. What are the five? The first is sensuous craving, which is also a synonym for greed. The second is ill will, which is a synonym of hate and violence, aggressiveness. The third is torpor and lassitude, or forms of laziness and lack of energy of mind. The fifth is elation and depression—the two are teamed together—or restlessness and depression. To be in *samādhi* is to be, at least temporarily, without these states or conditions. An important thing to note at this point is that these five states are said to be suspended or suppressed in *samādhi*. It is not that they are eliminated altogether. What is said, then, to have happened in *samādhi* is described in a simile. It is like throwing a pot into water covered by algae. The act of throwing such a pot in that setting makes a temporary clear patch of water pushing the algae aside. But the algae is not removed, is not eradicated.

---

[8] *The Visuddhi-magga of Buddhaghosa,* edited by C. A. F. Rhys Davids, London: Published by the Pali Text Society by Humphrey Milford, 1920, Vol. I-II. *Visuddhimagga of Buddhaghosācariya,* edited by Henry Clarke Warren, revised by Dharmananda Kosambi, Cambridge, Massachusetts: Harvard University Press, 1950. An English translation can be found at *The Path of Purification (Visuddhimagga) by Bhadantācariya Buddhaghosa,* translated by Bhikkhu Ñyāṇamoli, Colombo: Published by A. Semage and Printed at M. D. Gunasena & Company, Ltd., 1964 (?).

It is there but it is removed only from the place where the pot is. The undesirable states or factors are not eliminated, but only suspended.

Samādhi is supposed to require energy and exertion. That would remind you of the eightfold path of "right exertion." It also requires mindfulness or awareness (*sammāsati*). Such also is in the eightfold path. Also it requires one-pointedness of mind, as noted also in the eightfold path as right concentration (*sammāsamādhi*). Thus, under *samādhi*, we have the fourth, fifth, and sixth limbs of the eightfold path, which is the Buddhist middle way.

Another word for *samādhi*, as I noted above, is *samatha-bhāvanā*, the development of tranquility, that is, the tranquility which begins with the subsidence of the so-called hindrances, which extends then deeper and deeper and further. Most specifically, *samādhi* means the attainment of certain states of consciousness in which the content of consciousness becomes more and more attenuated, thinned, diminished. There are eight such states described. The first four of these are named "trances" (*jhāna*). They are called "trances of the fine material (*rūpa*) spheres." There are many complex matters associated with this, but it is not necessary here to go into them. We will rather just try to find out what are the main characteristics of each trance (*jhāna*) which constitutes *samādhi*. In each trance (*jhāna*) something of the normal content of consciousness is reduced.

In the first trance, the five hindrances are suspended or reduced, but everything else is there—the thought process is active, the emotions are active, one may feel pleasure or pain, but those five hindrances are reduced. In the second trance, in addition to those reductions, discursive thought, pondering and reasoning (*vitakka-vicāra*), is suspended. In the third trance with all of those occurrences, there is something more: the emotions of rapture are suspended. Again in the fourth one, in addition to all of that, pleasure and pain are not operative. They, too, are suspended. So as the trances advance, more and more of the activity of consciousness is eliminated or, rather, suspended.

These are followed by another four, which are not called trances (*jhānas*), but four immaterial spheres (*āyatanas*). Here, the fifth state, or the first immaterial sphere (*āyatana*), is called "the sphere of unbounded space." The sixth state is called "the sphere of unbounded consciousness." Consciousness is not perceived as finite or bounded. The seventh state is called "the sphere of nothingness." The last, the eighth, is called "the sphere of neither cognition nor non-cognition."

In short, what happens in *samādhi* is the abandonment of discursive thought and the progressive restriction of consciousness to its last frontiers.

The *Visuddhimagga* recommends for *samādhi* a scheme of forty topics for meditative training, that is, it mentions various devices designed to produce an image and to stay focused on that image, which is said to give way to the trances. Then, also, the *Visuddhimagga* recommends various kinds of reflection, for example the reflection on the impurity of the body, its impermanence, that unless one exerts continuous effort it becomes impure. The reflections on the Buddha, Dhamma, and Saṅgha, the gods, on death, on the body, on breath—a form of meditation made popular with a focus on the inbreathing and outbreathing—are also recommended. The *Visuddhimagga*, further, also recommends projecting thoughts of loving kindness, compassion, altruistic joy and equanimity, which are called the four sublime states. Those are the methods recommended for the development of *samādhi*.

In the Theravāda commentaries and in the *Visuddhimagga*, the performance of meritorious acts and also the observance of *samādhi* exertions are all regarded as the first of "the prior part of the religious observance." Meritorious acts, that is, for example the various ritualistic ceremonies, are also called the observance leading to heavenly places. But the real qualitative change of personality, according to the early discourses and also the commentaries, is not to be found in these—not in *sīla*, not in *samādhi*. Not even the highest *samādhi* is a guarantor of qualitative change. This is something that is important to remember.

We know that the *samādhi* meditations were actually not specifically Buddhistic. They were part and parcel of the Indian religious context even when the Buddha, as the prince Siddhārtha, was a seeker trying out the various religious systems that were in vogue at that time. He learned these *samādhi* meditations under two reputed religious teachers called Ālara Kālama and Uddaka Rāmaputta. The latter one, Uddaka Rāmaputta, was credited with knowledge of the highest *samādhi*, the one called "neither cognition nor non-cognition." The Buddha mastered that and soon, however, left Rāmaputta because, in the words of the texts, "this religious training is not conducive to detachment, to deep insight, to Nibbāna." And later, in the Pali discourses, the Buddha said again and again that the religious life is not lived for the realization of *samādhi* meditation.

There are higher concerns, and more refined ones. And it is for their sake that the religious life is lived. There are many discourses in the Pali canon where this kind of observation is made, but I will mention only one. In one of the discourses, every *samādhi* meditation is described as conditional, based on conditions, and dependent on conscious effort. As we saw, *samādhi* comes under "right exertion" in the eightfold path. Conscious effort is needed for *samādhi*, and therefore it is impermanent and liable to cease because whatever is dependent on conscious effort will cease to be when that effort is not there. What is conditional is not the highest truth. *Nibbāna,* for example, is not conditioned.

In fact, there is another interesting discourse in which the Buddha speaks to a monk and explains how the first four *samādhi* meditations are in the field of the unstable. He goes on to say to Udāyi, "aloof from pleasures of the senses one enters and abides in the first meditation which is rapturous and joyful. I say, this is not enough. Get rid of it, transcend it. And what is its transcending? A monk by allaying initial and discursive thought enters and abides in the second meditation." And again he says, "But I say this is not enough. Transcend it." This statement is then made successively for all of the *samādhi* forms, right up to the last one, right up to the *samādhi* meditation called "neither cognition nor non-cognition." And then he says, in effect, how does one transcend that? "As to this a monk by wholly transcending the plane of neither cognition nor non-cognition enters and abides in the cessation of cognition and non-cognition." It has also to be transcended. He continues, "It is for this that I speak even of getting rid of the plane of neither cognition nor non-cognition." Here the Buddha says that even that highest *samādhi* must be transcended, must be got rid of. "Now do you, Udāyi, see any fetter big or small of the getting rid of which I have not spoken to you?" So he puts down the *samādhis* also as a kind of fetter. In fact, the highest *samādhi*, that is, neither cognition nor non-cognition, is also called the ultimate attachment. That is, one could therefore still have attachment for these things. We know that the main thrust of the Buddha's message is to get away from all kinds of attachment. So the whole point I am trying to stress is that *samādhi* is not the ultimate purpose of the Buddha's message.

However, the canonical as well as the exegetical texts of the Theravāda express the idea that in *samādhi* the mind becomes supple, pliant, lustrous, firm, joyful and happy and the physical processes of the body, relaxed. The mind is composed, undistracted, integrated (the Pali word is *samāhita*) and inclined in such a direction that, in *samādhi*, the grip of all unconscious forces may snap at any moment. Now what are these unconscious forces? They are described in Buddhist literature in various ways: such as fetters, stains, defilements, intoxicants, latent dispositions and so on. There are stereotyped lists of each of these categories. For example, there is a list of ten fetters, the seven latent dispositions, the ten defilements, the four intoxicants. Basically, they are all similar. The shorter lists are usually compressions of the longer ones. All of them are metaphors for the self-same human predicament.

Generally, all of the fetters can be subsumed under three words: craving, violence or ill will, and unawareness or ignorance. Another important aspect of these fetters is measurement, that is, to measure others by my own yardstick, whether another person is useful to me or not useful, equal to me or not equal to me. These notions of equality or inequality, of similarity, all dualistic thinking would go under measurement. By dualistic thinking here I mean you separate yourself from all the rest and interpret your relationship to that as something outside. This is the basic sense. Then again there is among these things "view," "opinion" (*diṭṭhi*). But it is much more than that. This is a habit of the mind to entertain various opinions, biases, preconceived notions. It is not something that is consciously done. It is an unconscious force.

Then there is suspicion or doubt (*vicikicchā*), a very important matter. These, this sense of "view" and doubt, are not affected by *samādhi*, that is, they are not abandoned fully (*samuccheda*). Some of these, as we found in *samādhi*, are just suspended. Of course it is not held that in every instance the *samādhi* states are followed even by a complete suspension or by the state in which the mind is composed, undistracted, integrated and inclined in a direction that the grip of the unconscious forces may be snapped. The best that is expected of *samādhi* is that it puts the mind in such a state that the mind is inclined in a direction in which the grip of the unconscious forces may snap. It is not held that in every instance the *samādhi* states bring about such changes. Once those changes have happened in *samādhi*, if the *samādhi* has prepared the mind in that way, a series of new experiences or a series of changes take place.

The new order of changes is not quantitative. It is not that something gets entered on. On the contrary, it is a case of subtracting the drawbacks that hindered the mind's potentiality. We now turn our attention beyond the sphere of *samādhi*. We can see this from the simile used for this condition. The simile is that of gold ore from which impurities have been removed. The mind at this stage is so purified that it shines with its natural luster, as purified gold shines with its natural luster. Such gold becomes fit for the best work, and it can be used for whatever ornament one wants. In the same way the mind too becomes capable of action, pliable, a statement which underscores the ineffective crippled condition in which it hitherto was. Really, when you say that when the mind has changed with these meditations to a state of being capable of action, we know that until then the mind was ineffective and crippled.

The implications of these statements are far reaching. The references that follow next in these descriptions of meditation are in tune with these implications. They tell us that certain potentialities for extra-sensory perception now become actualized. This, then, is a result of the release from that ineffectiveness which disappeared with the mind becoming integrated. Each of these potentialities that are now awakened is called a knowledge (*vijjā*), but this is not a cumulative knowledge, not the knowledge that we acquire in class or in the pursuit of science in which past knowledge is built upon. Rather, this knowledge (*vijjā*) comes into being at the withdrawal of the mind's obstructions and represents an awakening of intelligence that was hitherto unavailable. So it is a case of subtracting the drawbacks and a new potentiality awakening.

And then comes the real breakthrough. The mind now inclines itself to shed the bonds that hitherto held it in their shackles. *Samādhi* was suspension of the bonds but not their dissolution; this means that their suspension now changes into dissolution. The wording is interesting at this point. "What it inclines itself to realize, it comes to the possibility of witnessing that state." In other words, the mind now witnesses the dissolution of the intoxicants. But, again, the supreme change is not an acquisition of quantitative knowledge. This transformation of the very basis of personality is an event of "penetration" (*paṭivedha*), a word that highlights its instantaneous nature. This instantaneous nature of the dissolution of the mind's pollutants is also reflected in the choice of words with which what are called the path (*magga*)-attainments are described, a complex subject which, unfortunately, we cannot consider in this brief presentation.

Penetration into the highest is usually described in the early strata of the texts as a "one-shot attainment." But in later texts, and also sometimes in the earlier, one finds this divided into four attainments: the first path (*magga*), the second path, the third path, and the fourth path—the stream-entrance, the once-returner, the non-returner, and the Arahant. So it is either described as enlightenment at one stroke or as in four stages. When one speaks of the four stages one speaks of the four paths. There might be some confusion between the eightfold path and the four paths. They are somewhat different. The four paths in this sense usually are interpreted as the result of being rightly on the eightfold path. Each of these paths is also supposed to be followed by a "fruit" (*phala*). The four paths and four fruits are combined with Nibbāna to make what is called the nine transcendent *dhammas*. What is important to remember is that the four paths ultimately lead to the realization of Nibbāna. In each one there is a perception only. Unlike the one-stroke instantaneous transformation, which is reflected in the references in the earlier texts, in these *magga* attainments, in the attainments of the fourfold path, the supreme transformation is broken up into four separate events, at each of which a given number of fetters is said to drop off. So with the attainment of the fourth state, the last of the fetters drops off.

The total and supreme stillness, the radical otherness that characterizes the emancipated mind, is reflected in many statements in the Pali canon; for example, take this verse: "As in the midst he no will breaks, and the water still, so still unmoving would the monk make not a stir, none wheresoever." And also one takes a statement like this:

> For him who clings there is wavering.
> For him who clings not there is no wavering.
> Wavering not being, there is calm.
> Calm being, there is no bending.
> Bending not being, there is no death and birth.
> Death and birth not being, there is no here nor
> yonder nor anything between.
> This, indeed, is the end of it.

There is another reflection of this otherness of the emancipated mind found in the discourse called the supreme descent into emptiness. This account begins with a reference to the various meditations of the field of thought, all of which are realized to be effected and thought out, that is, produced by the exertions of the mind. But whatever is effected and thought out, that is impermanent and liable to cease.

> Even as he knows and sees thus, his mind is
> released from the cankers of sense pleasures, of
> becoming, and of ignorance. In freedom he has
> the knowledge that it is freed. He understands
> thus: those afflictions that might arise from
> the cankers of sense pleasure, becoming and

ignorance [the three things] are no longer there.
There remain only these, namely, the afflictions
that might arise from the body with its six sense
spheres.

That means that although the mind has changed, although
there has been a complete transformation of the mind, the body's
afflictions will be there due to the fact that he is still alive. "He
realizes that this sphere of perception is empty of the cankers of
sensualities." That means that his mind is free of the cankers of
sensuality, of becoming, and of ignorance. "And there is non-
emptiness only due to the body with its sense pleasure." He sees
the fact of emptiness on account of that which is not there, that is,
the mind is free of the fetters and on account of that there is this
emptiness. As for what is there, remaining here, he realizes that
there are the bodily afflictions. "Thus there is for him this true,
unperverted, pure and supreme descent into emptiness in which
the Buddha, too, used to live as did the sages of the past." And the
highest privilege of the emancipated mind is that it has become
fit to slip into the non-mind state of *nirodha*, cessation, In other
words, to slip out of the field of thought. And when he is on the
summit of cognition, that is most pliant *samādhi*, it occurs to him
thus, "To be thinking at all is the worst state. Better it is not to
be in the field of thought. Were I to go on thinking and fancying
these ideas, these states of perception that I have reached, would
pass away but other coarse ones might arise." So at *samādhi* he
thinks that these fine experiences will pass away and others might
arise. "Let me therefore neither think nor fancy any more. And
he neither thinks nor fancies any more. As he neither thinks nor
fancies any more, those states of perception cease [or *samādhi*'s
perception ceases] and other coarse ones do not arise, he touches
the state of cessation." So the highest final change is cessation
(*nirodha*).

To conclude, we may say that what remains functioning all
the way from ordinary perception to the highest *samādhi* were
differentiates of the identical thing: consciousness of the field of
thought. The real other state is *nirodha* or cessation, where one
completely dies to perception and sensation in the normal sense
of perceiving dualistically, conditioned as it is by the unavoidable

influence of the latent disposition. It is when these dispositions are dissolved that one is liberated from the limitations of the field of thought. This is a wholly different dimension of being, where the information reaching the mind from the sense apparatus and from residuals of the previous operations of the sense apparatus cease to flow in. The mind is then not enmeshed in the picture of reality obtained from the senses, from these sources. It is alert in deep stillness, open to a wholly different kind of contact with reality.

CHAPTER VII

LIBERATION IN THERAVĀDA

Mahinda Palihawadana

Having considered some of the important teachings of the Buddha as remembered by Theravāda Buddhists and so ably communicated by Professors Wijayawardhana and Palihawadana, we are now prepared to come to the question of insight-liberation, paññā, the moment when a real qualitative change occurs. The questions and responses that ensue indicate the effectiveness of Professor Palihawadana's delicate interpretation of this transformative awareness.

What I will discuss in this talk is based on two articles that I have written: one is "'Liberation' in the Theravāda Buddhist Tradition," and the other is "Is There a Theravada Buddhist Idea of Grace?"[9] There are four major topics that I would like to address: "Liberation from What?"; "The Process of Religious Learning (*sikkhā*)"; "Aspects of Religious Learning: *samādhi* and *paññā*"; and the fourth topic, which asks "Is Liberation through Grace or 'Works'?"

Most great religions of the world have something similar regarding the notion of liberation. I believe that in the Christian

---

[9] "'Liberation' in the Theravada Buddhist Tradition," *Offenbarung als Heilserfahrung im Christentum, Hinduismus und Buddhismus*, edited by Walter Strolz and Shizuteru Ueda, Frieburg: Herder Sonderdruck, 1982, pp. 186-208. "Is There a Theravada Buddhist Idea of Grace?" *Christian Faith in a Religiously Plural World*, edited by Donald G. Dawe and John B. Carman, New York: Orbis Books, 1978, pp. 181-195.

tradition, it is what may be called salvation. In the Hindu religion, the same notion of liberation is found. These uses of the word are slightly different in the Buddhist tradition. In the Hindu case, the term used for liberation is *mokṣa*. The same word is used in the Buddhist tradition, but less so. It means 'to be free,' liberated.

In the religious traditions, the next question that naturally comes to mind is "what is one expected to be liberated from?" If you consider the Hindu tradition, especially yoga, it is cessation of the activities of the mind. The famous *Yogasūtra* starts with this. Yoga is close to the Theravāda tradition, but Theravāda is unique. In order to come to this, I will take you through a discussion which is found in the Pali canonical texts. This deals with perception, the way one experiences external reality.

Why should the Buddha have directed so much attention to perception? It becomes evident when you think of its implications. There is a story in one of the more profound discourses which is called "The Honey Bowl" in English. The Buddha was asked to tell what he taught, in simple words. The Buddha gave this cryptic reply, "I teach the way in which one does not get obsessed with images. If one follows this, that is the end of suffering."

So, at the end of this discussion, the man went away, probably without understanding. The Buddha reported this to the monks, and they did not understand this either. They asked, "What does this mean?" and he repeated what he had said but enlarged upon it. The monks then went to another leading monk and asked for an explanation and he gave a breakdown of the process of perception:

> a) When you see an object, there is sensory impingement leading to visual impression.

> b) With this perception there is always a feeling—pleasant, unpleasant or neutral.

> c) After this, the mind is focused on this object; it is cognized, but a vague impression.

> d) Then the process of thought works on this and the object is delineated.

e) Then the mind becomes engrossed in this delineated perception.

f) Upon that one gets a series of concepts and thoughts related to the object.

In other words, there is an observed mental state following the delineation of thought. Your mind is not free to see the next thing that happens, but is engaged in an internal process in which there might be all kinds of hidden emotions and affective attitudes related to that object. You might be reminded of something that happened to you relative to that object or something similar. You might feel anger; you might want to have it more. All kinds of things can happen.

Question: What do you mean by delineation?

What I mean is attention focused on that object and the consciousness which becomes more acutely related in order to obtain a clearer picture.

So, in the last three stages the various signs which are attractive or repellant are noticed, and the mind is fixed on the image and its signs; and a continuous inflow of mental states derived from past experiences takes place. These past experiences and their results are discussed in Buddhist literature over and over again. They are called latent dispositions, hindrances, fetters, defilements, intoxicants and so on. The basic event may change but the concept is the same. If you examine these perceptions, you find they are basically all the same thing. In this state you are not ignorant of these perceptions but you are not conscious that you are focused on them. Therefore, the thoughts that arise from these objects are unconscious. Unconscious thought takes place after perception.

This is not limited to one particular discourse. It is something that you find widespread in Buddhist literature. There is a tremendous amount of repetition in Buddhism because for a long time one had to learn these things by heart, as there was no written text. Everything had to be recalled from memory. This made it a very useful method of instruction. One formula that is repeated again and again is: "Having seen the object with the eye, one becomes attached to the pleasant object and repelled by the unpleasant one. Thus one is launched into attraction and repulsion."

I have spoken so far only about the visual aspect, the seeing. The same idea pertains for all the other senses, such as hearing. In the text, it continues to the auditory area and so on. In these discussions of perception the Buddha emphasized that whatever the sense in operation, the consciousness that arises is immediately tainted by unconscious factors. This is what constitutes the main problem. If this were not so, one would see the world anew each morning. This is impossible because of the constant flow of past experiences into the present. In the Buddhist view, every person is born with a drawback: the drawback is this ever-present factor of latent disposition. Because of it, one does not see clearly, but rather through the screen of past images. They evoke tremendous psychological pressure. What you see is not only pleasant or unpleasant but is also related to wanting to have it or not wanting to have it. Therefore, the past image, the "imaginary" image of these things is perhaps the most powerful image which touches all other things. This leads to "I want these things" and "I do not want them."

Now then, we can see from this approach found in the Buddhist texts that there is something significantly important: keeping free of this past. However powerful perceptions may be in light of past experiences, one must strive to get over this barrier.

There are many terms for this learning; one is *sikkhā*. What is learning? The religious process is to understand this situation and to learn to get over the barriers of these unconscious forces— this is the learning part. There is also a practical part, and this is to lead an uncomplicated, inwardly rich life (*caraṇa*).

If the problem is caused by unconscious factors, the latent disposition, the rush of past experiences into present conditions, then religious learning cannot be essentially of an accumulated nature, but is rather of an eliminative nature. At the highest level it certainly is eliminative.

We have seen that *samādhi* is where the field of thought is narrowed down, and unconscious forces are suspended, but not eliminated. This itself is unstable and can become a target for attachment. The whole purpose of *samādhi* is to concentrate on a particular topic or something, perhaps even an object, so that the mind does not go astray. In this way the mind is limited to particular topics. This is, however, a preliminary exercise. Nothing changes. The inward factors that create our problems are not eliminated in this way. Instead, one gets a temporary patch of clear vision, and the mind learns to savor that kind of clarity. We have seen how the tradition refers to this as though it is like dropping a pot into algae-covered water; for a short while, the algae opens to show the water, but it soon returns.

Now, you know that there are all kinds of meditations, levels of meditation. In each level there is greater refinement of concentration. The final one is described as neither perception nor non-perception. It is said that even the highest *samādhi* is not a complete change of personality, a transformation, because there is always the possibility that even that can become an object of attachment. One attains a certain kind of concentration and sees the power inherent in it, and then wants to have it. If all the other forms of attachment, all other forms of attraction are fetters, this too is a fetter. Therefore, it is not a qualitative change.

However, in *paññā*, there is a real, qualitative change. The process is awareness, where one really sees the operation of the mental factors at the right time. You have heard of the establishment of mindfulness. This is one of the gifts of the Buddha to his disciples. It stresses that the being is at all times aware of what is happening. That awareness deepens and there comes a moment when the unconscious forces are snapped and a qualitative change takes place and there is a different dimension of being, a different relation to reality, a new kind of mind emerges. This mind is not tainted by memories of the past. Potentialities that were inactive are now awakened and limitations of the thought-field are transcended. The mind, alert and deeply still, opens to a wholly different order of reality and being. Therefore, *paññā* is the real qualitative change, the real liberation. Once the mind has gone through the *samādhi* stage and the mind has become composed and undistracted, it becomes inclined in such a direction that the grip of unconscious forces are snapped, and great changes are underway. The similarity here is like that of gold, from which impurities have been removed. When the gold is so purified, it shines with its natural luster. It is then fit to be worked on. In the same way, the mind becomes capable of action.

We are told that certain potentialities of abstract perception now become actualized. This is the result of eliminating the ineffectiveness of the mind and its integration. The mind now inclines itself to shed the bonds. This is supposed to be something natural, it cannot be done externally. The will cannot achieve this because it is based on past experience. It is part and parcel of the thought-field which creates problems.

Something must happen naturally, without the person saying he will do so and so, or something will happen. In other words, the mind now witnesses the dissolution of the intoxicants, the unconscious factors.

Q:I am trying to get to the point where the mind naturally breaks through. Is this a similar thing—practicing the Tao is like trying to become involved in the present all the time?

MP: I don't know really what the Tao is. People have different ways of discovery in different parts of the world.

If it is not a question of adding something but more of subtracting, then the mind at this profound moment of inner change would be a mind that is deeply free. The Buddhist tradition speaks of emptiness—the empty mind. The *samādhi* process can never empty the mind, it can only concentrate the mind. The contents are there. In the other process, the one called *paññā*, the mind becomes emptied of its contents. It does not mean that the mind is not there, in a negative connotation. We do not know what the empty state is without experiencing it..

I would like to consider the description of the state of liberation, called the supreme descent into emptiness. It begins with various meditations in fields of thought, where thoughts are concentrated. *Samādhi* of this type requires you to make an effort. When all of these meditations are complete and found to be effective, then the meditator wonders what the words 'effective' and 'complete,' which the mind brings into being, really are. They are impermanent and liable to cease. Even as he knows and sees it thus, his mind is freed from the grip of sense pleasure, of becoming. In freedom he has the knowledge—it is free. Not "I am free" but "it is free." All that remains are the afflictions that might arise from his body. But if the body feels pain and discomfort, those kinds of affliction are there due to the fact that we are alive. What remains, he realizes, are the bodily processes. There is true, unperverted emptiness; this is called the supreme sense of emptiness. This use of the word "emptiness" was not so stressed in the Theravāda tradition as in the more philosophical Mahāyāna, though you do find it in Theravāda. The approach of Theravāda, as we have seen, is in this direction: that the mind must be free of its past legacy. Then there arises a new dimension of reality. In that dimension, one is not experiencing the world through the sphere of senses but by engaging another order of reality.

I believe that other great religious traditions also contain this, each in its own way. In some there is the notion of transcendence. The Theravāda has its own way of thinking and its own way of explaining this transcendence, which is achieved through the elimination of the power of the unconscious forces.

Now I would like to proceed to the final point here which asks: Is liberation through grace or "works?" I believe that some of the question has already been answered. Normally, no Theravādin would admit the aspiration, because grace is immediately associated with a being who grants grace. Indeed, in the *Bhagavadgītā* grace is very important, because through devotion to Kṛṣṇa (Krishna), and nothing else, one can be free of all one's evils. Such a thing would never be said in the Theravāda. But if we do not have grace, then what? We are used to this kind of dualistic thinking, either "this" or "that."

Q: What is the original meaning of grace, the etymological meaning?

MP: The meaning of grace is "*pasāda*," being pleased, or being satisfied.

I don't want to go into that deeper. I think we tend to think in terms of yes and no. Something is grace or it is not grace. If it is not grace then it must be works. Indeed, in the Theravāda tradition, you have to work. You have to work—yes! You cannot set your vision on a goal and then go to it because that vision is something which came out of your mind and if your mind is tainted, the vision is also tainted. Instead, you see what is there in you. In the process of seeing, naturally, a change takes place. Therefore, it is not "Works," but it is something that is inherent in things that works. In this sense, one might say that there is a kind of grace in the order of the universe itself.

I know most Buddhists would be very unhappy with this kind of explanation. There is another thing I want to pass to you. I do not know the exact words. It is from one of the early texts. Here the Buddha speaks of the importance of applying oneself to meditation, although a monk who does not apply himself to the development has the wish. He does not do anything, he only has wishes, would that the heart be freed of these attachments. His heart will not be free because he has not developed the four foundations of mindlessness. He must see beyond, he has not been aware. He has not applied his mind to be aware. He has not taken the trouble. It is like the faith of a hen who, after laying her eggs, keeps on wishing, would that my chickens break their shells and emerge safely, without sitting on the eggs to warm them enough for hatching. As the chicken will not emerge as wished for by the hen, just so is the monk who has not applied himself. He may wish that his heart be free of the taint, but he will not be free. If a monk has applied himself, even if he does not have the wish, would that my heart be free, still his heart would be free, as the chickens would come out after being warmed up enough for hatching, even without the hen wishing. This emphasizes the importance both of the work and that something that is not willed has happened. The hen has to sit. It is in the order of nature that the chick will come. Inner change, that the Theravāda tradition emphasizes through meditation, through awareness, is something that is there inherited in nature. You will find this under the word *Dhamma*. Step by step our changes take place. You do certain things as you are changing. If you do not do it there is no change.

We do not notice when things go away a bit at a time, but they continue to go until they are gone. Though a believer may not notice that so much of the taint has gone away today, so much yesterday, so much at another time, yet he knows that it is gone. He did not know the change when it was happening.

I have tried to show you why liberation is needed because of the inborn drawback, and from that background, the depths of our consciousness, urges come forward and merge with experience, and here we find all the trouble we have. We find a new way of viewing the world, experiencing the world; it can be possible only if the grip of the unconscious, of our latent mind, is broken.

QUESTIONS AND RESPONSES

Q: What you're saying is basically that liberation is attained in life and there is no difference between Nibbāna while living and Nibbāna while physically not in this life. At the end of existence, does Nibbāna change in any way?

MP: When the mind is so still in this new kind of experience, the latent tendencies of the mind have ceased, and another dimension has been reached. But the afflictions of the body, like pain, these are there. So when you say that Nibbāna in one's life is limited by the physical body, what is suggested is that Nibbāna after death is different in this sense.

Q: I have a question about the process of perception as it relates to mind. Mind is the sixth sense, right? I'm wondering, when you see something, the eye perceives the object and then the process occurs. How does this occur with the mind?

MP: We discussed two kinds of perception. One is the perception in which the past is part of the cognitive event. Another perception is when that does not happen. In this "wrong" perception, or normal perception, the past associations are associated. They are like any other perception. It is therefore implied that this kind of perception has deceased. I do not know if I have made myself clear.

The whole problem the Buddha has put into one very short description. A man comes and he tells him, I think I am not going to live very long, please give me some guidance because I am very interested in what you are teaching. The Buddha said this can't be done on the street. But the man insisted on getting a summary of what the Buddha did. In the seen, let there be just the seen, in the heard let there be just the heard, and he goes on with the senses, let there be just the sixth sense, the mind. What he is trying to say here is that in the seen here today, to us normally there is not merely the seen but much that is not seen. I see the tree, or I see the car. Memories of being in the car surge up. Therefore there is more than the seen. In the operation of the mind, there can be memory, there can be memory with which you associate yourself; you are involved. I see the car, it is just that. The mental experience is often associated with other past remembrances of cars and things. It can be that you just see without this. So there are two types of experience mentioned.

Q: So, the origin of thought would not be a useful question.

MP: Yes, that is the only approach. You can go on to historical analysis, and find different formulations at different times. And we can always ask, what went on before that, and on and on.

Q: There seems to be such an outstanding paradox here. If desires are fetters which should be eliminated, how can the ultimate desire for liberation be justified? There seems to be a contradiction.

MP: I would rather put it like this; that desire should be understood. In understanding, what is naturally necessary as desire, there should be a quantum of such a thought as desire for the human race, of living beings. There are also other desires which are added on as the process of perception goes on. If we are aware of the process of desire, I am sure that there is a mellowing, a maturing of desire, and a change takes place. So, the solution of having another desire for the elimination of one desire would be wrong. You will find that these desires will not work. You watch natural desires work and you develop an understanding.

Q: How does the realization of the truth of no-self (*anattā*) fit into the entire breaking-through process?

MP: Again, it is like when I said the natural order of the universe has a provision for change. We think what is being said is that apart from the thoughts, there is no other thing. So, in the case of this change, it is supposed that the thinker is part of the process. Apart from the thoughts, there is no other thinker.

Q: In an article you wrote, "Dhamma Today and Tomorrow,"[10] you mentioned the nature of Dhamma which lures, after the pursuer gets a taste of it, and calls one back for more. Today you mentioned that perhaps in the universe there is something inherent, which is akin to a concept of grace. Could you comment on whether there is a concept of grace in Dhamma which calls forth and helps the pursuer?

You said that desiring the mind to come back in another birth is a fetter, but then you also answered a question saying it is not abolishing this fetter of desiring but more a matter of understanding. So, in a way perhaps it is not too much of a contradiction.

MP: The mind savors, it feels, it knows the difference between a heavy mind burdened from the past and a light mind, free of the past. The natural thing is that when this is seen, the change takes place. And yes, I would say that the Dhamma has an inherent grace in it.

It is not just for myself, it is for everyone. It is not individual, it is religious.

Q: If someone was able to perceive the world without the past interfering, can one still speak of a memory?

MP: We are dealing with two kinds of memories, one which has no negative effect, for example a name you use. Without a necessary memory, then the whole academic enterprise is abolished. I think mankind has been provided with memory to make use of it. We can do without it, but there is no opportunity.

Q: Considering cause and effect, can you ever have a single condition which produces results?

---

[10] "*Dhamma* Today and Tomorrow," by M. Palihawadana, *Religiousness in Sri Lanka*, edited by John Ross Carter, Colombo: Marga Institute, 1979, pp. 129-147.

MP: If you mean a condition creating specific effect, yes. It is difficult to say how many causes there are.

Q: I am interested in the way one's thinking is transformed when the move is made from "I am free" to "It is free." You talked about not experiencing the world through the dimension of the senses, and I think I need some kind of visual image of this. My way of thinking, which may be completely opposite to what really is, is being aware of sitting here but being almost removed from your body, like standing away, being a third-person observer of your life and physical actions, or is it the complete elimination of that and just knowing that you are sitting, a complete elimination of why you are sitting and feeling you are sitting.

MP: This is a difficult one because I can only answer it within my own field of experience. I think most of us experience this personally in many ways. We get absorbed in this. It happens that you see something—a cloud or a sunset or a tree—and there are times when time passes by without you knowing it, until something "wakes you up." How could you describe this experience?

Q: If we are separating ourselves from our past experiences, from our memories, and we just see what we see and hear what we hear, how are we supposed to understand what is going on at the present if there isn't some kind of order given to us from the past?

MP: That is what I meant when I said it is difficult to describe. Your name, your social security number, these things are all part of the unnecessary world. All of these things can be brought into play. Most people have a fascination with ID cards, with photos and names. These are unnecessary parts of you, but there are necessary parts as well.

Q: So you distinguish between necessary memory and unnecessary memory, or is that part of the natural process—it just happens?

MP: I think it is for each one to find out what is necessary.

Q: But that is not an act of the will, that is something after meditating and focusing my mind that I will attain, that like a chicken attains a chick whether it wants it or not, it will just happen, and unnecessary memories will drop away?

MP: I think it is hard to know how much has happened. Later on you can see. I find that more enlightening than most other things that are indicative. You will find that some things are necessary but because the journey is not over, it is hard to say that different steps have occurred. For the last 50 years or so I have been trying this kind of thing, and a lot of things have gone away. I am glad that they have gone away. I can do without them and their not being there anymore is a form of great unburdening. Now I can say that all of those things were unnecessary, but I couldn't have said that back then. That is why I said it is a personal thing. Everyone experiences it differently.

Q: Do you have any desire to go forth, to renounce?

MP: No, I don't, but I think I should be doing it as I am.

Q: For another question, you said that our attempt to describe what we perceive is an interfering process and that by doing so we engage in this process by which we become "better," I guess. I wonder about the Buddha's own ability to relate his insight—the *Dhamma*—to us. In that case my language has to mediate his perception. How does this happen without damage, since it is interfering with our ability to understand the way it comes to us.

MP: Do you mean, how does one communicate?

Q: Yes, I guess so. I was wondering how one communicates *Dhamma*?

MP: I will try to answer that if I can. Language itself is tainted, because when you say "I am," it opens up many possibilities. The extraordinary perceptions do not use such language. Language is something that can interfere, that will interfere. That is why I said it is hard to describe. Now then, you ask me how did we communicate today? It is very interfering. If what I was saying was totally academic to me, I believe I would have communicated less. But, because it is not, I believe I have communicated more. There are possibly other factors borne in the communication process.

Q: My question has to do with the duality of grace versus works.
I was wondering if it could be overcome with the idea that,
and I think you suggested this, in practicing *samādhi* we
condition ourselves so that when that moment in the future
comes we will be prepared for it. Is that the idea—that the
moment we drop all fetters it will come naturally, not through
the will? Is there a notion that through practicing *samādhi* we
are preparing for that moment?

MP: Yes. I think you are asking me why you should not do
something that is divided.

Q: No, no, I am asking if that is how to overcome duality of grace
and works, seeing it as preparation for that future moment?

MP: Well, I would phrase it slightly differently. I would rather say
that one realizes genuineness and one tries various things. It
is suggested that this is a useful avenue to take. I shy away
from your way of putting it because it makes it one of the
desires. Too much effort. But, you are not far wrong.

Q: I know that the religious practices will not avail the final
goal. What is it that leads one to want to begin initially even
to offer a flower to a bodhi tree—at that level?

MP: Well, it is faith. I have never been able to understand what
saddhā is. I believe that, for example, a child is fascinated by
rituals, as temporal as they are. There is something beautiful
about the tree and the flower, so I suppose it is a kind of a
nice way to nudge us in that direction. But, I would not say
that that must be ruled out. If that is not done, perhaps we
would have too mundane a life. I certainly encourage going
to the temple and observing the rituals rather than not doing
so. But there is a better way in this life, on which we focus
attention.

CHAPTER VIII

THE CHARACTER OF BUDDHISM ACCORDING TO THE CANONICAL TEXTS (*TIPIṬAKA*)

Venerable Dhammavihāri

Moving from an introduction to the way the teachings of the Buddha contribute to the arising of a mind that is free from habituated preoccupations, leading to actions that are wholesome and also free from calculation, to tranquility, and to the arising of salvific insight, we now turn to a series of talks more topically focused beginning with a summary of the basic canonical texts (Tipiṭaka), and comments about how one might spot therein distinctive key Buddhist attitudes, by a great scholar of the monastic regulations (Vinaya), the late Venerable Dhammavihāri, who, prior to his entering the Order in 1990, was known as Professor Jotiya D. Dheerasekera and served as Director of the Postgraduate Institute of Pali and Buddhist Studies

I will attempt to address the contents of the threefold division of the Buddhist texts *(tipiṭaka)*, as an index to the character of Buddhism, that is to say; in the contents of the Buddhist texts there is an index to the character of Buddhism.

In the course of this discussion, I will be indicating some places and some areas in which, for one reason or another, there have been mistakes in the interpretation, in the analysis, of some of the basic viewpoints, even of basic texts of Buddhism, both in the hands of local Sri Lankan scholars, and of people of the

West. But this is understandable, because a hundred years ago the study of the Pali language was not as advanced as it is now. Much more than the difficulty of language, getting in alignment with strange ways of thinking was also not then prevalent. That was the way it was at the beginning, because the only way to measure and evaluate concepts developed in the Theravāda Buddhist tradition was by comparing them to one's own culture. This tendency appears, for instance, with T. W. Rhys Davids and the other academic pioneers in England and even in later scholarship. As a result, some of the vital bits of information contained in the Buddhist texts, which perhaps antedated some of the concepts of the West at the time, were lost.

I will give you one good example. The concept of "overtime work," namely, when a person works a fixed number of hours, beyond which he or she should not be compelled or forced to work, goes back to the time of the early Buddhist texts. This concept of releasing workers at the right time (*samaya*), with extra compensation due when working beyond the established time, is contained in the Pali texts which date not too far from the Buddha's death. About a hundred years ago, when Rhys Davids translated an important passage, he missed the point and translated what should have been, "release the workmen at the right time (*samaya*)" as, "give him leave from time to time."

The fixed time (*samaya*) is the eighth hour, when one is to be released. This is an important concept, simply misunderstood not only by Western translators but also by Sri Lankan scholars. At the work place, the workers are provided with meals; the workers ate at the workplace. So they said a worker is entitled to food and wages (*bhatta-vetana*). Now notice the confusion when one translated "food and wages"as "wages for food," implying that one can get money anywhere, wherever one likes, but one is to come out from the workplace and there is a canteen where one does not have to waste one's time or energy for food.

So we have "food and wages," and "wages for food." A misinterpretation between these two can yield confusion. And the books delivered the point that "food and wages" is the original understanding, brief but precise, dating back to the Buddha's own time. After a period of about 500 years commentaries on these old texts were written. The explanations of the commentaries demonstrates how the old concept was a living tradition—it did not change. Sometimes it was believed that these little statements in the earliest texts were mere extraneous statements, that they were just theoretical assumptions and did not reflect actual life. This is a mistaken assumption on the part of sociologists and historians, sometimes those of the Western world. I have researched this problem enough to show that the literary tradition on record, spanning about 200 to 500 years, is also a living, vibrant one. It is not divorced from life. In the original texts it was said that the employer shall provide "food and wages" for the workman—nearly 500 or 600 years later the commentary says "daily food and monthly wages." The continuity of the tradition is expressed very precisely.

What a wonderfully developed system! They would have had registers at the time. In this second phase of literature, the commentarial explanations, there are more details. When it comes to the question of wages, workers, and leave, the commentaries note there are two kinds of leave. One's Saturday and Sunday, say, are the regular leave days. But one also has festival holidays, which are also counted as leave—what we might find today at Christmas and Easter. These commentaries also specify the wages. One shall not only pay the workers their wages at the commencement of their holidays, but also one should give them bonuses and samples. What is meant by "samples?"—they are things to take home, not only for the workers, but also for dependents, particularly spouses. When one pays holiday wages, one is also to give clothing and alms for a worker's wife.

So, one is to feed a worker at the workplace. One gives the worker an allowance, festival allowances, and also material things to take home. Now, these are little insights that a student or scholar has to be careful about when reading about the culture in the past. In the process of study, one is to dig in and not throw the precious things over one's shoulder. This is the general impression that I would like to give interested persons who come from the West, not that they are careless, but to show that one will, with careful study, find many things about the practice of living life.

With this brief introduction and kind advice—not warning—
let us begin. The *tipiṭaka* is the threefold division of the extant
Buddhist texts. But remember, this division of the three is of the
recent past and is not of the very earliest strata. Buddhism did not
begin with a threefold definition of its literature or its contents.

What, then, is this division based upon, when the texts
were considered as one and then divided into two and then into
three? That is very interesting. The adequacy of the one is an
important matter. Because all that the Buddha did in becoming
enlightened, or in becoming the Buddha, was to find what he calls
the meaningful explanation of the phenomenon of life. And in
his own evaluation, he looked at life and made an assessment:
what is to be made of this—we go through the vicissitudes of
life, sometimes painful, sometimes something else, and so on
and so forth. His views of the world are recorded—persons and
their environment, not isolated but *in* their environment. People
might say that salvation in Buddhist thought is individualistic.
But remember, it is not considered apart from a social context.
The error in interpreting Theravāda arises because there is such
stress on the individual's working out his or her salvation that
he or she is cut off from society. Right from the commencement
of one's awareness to seek liberation, one is already in another
relationship with society.

The basic five precepts have social dimensions. The first
forbids the destruction of life. This involves respect for the whole
environment—human beings and animals—one's relation with
life. It also includes safeguarding one's own life. Associated with
these considerations is the notion of a *right* of positive living.
The second precept forbids stealing, and demands respect for the
ownership of property—here is another social dimension. The
third and often misinterpreted precept is also social in nature.
It calls for appropriate sexual relationships within society. This
is now interpreted in diverse ways which do not consider the
specific context in which the precept originated. The world of
the sixth-century B.C., in which the precept was formulated, had
attitudes concerning marriage and sex very different from the 20th
and 21st century. In this particular precept the Buddha himself
is reflecting the social relation of marriage and sex. In this way

we see that the Buddhist scheme of salvation, or emancipation, has to begin by getting oneself into proper social relationships with one's environment—human beings and animals. Initially, the psychological relationships that one establishes with one's environment gets one into this mess, what is called *saṃsāra*. The Buddha saw no reason to find an external reason or cause for this—it is the working of the psychology of the human being.

The Buddha had a new way of thinking about life in the world, about one's position in this life context and what one could do to make life better. The issue of salvation or release is directed to this end. This new approach is what we call the Dhamma which later, in the threefold division, is the *Sutta* (Skt. *Sūtra*), the teaching, of the Buddha.

Once there was a clear enunciation of what one is, what one makes of oneself, and what one should make of oneself—that was the Dhamma. That was enough, for one who takes life seriously, to start working on. This is why the early Buddhist texts are replete with references saying, literally, "having heard this Dhamma taught by the Buddha, a man who has gained conviction thinks, 'This way of life recommended for salvation is completely pure and wholesome and cannot be lived by a man who lives in a household.'"

In the Buddha's words one finds the needs and the necessities of household life. But if the demands of this life are allowed to commandeer too much, one cannot fully devote oneself to the practice leading to salvation. The layman and the monk do not have different goals. They seek the same goal but in different gears. One is the faster gear and the other, slower. There is a lovely simile in the Buddhist texts. It says that a beautiful blue peacock, with its crested head, will never equal the speed of the goose in flight. Likewise the layman living in the household shall never equal the monk who, living in the cloister, practices his whole life. They are on the same track; it is only a question of their being in different gears.

Now, having accepted that the more earnest of the Buddha's disciples has to be a little different from the layman, the community of the monks (*bhikkhus*) developed. Convinced of the necessity of proper conditions to achieve the goal that a monk sets for himself, he works earnestly and zealously. As long as the Buddha was living and his community of followers was practically within seeing distance of him, there was no need for elaborate monastic regulations. When questions arose, the Buddha would give his advice. This explains the reason why the monastic regulations, the *Vinaya*, comes on the scene at a later period, perhaps a decade or two after the Buddha's passing.

As the religion expanded and monastic communities arose at some distance and because more and more people joined— sometimes with less conviction and less seriousness, some seeking certain concessions—there was a gradual drifting away from the spirit of the Dhamma. The focused goal-orientation diminished. This is going on even today. With regard to our communal clashes, riots, and fighting, if one were to ask those who participated in them, they would say that they did it because the goal-orientation has gotten blurred—we do not know what we are living for anymore. What are the goals that we want to achieve?

Regulations appeared necessary when reports of a great many instances of contrary behavior appeared—that is, reports of behavior among followers contrary to that of the original disciples. In the early stage it seems that common sense prevailed. It might have been something like this: A monk engages in behavior contrary to proper goal-orientation. Other monks would say something like, "Look here, man, being a monk you can't do this!" That monk might reply, "There is no legal enactment against this behavior." "Rubbish! Why do you want a legal enactment?" For example, if one drives a car at night without lights one might hit a person, a tree, or a street lamp. For this sort of thing a rule should not be needed. But then we might argue that a society must see that legal provisions are in place to ensure that people follow even what seem to be common sense rules of conduct.

In this way, over time, the legalized form of what is called the *Vinaya* deveoped, out of a necessity to prosecute and punish in order to preserve the good name of the Order. The *Vinaya* probably never sent anyone to Nibbāna. It cannot. There are limitations of the *Vinaya*, while the Dhamma, the real texts, the scriptures, corrected the man in thought, word, and deed. That is the true medium through which a person can be corrected. We usually say it is adequate to focus on only two things: word and deed—not thought. One cannot legislate against thinking. And, in the *Vinaya*, the rules focus on activity of word and deed. However, in the *tipiṭaka*, that is, the Dhamma as *Suttapiṭaka,* the teaching is focused on correcting conduct through all three media: thought, word, and deed.

Always remember to interpret the *Vinaya-piṭaka*—the codified law which is the second group of the "three baskets" (*tipiṭaka*)—in relation to the Dhamma. In doing so, one sees the *Vinaya*'s character. It is designed to help the monk follow his spiritual goal and it also has a broad area of social considerations. There are goal-oriented precepts and more social-oriented precepts.

An example of the latter is the injunction that, on their alms round, monks are not to frequent a home or household that has lost its breadwinner. At no stage is a monk to become a pest like that, creating a hardship for the laity. Moreover, if a son of a family becomes a monk and the father of that family dies, leaving the mother a widow, there are provisions in the *Vinaya* for that monk to look after her at times. The old accusation made about the Buddha receiving these men into the order with the thought "Ah, we are getting rid of these families!" is not correct.

In considering the relationship of the Dhamma and the *Vinaya*, the conjunction "and" is important. The Dhamma and *Vinaya* are two divisions of discipline. Dhamma comprises ethical, moral, and mental directives. When it is legalized, codified, as a penal code, it is a *Vinaya*. That is why the Buddha, lying on his deathbed, said, as I paraphrase, "When I am dead and gone, think it not that you are without a teacher. There is the Dhamma which I have taught you, there is the *Vinaya* which I have laid down for you, codified." Sad to say, sometimes researchers have misinterpreted this statement to mean the Buddha laid down a doctrine only.

As I have said, the threefold division of *tipiṭaka* arose after the Buddha, post-*parinibbāna*. The *Dhamma-vinaya* was to regulate life, neither to run into conflict with society nor to run into conflict with the goal of Nibbāna. And, in a *sutta* almost at the close of the Buddha's life, there is a statement that records only two divisions of teaching: Dhamma and *Vinaya*. Then he passed away and three months later there was a congregational rehearsal, a *saṅgīti*, of the Buddha's disciples who assembled to put together all the teachings that the master had laid down: "Let us have it so that we can respect his word." When they got together they rehearsed it orally, repeated it, and codified it, without writing it down.

The earliest record of the Buddhist texts occurs in the report of the first Buddhist council.[11] Here we find a record of what took place. They asked, as it were, "Which of these two should we recite, the Dhamma or the *Vinaya*?" This is interesting. There were only two components. The living Buddha referred to two components and now at this assembly they also speak of two components.

One further point is of interest. Which of these two shall take priority? Which of the two is to be recited first? It is a question of priority. Whether this represents the very earliest tradition or is later is difficult to say. When the assembly considered this question they decided on the *Vinaya*—the codified law is the lifeblood of the religion. There was recognition of a need for the legal backing or the legal support even before one launches into the question of mental reflection. First, let there be regimentation, the *Vinaya*, the external grooming of the disciples. Then one can enter the practice. This does not indicate changing or fluctuating values in Buddhism: *Vinaya* first and Dhamma second. One has, as it were, to fence it all in first so there is no wild roaming-about.

Still, in our historical review, we do not hear of the *Abhidhamma*, considered the "third basket" of the *tipiṭaka*.

---

[11] *Cullavagga*, Chapter XI, *The Vinaya Piṭakam*, edited for the Pali Text Society by Hermann Oldenberg, London: Luzac & Company, Ltd., 1964, II, 284 ff., with an English translation in *The Book of the Discipline*, translated by I. B. Horner, London: Luzac & Company, Ltd., 1963, V, 393 ff.

Later, when we come to the commentaries and their observations on these things, we meet a different categorization: "Yes, they recited the Dhamma, they recited the *Vinaya*, and they recited also the *Abhidhamma*." As far as the records go, this is an accommodation of what apparently was a subsequent event. This is by no means to underrate the prestige of the *Abhidhamma*. A new scale of values developed.

In the earliest reference, in the *Culavagga*, only two elements are mentioned—the Dhamma and the *Vinaya*. The commentary on this, which is about five centuries later, says the *Abhidhamma* was also recited. While Upāli is recorded as being the leader regarding the recitation of the *Vinaya*, and Ānanda did the same for the *Sutta*, for the third one, the *Abhidhamma,* they assigned to Kashyapa. The texts of the *Vinaya* and the *Sutta* each give a reference to a spacific historical time and place. When the disciples considered *Sutta* they said, "Where was it recited?" At, for example, Sāvasti. "To whom? When?" There was a recorded method of establishing a historical setting for the *Sutta* and *Vinaya*.

When it comes to the *Abhidhamma*, one encounters some difficulty. Under the category of *Abhidhamma*, there are seven different books, more developed, almost encyclopedic works, that are presented as being recited. But places are not identified at which the words were spoken or persons to whom they were addressed. The doctrinal content may be found somewhere in the canonical literature, but the historical context or setting is not recorded. So, one has a beautiful theory in *Abhidhamma* that is not grounded in space and time. A new source for this collection needed to be found.

It is said that after the Buddha became enlightened, he suddenly became aware that his mother, who died some days after his birth, was born into a heavenly existence. So the Buddha, from a sense of gratitude, to repay his mother, is supposed to have traveled up to the heavenly world and to have preached this *Abhidhamma* specifically to her.

That is the mythological version. This is a great teaching, and who but a heavenly being would be able to comprehend it.

And in uninterrupted continuity, it is said that the Buddha wished that when he came down to earth, from time to time, he wanted—not in a tape recorder version—a created figure of the Buddha to continue the teachings. Then it is said that he came down to earth and passed it on to Sariputta who passed it on to Ānanda and so forth. So this is the mystical origin of the *Abhidhamma-piṭaka.*

The origin of *Abhidhamma,* as the later writers would make out, is hidden behind a veil of mystery and grandeur. The word "*abhidhamma*" seems to have some kind of relationship to Dhamma. The word itself is interesting because of the early occurrence of the term. We speak of it as being a later *piṭaka,* but the word itself is in early references, in all of which it points to a more profound content and method: a more analytical, sophisticated scanning and processing. So, *abhidhamma* is two things: as subject matter there is a profundity—not a collection of ethics, morals, psychology, and so forth—which moves over a deeper and more complex structure. It is also, in its method, a process of analytical examination.

At the time when the *Abhidhamm*a was not in existence as a body of literature, what about the question of salvation and of reaching the goal? There apparently was no difficulty at all. Perhaps more people attained Nibbāna and escaped the ills of life through *Dhamma-Vinaya.* As a salvation media, even at the time when *Abhidhamma* was not a separate body of knowledge, *Dhamma-Vinaya* seems to have worked well. There was no deficiency, no inadequacy. The fact that *Abhidhamma* was not in the early period did not mean that people did not attain Nibbāna. So, *Abhidhamma* is really peripheral in a way: the Dhamma and the *Vinaya* were equal to the task, adequate for attaining the goal.

In making this observation, we understand that the Dhamma is the main salvation medium. Using the word Dhamma and keeping in mind the goal, it is interesting to note that sometimes the attainment of the goal is called *dhamma-bhūto,* "become Dhamma," to become the Dhamma. That refers to a total grasp, a total conviction about Dhamma. This means that one comes to live the Dhamma, one is the Dhamma.

What one finds in this is the Buddha's way of looking at life. When one looks at life and its psychologically maladjusted environment and consequent abhorrences, which include the five constituents of an individual (*khandhas*), one intellectually comprehends a certain fact. But coming to terms with it is living it. Grasping (*upādāna*), leads on to the perpetuation of the life process. When grasping is abandoned, there is no longer a perpetuation of the process. So, one finds in Dhamma a theoretical evaluation of the life setting and a practical guide for living in it. This is why the higher truths of Buddhism are supposed to be experiential. For example, one comes to believe in the theory of *karma*, but there comes a time when this belief fades away and one knows *karma* with personal conviction. When the theoretical evaluation and the practical guide for living it become one, it is just like bringing two views into one focus. When one clicks one's camera—that is Nibbāna.

Sutta therefore had this aspect of imparting intellectual intimation of all of this and sufficient perseverance, an ethical earnestness to get on with it. It is like the beautiful imagery, found in a passage in the *Theragātha*, of a tree high upon a rocky crag being kissed by a cloud. What I am trying to say is that the inspiration that is there in the Dhamma, in the *Sutta*, is adequate to get a person across to salvation, because the truth, is communicated in the words.

The teachings of the Buddha were communicated through tutorials. When the Buddha preached his first sermon to a group of five people, it was a mixed audience. Throughout his preaching, the individual capacities of those hearing it were different. In the early Buddhist *suttas* it is said that there are two avenues through which you can receive the correct vision (*sammādiṭṭhi*). One is "the voice of another" (*paratoghoṣa*): one hears it from another, wherever one learns it. So the role of the teacher is brought into focus; one hears it from another, from one who knows. The second avanue, role of the individual, is also noted in the importance given to sustained reflection (*yonisomanasikāra*). In the earliest phase, this was entirely adequate. When it was systematically organized, it was provided in the dual framework of Dhamma and *Vinaya*.

CHAPTER IX

THE THERAPEUTIC QUEST

Padmasiri de Silva

Professor Padmasiri de Silva, formerly of the Department of Philosophy at Peradeniya University in Sri Lanka, more recently Research Fellow in the Philosophy Department at Monash University, Australia, has written widely on themes in psychology. Introducing points of convergence with some leading Western psychologists, notably Freud and Jung, Professor de Silva uncovers afresh Theravāda Buddhist contributions to resolving tensions and a sense of futility by pointing out a sense of a creative unconscious that can be seen not in a static sense of a self but in open-ended potentialities.

In this chapter, when I speak of therapy I am really speaking of therapy in a very broad sense. When we speak of therapy, immediately the word that comes into our minds is (1) sickness. In order to heal the sickness we need to have (2) a diagnosis that addresses the causes of the sickness. Then there needs to be (3) some techniques for healing, a process of therapy. The concept of sickness, the definition of what exactly sickness is, however, varies from person to person and culture to culture. Sickness, therefore, is also used in a very broad sense So we have a general idea of sickness, are aware that there are causes for it, and we need to know how to deal with it. But paralleling all of this is a necessity to have (4) some kind of concept of mental health. What exactly is mental health? Is it just functioning fairly well or is it merely social adjustment? Is it a state of being contented and happy, or is it general normality, or is it a very high ideal of perfection?

This fourfold classification of disease, which is found in the early Indian system of medicine, is fairly similar to the four noble truths, with which we are familiar. The Pali word for this general notion of disease is *dukkha*. It is rather difficult to translate. It really does not have just one meaning. Its meaning is multi-dimensional, in fact one might say it refers to the human predicament. Let us take it to mean sickness in a very general sense.

The first of the four noble truths is the existence of *dukkha*, which we may translate in this context as "unsatisfactoriness" or "a state of disequilibrium" or "lack of harmony." One could possibly come up with fifty English words for *dukkha*. It could mean "pain" in a very deep sense. *Dukkha* refers to all that is unsatisfactory in the human condition. The Buddha taught that craving and related concepts are the causes for it. He then developed a way of dealing with it, known as the Eightfold Path.

A problem is, of course, what one means by the concept of mental health. The Buddha had two concepts of mental health. One concept was meant for people like us, who have made a compromise with life—living in society with all the tensions and conflicts with some kind of attainable ideal of happiness—which the Buddha called harmonious and righteous life. Then, of course, he had a very high ideal of happiness which he called Nibbāna, which is a state of perfection in which there is no restlessness, there is no conflict with passion and so on. To sum up, the therapeutic method found in Buddhism begins with the recognition of one's unsatisfactory state, considers the cause for it, offers a means of dealing with it leading to the ideal of mental health, interpreted as of two dimensions expressed in two concepts. The difference between these two concepts need not be exaggerated, but roughly there is an ideal of living well in society and the far more difficult ideal of perfection.

We do not have space to go into great detail. However, I would like to draw our attention to a very interesting book written by Sigmund Freud towards the latter part of his life called *Analysis Terminable and Interminable*. Terminable means that something can be terminated; there is an end. Interminable means that something is unending; there is no end. This is one of the most fascinating works that he wrote on this question of mental health, and regrettably it is unknown to many people. Freud has been associated with just one factor, unfortunately, the sexual behavior of men and women, as though there is nothing else which influences the behavior of people. In fact, many years ago I saw a film, called "The Forbidden Passion," on the life of Sigmund Freud, which depicted only the first phase of Freud's psychoanalytical theory in which he claimed that sexuality was the most dominant part of human life. Reading his works very carefully, one realizes that Freud found that apart from sexuality there were equally strong, even stronger, non-sexual components in human personality. These are factors like narcissism, or self-love or egoism, and also strong impulses of destruction: to injure oneself and also to destroy other things. They are called the "libido," "the ego-instinct," and the "death-instinct."

In my work in Buddhist psychological ideas, I have found interesting parallels between these Freudian impulses and the three forms of craving. As we have noted, the cause of sickness is craving, which appears in (1) the drive for sensuous gratification, sensuous pleasure, sensuality; (2) the drive for egoistic pursuits; (3) the controversial instinct called the death instinct, which has come to be called *thanatos*. The Buddha recognized the urge to destroy oneself and also, when directed toward the world, to destroy unpleasant objects and people.

In *Analysis Terminable and Interminable* Freud discusses the therapeutic quest. In light of this rich and complex work, I would like to consider the therapeutic quest, the ideal of mental health.

I should first say a few words about the Buddhist concept of sickness. The Buddha was very concerned with sickness, *dukkha*, but with sickness in a qualified way. He distinguished three aspects or facets of this sickness: (1) physical pain, (2) psychological pain, and what we, for a lack of a better word, call (3) metaphysical pain. Beginning with specific instances of physical pain—like a tooth ache or other bodily ailments—we may then discern the more abstract facets of *dukkha* such as mental sorrow or frustration, conflict, tension, anxiety, restlessness and so forth. Metaphysical pain is the most difficult form of suffering to articulate. Perhaps it might be compared to the "sickness of the soul" in the writings of Søren Kierkegaard. It is a controversial kind of experience because empirical psychologists feel that its existence is speculative, and criticize the fact that it cannot be empirically examined or semantically analyzed. I think, however, there is something very rich in this concept. In fact, there is a kind of patient coming to the clinics today whose problem is neither physical pain nor a very specific kind of psychological pain, but some kind of unhappiness and discontent which has no name.

When we turn to Buddhism, we meet the mental states like unsatisfactoriness, disharmony, emptiness, and insubstantiality. *Dukkha* covers all these various facets of suffering. A careful reading of Freud's *Analysis Terminable and Interminable* reveals that his greatest contribution was his theory that there are psychological causes for man's unhappiness. He realized that people suffer because of *ideas*. So we have the physical ailments—brain disorders and so on—and also psychological problems, and thirdly, this very difficult to articulate kind of unhappiness.

Freud began his medical practice with neurology in Vienna. He encountered instances when people were suffering problems, but in whom he could find nothing physiologically wrong with the brain. While in France, he studied with people using hypnotism in their efforts to treat sick people. They discovered that by means of hypnosis artificial signs or symptoms of hysteria could be produced through suggestion and so on. By using this method Freud was able to get his patients to talk about their problems. After some time he saw that these patients experienced some relief because they were talking about it when they were under hypnosis. This process was called *catharsis*, which comes from a feature of Greek drama in which one identifies oneself with various emotions of pity, of terror, and the like, which are presented by various characters, and one feels that those emotive conflicts are also found within oneself. After leaving the theater one has a sense of relief because one's own conflicts have been dramatized. This is the kind of thing that was going on in France at the time. It was called the "talking cure," that is, through talking and moving on one could find relief.

Freud was very interested in this technique of hypnotism, thinking that it opened up a new understanding of aspects of human life that went beyond physiological study of the brain. After his study in France, he returned to Vienna and put what he had learned into practice, achieving some success. A famous case, and one which fascinated Freud, was the case of Anna, a girl who had a paralysis of the right arm. There was no physiological cause to be found. Freud thought he should use this technique of hypnosis. After studying Anna, Freud noted that causes for physical behavior are not always restricted to the anatomy itself. The cause of a nervous cough or some other symptom can be caused by some trauma which is really very deep in the past and buried by the subconscious. When a traumatic incident is brought to the surface and one becomes aware of it, there is some kind of relief and sometimes the symptoms disappear.

Freud, after some time, found that hypnosis had its limitations. Firstly, not everyone can be subjected to hypnotism. Secondly, under hypnosis the relief received was often only temporary. Thirdly, most importantly, a person who has received successful treatment may feel fine, but not know why this is the case. There is no self-knowledge. For example one sees a similar case in one's study of *bali* and other ceremonies of demonic possessions and the like in Sri Lanka.. One disadvantage in this is that the person feels fine but really he or she does not know why. Under hypnosis, there is no conscious encounter.

Concerned with these limitations, Freud developed a new technique called "free association." In free association one relaxes on a couch and begins just talking and one picks out various associations and then gradually one moves into deeper territory, going into deeper aspects of one's life. One of my favorite examples occurs in the film "Spellbound." In this film a man, when he shaves in the morning, faints. He just faints, falling down. Later analysis finds that he faints because he becomes terrorized when he sees black and white together—the image of white shaving cream on a black beard. Under analysis, it was found that ten years previously, while skating on ice with his brother—both dressed in black— his brother slipped and because of the accident died. He loved his brother so much it was a very painful experience. He tried to forget this experience and repressed it. In Freudian terms, this went into a very inaccessible part of the unconscious. After ten years, through analysis, this was brought to awareness. This was why the white/black image disturbed this young man. When he became aware of it the symptom disappeared and thereafter he could shave at ease. This was the result of a free association, when one thinks of white, one thinks of white but when one thinks of black and white, one's memory might become triggered to recall something else. This is the method of free association without obstruction, without any repression. One just relaxes and talks. In this process some kind of self-understanding, some kind of knowledge about oneself. arises. In this way, knowledge was liberating; it brought with it freedom, and autonomy, and self-understanding. Even if the patient had conflicts, he became aware of them. That is briefly a background to *Analysis Terminable and Interminable*.

With this technique, Freud did a tremendous amount of work thinking that he enabled people to give up their conflicts. But after some time he found that there was considerable repetition in all of this. People came to him with conflicts which could not be erased from their minds. He found in the nature of instincts something very fundamental and that always generated types of conflict. This was new for Freud. He said something like "I cannot make people perfectly happy, but I can convert hysteria into common unhappiness." At this point, Freud saw another dimension of men and women, some kind of unending restlessness. He noted a related problem of counter-transference. He found that people develop some kind of attachment to their therapists. In the therapeutic context whatever solution or cure that Freud was able to introduce, an uncomfortable feeling in the patient would remain. Something in the nature of these things was very difficult to conquer. It is with this background that his *Analysis Terminable and Interminable* was written.

Today, because of temporal and financial restrictions, therapy cannot be undertaken in time consuming approaches.

One cannot undergo prolonged therapy. Various short-cut or shorter versions of therapy, such as physical therapy, have been introduced. But Freud would devote a full lifetime to a person. Even the well-being of one human being is a matter of ultimate concern. When he wrote *Analysis Terminable and Interminable*, he raised the question whether there is a logical end to analysis. Whether, when a patient comes out of analysis has he or she really solved all of life's problems. In his book, one meets two conflicting concepts of disease and two conflicting concepts of sickness reflecting a dichotomy or tension in Freud's thinking. One concept is apparent when he said, "I do not doubt at all that it would be easier for faith than for me to remove your sufferings. But you will be convinced that much will be gained if we succeed in transforming your hysterical misery into everyday unhappiness." This is just to make life tolerable. Freud comments, further,

> Our aim will not be to rub off every peculiarity
> of human character for the sake of a schematic
> normality. Nor yet to demand that a person
> who has been thoroughly analyzed shall feel
> no passion, shall have no internal conflict.
> The business of analysis is to secure the best
> possible psychological condition for the
> functioning of the ego.

Here Freud presents a very attainable ideal of happiness. It is something like a do-it-yourself kit. More awareness arises. There is more of a reality feeling. One does not live in an imaginary fantasy field. There is the power to use reason, the power to face conflicts once more. Then one exits from the clinic. One faces one's problems and one becomes satisfied with some kind of attainable identity and human happiness.

On the other hand, toward the latter part of *Analysis Terminable and Interminable*, there is a deeper search in men and women, that is, they are not just satisfied with merely living with conflict but search for something far deeper. Freud said that when a patient steps out of the clinic, the great process of self-exploration has just begun. The person becomes qualified to become an analyst himself or herself. This is a completely different perspective and one that I have found extremely interesting in the light of Buddhism. Freud hoped that what was received in the patient's own analysis would not cease to be effective when the formal analysis ended. The process of ego transformation, Freud hoped, would grow of its own accord. And insofar as this happens, further experiences will be appropriately analyzed enabling the learner, who has learned through analysis, to become himself or herself an analyst.

Freud himself went through the deep process of analysis and he also underwent analysis by other people. He was trying to be heir of his own projection which he might bring to situations of analysis. There is this great process of self-transformation of which Freud could not see an end. This is really the kind of dimension that enables one to say that coming back to normality is a quasi-religious mission. Of course a lot of clinical psychologists and experimental psychologists might not like this observation. This is really the dimension in which I, myself, am interested.

Three significant contributions have been made to the subject of psychoanalysis and Buddhism. One is a study of psychoanalysis in relation to Zen Buddhism, edited by Erich Fromm, Suzuki and DeMartino.[12] That has influenced my own writings. Secondly, in my own work on Buddhist and Freudian psychology, I offered a critique of psychoanalysis from an early Buddhist or Theravāda perspective, the tradition which is found in this country, in Burma, and Thailand. As for the Tibetan tradition, there is a very interesting article by David Living in *Metaphors of Consciousness,*[13] an interesting and exciting article. So some work has been done from the Zen, Tibetan, and in my own work on Theravāda viewpoints.

If there is this question of continuous unrest, what are the causes for it? Freud turned to the libido, the sexual instincts which are repressed, blocked, and because one cannot satisfy them one creates them in one's fantasy world and works out defensive

---

[12] *Zen Buddhism and Psychoanalysis*, ed., D. T. Suzuki, Eric Fromm, and Richard De Martino, New York: Perennial Library, 1960.

[13] *Metaphors of Consciousness,* ed. Ronald S. Valle and Rolf von Eckartsberg, New York: Plenum Press, 1989.

mechanisms. One subsequently does not become a normal person. Such a person has many problems and neuroses generating various other forms of maladjustment. Freud later found that sexuality was not the only important thing in interpreting the psychological complexities of life. He found that there were certain forms of sexual problems where the problem was so dominant because of the ego rather than sexuality. This is found in Freud's paper on narcissism.[14] The term "narcissism" was coined by Freud due to his considerable acquaintance with Greek culture. Unlike most experimental psychologists or even clinical psychologists today, Freud had a tremendous background in the humanities and culture and religion. Narcissism refers, in Greek myth, to a youth, Narcissus, who was so fond of himself that he looked at his image in a pond, quite proud of his beauty. Then, because of this strong predicament of self-love, he could not love anyone else and he is supposed to have died and was turned into a flower, the narcissus. Narcissism refers to the tremendous predicament of a person in a state of self-love. Later Freud found that this deep unhappiness was not due just to sexuality but to sexuality as related to self-love. Later, still, he found the importance of ego-instinct—the drive for power, for status, for position and for self-preservation. This consideration of narcissism is one of the most important concepts in the psychology of Freud. He even has a definition of mental health in terms of narcissism. I have found his definition of well-being to be very much in line with early Buddhism. He says,

> Well-being is possible only to the degree to
> which one has overcome one's narcissism.
> Some say that well-being means finally to drop
> one's ego, to give up greed, to cease chasing
> after preservation and aggrandizement of the
> ego. To be and to experience one's self in the
> act of being, not having, preserving, coveting,
> using, and so on.

---

[14] "The Libido Theory and Narcism," in Sigmund Freud, *A General Introduction to Psychoanalysis*, New York: Horace Liveright, 1920, pp. 356-372.

So, one can say that there is neurosis to the degree that the ego dominates. Mental health in this sense is common not only to Buddhism but possibly to all religions. This is something like conceit, arrogance, which are qualities denounced by all religions. The precise metaphysical analysis of the ego might differ from religion to religion. But in some way, the notion of narcissism may have some kind of anchorage in a number of religions. It is the strong sense of narcissism in men and women that makes analysis interminable.

More controversial than narcissism is Freud's theory of the death instinct. He thought that people not only strive for pleasure but that sometimes they really enjoy pain. *Sadism* is when one inflicts pain on others and enjoys it, and *masochism* is when one enjoys inflicting pain on oneself. This death instinct is one of the most fascinating concepts in Freud. However, a lot of people have said that aggression is the most dominant form of behavior, that suicide or self-destructive behavior is reactive rather than habitual.

Now, the Buddha said that there are three important aspects of craving (*taṅhā*): (1) the drive for sensual pursuits (*kāma taṅhā*), (2) the drive for egoistic pursuits (*bhāva taṅhā*), and (3) the drive for self-annihilation (*vibhāva taṅhā*). It is possible that some of these comparisons might have come to Freud through Schopenhauer. Freud said that he had at one point refrained from continuing to read Schopenhauer because his own ideas very often were similar to Schopenhauer's.

This instinctual equipment is one of the very strong contributory factors to our unhappiness. A second contributory factor, which I mentioned earlier, is trauma, that is, early traumatic experiences, which cannot be erased from one's mind, and can be a very important reason for neurosis or hysteria. Finally, there is the conflict between the ego and the instinct.

This is a point where Freud came into a difficult problem, and I think he left the issue unresolved. The concept of the ego in Freud is beset with many problems. He uses the ego on the one hand as the principle of sanity and order, as something which shows the nature of reality. On the other hand, he thought the ego came from the *id*, from the passions, and then it was the precipitate of lost objects which come from the past. So he found that the ego was driven by passions and at the same time was the principle of sanity and order, while also articulating the voice of conscience and morality in the form of the super-ego. This idea of the ego has a precarious position in Sigmund Freud. A lot of the problems in Freudian psychology are due to the overworked semantics regarding the concept of the ego.

If there is a significant contribution in Buddhism, it is in the far deeper study of the ego. Even though ego-psychology has developed up to the present day, I think this development is not very satisfactory. There is a lot of confusion. If there is an interest in the study of Buddhist psychology it is in the nature of the ego. Nathan Katz has recently edited a book, *Buddhist and Western Psychology*[15]. In that volume there is a chapter, "Defensive Mechanism in Buddhism," written by the late Rune Johannson. This chapter takes this question into deeper territory. I do not say that the Buddhist contribution is perfect, but I think there is a very interesting study of the ego.

Finally, this does not mean that there are no basic differences between Buddhism and Freud. There are differences because the meditative culture or the way of meditation has a lot of differences from the work of Sigmund Freud. It has been noted that in Freud's personality there is a kind of coercive nature. Freud thinks that he knows the answer and he attempts almost to force it on the patient. Buddhism does not really force it on the person. The key idea is "letting go," so that generally the person is advised to find out answers for himself or herself. Encouragement is given to discover resources of one's own reason. And beyond "reason," the Buddha taught, there is something more. When one goes on developing one's powers of mindfulness there is some power, some skill, which is different from reason. It is a deep part of self-analysis, which, when developed more and more, becomes a kind of different dimension within oneself. It is something beyond reason. It is something very deep, which is something very difficult to discuss in terms of contemporary psychological systems. These contemporary systems do not accept anything

---

[15] *Buddhist and Western Psychology*, ed., Nathan Katz, Boulder Colorado: The Great Eastern Book Co., Prajna Press, 1983.

beyond reason, beyond self-analysis, and what are considered normal techniques.

This is where we come to a kind of end. We are considering a religious tradition which is offering something different. Buddhism is not that deeply and directly concerned with mere neurosis. In fact, the Buddha thought that all men in some way suffer from a neurosis in a deep sense. Similarly, in Freud's writings one finds reference to his opinion that all people are to some extent psychotic or neurotic.

I have not discussed the theory of motivation in Buddhism, how motivation emerges. I have not discussed emotions, although I have done some work on this. With our limited space, I thought it best to turn our attention to therapy as terminable or interminable, to the causes of neurosis and unhappiness, and wherein their sickness is constituted.

Today we see a new kind of patient coming to the clinic. They have plenty of wealth, even two television sets, two houses—one for summer and one for winter—they have everything. They are unhappy and they do not know why. Even this sense of alienation, this sense of emptiness, with which people are acquainted, remains obscure to them. There are a lot of business people who have plenty of wealth and do social service but their lives are compartmentalized, are not integrated. A lot of us live with these tensions and this emptiness. This new kind of patient is symbolic of our contemporary age and in that sense I think a larger framework for therapy is necessary, and I think the dimensions of therapy are widened. Especially in this last sense I think interest in Asian religions, in Zen, Tibetan and Theravāda Buddhism may be of great interest, although there are only very few people who have really integrated these ideas to therapeutic procedures.

When we turn to the therapeutic concept in Theravāda thought we find the issues of the concept of the unconscious, and whether there is a creative unconsciousness, and the Theravāda attitude toward the self are all connected. In Theravāda, there are two facets of the unconscious. One is the aspect of the unconscious which cripples and obstructs the personality. In a way similar to Freud's discussion of the concept of the unconscious, the early Buddhist tradition developed a number of concepts addressing deep proclivities, deep tendencies in personality development. In fact, it is said that even a baby lying in a cot will have potential seeds of malevolence and passion and the like. The difference from Freud's thought is that in the Buddhist case these unconscious tendencies are not limited to one birth or to a single trauma.

A criticism Jung raised against Freud was Freud's neglect of the creative aspect of the unconscious. But in the Buddhist context, the good aspects are discussed as "powers" (*bala*). There are tremendous powers within us. For instance there are stories of Agulimāla, a thief, who went on killing many people. But after he encountered the Buddha some aspect of his personality which was not tapped, a germinal aspect for good, became tapped. The Buddha said that such dispositions can either be towards good or bad. So there are really strong tendencies, potentialities, within human beings. Perhaps one might not use the word unconscious for this. But there will be deep potentialities within us, for good or ill, and to that extent there is some agreement between Jung and Buddhist thought.

The *id*, so often associated with Freud, is something like a cauldron of excitement and passions. It is more like powers (P. *saṅkhāra*). *Saṅkhāras* are conative dispositions which can be either good or bad. There are massive semantic problems involved with the notion of "self." The Buddha would say that people should have a sense of direction, purpose, targets, goals, and coherent life styles. That is accepted. The fact that the Buddha said one should achieve a sense of egolessness does create confusion. For example, a friend of mine, who was doing some meditation work with meditation students in Texas, wrote to me to say that some students who came to practice meditation and who were introduced to the doctrine of egolessness liked it very much because their own lifestyles were so chaotic. Egolessness does not mean that there is something noble in having a chaotic lifestyle. The fact that there is no permanent ego, does not give rise to anarchy, impersonalism, and chaos. The doctrine of egolessness definitely leaves room for coherent lifestyles, targets, and goals. And sometimes the Buddha spoke about self-development, self-interest. This means that there is a sense of direction, a sense of purpose. But on the other hand, this sense of purpose has to be very carefully considered so that one does not fall into the trap of the doctrine of a permanent self or soul.

The Buddha said there were two extremes about which one is to be careful: one extreme is eternalism and the other is anihilationism. The fact that one rejects eternalism does not necessarily mean that one lands in anarchy and nihilism. The fact that there is a doctrine of egolessness does not mean that there need not be a concept of self. The only problem is what kind of self does the Buddhist accept. It really means that there are certain potentialities within oneself: the potentiality for compassion, the potentiality to help others, to understand—rationality.

These potentialities can be developed, but at each moment one has to be careful that one does not fall into conceit. It is said that even for a monk in meditation, he must be careful not to think *I* am a great master in meditation, *I* am achieving this state, *I* am far higher in a moral order than other monks. At every moment one must be very careful not to cling to a wrong conception of the self. It is one of the trickiest, one of the most difficult facets to understand in Buddhist psychology.

In Buddhist thought there is an acknowledgment of a creative unconscious. The *saṅkhāras* or dispositions can be either good or bad. On this, I think the Buddha is somewhat closer to Jung than to Freud. But regarding the concept of the self, I think a line has to be drawn. If a person is walking on a narrowly drawn line, he or she has to be careful not to fall on this side or that side. So the doctrine of egolessness is a kind of very narrow way of proceeding where one must be very careful to avoid eternalism and nihilism or anihilationism. This is relevant for us today because we meet a tremendous amount of impersonalism, a tremendous amount of anarchy. It may be that people today associate egolessness with this. That would be the other extreme.

There remains much for us to continue considering about the therapeutic quest in a comparative perspective.

CHAPTER X

THE PLACE OF ETHICS AND MORALITY
IN BUDDHIST THOUGHT

P. D. Premasiri

It is characteristic of Theravāda Buddhist thought that one does not begin one's reflections about the religious life in the abstract, or one's considerations about moral living by debating speculative opinions, but by carefully analyzing the nature of reality, which, as Professor P. D. Premasiri, previously Professor of Philosophy, now Professor emeritus of Pali and Buddhist Studies at Peradeniya University, shows us is none other than the nature of the human predicament. One aspires to moral perfection and these aspirations have a rational basis. The Questions by students run the gamut from doing good for the sake of the good, about self and others, and of the notion of no-[substantial]self and other matters of an ethical position.

I have approached the study of ethics mainly from a philosophical perspective. Consequently, my studies on Buddhist ethics have a philosophical bias. But I will not make my presentation in this chapter a philosophical one, although I might raise certain issues which are philosophically significant. Now when, as philosophers, we look at ethics as a branch of philosophy we make a distinction between normative ethics and meta-ethics. By normative ethics we understand the first order moral judgments, ethical injunctions, moral rules, moral advice given by moral teachers—all that comes under normative ethics. But there could be a philosophical aspect to normative ethics as well. Now suppose someone attempts to justify certain general normative principles, like, for instance, the utilitarian principle or the deontological theory of ethics. Then one is doing philosophy.

But when one says that one is approaching ethics from a meta-ethical standpoint, one, as a meta-ethicist, is not expected to commit oneself to any moral theory as such. A meta-ethicist need not be concerned about any normative commitment as such, but such a philosopher, as a meta-ethicist, examines the meaning of ethical terms and the nature of ethical propositions; their logical status, what kind of reasons can be counted for the justification of moral judgments—that is the kind of issue that is raised by a meta-ethicist. And a meta-ethicist may even come to the conclusion that we cannot have any moral knowledge, that knowledge is impossible in the area of ethical judgments, that they are merely a way of expressing our emotions or expressing our commitments to certain principles which cannot be in any way logically validated.

Now to me, Buddhism seems to be important as an ethical system, not mainly as attempting a meta-ethical analysis of morality. I do not think Buddhism has taken this philosophical approach, trying to examine the meanings of ethical terms. Although there may be in the Buddhist approach certain meta-ethical aspects, that does not seem to be the main purpose of Buddhist analysis of morality. I would describe Buddhism as primarily a normative ethical system.

A part of the Buddha's teachings can be said to be for the purpose of explaining the nature of reality. Now of the Four Noble Truths, at least three of the four attempt to explain the nature of reality: that life in the unenlightened condition is suffering, that is the first of the four Noble Truths. Then the second, that there is a certain cause for it, and the cause is desire, and attachment and craving. And the third is that it is possible to put and end to this unsatisfactory state of affairs. The fourth, I would say, deals with morality because it shows a certain right way, a correct way, which is called the *sammāpaṭipadā*, the correct path, the right path to overcome suffering. And if one questions what is the best way for a Buddhist to live the Buddhist answer is that it is a life in accordance with the Noble Eightfold Path. So the Noble Eightfold Path can be said to be the quintessence of the Buddha's ethical norms.

So we have a certain statement of the nature of reality in Buddhism, and based on the descriptions of the nature of reality, or based on the analysis of the nature of reality, the Buddha lays down a certain way of life which is considered to be the good life. So morality in some sense follows from, or is dependant upon, what the Buddha considers to be the nature of reality, or in other words, the nature of the human predicament.

What I would like to do in this chapter is to express my own view about the place of ethics and morality in Buddhist thought, what place ethics and morality occupy in the entire system of thought which we call Buddhism. And, secondly, I would like to examine the rational ground for laying down such moral principles, such moral standards or such a normative system. What is the rational ground for it? And then, thirdly, to present briefly what constitutes virtue from the Buddhist standpoint. What is virtue, what is morality, what is the good life? And fourthly, to take up one of the most relevant issues with regard to Buddhist ethics in the context of certain critiques of the Buddhist ethical system, its social relevance, or how far can Buddhist morality be considered as having social relevance. Is it just a prudential ethical system which looks after the individual's own aspiration to save himself or herself? Or is it something more than that? Is there something more than a prudential approach in Buddhism when we talk about Buddhist morality? So these are the four main themes that I would like to touch upon in this chapter.

With regard to the first issue that I raised, that is, the place of morality in Buddhism, in my view the ultimate goal in Buddhism can in a certain sense be described as moral perfection. So if moral perfection itself is the ultimate goal of Buddhism, I think it follows that morality should occupy a very important place in Buddhism. As we all know, Buddhism has Nibbāna, or the peace of Nibbāna, as its ultimate goal. Now, leaving aside all the metaphysical problems about Nibbāna, there are a number of instances in which the Buddha himself characterizes the nature of

Nibbāna in a certain way. *Nibbāna,* according to the Buddha's own definition of it, is absence of greed, absence of malice or hatred, and absence of ignorance or delusion. According to Buddhism, human behavior is determined by mental conditions—behavior is a consequence of our mental nature, or psychological nature. So when the Buddha is asked what is good, or *kusala,* he says, *kusala,* or goodness, can be briefly stated as the absence of greed, absence of hatred and absence of ignorance or delusion. Whatever Buddhism considers to be evil is actually a consequence of the presence of these three unskilled or unwholesome states in our minds. What is needed, from the Buddhist point of view, is to gradually eliminate these unwholesome traits of mind. So they are called the *akusala,* and there are various byproducts of these unwholesome or evil states of mind. And they have to be gradually eliminated. So the Buddhist path is actually a practical means by which these evil mental states are eliminated, and they are replaced by the more positive and the more wholesome states of mind. So instead of greed, hatred and delusion, we have generosity, compassion and understanding.

Buddhism has made use of two main ethical terms in talking about the moral life. One is the term *puñña,* which originates in the Indian, Hindu, Vedic system. The word *puñña* (Skt. *puṇya*) has a long history and in Vedic times it was associated mainly with certain practices in religious ritual like the performance of sacrifices to gods in order to achieve certain benefits, which are sometimes of a very worldly nature, not even of any spiritual nature. To increase one's offspring, or to have good offspring, to have more cattle, more wealth and so on, one is expected to do acts of *puñña.* In Buddhism also, we find the term *puñña,* but with a totally different meaning, a totally different sense and significance. *Puñña* acts for Buddhism are acts like generosity, charity, *dāna. Dāna* is one of the foremost acts of *puñña.* Conforming to the *sīla,* like abstention from killing, abstention from stealing, would also be a way of increasing one's *puñña.* Then doing work that is beneficial to others is a way of increasing *puñña.* Its opposite is *pāpa.* So all acts which are harmful to oneself and harmful to others are considered as *pāpa* deeds, which are evil; *pāpa* meaning "evil."

From the Buddhist point of view the concept of *puñña* is closely associated with the doctrine of *kamma* and rebirth. It is the increase of *puñña* or acts of *puñña* which produce *kamma*, which is productive of happy consequences, of felicitous consequences in the future life. So if one has done a lot of *puñña* deeds or acts of *puñña*, then karmically, one is destined to be reborn usually in a heavenly sphere of existence, or what is called *sugati*, a form of existence which is of a higher order than the human form of existence. And if one has a weight of *pāpa* on one's side, then one is destined to be reborn in the lower forms of existence, even as an animal or in some kind of sphere in which there is more suffering then happiness. There is an encouragement in Buddhism to do acts of *puñña*. It is said if one increases one's *puñña*, it is for one's happiness.

Now when one looks at the concept of *puñña*, one might get the impression that this is totally a morality which is concerned about the individual's well-being, that is, it is a prudential morality which encourages a person to increase his or her happiness by performing certain types of action. The idea of doing good for the sake of doing good, or goodness for the sake of goodness one may say is lacking in Buddhism because morality is introduced primarily as a prudential approach to life. To improve one's condition in *samsāra*, to have more wholesome karmic accumulation, is what the concept of *puñña* encourages a person to do. But of course there is a point in the Buddhist way at which the Buddha recommends that both *puñña* and *pāpa* must be left aside. That is, for a person to be perfect one should lose interest in *puñña*. One should transcend one's attachment even to acts of *puñña*. So one comes to a stage in the path of spiritual development where one gives up both *puñña* and *pāpa*. The perfected person is said to be beyond *puñña* and *pāpa*.

Some commentators on Buddhism, who paid attention to this statement of the Buddha, thought that in Buddhism morality is only a means, that the final goal amounts to a transcendence of morality. One goes beyond both good and bad when the person is perfected. This is a point of view which I have, in my own writings, criticized. I do not feel very comfortable about taking "going beyond *puñña* and *pāpa*" as in some way transcending good and bad, or transcending good and evil because the term *puñña* has a particular connotation in Buddhism. It is associated with the theory of *kamma*, the theory of rebirth, and one cannot just simply take it as "good," in the English sense, good in the sense of moral goodness. And it is also important to note that there is another term that Buddhism uses, the term *kusala*. Acts of *kusala* are usually those acts which have a spiritual quality. The development of compassion would be *kusala*. In brief, as I noted above, *kusala* is absence of greed, absence of hatred, absence of confusion or ignorance. The aim of Buddhism is to develop *kusala* to the highest, and one who has developed *kusala* to the highest is supposed to be endowed with *kusala* all one's life. One does not, like *puñña*, give up *kusala*. *Kusala* is a characteristic of that person as long as that person lives.

The Buddha is described as a person who attained the culmination of *kusala*, for he is the very embodiment of *kusala*. There was no further point in his life for a further development of *kusala*, because he had reached the highest point of the development of *kusala*. Now, Arahantship, or sainthood, in Buddhism is a stage at which *kusala* comes to perfection and at that stage one goes beyond the stage of committing any willful misdeed. One is incapable of committing any act of evil deliberately. One transcends that stage. Goodness becomes spontaneous to such a person, that is, one does not have to engage in a kind of moral struggle between what one conceives to be the right thing to do and one's inclination. That moral struggle between inclination and what is right, or what one considers to be right does not exist because one is naturally good. So that is the stage of moral perfection that Buddhism speaks about. And this does not mean that one goes beyond morality; actually the perfected person is the very embodiment of moral goodness. There is no question of leaving aside morality, and there is no question of using morality for some other goal to be achieved. So the idea that morality is really a means to an end does not seem very fitting with regard to the Buddha's teachings. Morality, in a sense, is the end itself. To become morally perfect can be said to be the end itself. So in this sense I consider Buddhism to be a system which gives a very important place to the moral life.

Regarding the Buddhist path of moral progress, I think there is a very important psychological analysis given by the Buddha. If we approach from the side of moral evil, which according to Buddhism is the cause of human suffering, moral evil, according to the Buddha, can exist at three levels in our personality. The most, one might say, subtle level at which moral evil exists is the dispositional level. Buddhism has a term for that: the *anusaya* state, *anusaya* meaning "dormant or latent." At this moment, for example, we do not express any forms of behavior which can be called morally evil. We are not being violent at this moment, we are not stealing anything, or we do not even have these thoughts in our minds at this moment, but the tendency to commit all these acts is still lying dormant in ourselves. That is the most deep-rooted level at which moral evil exists from the point of view of Buddhism. Enlightenment is a stage at which moral evil is eradicated even at this deep-rooted dispositional level, or at the level of latent tendencies. Then the second level at which the presence of moral evil can be felt is when we feel the disturbance of greed, attachment, jealousy, all the evil states arising within us. The person who has them feels the turbulence of those emotions. But one who is looking at such a person from outside may not notice it, because it is something that is festering within the individual's mind. An individual may suffer intensely with evil emotions, unwholesome emotions. That is the second level at which moral evil can exist. It does not boil over in terms of actions, verbal or physical, which can affect human relationships in society. There is a third level, the grossest level, at which moral evil can be noticed in a human being, That is at the level of verbal and physical action. So evil is found in our personality in a latent state. Then when we face certain situations in life there is the excitation of the unwholesome emotions in ourselves in the second level which is activated. Then at the third level we act verbally and physically and those actions become socially significant. Because then we interact with society, the moment we open our mouths, the moment we use our limbs, our body to do something, then our behavior becomes socially significant. But of course it all springs from thoughts and certain mental dispositions.

Buddhism has a threefold way to tackle this problem, and I think that threefold way is also characterized by some kind of systematic approach to deal with moral evil. When we deal with moral evil we do not first go to the most subtle level at which moral evil operates, but we take up the gross level, and we try to condition our behavior at the grossest level at which behavior expresses itself in morally evil ways, that is, by regulating our verbal and physical behavior. And *sīla* is meant primarily for that.

The purpose of *sīla*, wholesome practices, which one cultivates, which one consciously adopts, is to regulate one's day-to-day behavior. Abstaining from acts of violence, abstaining from injury to living beings, is the first *sīla*. Whether it is for the layman or for monks, that is the first *sīla* that Buddhism introduces. Then abstaining from dishonest acts, stealing is the second *sīla*. Then abstaining from unchastity is the third *sīla*. So in this way there are several lists of *sīla*s.. But what I want to point out here is that the purpose of *sīla* is to regulate the gross expression of moral evil through words and deeds, that is, physical and verbal expression of moral evil. I think the important psychological point that Buddhism tries to make, in making *sīla* the basis on which all elimination of evil is to be attempted, is that it is in doing things that we cultivate these dispositions. Each act of ours, whether it is verbal or physical, feeds the dispositions that we have already acquired. So every act has the tendency to repeat itself.

When we perform an act in a certain way, we are inclined to repeat a similar deed on a future occasion when we are faced with similar circumstances. So what *sīla* attempts to do is to condition the verbal and physical aspects of human behavior in such a way that the dispositions which are said to be evil or unwholesome do not get further feeding from our behavior patterns. So we try to weaken the dispositional structure of our personality by regulating our behavior in a morally different way. That is why *sīla* is foremost. The Buddha very emphatically says that *sīla* is the foundation for all spiritual development. All other higher states of spirituality are to be based on the cultivation of *sīla*. Just as everything that grows on earth grows with the earth as its foundation, its basis, so all spirituality grows with *sīla* or these wholesome practices which are cultivated consciously as its foundation.

Then the next stage is *samādhi*, mental training. Now that obviously is a higher stage which needs more introversion, getting back into one's own inner nature, and trying to compose one's mind, the scattered mind. What happens in *samādhi* is that, at least temporarily, the activity of the unwholesome emotions gets settled. Unwholesome emotions do not get an opportunity to be excited in a *samādhi* state. Very clearly in the Buddhist tradition it is said that *samādhi* leads to pacification of the mind. It leads to the achievement of tranquility of the mind because the disturbance of the passions may not find an opportunity within the *samādhi* state.

Finally in the *paññā* stage, where one develops insight into the nature of reality, moral evil is totally cut off from the dispositional level itself. So when one understands the nature of things, there is no occasion for moral evil to arise. That is why there is this systematic path consisting of *sīla*, *samādhi*, and *paññā*. One has to develop them one based on the other, but that does not mean that one develops one thing then gives it up and then takes the second one and goes like that. They have to be developed concurrently. But if one takes the order of development, it has to be *sīla*, *samādhi*, and *paññā*. But that does not mean that one does not take care of *samādhi* until one attains complete purity of *sīla*. They have to be concurrently developed. Sometimes the Buddha speaks of *sīla* and *paññā* as two things that mutually support each other. One has to clarify or purify one's wisdom by means of *sīla*, and one has to purify one's *sīla* by means of *paññā*. They are mutually supportive.

Space does not allow a detailed analysis or detailed enumeration of all the moral virtues recognized in Buddhism. There are ten *kusalas*, of which there is a standard list in the canonical sources, the so-called ten *kusalas*: abstention from killing, abstention from stealing, abstention from unchastity, abstention from harsh speech, abstention from frivolous talk, abstention from slanderous talk, abstention from intense desire, abstention from malicious thoughts, abstention from wrong views.

What is more important from my point of view is the rational basis for recognizing some things as evil and other things as good. One instance in which the Buddha's reasoning with regard to moral rightness or moral right and wrong is the *Kālāmasutta*,[16] which is I think justly famous for the kind of free thinking which it recommends. In the *Kālāmasutta* it is recorded that the Buddha went to a certain village where the people were known as Kālāmas. They came to the Buddha and said that many teachers visited them and taught them different moralities. Some people said these are the things that are good and others denied those very things, and maintained that there are other things that are good. The Kālāmas said that they were confused and were unable to know how they ought to live. The Buddha told them that their puzzlement was quite understandable. He also pointed out to them that in determining what is right and wrong one should not go by hearsay, by report, by revelation, by authority of scriptures. One should reject all those extraneous or external means by which one comes to determine what is right and wrong. Instead one should use one's own experience and reflect on one's own experience. And the Buddha asked them whether in their own experience intense greed results in happiness and well-being of oneself and well-being of others. So they came to realize that if one has intense greed, it does not conduce either to the well being of oneself or to the well being of others. Then the same was said about hatred, malice and a confused state of mind. The Buddha finally told them that by this means one could find out for oneself what modes of behavior are right and what modes of behavior are wrong. If greed does not conduce to one's own well-being or to the well-being of others, then any act that proceeds from greed is wrong, or greed itself is wrong. In this way the Buddha recommends that one should examine the nature of right and wrong in light of one's own experience. There are other instances also in which similar advice is given by the Buddha. That is one criterion that the Buddha uses to distinguish between what constitutes good and bad behavior.

---

[16] *Aṅguttara-nikāya*, edited by the Rev. Richard Morris, with the second edition revised by A. K. Warder, London: Luzac & Company, Ltd., 1961, I, 188 ff. with an English translation in *The Book of the Gradual Sayings*, by F. L. Woodaard, for the Pali Text Society, London: Luzac & Company, Ltd., 1960, pp. 170 ff.

The second criterion, which I find very prominent in the Buddha's teaching, is what we usually call the Golden Rule criterion, that is, doing unto others what you would like others to do unto yourself, as for example, if you, in your own experience find that others should not torture you, then you yourself should not torture others. If you yourself want to live a happy life, then you should not prevent or be an obstacle to the other person living a happy life. So that kind of mutual sympathy, mutual care the Buddha says is the foundation of all moral rules. He says that even *sīla*, the Buddhist precepts, can be traced to this criterion, this principle.

It is by the combination of these two criteria that almost all ethical injunctions and ethical rules in Buddhism are formulated. One is the criterion which is similar to the utilitarian criterion—I would not say it is totally utilitarian (because utilitarianism can suggest other meanings). The other is the Golden Rule criterion. It is by the combination of these two criteria that Buddhism derives its moral roots or its ethical system.

Then regarding the social aspect of Buddhist ethics, it is often thought that Buddhism is a "salvation religion." I think there are some writers who have called Buddhism a "life denying, asocial salvation religion." I think this is being contested by many scholars today. It is pointed out that this is a total misrepresentation of the position of Buddhism or Buddhist morality.

I think it is important to realize that Buddhism places more importance on the spiritual transformation of the individual, that is, Buddhism does not begin with social concerns. What is striking to anyone who takes note of the Buddhist priorities from a comparative perspective in relation to certain other systems is that Buddhism gives priority to the moral development of the individual. Buddhism does not begin with social commitment as such, but begins with the commitment of the individual to one's own spiritual well-being. That is what is puzzling to most enquirers into the nature of Buddhist morality.

I find an interesting passage in the canonical sources, which says there are four types of people in this world. The first type are people who are neither interested in their own well-being nor the well-being of others. The second are those who are interested in the well-being of others but not in their own well-being. The third are those who are interested in the well-being of themselves but not that of others. The fourth are those who are interested in the well-being of themselves and in the well-being of others. The Buddha says that the fourth type is the greatest, the highest. I think he would have considered himself as belonging to this fourth category. Taking the second and the third, he says the third is better than the second, which might not seem acceptable from a moral point of view—that is, that those who take care of their own well-being but not of others are higher than those who do not take care of their own well-being but are concerned with the well-being of others.

The Buddha's position was that the third type is better than the second type. Of course, he condemns the first type outright as the useless type. But why is the third better than the second? I think this is explainable only in terms of other teachings of the Buddha relevant to morality and social concern. There is a *sutta* called the *Sallekhasutta* in the *Majjhima-nikāya,* "the Middle Length Sayings,"[17]—*Sallekha* means the removing of all the evil traits of mind like the surgical removing of a cancer by a skilled surgeon; one just erases the evil traits systematically. At the end of this *sutta* the Buddha says that a person who is sunk in the mud cannot pull out another who is also sunk in the mud. Very often, we have a great sense of social commitment, but we do not have the basic qualities necessary for bringing about that well-being which we desire for others because sometimes it may be mere pretense or a facade. We think that we are on a path which is characteristic of our social commitment, our moral commitment, but we deceive ourselves. We just want to become great. We just want to show others that we care for them, but we may be, underneath, seeking for our own gain, our own power. This is what happens to many social movements which begin as liberation movements. They very unconsciously, or consciously,

---

[17] *Majjhima-nikāya*, edited by V. Trenckner, Published for the Pali Text Society by Luzac & Company, Ltd., 1964, I. 40 ff., with an English translation in *The Collection of the Middle Length Sayings*, by I. B. Horner for the Pali Text Society, London: Luzac & Company, Ltd., 1954, I, 51 ff.

get corrupt, they get reduced to this kind of facade. But the Buddha says, one must first purify one's own inner nature.

This is quite characteristic of the Buddha's approach when he advised sixty saints to go in different directions and work for the well-being of mankind. The statement that he makes in that context is, "I am totally free of all bonds, and so are you." Therefore, in effect, he said, "You must go in different directions and serve humanity." So the importance of being free from bonds, the importance of being morally pure, from the Buddha's point of view is a necessary precondition for social commitment. This does not mean that one has to wait until one becomes an Arahant to work for society, but one's social commitment and one's own spiritual culture should be mutually enriching. That is, I think, the Buddhist approach with regard to that issue. As the Buddha says, "One who looks after oneself looks after others," or "one who cares for oneself cares for others and one who cares for others cares for oneself." They are mutually supportive, mutually enriching.

The Buddha is very concerned about the individual's moral culture. If there are more cultured human beings in society, there will be less suffering in society because from the Buddha's point of view, human beings not only suffer but they also create suffering. With regard to the suffering that we ourselves experience and the suffering we cause for others, the causal factor that is related to both these types of suffering is the moral depravity of men and women. So what Buddhism considers to be foremost is the importance of getting rid or tackling this moral depravity. Leaving aside all other types of commitment, Buddhism insists that we should give priority to commitment to the cultivation of our inner spirituality.

Questions and Responses

Q: Within the system of Buddhist ethics, it seems to me as though gaining merit for rebirth in a better position than I am now is contrary or counterproductive to the final goal of

doing good things for their inherent goodness. How would
you comment on this?

P. D. Premasiri: According to some scholars there are two
different paths in Buddhism: the Nibbānic path, which is
meant for a person who renounces the world, who does not
care about *kamma* and is concerned about meditation and the
higher spirituality. This kind of dichotomy is emphasized
by scholars like Melford Spiro, who wrote on Buddhism
and society based on his anthropological investigations into
Burmese Buddhist society. According to his analysis, there
is another type of Buddhism which is called "Kammatic
Buddhism," in which primarily there is interest in the
improvement of one's store of *karma*. Now I personally do not
see these two ways as mutually contradictory, or as mutually
opposing. I think it is the very same causes or motivation of
action which are considered as both nibbānically inclined
and which also produce wholesome *karma*. Now if one takes
dāna or liberality, *sīla*, the cultivation of virtue, and *bhāvanā*,
meditation; although they are three of the foremost *puñña*,
meritorious acts, they are also the methods of progressing
towards Nibbāna. If *dāna* is cultivated, if *sīla* is matured,
and *bhāvanā* is practiced, then one gets closer and closer to
Nibbāna. But, of course, there is this final point at which one
should not cling to merit because clinging to merit involves
attachment to further rebirth in *saṃsāra*, the cyclic process
of birth and death. So, one totally loses interest in *puñña* at
the final point of one's spiritual progression. But *puñña* is
actually a means by which one approaches the nibbānic goal.
So without cultivating *puñña* one cannot progress towards
the nibbānic goal.

There is an interesting work by Damien Keown on Buddhist
ethics.[18] He discusses the concept of *puñña* and the concept
of *kusala*. He has some references to what I had written some
time ago also. There are certain points at which he does not
agree with my own interpretation. But this book is also very
interesting.

---

[18] Damien Keown, *The Nature of Buddhist Ethics*, London: Allen & Unwin, 1992.

Q: You said that in the Buddhist tradition priority is given to developing one's own inner nature. You said that the Buddha said that by caring for oneself you are caring for others. I feel like there is a very close relation between the self and others. But I feel that although there is this close relation, it is still somewhat separate. I feel like there is a closer relationship between an individual and others. In a sense others define the individual. Others are so important in defining the self.

PP: Yes that is true. If we apply the Buddhist notion of dependent existence or dependent origination our tendency to make a very sharp distinction between self and others itself seems an illusion because we are so interdependent, not only dependent on other persons but also dependent upon so many other natural conditions. We ourselves are a product of a variety of conditions. Buddhism recognizes this very clearly. So in that sense, I think that Buddhism goes beyond this self/other distinction and recognizes the mutual relationship between one's own existential condition and other dependencies, the multiplicity of the variety of dependencies. In recent times much emphasis is made on environmental dependencies and it is suggested that the Buddhist notion of dependent origination has a very sound metaphysical basis for a very wholesome environmental ethic because it does not consider the individual as a self existent, insulated being but as a dependent phenomenon. The individual himself or herself is a dependent phenomenon. So in that way the point that you raised is relevant.

Q: Did the Buddha say that you can love some people more than others and how does that apply to the relationship between family and others?

PP: This is a question regarding what one is naturally capable of doing and what one ought to do. If it is a question of "ought," I think the Buddha would say that complete equality is the proper mentality to be developed, that is, without any distinction between one who is close to me and one who is far away from me. In cultivating *mettā*, one cannot have any boundary, that is, it is a matter of boundless compassion. It should extend to the whole universe without any bounds.

But, of course, psychologically we are inclined to have more concern about those who are closer to us. That is a psychological fact. So, even when developing *mettā* we have to begin with ourselves, then extend it to our close associates, and gradually extend it to the whole universe.

Q. Right, because you were talking about Buddhism as being a normative ethic. That would mean that you would have tendencies to love your family more. But maybe as you would strive to Nibbāna you would extend this sense of *mettā*.

PP: Right. Now for the layperson, it is a priority to care for one's own family, looking after one's own children, looking after one's wife. Those are priorities for the lay Buddhist. But when one becomes a monk, one's attachments to family are gone. That attachment is renounced and one is at a different plane.

Q. Must it happen naturally so that it is not a decision?

PP: Initially it is a decision. That is, if one desires to leave the family and take the path of a recluse, then one makes that decision, but one may still be psychologically bound. But that has to be overcome by progressive training.

Q. How does the concept of *anattā*, no soul, fit into Ethics?

PP: I think that can be related to the point I raised earlier. A*nattā* is very closely related to the dependent origination doctrine. Actually Buddhism does not think in terms of a particular soul or self or individual who is becoming perfect and who is saving himself or herself. The thinking is in terms of elimination of suffering in the world. It is elimination of suffering and not the elimination of suffering of a particular individual. So in that sense the concept of *anattā* is important, but the question has been raised whether in the absence of a person, an individual, is it possible for someone to have any moral consciousness, that is, without there being persons, selves. This, of course, is not a problem for Buddhism because for all practical purposes Buddhism admits the existence of individuals in our practical life. We make a distinction between myself and the other, and there is a basis on which that distinction can be maintained. But it doesn't take the idea of a pure ego or an indestructible self or a metaphysical soul. That kind of view is not entertained.

Q. Do you think it is possible for an individual living in American society to live a life which follows the Four Noble Truths in a way that the Buddha would have wanted you to? Is it possible to live, surrounded by people who are so attached to material possessions and making a lot of money, to think that you must live a simple life in order to make it meaningful or could you just realize that these material things around you are not too important and still continue to live a life like the Buddha would have wanted?

PP: Buddhism becomes more meaningful to people who live in affluent societies because of its very starting point, if you consider the life of the Buddha himself. He was born in a family which had all the riches and enjoyments of life. What he realized was that despite all these material riches there was no satisfaction. There was frustration. There was anxiety. I think in materially developed societies this reality is felt more than in a society that is still trying to get there.

Sri Lankan people, although they are traditionally involved with Buddhism, are not seriously involved because they do not feel that urgency. But when you have tasted the highest level of material wealth and progress and when you still cannot find satisfaction, when you cannot find happiness, then you have to look for some other alternative. And the alternative for some people is found in other kinds of experience, like the experience induced by drugs. When they cannot find happiness in material possessions, they look for something else. I think Buddhism presents an alternative for such people. It could be more meaningful for American society than for Sri Lankans who are still struggling just to gain the level that America has already reached in terms of material wealth.

Q: According to the Buddha, what is the basis for morality? Do values evolve or is there some alternate way that just exists because it just is?

PP: I think Buddhism takes the position that values do not subsist somewhere in nature as such, but emerge from the very conditions in which we live. Suppose there was no jealousy, no ill-will among humankind, that everyone was naturally kind, naturally compassionate and there is no competition for things, then what is the necessity of having a system of values? But our condition is such that there is enmity, there is cruelty, anger, jealousy, all these things are there, and it is in that natural condition that we need values. So, I think from the Buddhist point of view it is a contingent fact. Values become significant in terms of the very nature of the human predicament. If everything was very cozy for us, and nothing was wrong with us, then I do not think we would have gone in search of values.

Q: You were talking about dependent origination. You said you were interdependent with other people. But in the nature of dependent origination shouldn't you be dependent rather than interdependent?

PP: The kind of dependence that Buddhism recognizes is not just dependence in a chain fashion. If you think in terms of a causal chain, that is A causing B and B causing C, and so forth, it is not that kind of dependence that Buddhism is talking about. It is a kind of dependence wherein if you keep three sticks together and you pull out one, all three fall. So they are mutually dependent. Actually that simile itself has been used in the Buddhist scriptures. Everything that exists can be compared to three sticks put together. They stay in that position through mutual support, interdependence, not just one causing the other, but there is mutual dependence.

Q: Obviously people need moral values, but they are not going to listen to anything under the heading of "spirituality." What do you think the solution is?

PP: I think that people need, in my opinion, to understand themselves. If I may use the simile of the mirror, they need to see their own reflection in the mirror and then correct themselves, that is, get rid of whatever seems ugly in the mirror image. What is most difficult for us to see is our own real nature. We try to deceive ourselves. The other thing is that we try to understand everything other than ourselves. Actually modern knowledge is mainly knowledge of the other, but not knowledge of one's own nature. The latter knowledge is what is most needed in terms of spirituality.

Q: If I become a Christian pastor, what type of person would you look for to provide that kind of guidance?

PP: If I may use the Buddha's own guidance with regard to this type of question, you should not follow anyone blindly, but you should investigate the nature of the guide himself or herself, that is, you have to watch very carefully whether the person who wants to guide you is trying to guide you for his or her own benefit or whether it is through compassion that he or she is guiding you. So one has to observe the behavior of the person for a long time and be very careful and judge from his or her words and deeds. Very often you find a big gap between words and deeds. This mutual agreement between words and deeds is very important.

Q: What about the case of the person who guides, who leads? Like a pastor?

PP: Not to be dogmatic is a very important precondition; that is, being free from being dogmatic. Being open to whatever is reasonable and to try to examine the situation in the light of your own observation and experience—that is very important, without running after dogmas. That kind of spiritual environment was there even at the time of the Buddha when there were so many people teaching so many different things. That is probably why the Buddha very strongly recommended a non-dogmatic approach to the spiritual life. He said that even his teachings should be used in the sense of being merely a raft to cross over, but not to be carried thereafter on your back. The teaching, as a raft, is to be used as a practical device, to cross over. So you should constantly watch your own experience, your progress, your shortcomings, whatever system you adopt for spiritual culture. The criterion should be your own observation and experience.

CHAPTER XI

BUDDHIST INSIGHTS INTO HUMAN RIGHTS

L.P.N. Perera

The late Professor L.P.N. Perera, formerly of the Department of Pali and Buddhist Studies of Sri Jayewardenepura University, shows the relevance of Theravāda Buddhist thought to the key social issue of human rights. Drawing on foundational insights underpinning the Four Noble Truths, weaving the assumptions reflected in the precepts with the virtues of compassion and sympathetic supportive involvement with others, Professor Perera points out the depth of commitment to the principle of equality among men and women.

I have been interested in the theme of Buddhists Insights into Human Rights for some time. I have had the opportunity to write a number of articles dealing with issues of human rights for The Center for the Study of Human Rights, which opened some years ago at the University of Colombo here in Sri Lanka. We are going through a period of history in the world when practically everyone is interested in the subject of human rights. Human rights are now of central importance in international law, politics, and legal philosophy among other disciplines. Even in today's papers in Sri Lanka one finds references to human rights. In India human rights are being violated in Kashmir. We in South Asia have indeed been in the limelight of human rights, but on the wrong side. For us it is of immediate as well as a universal concern.

The traditional debate on human rights between the advocates of the liberal conception of rights and those of a socialist conception of human rights is fast disappearing. In Europe, under the aegis of the Conference for Security and Cooperation, there was talk of creating a charter of human rights for the whole of the continent. It would have, of course, been impossible to do this over such a vast ideological divide as had existed in the past.

Now that the United Nations is sincerely interested in enforcing the mechanisms for the protection of human rights, the relationship that human rights could have with the major religions of the world should be a major focus of study. My small contribution has been in writing about human rights from the Buddhist point of view. As religious fundamentalism grows, finding commonalities between religions in order to foster interreligious dialogue has become increasingly important. The social doctrines of the world's religions and their perspectives on human rights are naturally a good place to begin searching for points of agreement.

What I will do here is examine articles from the UN declaration on human rights of 1948 from the Buddhist ethical perspective. I could have written generally on Buddhism and human rights, but I thought that this approach would be more concrete and useful as these UN articles are known throughout the world. They are commonly now a part of some government constitutions.

I should first qualify that Buddhism is concerned not only with the human being but with all sentient beings. We need to remember that; Buddhists are concerned with all sentient beings. Therefore, Buddhists have to be concerned with human rights and much more, naturally, if we are concerned with all beings. Buddhism's concern for human rights finds expression through the value system and norms that Buddhism upholds and considers salutary for humankind. This therefore involves the social philosophy and the ethical dimensions of Buddhism. Buddhism is concerned with two spheres of welfare: human welfare while one is alive, and one's welfare after one dies. Living one's life righteously, and therefore successfully, aids a great deal in ensuring that one's existence after death will be a pleasurable one.

The expression "human rights" originated in the West, and it is in this Western sense that I use the term here. Human rights have historically been respected in Eastern cultures, and especially in Sri Lanka. The term "rights" has so vociferously surfaced in industrialized civilizations because of the avarice which has led to exploitation. Industrialists blinded by greed care little for the well-being of their employees. Concepts like "surplus value" and exploitation are all but unknown to us here. They come from a Marxist concept, which is foreign to this country. Indeed the recognition of the importance of human rights is part and parcel of the Buddhist and Eastern ethos in general. Through the discharge of duties and obligations espoused by Buddhists, generally, in the cultural ethos of Sri Lanka, our rights are also fulfilled. As we have not been denied our basic rights, the issue has never emerged in the urgent and formal manner which it has in the West.

Any careful student of Buddhism will not fail to note that the concepts and concerns of the universal declaration of human rights (adopted by the United Nations in 1948) are enshrined in the teachings of the Buddha. The basic principles of the declaration are fully supported and reinforced by the Buddhist canonical and historical literature, the earliest teachings of which date from the 4th or 5th century B. C. One would not expect "human rights" to be expressed then in the terms which we use today. But the values upheld in those teachings and since are very much akin to the more recent concept of "human rights."

The Buddha was articulate and eloquent in these matters when they arose in his discussions with others and in the course of his preaching. In Sri Lanka, some time ago, we had a seminar on human rights in which I examined the United Nations declaration of 1948 from a Buddhist perspective, as I am attempting to do here. Naturally I faced some critics who said that from the religious point of view this declaration is a failure. Not only some Buddhists but also some Roman Catholic representatives said that the declaration was too individualistic in its approach and that religious insights were not to be found in it.

I need not mention that before the 1948 UN declaration there were other attempts at securing human rights by written decree. One recalls the Magna Carta of the English in 1215, and the Declaration of Human Rights of Man of the French in 1789, among others. However, it is only with the adoption of the 1948 declaration by the United Nations that for the first time in history a document has expressed in simple and succinct terms the inherent civil, political, economical, social and cultural rights to which the whole of humanity is entitled. Accordingly, this universal declaration provides a yardstick by which men and women can judge for themselves the extent to which their rights and freedoms are respected by their governments, by organizations and other groups, as well as—very importantly— the degree to which they themselves are respecting the rights and freedoms of others.

Though it has been over half a century since this declaration was made, the concept of human rights is still evolving; people are talking about it, debating it—this is important to remember. Discussion of this subject is continuing and students of the subject now note with concern limitations inherent in the declaration. No human act is perfect. But this discussion about it is a very good thing. There is a good book related to some of these issues edited by B.G. Ramcharan[19], *Human Rights Thirty Years after the UN's Declaration*.

There are altogether thirty Articles in the UN declaration (though the thirtieth is actually a summary). The articles make broad claims which do not reference any one culture or religion. For instance, it has been noted that the declaration does not contain any provisions specifically for the protection of minorities. Neither is there any mention of the right to petition, even at a national level. These can be seen as limitations of the declaration as a whole. While we recognize its importance as a common standard of achievement for all peoples and all nations, one may agree with one Roman Catholic critic who declared that the document "tends to be juridical in its expression, individualist in its emphasis and restricted in its perspective on community." This is only one of many criticisms that have been levied against

---

[19] *Human Rights Thirty Years after the UN's Declaration, Commemorating the Occasion of the Thirtieth Anniversary of the UN's Declaration of Human Rights*, ed., B. G. Ramacharan, The Hague: 1979.

it. Those studying religion in Sri Lanka seem to say that the declaration lacks both depth of perception and insights, which religion alone can provide. However, we must not underestimate the importance of this declaration and its great value.

From a Buddhist perspective, the UN articles on human rights are considered a more or less imperfect reflection of ideas and concepts which in their pristine form are also expressed in the Dhamma. The Dhamma articulates these thoughts in a more humane and more philosophical way than we moderns have managed. These principles operated during the time of the Buddha in a social context which we, in our age of science and technology, may see as worth retrieving and reviving.

Fritjof Capra, a Hungarian physicist who has written a number of books from the religious point of view, sees mystic traditions, particularly Eastern traditions, as converging with modern science. He is very critical of what I call the Newtonian and Cartesian reductionist science, what we now call the "new science." One of his books is called *The Tao of Physics*, about Taoism, a religion in China.[20] Another one of his books, published in 1982, is called *The Turning Point: Science, Society and the Rising Culture*.[21] Here he anticipates a great change very soon in the way that science looks at the problems of humankind today and how we live. He and others like him seek to go beyond Newton and Descartes in an attempt to reconcile modern science with religious insights. Capra's third book is *Uncommon Wisdom*.[22] These three publications are very readable.

In determining morally sound action, Buddhism considers, among other things, humankind's view of the universe and our place therein, and the assessment and appraisal of human life now and hereafter. These considerations have contributed to a concept of human rights with an entirely different emphasis and sense of direction than have some concepts which are now popular in academic discussion. Over time, a retrograde shift in emphasis has occurred in the understanding of human

[20] Fritjof Capra, *The Tao of Physics*, London: Wildwood House, 1975.

[21] Fritjof Capra, *The Turning Point: Science, Society and the Rising Culture*, New York: Simon & Schuster, 1982.

[22] Fritjof Capra, *Uncommon Wisdom*, New York: Simon & Schuster, 1988.

rights. Those features which are grounded on selflessness and the affirmation of the perfectability of human beings have been replaced by vociferous demands for individual rights in modern times. Modern human rights are, as we see, of a legalistic nature. Human rights derive their power from courts and governments. This is not how human rights were conceived in the Dhamma. While appreciating the value of human rights in their present form, this difference has to be stressed because it is of utmost importance. It is the most important message I have to give you from the point of view of Buddhism.

This distinction is apparent in the restricted role that religious and philosophical considerations play in the 1948 UN declaration. From a more universal, religiously comprehensive view, one might say that the declaration appears rather cynical. While this critique deserves further separate consideration, it is not inappropriate to examine the declaration's various articles from the point of view of Buddhist thought, and to see what support Buddhist thought, traditions, teachings and practices could provide for the declaration, and for discourse on human rights in general.

Buddhist views on human rights emerge from two basic assumptions: one philosophical, the other ethical. The first one, the philosophical assumption, is that all human beings are born with complete freedom and responsibility. Buddhism is a non-theistic religion in the sense that it does not maintain that a being created or sustains the universe. Buddhism therefore regards humans as being subject only to a set of non-deterministic causal laws. Human beings' destiny rests in their own hands, as they have the power to discover the causal order of the universe. The *Dhammapada*, translated by Professors Carter and Palihawadana, contains a famous line: "Oneself indeed is patron of oneself" (*attā hi attano nātho*, v. 160).[23] As individuals truly are their own patrons, and are not subjects of external agency (except insofar as we are restricted by the causal laws which govern the universe), human beings are free to attain the highest good materially, mentally, morally and spiritually.

---

[23] *The Dhammapada*, translated by Carter and Palihawadana, v. 160, pp. 40, 226.

The ethical assumption is more relevant at the social level than the philosophical assumption. It is the insight that humans and all other living beings desire happiness. The *Dhammapada* also carries a phrase, "beings who desire ease" (*sukhakāmāni bhūtāni*, vv. 131, 132).[24] This refers to all living beings, including the animal realm also. There are five levels of existence: the human, the divine, the world of the departed spirits, the animal kingdom, and states of woe where there is great suffering. One is not destined, for example, to be in a state of woe forever. One is in the process of becoming and it is always possible that a person or other living being can change. As Buddhism contains a doctrine of rebirth in which humans are reborn in various realms with various degrees of potential for living a happy life, the Buddhist approach to human rights is naturally more humanistic than legalistic. With these two basic assumptions, philosophical and ethical, Buddhism looks upon men and women as quite competent in the task of insuring for themselves and their fellow beings success and happiness in this world, as well as in securing for themselves emancipation from the turmoil of existence.

According to Buddhism, worldly success itself is to be righteously achieved. One can achieve "success" through black-marketing or pillaging, but these are dishonest means. Buddhism admits the necessity of some material things, but that which one needs one must earn "by the sweat of one's brow." Righteously achieved success, in Pali, is called *dhammaladdha*, what one has obtained according to Dhamma, according to righteous living. The Buddha's teachings are partly directed toward this objective. Failing to make a righteous success of one's present life may mean unhappy future lives.

It is here that human rights need to be seen in a social context. Worldly or mundane success in particular demands the reciprocal recognition of, respect for and the observance of the rights of others. While these philosophical and ethical considerations of Buddhism gave rise to humanistic concerns in this sense of righteous achievement, they were further bolstered by kindred values generated by Buddhism through its reaction to social problems at the time of its inception. The religious and

---

[24] *Ibid.*, vv. 131, 132, pp. 35, 203.

social climate of north India, during and after the rise of Buddhism and other allied religious systems, was generally one of reaction against the limitations imposed on the rights of people by the then prevailing value system (Brahminism, its accompanying caste system and so forth). The activities of the Buddha and his early disciples in this context were directed toward the acceptance and practice of principles of human rights in a very practical way, not only as a desirable effort at social restructuring but also in recognition of its ultimate spiritual value. Furthermore, Buddhist social philosophy demands that conditions in society be conducive to the continuation of the Buddhist social ethic, as required by the Buddhist moral life. Buddhists have to be able to live as Buddhists, practicing the social ethics enunciated by their teacher.

The social ethic of any given religion could be achieved mainly through the economic and political needs of the people. It has to be remembered that in this exercise of practicing the social ethic, the identification, the recognition, and effective implementation of human rights concepts have a major role to play. It is from the needs of the people that rights will emerge. As long as one has needs legitimately to be fulfilled, one certainly has rights. The idea that Buddhists have only duties and obligations is a narrow way to consider the matter. Duties and obligations have been emphasized in Buddhism a lot; so also in Hinduism—it tends to be the Eastern tradition.

But, in this context there is a much broader perspective than focusing on duties and obligations. The Noble Eightfold Path, enunciated by the Buddha as the path to salvation, is fundamental in Buddhist thought. There are also the key concepts of the five precepts, the *pañcasīla*, which every Buddhist is expected to observe. There are also important Buddhist virtues like benevolence, which are implied by a number of words: "loving-kindness" (*mettā*); "sympathy" (*karuṇā*); "compassion" (*anuddayā*); *muditā*, something like *mit Freude*, in German; and "non-injury" (*ahiṃsā*). Also there are the more apparent social virtues one will note in Sri Lanka, like "liberality" (*dāna*), which is the basis of altruism in Buddhism. *Dāna* is not simply giving food to the Buddhist monks. It is much more than that; not only food but material gifts. In fact, the highest gift is *Dhammadāna*, giving Dhamma. Other key virtues are gratitude, reverence, courtesy, humility, toleration, and veracity or sincerity. All of these constitute the fundamental moral basis of one's relationship with one's fellow beings. This whole list, coming under benevolence, would serve to give acceptance of human rights. If one accepts these virtues, one cannot brush human rights aside.

The five precepts (*pañcasīla*), from my point of view, embody all human rights.[25] If one follows the five precepts of Buddhism—there is nothing Buddhistic about it—one does not thereby become a Buddhist. One becomes a Buddhist by accepting the Buddha, Dhamma, and Saṅgha, the three gems, as one's guide. These precepts are taken upon oneself by oneself. They are not enforced from outside. All human rights can be broadly put into two divisions: right to life and right to property. (1) Refraining from taking life—here the right to life is recognized. (2) Refraining from taking that which is not given, i.e., theft—here one notes the right to property. (3) Refraining from wrongful indulgence in the passions, a precept having mostly a sexual significance. For the Buddhist clergy, the point is to refrain from all sexual activity. For the laity, it has a special significance for sexual morality. This actually also refers to the right of property. One has no right to misbehave with regard to another person or another person's spouse. (4) Refraining from falsehood—this has to do with both right to life and right to property. Through falsehood, someone might get killed, and through falsehood someone might possibly lose some belongings. It cuts both ways. (5) Abstaining from alcoholic drinks. Alcohol and drugs affect one's health, which has to do with the right to life, and also one's wealth, which involves right to property.

I mentioned at the beginning of this chapter that Buddhism is concerned with the welfare of all sentient beings. That the Buddhist conception of rights embraces all living beings is borne out by the fact that a universal monarch (*cakkavatti*) is expected not only to provide protection for human beings, but also for all beasts and birds. Rights are also for other living creatures.

---

[25] See also the discussion of the precepts given by Lily de Silva in her chapter "Wherein Do We Most Frequently Fail to Live as Buddhists."

Indeed this was observed throughout Buddhist history. In Sri Lanka in the past, some kings ordered by royal proclamation that on certain days no slaughter of animals was to take place. Even quite early, in India, one of the great Buddhist kings, Aśoka of the third century B. C., is supposed to have established dispensaries and hospitals where veterinary surgeons were appointed to attend to animals. Now the matter of the rights of animals is being recognized once again, as is evidenced by the many animal rights groups which have emerged in a number of countries.

Let me move to bring to a close this chapter by reviewing two articles specifically from the 1948 UN resolution. One article contains the quotation:

> All human beings are born free and equal in dignity and rights. They are endowed with reason and conscience and should act toward one another in the spirit of brotherhood.

This article and its sentiment is basic to all human rights, and it is in complete accord with Buddhist thought. There is no dispute with that article. In conception, I should say, it is not a new idea to Buddhism. Our concern here, with this article, is the philosophical assumption. This article upholds that every human being is born with complete freedom and responsibility. This implies that one's destiny lies in one's own hands. The freedom of human beings, as commencing from their very birth, and the recognition of their equality, dignity and rights by Buddhism are clearly reflected in the Buddha's emphasis on the following matters. (1) Self-reliance. If one is not the handiwork of a creator, obviously for one's emancipation one must rely on oneself. The Buddha extolled what he called "personal endeavor" (*attakāra*). (2) Second, he taught "human effort" (*purisakāra*), and also "human strength," "human energy," "human valor," and "human responsibility." These concepts are reinforced by the further teaching that Buddhahood itself is within reach of all human beings. One may not become a Buddha in one's present life, but by gradually perfecting oneself one ensures one's welfare in some future rebirth—at some point further along in the stream of becoming. An intelligent human being must try to take at least one step, if possible, towards Nibbāna, although one might not be able to attain it. If one is one's own master or is patron of oneself, as in the *Dhammapada*, and if one is born free, and if all can attain Buddhahood, one would simply ask, what greater equality, dignity and rights can there be. It is a reflection of a fundamental belief in universal equality and dignity to say that *all* human beings are capable of attaining Buddhahood.

"Reason and conscience," the article in the declaration says, are endowments of human beings. Buddhists agree. Nowadays, people associate "conscience" with the Christian faith. The word for us that is closest is *dhammavitakka*, "analysis in light of Dhamma," or "righteous thought." There is another word, *dhammādhipateyya*, meaning something like the rule of Dhamma or sovereignty of Dhamma. These subtle concepts are in the canonical texts. They just need to be uncovered and elaborated. "Reason and conscience" go together. They both constitute the awareness of right and wrong. They both are used to judge the moral worth of an action.

We also see the importance of mutual relations. The spirit of brotherhood is validated in this article. The Buddhist word is *mettā*. It goes beyond brotherhood—it means "universal loving-kindness." In fact this concept of brotherhood, when one thinks about it, has a narrower sense. Although we use this word in Buddhism, as in the Buddhist Brotherhood, as do others also— the Islamic Brotherhood, and so forth—we have to go beyond it. It seems that the idea of Brotherhood is primarily, I think, theistic. One talks of a common brotherhood when there is a common fatherhood. We are all brothers when we are all children of one father. Brotherhood seems to be a Western concept and although we sometimes use it, too, we need to go beyond that.

We must remember that "equality" is always circumscribed by certain limitations. It is impossible to say that two people are completely equal. The claim that human beings are equal, in my view, is more prescriptive than descriptive. "Equality" really means that there are various respects in which no difference ought to be made in the treatment of or consideration given to all persons. Whatever difference is referred to in the Buddhist texts is the difference between individuals. No two people are equal. There is a Pali word used to specifically recognize this fact, *puggalavemattatā*, which means "differences between individuals." While recognizing these limitations, Buddhism posits a basic equality between all human beings in respect to their essential nature, and therefore sees all persons as equal in dignity and in rights. This basic equality, according to Buddhist thought, stems from a number of factors. The most important factors in which people are equal are biological and anthropological, among many others such as moral, legal, ethical and so forth. Space does not allow a further discussion on this particular matter.

This sense of equality among human beings is further reinforced by the Buddhist view that all human beings, in the final analysis, face the same basic problems of birth, decay, and dissolution. That is the first noble truth of Buddhism, the universality of dukkha, "suffering." We are all subject to this same basic plight, and yet we are all in a position to overcome suffering, death and rebirth by attaining the very highest, morally and spiritually, through development of human potential. The answer to the question, "What is Buddhism?" can be answered simply, "a doctrine advocating the development of human potential through an extension of human capacity which is done from within." Human life is so placed in the cosmic scheme of things that human beings alone enjoy the opportunity of transcending the unsatisfactoriness of existence.

CHAPTER XII

WHEREIN DO WE MOST FREQUENTLY FAIL TO LIVE AS BUDDHISTS?

Lily de Silva

Having followed the presentations of five distinguished scholars and committed Sinhala Theravāda Buddhists, we have clearly set before us the basic tenets of this grand religious heritage. Now Professor Lily de Silva, Professor of Pali and Buddhist Studies emeritus of Peradeniya University, reviews the key themes of doctrine and practice to consider them in light of one's understanding of how most adequately to live one's life. Once again, and in an engaged way, we see how pertinent the teachings received with optimism from the past are for living life well today.

In this chapter I will address a rather unusual subject given to me, "Wherein Do We Most Frequently Fail to Live as Buddhists." I thought this an unusual subject because normally we are interested in the academic aspects of Buddhist Studies. But this topic makes me feel that we are now interested in soul-searching *as well*. That is why, I think, a topic like this has been suggested for discussion.

Actually, there were no Buddhists as such at the time of the Buddha because the Buddha did not preach a religion as such. Rather he preached a way to make one's life happier and happier until at last one comes to a stage where the happiness never fails but stays with one forever. So it is a progressive form of happiness that the Buddha taught and he did not speak only to

Buddhists because there were no Buddhists as such at the time. People from all walks of life came to him and he showed the way how not to be unhappy, how to be happy.

Once the Buddha divided all people into four categories: (1) those proceeding from darkness to light, (2) those who are proceeding from light to brighter light, and the other way around also, (3) those who are proceeding from light to darkness, (4) those proceeding from darkness to further darkness. This shows that there are people who are progressing as well as those who are regressing. I will return to this later.

In the *Aṅguttara-nikāya*,[26] there is a discussion of the cause, the antecedents to, moral degradation. The Buddha said that the absence of a sense of shame and of the fear to do wrong leads to the absence of sense control. We are constantly working under the influences of our senses; we want to see things, we want to hear things. But if we do not have a sense of shame and the fear to do wrong, we will be dominated by our senses to an even greater extent, causing embarrassment, litigation, etc. And if we are dominated by our senses, if we do not have sense control, there arises the absence of moral virtue. We cannot have moral virtue if we do not have sense control.

If one does not have moral virtue, one cannot have concentration. Concentration is very much needed for one to understand truth as it is. Even if one is working on a mathematical problem, one will not be able to see all the angles in solving that problem if one is not mentally concentrated. One has to have concentration in order to see things as they are—whatever one is doing. Even in the ultimate sense, if one wants to see truth as it is one must be concentrated. If one does not have the ability to see all dimensions of the problem of life then one will be so much attached to life that one will not be detached from life. It is important to be detached from life because it is attachment that causes all the misery. I am attached to my possessions—this bracelet is very dear to me, the moment I lose it I become very

---

[26] *Aṅguttara-nikāya*, edited by Prof. E. Hardy, published for the Pali Text Society by London: Luzac & Company, Ltd., 1958, IV, 99 ff., with an English translation in *The Book of Gradual Sayings*, translated for the Pali Text Society by E. M. Hare, London: Luzac & Company, Ltd., 1955, IV, 63 ff.

sad about it. So it is attachment to various things, to our family, to our wealth, to our fame, that causes unhappiness. So, one will not be able to take a detached view of things if one is not able to see things as they are and if one does not have concentration. So if one does not have detachment one will not have emancipation, which is the ultimate goal of Buddhism; emancipation from *dukkha*, from suffering. One will not have happiness if one does not have the causal antecedents mention in this *sutta*: the process beginning with a sense of shame and the fear to do wrong.

There is a path leading to liberation or emancipation or Nibbāna, a progressive path leading to this ultimate goal. That path is called the eightfold path, which is divided into three groups: *sīla*, virtue, *samādhi*, concentration, and *paññā*, insight-wisdom. I have tried to see wherein we fail to be Buddhistic most frequently with reference to these three dimensions of the path. Let us begin with virtue.

A Buddhist is expected to follow the ethical code of the five precepts. The first, as we have seen, is abstaining from killing. Is it possible to say that humankind is abstaining from killing in light of the fact that we are killing by the thousands, by the millions, for food, for clothing, even for making cosmetics? Slaughter is going on in an unprecedented level. Animals are raised for these purposes and without any qualms we kill them. So the very first precept we violate in this manner. We think we need meat and fish for protein. Methodically we indulge in killing without any reservations.

Apart from that, we spend by the billions to manufacture various kinds of war machinery and lethal weapons and so forth. Every country spends so much for defense as well on offense. With a weapon, what can you do other than kill? It is all designed and utilized for killing. This is justified for various reasons, often for perpetrating ideologies. Capitalists say, "Capitalism is the best form of government, and the best method for bringing about social equality and the highest standard of living." Socialists will say "Socialism is the best form of life for people and will lead to happiness." And both sides compile weapons and spend so very much money. The first precept has hardly touched the lives of modern humankind. What about terrorism, wars, and bomb blasts that are going on in the world? The newspapers are filled with accounts of violence. It is not that the first precept is not known. It is that it is never cared for. What about the crime rate in all countries around the world? Do not think that these things do not happen in our country because it is supposed to be a Buddhist country. We have failed to heed the first precept and hence fail to be Buddhistic in this respect.

It is the same with the second precept; not to take that which has not been given. What about all the highjacking, blackmailing, and organized robbery that is going on throughout the world? It may be that I will have qualms about taking a bit of chalk from a classroom, but some people will not have qualms about robbing banks. We have hardly paid heed to the second precept.

The third precept is about sexual misconduct. There is permissiveness all over the world today. In earlier days, gossip served as a social regulator. When someone misbehaved; people would start talking. The wrongdoer would become very uncomfortable. It was a form of social control, not that gossiping is a good thing. But it has its good effects, too. Now society has accepted permissive moral standards—or may I use the word immoral. Even society cannot control this permissive behavior. We have paid dearly for this. Consider the number of broken homes and the divorce rates. A broken home means broken individuals as well. When the home is broken the life of the child is broken. Consider the spread of sexually transmitted diseases which are running rampant in society today. Some virulent forms are not responding to known forms of medical treatment. We read about this in the papers. It is not restricted to the West. This is happening here in our own society.

Troubling situations are no longer isolated to or contained in their place of origin. In the "good old past" the impacts of a war in one part of the globe would not be felt in another, distant part of the world. Methods of communication and forms of interaction were not as developed then as they are now. Wars, standards of permissive behavior, and many other things are now experienced around the world. We have our own share of this here as well, which we received mostly from the West. Because the third precept is not followed, we once again fail to be Buddhist.

Where lying is concerned, I have to give credit to the West. They are in general much more honest than people here. When I was in the West, sometime back, I used to see newspapers just left on a pile. A person would just take a paper and leave the proper amount of money. That kind of thing would not happen in our part of the world. It seems that the case of a work ethic is similar. We hardly have a work ethic as such because people do not have the consciousness that one has to work for the pay that one gets. Generally we are very slack about work, about not working for what one receives, which is a form of lying, a form of dishonesty. Corruption is found in all government departments in our country. We have failed to be honest, too, and in that respect we have failed to live up to the fourth precept.

The last precept is not taking liquor. The world is actually seething with alcohol and drugs. It is said that one's conscience is soluble in alcohol. Actually one's conscience is now dissolved. In such confused state it is difficult to find out what is right and what is wrong. What does it mean for one person to be addicted to alcohol? It means that that person has no strength of character. He or she is addicted to something. If there is no strength of character he or she is only a puppet in the hands of his or her own senses.

The Pali word for senses is *indriya*. It is an interesting word. *Indriya* are one's eyes, ears, nose, tongue, body, the mind, which is also one of the senses. The word *indriya* comes from the word *indra*, which means "lord," "the master." So, *indriya* are "lords" which are acting as our masters. We are actually working under the influence of our lords; my eye is dominating me, my nose is dominating, my tongue is dominating me. Is it for my health when I am overwhelmed by my senses? Take just one of the senses: my tongue. I like to eat so many sweet things, fried things—so very much. What happens? Ultimately, I cut my neck by my tongue. Why? I fall ill with diabetes, heart disease, all kinds of things because I did not control my tongue. I have actually become an addict to food. Because of that, obesity overwhelms me which makes me unhappy. If I want to be a happy person I have to learn to control my senses, and the tongue is one of them. To be distracted through these senses is not to have concentration. Any form of addiction, including smoking, of course, means one is out of control of oneself. But why are we getting addicted to these things? It is because we do not want to accept the reality about ourselves. We want to run away from reality. We want to forget ourselves. It is because of this that we take to drugs, alcohol, even smoking.

One has to practice these virtues oneself. One cannot change the outside world. It is in individually practicing that the world and society become gradually changed. It is pointless having vast plans to change society without changing oneself. Individually one has to change oneself and then automatically society will become changed because society is a collection of individuals. These virtues have to be inculcated and cultivated and practiced individually. One can influence another, of course, by indicating how one's life has become happier by following these precepts. That is how one can improve oneself as well as society. But one cannot have master plans on the one hand and, at the same time, practice something else—it is hypocrisy. One cannot do that. It will not work.

Beyond observing the five precepts, from time to time in our society, people observe *sil*, as we call it (from P. *sīla*). That means that one takes upon oneself, on special *poya* days—the new moon day, the full moon day, and so forth—*sil*, that is, one takes up *more precepts* than five; generally eight precepts. This means that one wants to practice sense control at least once or twice a month. It would be much the better if one could go on with sense control all throughout one's life. That would be conducive to one's happiness. But if one cannot do that all throughout the month, at least twice a month or once a month one could try sense control. On that special *poya* day one abstains from eating after twelve noon. One abstains from luxurious furniture. One abstains from wearing ornaments, using cosmetics, and so forth. We love to wear ornaments and use cosmetics because we have a particular image of ourselves. Each one of us has a self-image and according to that we dress, we eat, etc. We wish to maintain certain standards in society and so forth.

This reminds me of a story a professor from the United States told about a special mirror that could be adjusted to gauge the self-image of a person. This mirror was such that you could adjust it vertically as well as horizontally. So while standing before the mirror you can adjust it in such a way that it reflects what you thinks is your correct height and your figure reflects your own idea of yourself. The professor said that not a single person standing before this mirror adjusted it accurately according to his or her personal dimensions. Depending on their ambitions, various motivations, inhibitions and so forth, people have a different self-image of themselves. No one knows what they really are.

By these restraints of *sil*, people cut down that false self-image. They seek to enhance sense control, at least during certain days of the month. Sense control is absolutely essential in order to attain *samādhi*, concentration. Lack of concentration means that we are dominated by what are called the five hindrances (P. *nīvaraṇa*). Normal, average human beings are dominated by certain desires and impulses which act as hindrances for the exercise of their mental capacities. The first hindrance is sensuality; the second is ill-will; the third is indolence, laziness; the fourth is anxiety, worry; and the fifth is doubt.

The state of our minds when dominated by these hindrances is beautifully explained by a water simile. This simile is taken from the ancient practice of using a bowl of water as a mirror. If the bowl had muddy or colored water it would not give a clear reflection of the face. When the mind is dominated by sensuality, the mind is like a bowl of muddy or colored water. It will not be possible to get a true reflection or perspective of anything. The mind that is dominated by ill-will is like a bowl of boiling water. With the mind boiling with anger, ill-will, malice and jealousy, it is difficult to solve even a mathematical problem or to do anything that requires concentration. Concentration is far away if one is angry. If one is lazy one cannot do anything at all. That mind is like a bowl of water which is covered with moss. This, too, will not give a true reflection. When one is saddled with anxiety, worrying over something, it is like water that is turbulent or disturbed. This, too, will not give you a true reflection. The mind that is in doubt is like water that is kept in darkness. These are the hindrances which will prevent you from concentrating your mind.

The *Samaññaphala Sutta*[27] gives another set of similes which will help us understand the sense of relief we experience by the elimination of these factors. It is said that if we are not troubled with sensuality, we will experience a sense of relief like a man with a profitable business who is able to pay back the money he borrowed to start it. He experiences a great sense of satisfaction and relief. A person who has gotten rid of ill-will experiences relief in the same way as a person who has regained good health after a protracted illness. A person who has eliminated indolence is like a person who has been released from prison. The one who has gotten rid of anxiety is like one who has been released from slavery. The case of the last one, one who has become free from doubt, is like a person who had been lost in a desert and at last finds the way to security and safety.

People today are not free from these things and that is why they tend not to be at peace with themselves. They cannot experience the relief suggested in the similes. Therefore they want to run away from themselves. They often return to tranquilizers, alcohol, drugs, and permissive behavior because they are not at peace with themselves.

We have failed to be Buddhistic in all the aspects mentioned—all the ways in which we have failed to be peaceful human beings.

The third dimension is *paññā*. Do we have wisdom? People today have a great deal of knowledge. Though we have accumulated so much knowledge and have even been to the moon, still we lack wisdom. There is a difference between knowledge and wisdom. Wisdom wells up from within if one has concentration. If you cannot observe *sīla*, moral virtue, you will not have concentration and will be plagued by the hindrances. Ultimately it comes down to the fact that without virtue, concentration and wisdom cannot arise. When we do not have *sīla* we are without virtue—this is the root cause of all problems. Why do we not have *sīla*? It is because

---

[27] *The Dīgha Nikāya*, edited by Prof. T. W. Rhys Davids and Prof. J. Estlin Carpenter, London: Luzac & Company, Limited, 1949, I, 47 ff., with an English translation in *Dialogues of the Buddha*, translated by T. W. Rhys Davids, for Sacred Books of the Buddhist, London: Luzac& Company, Ltd., 1956, I, 56 ff.

we are dominated by our senses. Why are we dominated by our senses? It is because our characters are weak. Everything boils down to virtue, which is the very basis for spiritual progress. With wisdom, *paññā*, we see things as they are. How do we see things this way? It is because with wisdom we act under the influence of non-greed, non-hatred, and non-delusion. The untrained human being acts under the influence of greed (*lobha*), hatred (*dosa*) and delusion (*moha*). But the trained person, the one who has concentration, the one who has based himself or herself on virtue, acts under the influence of non-greed, non-hatred, and non-delusion. We are in the habit of accumulating so many things around ourselves: TVs, cars, this and that. Some things we do not even use but we keep them as ornaments or hang on to them as possessions. We act under the influence of acquisitive instincts. Through this greed for possession, we exploit nature. The exploitation of nature has gone on to such extent that nature is responding—many kinds of pollution now confront us. Nature is becoming incapable of supporting healthy life on this planet.

H.M.S. Karunatillake, in *This Confused Society*, has written an important observation that relates to what I have tried to say. Since this work is very hard to find, let me quote from it here.

> The problems of environmental pollution,
> depletion of non-renewable resources and
> the rapid exploitation of natural resources
> are the outcome of man's greed, avarice and
> his acquisitive instinct. This fundamentally
> reflects a serious imbalance in man's orientation
> towards nature. The Buddha does not say that
> one should not produce goods and build up
> assets by energetic efforts and the sweat of
> one's brow. But what he does not advocate is
> the excessive domination of the personality by
> greed of any kind. His doctrine is based on the
> premise that it is not maximum production that
> matters but optimal human development.

This reminds me of the *Agañña Sutta*[28] which says that moral degeneration of persons has its counterpart in nature with the depletion of natural resources. This is given in the form of a legend, but when one fine tunes the legend and gets down to the facts, the point is made that moral depletion leads to a corresponding depletion of nature.

What about ill-will? There is so much competition in society today. It is the aggressive person who progresses in society these days. We have to push in order to get what we want. Because of this competition we become anxiety ridden and we want to drown ourselves in alcohol and drugs and the like. We keep on coming back to these problems because we are not working with non-greed, non-hatred, and non-delusion.

Insomnia is rampant today. So, people seek out Valium or some such thing in order to sleep. The tranquilizer industry is thriving. It is said that the United States alone consumes so many tons of tranquilizers every day. This shows that we are so anxiety ridden, so anxious and unhappy. If Buddhism is a way of showing how we can be happy, then let us try to practice it, try to become virtuous. It is not an "-ism." It is a way of making one a happier, more contented human being.

There are extremes that Buddhism renounces: the extreme of self-indulgence and asceticism. Self-indulgence is like an ant that has fallen into a pot of honey. The ant is drowning in the pleasure it is trying to enjoy. Men and women are like this: happy because they are indulging in the senses while drowning in the pleasure, not getting anything out of it. That is why people are trying to escape from themselves.

We have delusion, *moha*. We do not actually know what will make us happy. We do not know what will make us contented. We do not know that it is sense control that will provide lasting happiness.

---

[28] *The Dīgha Nikāya*, edited by J. Estlin Carpenter, London: Published for the Pali Text Society by Luzac & Company, Ltd., 1960, III, 80 ff., with an English translation in *Dialogues of the Buddha*, translated by T. W. and C. A. F. Rhys Davids, Sacred Books of the Buddhists, London: Luzac & Company, Ltd., 1957, III, 77 ff.

This, in outline, indicates for us the idea that from beginning to end we are not being Buddhistic nowadays and that is why there are so many problems.

Questions and Responses

Q: What, exactly, is sexual misconduct, and what is the origin of the definition of what constitutes sexual misconduct?

Lily de Silva: The Pali phrase that is used is *kāmesu micchācara*. It means "with reference to sense pleasures, wrong conduct." You could interpret this in two ways. One way is to act contrary to what is accepted in a particular society. In a Muslim country, say, it might be possible to have four wives. Buddhism would favor one wife. It is possible to interpret this according to accepted norms regarding sexual behavior. Humankind has, in the long run, evolved several ways and means of satisfying sexual drive which is to the best advantage of humankind itself. Buddhists tend to interpret this in a way that relates it to enhancing human relationships and developing spiritual progression. If you tread upon what rightly belongs to somebody else, you are hurting another, that is, if you rob, as it were, someone else's spouse, you are hurting that person. If you take a spouse who does not belong to another, then one is not hurting another. It is possible to hurt yourself as well as your spouse by overindulgence.

According to Buddhism, the best way is monogamy. It is not just the satisfaction of sex alone that matters. It is a personality adjustment. Married life is also a method of cultivating yourself to become a better personality, to spiritually progress along the path. Married life brings its own responsibilities as well, namely, children. You then forget about yourself and focus on the needs of the children. You have to make your interests subservient to the interests of the child. That means you are being less selfish when you have a child, because you have to devote selfless service for the child. Married life, therefore, is not sexual life only. It is a much broader adventure in which you progress spiritually.

A marriage has succeeded to the extent that it has produced the *brahmavihāras* within that family: loving kindness, compassion, sympathetic joy, and equanimity.

Sex by itself is not something that will give one satisfaction. It is like drinking salt water for thirst. One wants more and more water.[29]

Q: You said that in order to get concentration sense withdrawal is absolutely necessary. It would seem like this could be something like blind control without understanding why.

LdS: You must have understanding. When you take the eightfold path, proper view, *sammādiṭṭhi* comes at the very beginning. That is, theoretical understanding must be there. Otherwise you do not know what you are and why you are doing it. It is important to know why you are doing something. For example non-sensuous aesthetics, such as painting and music, are for sense control and concentration.

Q: It seems more like a theoretical understanding than a meditative understanding.

LdS: That's right. Theoretical understanding is necessary. If you stop there, it has not touched your personality. You have not really benefited from that. If you move beyond the theoretical level to practice, it is as if moving from darkness to light.

Q: Even the Buddha realized that such practices were against humankind's tendencies. It seems now that the modern age is perhaps more decadent than the past—but still we are better off than what we've come from: we have no slaves, we have human rights and the like. Would you say that it will become easier and easier to practice with gradual evolution?

---

[29] There is interesting related information found in the Pali texts. See, for example, *The Dīgha-nikāya*, III.73 ff., with English translation in *Dialogues of the Buddha*, III. 71 ff., and *The Sumaṅgala-vilāsinī*, the commentary on the *Dīgha Nikāya*, edited by W. Stede, London: Published for the Pali Text Society by Oxford University Press, 1932, III. 853-4, where it is noted that sexual abnormalities lead to the development of weaponry and of war. Also, *The Aṅguttara-nikāya*, edited by the Rev. Richard Morris, London: Published for the Pali Text Society by Luzac & Co., Ltd., 1961, I. 160 ff., suggests these abnormalities lead to inhospitable weather patterns and to crime.

LdS: We have come from human duties to human rights, which is not a healthy thing at all. The five precepts, *pañcasīla*, actually comprise human rights as duties and responsibilities in a more comprehensive way than merely speaking of "human rights."

Q: Is the next move from human rights to human responsibilities?

LdS: We have actually come *from* human responsibilities to human rights. During the time of the Buddha what was emphasized was duties and responsibilities. In the *Siṅgalovada Sutta*,[30] the duties of the wife towards the husband, the responsibilities of the husband to the wife are noted. Nowadays it is the wife's rights and the husband's rights. So it is contentious.

Q: Do you see our age in sort of a downswing and ready for change?

LdS: I think the upward swing is also gradually taking place. Meditation centers are found all over the world. And you are also interested. That is why you have come here to learn alternative orientations to enhance our lives.

Q: Does the Buddhist tradition hold the only answer or does each individual develop an answer.

LdS: No true religion will teach you anything immoral. Each religion will have its own goals and a certain set of procedures. Where the ethics are concerned, I think all religions are in agreement.

---

[30] This appears as *Siṅgālovāda-Suttanta*, in *The Dīgha Nikāya*, III. 180 ff., with an English translation in *Dialogues of the Buddha*, III.173 ff.

II

IN PRACTICE

Religious rituals and practices enable one to realize shared expectations in behavior with others and, at the same time, to rediscover a dimension of awareness that is profoundly personal. In temples, alone and in public, surrounded by sounds of chanting and smells of incense, listening to sermons and in silence, men and women in Sri Lanka have found continuity in memory rekindled through the repetition of religious practices and have not been cut adrift from history.

CHAPTER XIII

BUDDHIST BELIEFS AND PRACTICES

G. D. Wijayawardhana

Running through the previous chapters, beginning with the first, we see the importance placed on a focused awareness of the quality of one's actions. We have seen emphasis consistently placed on the importance of moral virtue and the significance of developing what is wholesome in thought, word, and deed, in one's own life and in relations with others. Professor Wijayawardhana turns our attention now to ritual in the religious life of Sinhala Theravāda Buddhists.

The Theravāda tradition in Sri Lanka today consists of two categories of practices. The first are those which are confined to the Saṅgha, the community of monks. These are monastic practices concerned with the monastic code (*vinaya*) by which the monks are expected to abide and by means of which they contribute to the perpetuation of this monastic order. Here I will consider those practices concerned with ordination of a person just entering the monastic life and the *upasampadā* (the higher ordination by which a monk receives the full-fledged position of a full monk, *bhikkhu*) and the *uposatha* ceremony, which the monks are expected to perform regularly according to the monastic rules laid down in the *vinaya*. The lay community has almost nothing to do with these practices. Most are observed by the monks themselves and no lay people are expected to be present. Very few of such practices of the Saṅgha have to do with lay people in general. Apart from the exclusive ceremonies of the

185

Saṅgha, there is another set of beliefs and practices in which the laity is involved. In these the Saṅgha plays an important role. In this chapter I will place more emphasis on the practices that the lay followers are expected to follow.

Theravāda Buddhism is said to be a religion with no place for ritual as such. It is said to be a philosophy with the goal of attaining spiritual release through meditation and insightful thinking and by individual effort. Thus it is said that there is very little place for ritual in the Theravāda Buddhist tradition. However, as time passed, Buddhism has transformed itself into a popular religion—a system of philosophy cannot be expected to have a very wide appeal. In order to cater to the needs of the wider population, the Theravāda tradition has developed certain practices that have become formalized over the course of time. This may have been the result of the influence of Hinduism or perhaps Mahāyāna Buddhism. Whatever their origins may be, the literary sources as well as historical rock inscriptions make mention of several formalized observances in the Theravāda tradition of Sri Lanka which have been passed down and which are still practiced today.

Theravāda Buddhists maintain that their ritual practices have their basis in the Buddhist scriptures. Most of our practices are based on some of these well-embedded beliefs. First and foremost are the beliefs in *karma* and re-birth. Theravāda Buddhists believe in a samsaric process of existence wherein a person is reborn indefinitely until his or her karmic force is exhausted. At this point he or she has reached a stage which we call Nibbāna. Only then does a person become free from this continuous cycle of *saṃsāra*. We discussed previously, in the talk entitled "Kamma," the forms of action known as *kusala* and *akusala karma*, wholesome and unwholesome action. In the popular language of Sinhala Buddhists there is another set of terms generally applied to these deeds: *pin* and *pau*. *Pin* (P. *puñña*) means wholesome, meritorious deeds, and *pau* (P. *pāpa*) means the unwholesome or unmeritorious deeds which result in demerit or sin. Theravāda Buddhists believe that *pin* or *pau* deeds will lead to wholesome or unwholesome results as the case may be, both in this life and in one's future existences.

The notions of *pin* and *pau* are impressed upon us as Sinhala Buddhists beginning at a very young age. It is part and parcel of our lives. What makes us do good or evil is this notion of *pin* and *pau*. Our parents will always exhort us to do deeds which count as *pin*, saying that this will help us to lead a better life here and hereafter; while if we do *pau*, if we harass animals and the like, these actions will produce the opposite fortune. The child growing up in the Theravāda Buddhist tradition first acquires this notion of *pin* and *pau* from his or her parents or elders or from the Saṅgha. The whole idea of *karma* is involved with this, so much so that our moral code is based on this notion of merit and demerit.

One could commit an act of *pin* by oneself or as a part of a community. For example, a *dāna*, an act of giving, could be a personal act or a collective act. In certain instances, the Buddha said that this collective performance of good actions is even more praiseworthy than individual acts. So one who enables others to join in observing the eight precepts (Sinhala: *aṭa sīl*), or encourages others to perform an act of *dāna* along with oneself is doing another additional good deed. Even an act of meditation (or purification of the mind), *bhāvanā*, is considered an act of merit capable of yielding beneficial results in a future state. This whole process of doing something good or bad, favorable or harmful, is involved in the notion of *pin* and *pau*—good and bad deeds will naturally have their own results.

The general Buddhist belief is that when performing good deeds and accumulating merit will lead to one's taking birth in better circumstances in the future. Being born in favorable circumstances increases your likelihood of attaining Nibbāna. The fruits of *pin* acquired in various ways will take you to this ultimate goal.

It is generally believed that Nibbāna can be reached in three ways: by becoming a Buddha, by becoming a Paccekabuddha (one who realizes Nibbāna on his or her own but is not in position to lead others to salvation), or by becoming an Arahant. By any of these three ways one can attain Nibbāna as a result of the accumulated meritorious deeds performed. Hence, many Buddhists are inclined to view every practice of *pin*, even the smallest observance, as an act of merit. Even going to a temple to worship the Buddha or the Saṅgha is considered meritorious and is on the side of *pin*.

The other belief that is basic to most Theravāda observances is the power of the *tisaraṇa*, the threefold refuge. In common Buddhist parlance, they are referred to as the *tiratana*, the three jewels: the Buddha, Dhamma, and the Saṅgha. We believe that the triple gem has the power to help us in an hour of need, to ward off any evil that might fall upon us, and it has a protective effect over the affairs of those who wish to go to them as refuge. So whenever a person starts out on a journey or on a new venture of some kind, their mother or someone elderly would say, in Sinhala, *triruvan saraṇayi*, which means approximately "may the refuge of the triple gem be on you." We are frequently reminded of the power of the triple gem throughout our lives. One's behavior toward the triple gem, the Buddha, Dhamma, and Saṅgha, normally determines whether you are considered a good Buddhist, whether you keep the triple gem, the *tiratana* in mind.

This leads to the act of *pūja*, of paying homage to the triple gem. It is a wholesome (*kusala*) act, an act of merit, if one pays homage to the triple gem. When a Buddhist enters a temple he or she has this sense of *pūja* in mind, a sense of homage to the triple gem. The act of *pūja* is seen in the offering of flowers, and offering incense to the Buddha, which would be an act of *pūja*, an act of merit.

Religious observances follow the four quarters of the moon. Visiting a temple is the most basic observance a lay Buddhist performs and is most significant on a full moon day. The first place to visit is the *stūpa* or *dāgoba*, which contains a relic of the Buddha. Next would be the Bodhi tree. At each of these places we would offer flowers, burn incense, or light an oil lamp. Then we would go to the shrine room containing the image of the Buddha. Most commonly, flowers are offered there and incense is burned. Then we light a traditional oil lamp to show respect to the Buddha. Acts of *pūja* performed on the full moon day are all the more praiseworthy. In the same way, acts of *pau* on a full moon day are considered more severe. The full moon day is considered of most importance in connection with these religious observances. From the day we were small children we were taught the full moon day should be set aside to visit the temple and to perform good deeds.

Observance of the eight precepts (in Sinhala the *aṭa sīl*) is an important practice. Normally, Buddhists are to observe the five precepts in their routine life. On a full moon day, a good Buddhist makes an effort to go to a temple and to observe the *eight* precepts. A very devout Buddhist would consider observing the eight precepts on other *poya* days (lunar-related days of the moon's quarter phases). But the most common lay practice is to go to the temple on the full moon day and then to observe the eight precepts.

This *pūja*, or worship of the Buddha, is generally believed to be of two kinds. There is the *pūja* performed by offering something to the Buddha, or by giving a gift to the Saṅgha. Worshiping by offering some material item is referred to as the *pūja* of observances. But we believe that the *pūja* of practices is greater than the *pūja* of homage or of material offerings. By observing the eight precepts, by meditation, or by listening to Dhamma—although not involving anything given materially—these are also acts of *pūja*, specifically *praṭipatti pūja*, "*pūja* of practices." This is the more important type of *pūja*.

The major belief that forms the basis of most of the religious practices performed in Sri Lanka today is the concept of *dāna*, which is making a gift to the Buddha, Dhamma and the Saṅgha. As it is the easiest observance to perform, people take recourse to this act of giving more than to any other. The act of giving constitutes an act of *pin*.

A common belief is that one is able to participate in another's act of *pin*. Having committed a good deed, one can share the merit accumulated. We call this *anumodana*. "*Modana*" is an act of rejoicing, an act of being happy—the root meaning of "*anumodana*" is an act which involves "being happy along with." If one performs a good deed, an act of merit, one can always get others to rejoice in this act. In doing so, these other persons participate in and therefore benefit by this act. At the same time, if one rejoices in another person's meritorious act that would be conducive to one's own happiness. At the end of a *dāna* or any other meritorious deed, one always makes a point to utter some Pali stanzas wherein one calls upon other people, as well as departed relatives and gods who look over the affairs of the human world, to be happy in this act of merit. Actually, the idea of *anumodana* produced a number of practices connected with death, rituals and rites of passage. When a person who has died is born in a miserable state where he or she is uncomfortable, there is the possibility that if this person rejoices in a *dāna* or other meritorious deed their unfavorable existence could be improved. This belief forms the basis of several practices concerned with the dead.

As soon as a person dies, or when he or she is buried or cremated, monks are invited to the home to sit in front of the casket. Having given the Saṅgha some suitable refreshments, one must give a length of white cloth, called *paṅsukūla*, "a cloth from a dust heap" because in the early accounts monks were to wear discarded robes picked up from cemeteries and elsewhere to indicate their piety and absence of desire. The chief monk who participates in this ceremony will preach a short sermon on the impermanence of life, the certainty of death, the effects of *karma* on future births, and the nature of our samsaric existence. Then those present are called upon to meditate on the fact that life is impermanent and that the time of one's death can never be predicted.

The act of giving, *dāna*, and observing the five precepts, *sīla*, as well as the practice of meditation, *bhāvanā*, are all viewed as acts of merit. During the observance of *anumodana*, one calls upon the departed ones to rejoice in the quality of the acts performed. Similarly, after a death, at a prescribed period of time—one month, three months, one year—one would want to have a *dāna*, an act of giving alms to the monks, by virtue of which one acquires merit and consequently transfers that merit to the departed relative. The *dāna*, gifts of food and other items, could be taken to the temple and offered there, or the monks could be invited to the home where the death took place and then the *dāna* could be performed there. When the observance is held in the household, usually the relic casket in the temple (believed to contain some relic of the Buddha) is brought into the house, signifying that the Buddha himself has arrived to take part in this meritorious deed. First, offerings of food are made in small quantities to the Buddha, followed by offerings to the Saṅgha. This is called *Buddhapūja*, homage to the Buddha. Then the gifts to the Saṅgha are given. At the end of the *dāna*, the chief or senior monk presents a short discourse, *anusāsana*, outlining the good results of this particular act of *dāna* and the associated thoughts. Again the ceremony is concluded by *anumodana* in which the departed relative is invited to take part in the meritorious act which has been performed. If the departed is in an unfortunate existence, this act would contribute to improving that existence.

Of course, a departed being is not in position to accept the merit in each and every place in which he or she is born. If he or she is born in the heavenly worlds, it is said that no *pin* is necessary. If he or she is born in the animal world, this act of transference is not going to help very much, or similarly if he or she has gone to a state of great suffering. But we believe that there are certain existences where this transference of merit is beneficial. This is not really in keeping with the spirit of pure Buddhism. I think that Buddhism in its pure form would maintain that a person will have to see to his or her own liberation and that an act by another would not help much in one's journey through *saṃsāra*. Merit transfer is not perhaps in keeping with the pure spirit of Buddhism, but the practice has grown over the years so that now Buddhists practicing the Theravāda tradition in Sri Lanka will consider this act of performing a good deed and enabling others to rejoice and be happy as a consequence of a particular meritorious act to be of great importance.

The offering of a robe to a monk at the end of the rainy season is an act of *pūja* of great consequence. Buddhist monks, from the time of the Buddha, kept the practice of going into retreat during the rainy season. In the Sinhala language he is said to be observing *vas* (P. *vassa*). During this time, approximately between August and October, they are expected to live in a monastery without leaving for any length of time. They are expected to lead a very religious life, performing the monastic practices even more diligently. It is a period in which the monastic discipline is followed very carefully. At the end of this season, lay people offer the monks a particular robe, called *kaṭhina cīvara*, an act which is thought to be of great merit, even more than perhaps any other gift given to the Saṅgha. This is a communal activity in which the whole village participates.

CHAPTER XIV

WOMEN IN BUDDHISM

Lily de Silva

Often presentations of the Theravāda tradition tend to draw attention either to the monastic tradition and the monks, or to anthropological studies that focus on contemporary village life. Frequently left out is a meaningfully interpretation of the life of women in the household—as mothers, daughters, wives, single women, or working women. Professor de Silva offers numerous examples of the role of women in the Theravāda frame of reference, both in the social setting and in the soteriological process, in accounts from the past and held before us anew today.

To be born human means to be born a male or a female. Sex difference is common to almost all animate things in nature. Males and females are both made for the propagation of the species. Individually, neither party can make life go on. Therefore each party is a complement of the other for the purpose of propagation. Thus, according to nature, there is nothing high or low between these two divisions. Though sex as such is natural, history shows that the position of women has fluctuated from culture to culture. To a large extent it has depended on the social organization of the family in various societies. In some matriarchal societies, not only was the position of women quite high and wealth was inherited matrilineally, the husband had no important legitimate place in the family. The Dobu Islanders of southeastern New Guinea are a good example of this type. In some patrilineal societies, sometimes the woman's position was so low that she was considered living property of the man. Both these family types seem to ignore the natural complementary role of the two sexes; they favor one or the other, thus preventing a normal natural balance.

Religious ideologies, too, contribute to the fluctuating status of the sexes. In pre-Buddhist India, the position of women varied from time to time, depending on changes in religious ideologies. In ancient Vedic India, woman had quite an honored position in society. Though the Vedic Indians generally prayed to gods for more and more sons, they did not despise as unlucky the birth of a daughter. Learned ladies who had risen to the level of sages known as *ṛṣikās* and *brāhmavādinī* were even honored as composers of Vedic hymns. Romasā, Lopāmudrā, Vishvawārā, and Kadrū are some of these learned women. In religious ritual, the wife occupied an equal position with the husband. Unmarried women performed sacrifices alone. Though women held an honored position according to most hymns of the *Ṛig Veda*, there were signs of their position being weakened according to some hymns.

In a hymn of the eighth *maṇḍala* of the *Ṛig Veda*, Indra has declared that woman has an untamable mind and that she is unintelligent. It was not possible to maintain a long-lasting relationship with women and they had hyena-like hearts says a hymn in the tenth *maṇḍala* of the *Ṛig Veda*. These are but fore-warnings of the ideas emerging in the *Brāhmaṇas*, another set of ritual texts.

The meticulous performance of the sacrifice itself became the central theme of the *Brāhmaṇas*. There, the ordinary layman was considered incapable of performing the sacrifice with the required precision and rectitude. Therefore, the Brahmins appropriated the right to perform sacrifices. They styled themselves as gods on earth. A Brahmin descending from a *ṛṣī,* that is, a seer or sage, was regarded as even higher than gods. When the position of the Brahmin in domestic ritual thus became consolidated, the position of the husband also suffered serious setbacks in home rituals. The woman was relegated to a very low position. During the Brahmanic period women suffered a great deal and they were classed together with the sinful *Śudra*, the dog, and the crow. The sacrifice constituted the truth, and in contrast woman was considered the epitome of the untruth and sin. There is a statement in the *Śatapatabrāhmaṇa* which is like a religious sanction given in order to keep women in subjugation. Ghee is poured into the sacrificial fire. Gods discipline their wives by beating them. Wives who are weakened thus by such assault do not even own their bodies. They have no claim for any other heritage either. This is a statement taken straight from the *Śatapatabrāhmaṇa*. If a wife is unfaithful to her husband, some ritual or some sacrificial rites make it imperative that she confesses it in public. Thus, the position of woman was really pitiful during the *Brāhmaṇa* period.

Brahmin superiority was challenged by the *Upaniṣads,* which questioned the very core of the Brahmanic ritual system. They questioned the validity of sacrifice and the existence of the gods to whom sacrifices were offered. As a result of free inquiry in Upanishadic thinking, woman started regaining the privileges she lost during the preceding age. The characters of Gārgī and Maitreī show that there were women who could hold their own in prestigious philosophical circles. They took part in learned debates with men regarding abstruse metaphysical problems, but the *Upaniṣads* were not powerful enough to completely change the attitude molded through a long period of Brahmanic supremacy.

Generally, these comments provide us with a rough outline of the history of the role of women which forms the background of the rise of Buddhism.

In contrast to this, the Buddhist theory of evolution of humankind and society recorded in the *Agaññasutta* of the *Dīghanikāya*, to which we referred in the talk "Wherein Do We Most Frequently Fail to Live as Buddhists," has an important contribution to make regarding the status of the sexes. According to this legend, beings at the primordial times were self-luminous. They subsisted on joy and were able to traverse through the skies. They had spontaneous births and were sexually undifferentiated. There were no males and females; there were just beings (Skt. *sattva*). As time went on, they tasted the flavorsome earth-substance and were overcome by greed. They started taking this tasty substance as food, and the quantity gradually increased. Their bodies became coarser and coarser. Their self luminosity diminished and vanished, and so did their ability to move in the sky. As time went by, sexual differentiation manifested and spontaneous birth was replaced by sexual reproduction. Thus the manifestation of both sexes, male and female, was the result of moral degradation. Therefore, one sex had no claim to superiority, both were equal in status and had complementary roles to play in the propagation of the species. The acceptance of this fact had considerable impact on the position of women in society. The point I am trying to make is quite clear. Because of moral degradation—greed descending into those beings who were originally sexually undifferentiated—sexual differentiation appeared and, therefore, there is no superiority or inferiority attached to the sexes. Both are equal because they manifested themselves under the same circumstances.

There are several words in Sanskrit and Pali which denote the female of the species, and these seem to reveal the natural biological function of the woman. The commonest is *strī*. This is related to the word, *stṛ*, "to spread." Her function as the propagator of the species seems to be reflected in it. *Matugāma* means "the one who is destined for motherhood." And there are several other words: *vanitā* means a woman, and that comes from the root *van*, "to desire, to win over." *Kantā* comes from the root *kam*, "to desire." And *mahilā* comes from a root also meaning "to excite, to desire." *Yoshitā* comes from a root meaning "to take delight in." All of these record the fact that the woman is an object of desire.

Sanskrit words denoting family relationships also seem to reveal quite a bit of the traditional views regarding the functional roles of family members. *Mātā* comes from the root *mā*, "to create." It is the mother who augments the family, therefore she is called *mātā*, literally, "creator." It may also be interpreted as from the prohibitive particle *mā*, which means "don't." This indicates a prohibition for other males than her husband of any claim as the father of the child, to have recourse to her. "Father," *pitā* comes from the root *pā*, to protect, as the father looks after the family, keeping the wolf away. The husband is called *bhāta*, meaning "the one who supports," and the word is derived from the root *bhṛ*, "to bear," the one who supports the woman and the family. The wife is called *bhariyā*, "one to be supported." If we take the literal economic aspect only, it appears inadequate and somewhat derogatory. It can also be interpreted to mean the one fit to bear, not only children, but also the husband's confidence. The sage Mahosada, according to a story in the *Jātaka*, did not see even his wife as fit to be entrusted with guarded secrets. According to the Buddha, the wife is the friend par-excellence, *bhariyā paramā sakhā*.[31]

The daughter in the Indian social context seems to have been looked at as an economic drain. She is called *duhitṛi* because, according to the Monier Williams *Sanskrit-English Dictionary*, she draws milk from the mother, but surely the son also does the same as an infant. Perhaps the daughter was so-called because it was her duty to milk the cows at home. This is from the root *duh*, "to milk."[32]

In the Buddhist household, the daughter held quite an honored, affectionate position. There is one recorded instance of displeasure expressed at the birth of a daughter. Once, King Pasenadikosala was displeased with the birth of a daughter. The Buddha explained to him that the value of a human being does not depend on sex, but on spiritual quality.[33] If a woman is endowed with virtue and intelligence, and if she can get on with her relatives and friends harmoniously, such a woman is even more valuable than a male without such qualities. In Brahmanism, the preference for a male child was very strong as it was believed that the happiness of a man in the afterlife depended on the funeral

---

[31] *The Saṃyutta-nikāya of the Sutta-Piṭaka*, edited by M. Léon Feer, London: Published for the Pali Text Society by Luzac & Company, Ltd., 1960, I. 37, with an English translation in *The Book of the Kindred Sayings*, translated by Mrs. Rhys Davids, London: Published for the Pali Text Society by Luzac & Compay, Ltd., 1950, I. 57.

[32] Sir Monier Monier-Williams, *A Sanskrit-English Dictionary*, Oxford: the Clarendon Press, 1960.

[33] *The Saṃyutta-nikāya*, I. 86; *The Book of the Kindred Sayings*, I. 110-111.

rites performed by a son. A daughter was incapable of performing this ritual.

Buddhism entertained no such belief and funeral rites could be performed by anyone, be it a daughter, widow, or any other interested relative or friend. Therefore, in Buddhism there was no religious prerogative which required the birth of a son as against the birth of a daughter.

Childless couples wished for a son or a daughter, as is seen in the episode of Cakkhupāla the Elder,[34] and as also noted in the *Jātaka*.[35]

The word *putta*, which strictly means "son," also seems to have been used in the sense of "child," which reveals that there was no obsessional preference for male children, or prejudice against female children. In fact, there are a couple of recorded cases where girls have been adopted as daughters.

As wife, woman plays the role of a companion to her husband. It is a relationship of mutual love and understanding, fortified by the discharge of duties towards one another. The *Sigālovādasutta*[36] clearly defines the duties of the husband and wife. The husband should respect the wife, should be courteous to her, should be faithful to her, should hand over authority to her and provide her with things of beauty. The wife's duties toward the husband comprise the maintenance of a well organized household, treatment of servants with kindness and hospitality,

---

[34] *The Commentary on the Dhammapada*, edited by H. C. Norman, London: Published for the Pali Text Society by Luzac & Company, Ltd., 1970, I. 3, with an English translation in *Buddhist Legends*, translated by Eugene Watson Burlingame, Published for the Pali Text Society by Luzac & Company, Ltd., 1969, I. 146.

[35] *The Jātaka together with Its Commentary*, translated by V. Fausbøll, London: Published for the Pali Text Society by Luzac and Company, Ltd., 1963, V. 110-111, with an English translation in *The Jātaka or Stories of the Buddha's Former Births*, translated by Professor E. B. Cowell, London: Published for the Pali Text Society by Luzac & Company, Ltd., 1969, V. 59-60.

[36] *The Dīgha Nikāya*, edited by J. Estlin Carpenter, London: Published for the Pali Text Society by Luzac & Company, Ltd., 1960, III. 180-193, with an English translation in *Dialogues of the Buddha*, translated by T. W. and C. A. F. Rhys Davids, London: Published for the Pali Text Society by Luzac & Company, Ltd., 1957, III. 173-184.

being faithful to her husband, safekeeping of the family wealth, and conducting herself with dignity and dexterity in all affairs. Now, I would like to make a comment here. According to the *Siṅgālovādasutta* of the *Dīghanikāya*, the man who earns the family wealth must hand over the wealth to the wife. It is the wife who budgets and meets the household expenses and so forth. But it is the duty of the husband to provide the wife with things of beauty: clothes, ornaments and so forth. I think this was a very prudent, cautious method of divided responsibility, because the possibility may be there, had wealth been fully in the hands of the woman, she may overspend on clothes. Therefore, it is not she who has the responsibility to provide herself with finery and so forth. It is the man who does that, and in doing so the man has the opportunity to show concern and affection to her. What is given by him is much more precious to her. I think this was a very subtle way of maintaining income at a manageable level in the household and also showing the man's concern and affection toward the wife.

The conjugal duties enumerated in the *suttas* show that the husband and wife are partners of a joint venture, with shared responsibilities and interests. The wife, in such a setup, has a full active role to play, exercising her authority and discretion with prudence and heedfulness. She is not only accepted and respected as a full person. She is even depended upon as a helpmate who has a unique contribution to make. There are no religious sanctions which make her position inferior to that of her husband. Buddhist texts show Nakula's parents as ideal spouses with a well adjusted matrimonial relationship. They live a beautiful life with great mutual love, respect and understanding. In their old age they entertain the wish to be reunited in the next life as husband and wife, and they sought the advice of the Buddha on this matter.[37] The Buddha said that their wish would materialize if they equally shared the qualities of *saddhā*, "mutual confidence,"

---

[37] *The Aṅguttara-nikāya*, edited by Rev. Richard Morris, London: Published for the Pali Text Society by Luzac & Company, Ltd., 1955, II. 61-62, with an English translation in *The Book of the Gradual Sayings*, translated by F. L. Woodward, London: Published for the Pali Text Society by Luzac & Comopany, Ltd., 1962, II. 69-70.

sīla, "moral conduct," *cāga*, "self-denial," and *paññā*, "wisdom." If these spiritual qualities are present in both husband and wife, it is possible that this relationship will survive death.

Here, a word might be necessary on the meaning of *saddhā*. It is translated as "faith," faith in whatever religious affiliation one has—faith in that. In Buddhism it is the faith in the Buddha, the Dhamma and the Saṅgha. Here in this particular context as well as in other contexts, *saddhā* is not confined to faith in the religious sense. It also means confidence, to have confidence in one another. That is very important in this particular respect.

Another word here is *cāga*, "self-denial," that is, what I mean by self-denial here is that one always puts the interest of the other before oneself. One does not consider oneself in terms of selfishness, but one considers always the interest of the other as coming first. Maybe in the choice of food, or the choice of anything else, one will think "I will keep the better thing for the other person." Always, that amount of self-denial shows the amount of love one entertains for the other.

These are the spiritual qualities which make married life a success, insuring a long-lasting, mutually enriching relationship. They provide a healthy environment for the nurture of children, thus contributing to harmony in social life. What is more, they contribute to the spiritual growth of all members of the family, to advance from light to bright light *joti, jotiparāyaṇa*, towards the ultimate goal of Nibbāna. Thus in the creation of a spiritual unit called the family, both men and women have equally grave responsibilities to perform with mutually complementary roles to play.

As mother, woman has definitely an honored position, and her position was unassailable. Parents are like gods unto their children *brahmāmātāpitaro*. When a child is small, the children are called with terms of affection, but supposing the parents do not show love for the child, especially when the child is very small, the child feels rejected by the entire world. So, the affection that the parents give make the child feel that the parents are like a God—here I spell the word "God" with a capital "G."[38] Their sentiments

[38] *The Aṅguttara-nikāya*, I. 132, with an English translation in *The Book of the Gradual Sayings*, I. 114-115.

toward their children are equated to the sublime modes of conduct called *brahmavihāras*. They entertain thoughts of benevolent loving kindness (*mettā*) towards their children. Their compassion (*karuṇā*) knows no bounds when children are in distress. They experience selfless joy (*muditā*) in the success and happiness of their children. They experience equanimity (*upekkhā*) if their children are engaged in a wrong course of conduct. Just because a child goes wrong, a parent cannot hate that child. The parent will try to correct the ways of the child. If they fail, the parent would rather entertain an attitude of equanimity.

Thus parenthood is an opportunity for the natural unfolding of noble spiritual qualities in the human heart. Of the two parents, the mother is held as even superior to the father in these qualities. In fact, *mettā* is defined in terms of the love a mother has towards her one and only child. The mother is the mentor and the *guru* of the child.

Here, I am reminded of the Sinhala word for mother, because I am talking about women in the Buddhist tradition, and I thought I might as well use the Sinhala word for mother, which is *ammā*. I truly feel that this is a sacred word from a philological point of view. The word *ammā* starts with the guttural vowel "a" and the word ends with the labial nasal, at the lips. Try to pronounce *ammā*: note that it starts in the larynx and it ends at the lips breathing through the nose. That is, it joins the two ends of the vocal organs. When you pronounce this word, the tongue rests in the mouth. It does not touch any part of the palate. It is as if to say, you should never bend your tongue to speak ill of your mother. I call this a full-mouthed word. It must not get sullied by coming into contact with the axe in the mouth. The tongue is called *kuthāri*, "axe," because it can play havoc if it is uncontrolled. This is why the Sinhala Buddhist tradition maintains that there is a Buddha in every household, *geingetabudu*. Though the *Sigālovadasutta* sketches the outlines of reciprocal duties of parents and children, it is strange to find that there are no recorded codes of conduct for the upbringing of children. The Buddha maintains that the parent has to look after the child, physically as well as spiritually. Most parents endeavor to keep after the child's physical needs but they are not aware of the nourishment the child needs mentally and spiritually. In order to understand the full significance of the idea meant here, one must investigate the developmental process a child goes through from conception to adulthood, especially according to the theory of *anattā*.

This is how I see a child going through the developmental process. A fetus in the mother's womb is most selfish. It cares not what happens to the mother. It leads a parasitic life, completely unconcerned about what happens to its surroundings. The baby in the womb draws nourishment for itself, irrespective of whether the mother can afford to let it or not. After birth, the baby is dependent on the mother for its food. By and by, the child is weaned and learns to be less selfish. Playing with siblings and peers, he or she learns to share toys and goodies, thus becoming more and more unselfish. In society, a growing child learns to appreciate the fact that he or she is better accepted by his peers to the extent that he or she is selfless.

As an adult, he or she learns to love and cherish one of the opposite sex, making adjustments in his or her lifestyle, habits, likes and dislikes. The selfish person is a boor in love-life. He or she spells disaster for himself or herself and his or her partner. When the couple enjoying conjugal happiness realizes that the satisfaction of the other is the whetstone for one's own happiness, such love is akin to—develops into—*maitrī*, cementing the relationship between the two. This emotion, which I venture to characterize as *maitrī*, is qualitatively different from *mettā*, "benevolence," with which one is expected to supply the whole world. I use the Sanskrit word *maitrī* for want of a better word, in my own interpretation. *Maitrī* generally means the friendliness towards everybody, and to express that I use the word *mettā* in Pali. To express all the emotions I want to express, there is hardly any word. I use *maitrī* for want of a better word as I wish to synthesize in it all the qualities which, according to the *sutta* delivered to Nakula's parents,[39] carry conjugal love beyond death. Not only love in the sense of the sentiment between two people of the opposite sex but also *saddhā*, "mutual confidence,"

---

[39] *The Aṅguttara-nikāya*, II. 61-62, with an English translation in *The Book of the Gradual Sayings*, II. 69-70.

sīla, "moral conduct," *cāga*, self-denial, and *paññā*, "wisdom." Without wisdom it is difficult to go through married life.

When the couple is blessed with a child they forget their own convenience. They plunge into the depth of selfless love as the child is but the creation of their own love for one another. Throughout life they make various economic sacrifices for the well-being of the child which ultimately culminate in handing over all of one's earnings and savings. Parents make an emotional sacrifice, too, when they get a suitable partner for their child to love and cherish. Incidentally, it is the mother who cannot wean the child emotionally, who becomes the target as the proverbially abhorred mother-in-law. Thus, the march from womb to tomb is marked by a successively progressive elimination of self-love and the cultivation of selfless love.

The root of life is love, and the divinity that is infused into it is selflessness. This is the crux of the *anattā* theory in Buddhism. If one understands the theory of *anattā* in this life, one can gain the fruits of Buddhism in double quick time. In this case, the woman is at an advantage. She has the natural capacity to love selflessly. Here I bring in my own experience too. I, being a woman who has borne four children, felt, at the birth of my first child, a great thrill at being able to bring forth life into this world. The flow of milk made me feel that life sustaining energy was flowing from my breast. I was jubilant at being a woman as no man can have this soul-stirring, exhilarating experience.

If a woman realizes her value as mother, she can raise a family from the depths of poverty to the height of affluence, both physically and metaphysically. It is love that stirs woman to action, whether making *hoppers* (rice flour pancakes) or writing books; whether stimulating flagging courage or bolstering upward-directed mental energy. When a woman loves a man she does not just love his body or money. She sees something beyond the body and wealth—something unfathomable yet tangible to her sensitive heart. She sees the potential, the unmanifest, and strives hard to bring to the surface what she alone can sense. If the man is dense and cannot understand her, she does not lose heart. She achieves her desire through progeneration. She passes her own vision genetically to her children as a birthright and through exemplary conduct.

The Buddha categorizes seven types of wives. They are "the nagging killer type," "the faithless robber type," "the domineering fussy type," "the mother type," "the sister type," "the friend type," and "the slave or servant type."[40] Here the seven types are given in ascending order of importance or desirability, and one begins to wonder whether the seventh type is the best. To my mind, it certainly is not so. The "friend type" is undoubtedly the best. But in practice, as the time and occasion demands, the best type is also likely to assume features of the other types temporarily, in decreasing degrees as the list works in the reverse order, perhaps with the exception of the "robber type." "The slave or servant type" is listed as last as this type calls for great strength of character and moral stability, if the husband happens to be callous and undependable. In that case, in order to keep the family fires burning and to give the children a home, the "slave or servant type" has to exercise great patience and maintain spiritual values. That is the reason why the "slave or servant type" is listed last. Especially if she is not working and does not have the means to maintain the family, she has to somehow depend on the man and look after the children.

In the Sanskrit epics of the *Rāmāyana* and the *Mahābhārata*, the heroines, Sīta and Draupadī, are depicted as women who allowed themselves to be cast off or used as stakes in a game of dice. In the *Rāmāyana*, Sīta was abducted by Rāvana and brought to Sri Lanka and later on she was rescued by Rāma. But she could stay in the household only for a short time because the people suspected her purity and Rāma was obliged to send her into exile. Sīta, though a virtuous, pure woman, had to endure being chased out of the house, sent into exile. In the *Mahābhārata*, Draupadī had five husbands, but the first one staked her at a game of dice and lost her. She could even be staked at a game of dice! This showed the position of women according to the two famous epics.

---

[40] *The Aṅguttara-nikāya*, edited by Prof. E. Hardy, London: Published for the Pali Text Society by Luzac & Company, Ltd., 1958, IV. 92-93, with an English translation in *The Book of the Gradual Sayings*, translated by E. M. Hare, London: Published for the Pali Text Society by Luzac & Company, Ltd., 1955, IV. 57.

These women appear to be completely at the mercy of their husbands. But the Buddhist *Jātaka* tales depict the wife of a Bodhisatta as a faithful companion and a trusted helpmate who emulates his exemplary conduct. Even after Prince Siddhārtha's renunciation, Yosodhāra is said to have followed his practice of donning the yellow robe, shaving the head, partaking of a single meal a day and sleeping on the floor. This she did, not because she felt she was forsaken but because she understood, through eons of association with the great being, that renunciation was for a greater and a nobler achievement.

If a woman is single she does not have to mope that she is unmarried. She can sublimate her emotions to gain knowledge or serve the disabled. Such women do not reserve their love's vitality to one family, but enlarge it to envelope humanity. Mother Theresa, of world renown, was a woman who devoted her entire life to serve humankind in such a manner, in a manner that no other human being has done in recent time. In any case the love a woman's breast holds had to find expression in a manner most suitable to her self-advancement. Mother Theresa's life was not just spent in serving the disabled, she thereby ennobled her own life for a path higher than this world can dream of. She had the strength to command the inner resources which lie hidden in the human heart. When a woman is in despair she gains vigor from unfathomable depths and strange leaps of strength are recorded in world annals. These inner resources have to be tapped even for day-to-day affairs, if the woman wishes to make the best of her life situation.

There is very little evidence regarding the position of working women in Pali texts. Poor women have worked as domestic servants and the *Siṅgālovādasutta* clearly defines the duties of employers towards their subordinates. But from incidental references it is possible to surmise that employment for women was not looked down upon in Buddhist texts. When Nakula's father was seriously ill and his wife noticed that he was full of anxiety, she tried to pacify him. One thing that she thought worried him was the family income. She assured him that she was capable of spinning yarn to make a living and look after the family, and that he should not worry on that account.

This assurance given by Nakula's mother at a critical moment of their lives shows that there was no social stigma or taboo against women working.

Well-to-do women may not have worked beyond their normal household tasks as wife, mother or daughter. Among the poor there were women working in the fields. There is also reference to women acrobats and several references to women in the profession of dancing. They were well accepted in society as individuals who had a chosen contribution to make. Widows were not despised as evil omens in society, as was done in the Brahmanical circles. And widow-burning, *satipūja*, is nowhere heard of in Buddhist texts. It was practiced in Hindu India. Widows were integrated as family members in the household of either their parents or their children. There was nothing against widow re-marriage either. *Satipūja* is really venerating the memory (P. *sati*, Skt. *smṛti*) of the husband. When a widow misses the companionship he gave, she does *satipūjā* properly.

When attention is paid to the issue of women and the spiritual path, it has to be emphasized that *vipassanā* meditation provides the housewife with opportunities for spiritual development, while being engaged in household activities such as cooking, cleaning, washing, and childcare. While cooking, and so forth, if she can keep her mind occupied with the work and dwell in the present moment, she is being diligent—*appamāda.* Cooking, washing, etc., can be meditative activities if an attempt is made to be engaged mentally in the activities at hand.

Another important aspect is to be satisfied with what one has to do rather than to be resentful that one could not do one's studies to have a career as successful as the lady next door.

One of the frames of the human mind is to want what is not, to hanker after what one does not have, be it position, wealth, power, or leisure. The career woman envies the housewife who she imagines has all the time for keeping a well-ordered house, shopping, etc. The housewife envies the career woman that she has all the freedom and the money to do whatever she wants without having to answer to the husband—so on and so forth. But *vipassanā* meditation trains us to be satisfied with our lot in life.

Let us consider child bearing. How can we set about it so that it ennobles us spiritually? Buddhism believes that during pregnancy a mother can transmit emotional qualities to the child in the womb. It is the mother's blood that nourishes the baby, and emotional imbalances do affect the baby. Therefore it is the duty of the mother to be emotionally balanced, not to flair into temper tantrums if she wishes her child to be healthy in body and mind. The mother must think healthy, kindly thoughts and regard the baby in her womb with love and care. It is not only with healthy food that the mother can nourish the child. Healthy thoughts are much more important. Healthy habits can also contribute a great deal. Nursing the baby, too, is a duty a mother should not neglect. Thereby she nourishes not only the baby's body, but the mind too. The baby is made to feel wanted, cared for, and tenderly loved in the most intimate manner. Attending to a baby's needs, too, can be a spiritually enriching experience. If the mother does the chores such as changing nappies, soothing a crying child, etc., with great love and compassion, the mother not only helps the child to have emotional security, the mother too grows in selfless love.

The Buddha accepted the view that femininity is no obstacle to spiritual development and attainment of Nibbāna. Therefore, he admitted women into the order, though after some hesitation perhaps due to the social environment of the day. He laid down eight extra rules[41] the observance of which was incumbent on the nuns. Arahantship or Nibbāna is the highest goal that has to be attained with utmost human perseverance, subtle awareness and penetrating wisdom. Femininity does not prevent women from exploiting these potential human capabilities.

That women are not deficient in wisdom is amply testified to by the Buddha's own words. The nun, Dhammadinnā, attained Arahantship shortly after entering the order. Her former husband, the householder named Visāka, who had himself attained to the third stage of sainthood, wished to find out if she had attained some spiritual distinction. He asked her a series of questions, and

---

[41] *The Aṅguttara-nikāya*, edited by Prof. E. Hardy, London: Published for the Pali Text Society by Luzac & Company, Ltd., 1958, IV. 276-277, with an English translation in *The Book of the Gradual Sayings*, translated by E. M. Hare, London: Published for the Pali Text Society by Luzac & Company, Ltd., 1955, IV. 183-184.

she answered them with commendable ease and understanding. The last question was about Nibbāna and she said that it transcends verbalization and advised him to meet the Buddha if further clarification is needed. Visāka reported to the Buddha the entire conversation, and the Buddha commented that he too would have answered those questions in the same manner. He further added that the Dhammadinnā is a lady of great wisdom.[42]

Khemā was another who attained the goal within a short time. And the Buddha ranked her as the foremost among his female disciples for great insight. Khemā was a queen; she was very, very beautiful. She heard that the Buddha spoke ill of beauty and therefore she did not wish to meet him. Somehow through the persuasion of her husband, King Bimbisara, she one day approached the Buddha. The Buddha knew that she was coming and he contrived a miracle. He created the figure of a beautiful woman standing beside him, fanning him. And when Khemā came to see the Buddha and saw this woman she was just spellbound. She kept on gazing at this woman because she was so beautiful. And gradually this woman went through the ages of youth, middle age, old age and then she became a decrepit old woman and after hours maybe she fell dead. And thus Khemā realized, as if through cinematography, that beauty is but evanescent. It is impermanent; it ends in old age and death. She was not only convinced, she wanted to become a nun and shortly afterwards she became an Arahant. She had a reputation of being wise, erudite, intelligent, learned and a brilliant speaker with originality of ideas.[43]

Khemā and Uppalavaṇṇā were the chief female disciples of the Buddha. Uppalavaṇṇā was declared foremost among

[42] *The Majjhima-nikāya*, edited by V. Trenckner, London: Published for the Pali Text Society by Luzac & Company, Ltd., 1964, I. 299 ff., with an English translation in *The Collection of the Middle Length Sayings*, translated by I. B. Horner, London: Published for the Pali Text Society by Luzac & Company, Ltd., 1954, I. 360 ff.

[43] *The Saṃyutta-nikāya*, edited by M. Leon Feer, London: Published for the Pali Text Society by Luzac & Company, Ltd., 1960, IV.374-380, with an English translation in *The Book of the Kindred Sayings*, translated by F. L. Woodward, London: Published for the Pali Text Society by Luzac & Company, Ltd., 1956, IV. 265-269.

those proficient in psychic powers. When Mahāpajāpatī Gotamī approached the Buddha to get permission to enter Parinibbāna, that is, "final passing away," the Buddha requested her to perform miracles, to remove the doubts of those who were skeptical about the intellectual and spiritual attainments of women. The miracles she performed were not second to those of Moggalāna in splendor.

Visāka, the female lady disciple of great repute, was another lady who won the admiration of the Buddha and his disciples. Once the Buddha questioned her as to why she performed great meritorious deeds by making lavish offerings to the Saṅgha. He inquired about what she saw as the advantage of such generosity. In reply she made a detailed analysis of the reasons with deep psychological insights. The Buddha was so pleased with her erudite reply that he expressed approbation by exclaiming, "*sadhu, sadhu, sadhu.*"[44]

The philosophical maturity of the ideas set forth in the *Therīgātha* is not second to the *Theragātha* or, for that matter, any other book of the Pali canon. The *Therīgātha* is translated as *The Psalms of the Sisters*, poems expressed by Arahant nuns of the Buddha's time, or maybe a tribute to them, we do not know.[45] The poems recount the experiences the nuns had prior to their ordination, the luxuries they enjoyed, the turmoil they faced, etc., with such detached equanimity that their attitude itself is an unmistakable index to the spiritual heights to which they had risen. Recalling those bygone incidents they experienced no regret, no elation, no grief. They displayed limitless equanimity and a deep sense of joy born of full emancipation.

---

[44] *The Vinaya Piṭakaṃ*, edited by Hermann Oldenberg, London: Published for the Pali Text Society by Luzac & Company, Ltd., 1964, I. 294, with an English translation in *The Book of the Discipline*, translated by I. B. Horner, London: Sacred Books of the Buddhists, Luzac & Company, Ltd., 1962, IV. 419

[45] *The Therī-gāthā*, edited by Richard Pischel, in *The Thera- and Therī-gāthā*, edited by Hermann Oldenberg and Richard Pischel, second edition with appendices by K. R. Norman and L. Alsdorf, London: Published for the Pali Text Society by Luzac & Company, Ltd., 1966, with an English translation by Mrs. Rhys Davids in *Psalms of the Early Buddhists I.—Psalms of the Sisters*, London: Published for the Pali Text Society by Luzac & Company, Ltd., 1964.

Ambapālī was once a courtesan who entertained those around her with her physical beauty. In her poems she recounts her bygone beauty of form and the ravages of old age with deep equanimity fully substantiating the words of the Master. Poems of Uttārā, Sakulā and others, reveal that their spiritual insight and attainment lacked nothing due to their femininity.

The spiritual attainment summarized by the words *tisovijjā anupattā kataṃ buddhassa sāsanaṃ*, meaning, "the threefold knowledge has been mastered and the message of the Buddha has been accomplished," is a refrain common to both the *Thera-* and the *Therīgātha*, that is, the psalms of the brothers as well as the sisters.

The beautiful nun, Subhā, of Jīvaka's mango grove, is an epitome of strength of character and determination. She was weary of worldly pleasures and became a nun in early youth. She was accustomed to meditating in seclusion in Jīvaka's mango grove. Once, a youth who saw her fell in love with her and entreated her in various ways to leave the yellow robe and become his spouse. He promised her cashmere silks for clothing, gold ornaments, a palace to live in, luxurious furniture and servants to be at her beck and call. Not only these, he pledged his lifelong love and loyalty to her. But Subhā remained calm and firm. Unperturbed, she inquired from him what he saw as being worthy in this rotten body which is full of impurities, which has the nature of disintegration, and which only helps to fill the cemetery. He replied that he is infatuated with her mermaid-like eyes. The more he sees them, the more his love grows. With undaunted conviction and determination Subhā replied, "You are like one wanting to play with the moon, you are like one trying to jump to the top of Mt. Meru, in that you desire to espouse a child of the Buddha. If you are so enchanted by the eyes, here is the eye seeping with tears and yellow matter, take it and go away." So saying, she plucked off an eye from its socket and gave it to him.

Strength of conviction knows no sex barriers as Subhā and many other women in the Buddhist tradition have proven by their heroic characters.

CHAPTER XV

THE CEREMONY OF PROTECTION (*PIRIT*)

Lily de Silva

The Ceremony of Protection, about which Professor de Silva has written a standard work related to the Sinhala Buddhist case, is an old and very important religious ritual practiced by Theravāda Buddhists. It is a religious ritual which addresses uncertainties, with which men and women are familiar, that have to do with one's own welfare and the welfare of others ranging from the safe landing of men on the moon to building the next floor to a high rise building, from a birthday celebration to a death anniversary, and from seeking protection for one traveling abroad to obtaining protection from the evil intent of spiritual forces in the world. Reflective persons have discovered through this ritual that in the final analysis truth is efficacious in enhancing life.

In this chapter, I want to talk about the *pirit* ceremony of Sri Lanka, which is a very popular Buddhist ceremony in Theravāda countries. The Sinhala word *pirit* actually comes from the Pali word *paritta*. *Paritta* comes from the root "*trā*" plus *pari,* meaning "to protect." Both *pirit* and *paritta* refer to the same ritual. These are ceremonies performed for protection which we may accordingly call "prophylactic" ceremonies.

The most important aspect of the *pirit* ceremony is the recitation of extracts taken from the Pali canon, which are collected in a book called the *Piritpota*: "Book" (*pota*) "of Protection" (*pirit*). This ceremony pivots around two important

211

themes: the power of truth, *satya* (P. *sacca*), and the power of amity, *maitrī* (P. *mettā*). Ancient Indians believed that truth, when uttered with sincerity and conviction, had an almost miraculous power. What was called an affirmation of truth (*saccakiriya*) was done in order to bring about whatever results one desired. If a child was bitten by a snake, for example, the mother would make an affirmation of truth. She may have said she had such and such a personal quality, *"and that is the truth*—by the power of the virtue of this truth—that there is, indeed, this virtue in me—may the child be free of the venom." By this means she hoped to cure the child.

The truths recited in *pirit* are the noble virtues of the Buddha, Dhamma, and the Saṅgha. The Buddha is the Enlightened One, Dhamma is teaching, leading to liberation from *dukkha*, and the Saṅgha is a community of monks who have realized the benefits (*maggaphala*) of following Dhamma. One particular *sutta* recited at *pirit* ceremonies states, "By the truth of the virtue of these three may there be happiness and well-being."

Mettā is the other factor on which this ceremony pivots. *Mettā* comes from the Sanskrit word *maitrī*, which is derived from the word *mitra*, which means "friend." *Mettā* refers to the friendliness that people possess—the benevolence, the loving kindness—that, when extended to everyone, brings about closer sympathetic interpersonal relations.

Parittas, or pirits, can be performed on a number of occasions. These may be domestic, social, political, or religious. Parittas can be undertaken with great simplicity or with grandeur. Sometimes they may take only an hour, which are called "sessional" parittas. This may include one hour in the morning, one hour in the evening, and one hour the following day. During these sessions, suttas concerning *sacca, mettā,* and social ethics are recited. The suttas relating to *sacca* are contained in the Ratana Sutta, those dealing with *mettā* are in the Metta Sutta, and those concerning social ethics are in the Maṅgala Sutta. Collectively these three suttas are called Mahāpirit, the "Great Paritta."[46] Although

---

[46] See *Catubhāṇavārapāli: The Text of the Four Recitals or The Great Book of Protections*, with English translation by Lionel Lokuliyana, Colombo: by the Mrs. H. M. Gunasekera Trust, at the Printing House, n.d. See also *The Book of Protection*, translated by Piyadassi Thera, Colombo: Union Printing Works, 1975.

lay people can perform the paritta ceremony (in which case it is called in Sinhala "gihipirit"), this is a rare occasion. Though nearly all Buddhists in Sri Lanka know the three suttas used in the Mahāpirit by heart, and do recite them on their own from time to time, monks perform the paritta or pirit ceremony at the request of the laity.

In its domestic purpose, a *paritta* ceremony may be performed just before the birth of a child in order to bless the mother and the babe. She is thought then to have the protection of the power of the recited truths. The Agulimāla *paritta* is recited especially for this purpose. Immediately before a wedding ceremony, a *paritta* will be performed to bring blessings to the couple. A *paritta* may be performed to ward off evil spirits during an illness. When a person is near death, the ceremony can be useful in diverting the attention of the dying person from evil thoughts towards the more wholesome thoughts of the Buddha, Dhamma and the Saṅgha. Political occasions, independence celebrations and so forth are celebrated with *paritta* ceremonies. In a way, the *paritta* ceremony is like a sari—one can wear it on any occasion, though the texture of the chosen material and color will differ, appropriate for the occasion. Likewise, various *parittas* are performed on many different kinds of occasion.

Besides chanting the *suttas*, *parittas* generally involve a pot or jug of water, some white thread woven in three strands, round a betel leaf. The pot of water is placed on a table, and monks, sitting on chairs, recite the *paritta*. The belief is that the water gets charged with the potency of the recitation, and that this power transforms the water into a salubrious elixir/holy water. The thread is moistened with this water, and is generally worn round the wrist or neck, thus forming a sort of a protective circle for a person. The thread always has three strands, which I believe represent the Buddha, Dhamma, and the Saṅgha. This practice is derived from an Indian custom where there is the ritual of tying cords for protection during particular ceremonies. Yellow thread is used in Hindu *tovil* ceremonies for ritual practices. White thread is always used for the Buddhist *paritta*.

More elaborate *paritta* ceremonies are more grandiose affairs which last the whole night. A temporary pavilion or *maṇḍapa* is erected within which the monks sit and chant the *paritta*. This *paritta-maṇḍapa* can be designed according to one's personal taste. It can be decorated with paper, it can simply be an enclosure with white cloth, or it can be made with tender coconut leaves. Decoration with tender coconut leaves is a special art. If possible, the entrance to the *maṇḍapa* is made to face the east (if the *paritta* takes place in a house it is done in the room with an entrance facing east, if possible). This is done because the Buddha is said to have attained enlightenment under the Bodhi tree while facing east. The *maṇḍapas* can be octagonal or square. There are a minimum of eight chairs within, and a maximum of usually 16, depending on the size of the *maṇḍapa*. There are two chairs kept at the entrance called *ugaputuwa*, "the double or twin chairs." These two chairs are tied together, and then a structure called the *indrakīla* (*indra* meaning "lord" and *kīla* meaning "post") is constructed above them.

The fact that it is called the *indrakīla* is a problem which I have tried to explain in my book on *pirit*.[47] It means something like "chief post" or the "lordly post." In the construction of a *stupa*, a monument of the Buddha's *parinibbāna*, there is in one case a huge pillar (which one leading scholar says weighs as much as twenty tons). This *indrakīla* is placed inside the dome, and the *indrakīla* really gives character to the *stupa*. This we can trace back to the Vedic sacrifice, during which time there was a post (*yūpa*) to which the sacrificial animal was tied in the *yāgaśala*, the sacrificial hall. The *yūpa* has cosmic symbolism: when the *yūpa,* made of a straight tree, is felled, the sacrificer would call out to the *yūpa* telling it not to rend the heavens as it falls. It is from the *yūpa* that the *indrakīla* evolved.

Indrakīla is also called the *kapagaha. Gaha* means "tree," and *kapa-gaha* relates to the cult of *kalpa-vṛkṣa*, a mythical tree which grants all one's wishes. In a text compiled by Mānasara[48] regarding architecture, it is said that the Buddha's standing

[47] Lily de Silva, *Paritta: A Historical and Religious Study of the Buddhist Ceremony for Peace and Prosperity in Sri Lanka*, a publication of the National Museums of Sri Lanka, "Spolia Zeylanica, Vol. 36, Part I, 1981

[48] *Architecture of Mānasāra*, translated by P. K. Acharya, Oxford University Press, 1933..

and seated images are worthy of being distinguished by the *kalpavṛkṣa*.

The functional purposes the *indrakīla* as well as the process of its construction are significant to understanding the symbolic significance of its place in the *paritta*. When the *indrakīla* is constructed it is made of pleated cloth which fluffs out like a fan. Behind the *indrakīla* structure is the arecanut palm, which symbolizes the *kalpavṛkṣa*. To make a long story short, I have discovered that the *indrakīla* itself has four symbols in it.

One is (1) the symbol of stability. It is said that when the Buddha stepped in a village, he placed his foot on the *indrakīla*. *Indrakīlas* were formerly placed on the ground, such that they would never shake. (2) *Indrakīlas* also marked the limit to the city, which is their second symbolism. At the time of the Buddha, the *indrakīla* was erected at the entrance to a village or city so that it stood as a pillar or post imbedded in the ground onto which one could step. It was a sort of stone meant to demarcate the village or the settlement from the rest of the forest. The third and fourth symbolisms are those of (3) authority and of (4) the center. When an *indrakīla* was erected at the entrance to a city, the authority of the king was therein symbolized. In the *paritta* ceremony, this symbol has been appropriated to indicate the authority of the Buddha. The "center" symbolism derives from the fact that *indrakīla* is another name for Mount Meru, the mythological center of the earth.

Through its composite symbolism, the *indrakīla* erected in the *paritta-maṇḍapa* metaphorically recreates the place where the Buddha attained enlightenment—the *Bodhimaṇḍa*. Accordingly, the *Bodhimaṇḍa* is related to the notion of stability. The legend of the Buddha's enlightenment recalls that at the moment of his enlightenment there was an earthquake which made the whole earth tremble. The entire world system also trembled because of the power of this spiritual explosion. As the rest of the earth quaked, the place where the Buddha was seated remained steadfast. It was the only *acalaṭṭhāna*, "the place which does not shake," in the whole world.

It is from the *Pūjāvaliya*, a classical Sinhala text, that the symbolism of "the limit" derives. Therein it is said that the *Bodhimaṇḍa* was like a fortress made of the *pāramitās* of the Buddha. *Pāramitās* were the perfections that the Buddha completely fulfilled during his prior lives in order to become eligible for Buddhahood. Those *pāramitās* formed a sort of fortress around the *Bodhimaṇḍa*, which extended from the ground up to the cupola of the brahmā-world. This is the basis for the symbolism of the limit represented by the *indrakīla* in the ritual recreation of the *Bodhimaṇḍa*.

The symbol of authority finds its origin in the story of Māra coming to fight the Buddha under the Bodhi tree. Māra could not enter the *Bodhimaṇḍa* because there the authority that the Buddha held was supreme. Also, like Mount Meru, the *Bodhimaṇḍa* is a symbolic center of the earth.

One may wonder where the Bodhi tree is amidst all this symbolism. After all, it was the Bodhi tree that gave special character to the *Bodhimaṇḍa*. The Bodhi tree retains special significance for Buddhists, many of whom do not dare to cut even the branch of one. The Bodhi tree is represented in the *maṇḍapa* through the requirement that the *indrakīla* be made of a straight, freshly cut *suriya* branch (*Thespesia Populnea*). This *suriya* tree has leaves somewhat similar to those of the Bodhi tree. Also, the same words which refer to the Bodhi tree in Sanskrit are used for the *suriya* tree. We can conclude that the *paritta-maṇḍapa* symbolically recreates the *Bodhimaṇḍa*, the place where the Buddha attained enlightenment.

The Buddhist trinity of the Buddha, the Dhamma, and the Saṅgha is also symbolically present. Relics of the Buddha in a casket are placed on a table inside the *maṇḍapa*, thus representing the Buddha himself. Dhamma is represented by the *paritta* texts. Generally for an all night *paritta* ceremony an *ola*-leaf (palm-leaf) *paritta* text is used. The Saṅgha is represented by the *bhikkhus* (Skt. *bhikṣus*), the monks who recite the *paritta*. The water and the thread are there to absorb the potency of these three jewels.

Placed around the *paritta-maṇḍapa* are, in Sinhala, *punkala* (P. *punnakata*; Skt. *pūrṇaghata*), "filled vases," which are small earthenware jars or pots into which coconut flowers are placed. This is a symbol of prosperity, and plays a part of the *paritta* ritual specifically representing the earth goddess who bore witness to the Buddha's performance of the *pāramitās*, especially the *dāna pāramitā*, the perfection of generosity.

There are other ritual appurtenances used inside the *paritta-maṇḍapa*. Those items can be divided into two parts: those intended to ward off evil, and those intended to herald prosperity. Mustard seeds, which are scattered inside the *maṇḍapa*, are called "demon killers." They are thought to have the power to drive away demons. A particular kind of grass called "killer of evil spirits" is also used. Jasmine buds are believed to bring prosperity. Betel leaves and tender leaves of the ironwood tree are hung on the canopy of the *paritta-maṇḍapa*. Those particular leaves are most likely used because the word "*nāga*" occur in their names. The *nāgas* of ancient *nāga* worship became represented in temple architecture as protectors of the Buddhist tradition. That is also why the guard stones at the entrance to the temple are called *nāga* guards.

The *paritta* ceremony itself can be performed on a very grand scale, lasting even a whole month. At such protracted ceremonies a messenger to the gods, called *dēvadūtayā,* is introduced who invites the gods to attend. Space does not permit a more detailed presentation of the ceremony itself. These are some of the key ideas about the purpose of, and some general overview of the symbolic significance related to, the *paritta* ceremony as practiced by Buddhists in Sri Lanka.

CHAPTER XVI

BUDDHIST TEMPLE WORSHIP

W. S. Karunatillake

with Venerable Dhammarakkhita

The late Venerable Dhammarakkhita, head of the Vidyalankara Pirivena (a prestigious monastic educational center in Sri Lanka), a leader of those restrained in speech, mind, and deed, extends a welcome to the site of a talk by Professor W. S. Karunatillake, Professor of Linguistics emeritus of the University of Kelaniya, formerly Vidyalankara University, on worship in a Buddhist temple (pansala), a symbolic spatial representation of the Buddha, the Dhamma, and the Saṅgha. We quickly discern a perspective of the laity and note a deep respect for this worshipful practice.

I

*Introductory Remarks by
the Venerable Dhammarakkhita of Vidyalankara Pirivena
(Professor W. S. Karunatillake, Interpreter)*

Sri Lanka is a country that has been well known as a cultural center, especially in the Orient. As a result, many cultural missions have come to our land from distant countries, eastern and western, far and wide. Most of those missions, as far as I can remember, have visited the Vidyalankara Pirivena and have been especially interested in Oriental studies.

As a result of the religious missions sent by Emperor Aśoka to Sri Lanka, this country inherited the Theravāda Buddhist tradition. Thinking he should send the best of those missions to Sri Lanka, Aśoka actually sent a royal mission, which was received upon their arrival by a royal mission headed by King Devānampiyatissa. The missions sent by Emperor Aśoka visited other places and carried with them the first recognizable form of Theravāda Buddhism, though it has since become mixed with other beliefs and philosophies. Therefore, many people believe that Buddhism in its most pristine form is preserved only in this small island of Sri Lanka.

It is because of this inheritance of the Theravāda tradition that we here at Vidyalankara have taken steps to propagate Buddhism abroad as it is taught in this country. It is now well over a century since the inception of Vidyalankara, and during these years we have taken great efforts in teaching the *Buddhadhamma* and Oriental Studies in this country. There are presently many students who have graduated from this institute teaching the essentials of Buddhism in different countries throughout the world.

Since the founding of this *pirivena*, we have built up our own identities and traditions. From its beginning to the present day highly erudite scholars have served the institute. They have written a large number of works and treatises on Sanskrit, Pali, Prakrit, Buddhism, and Sinhala. Among these scholar-monks, one would consider Venerable Ratmalanē Dharmārama Nāyaka Thera as the crest gem of scholars because of his careful, scholarly writings, textual criticism, and his profound knowledge, especially of Sanskrit. In our curriculum today are subjects like Sanskrit, Pali, Prakrit, Sinhala, Hindi, Tamil, English, and of course, Buddhism. This *pirivena* is also a training center for Buddhist monks who have completely dedicated their lives to the cause of *Buddhadhamma*, and its propagation through teaching.

We have taken upon ourselves the responsibility of training young monks in all the ways that a monk should be trained: for example, in teaching, preaching, chanting *pirit*, the mode of deportment and in moral conduct. The life we have entered, which is called "monkhood" (Sinhala: *bhikṣutva*), is something really difficult in this world. We have become deprived of all the beauties of life in a physical sense, but not, of course, in an ethical sense. Ours is actually not a natural way of life. It is something constrained and tough, and we have voluntarily taken it upon ourselves.

This requires of us to live with a group of people who are also restrained, not only in outward appearance but also in mind. It is people of this type, who are treading the Buddhist path of life, who will be able to see more clearly the highest experience in Buddhism, which is called the state of an Arahant, sainthood. The etymological sense of the word *arahant* indicates that such a person is "suitable," one who "deserves," who is "benefitting" the entire world. With this thought in mind we train ourselves every moment and we also train the younger monks in that path.

II

W. S. Karunatillake

We thank Venerable Dhammarakkhita Thera for his remarks. Before turning to the primary subject of this chapter, I will offer some introductory observations about why this *pirivena* has been selected to provide the context for our consideration and why it is admired by Buddhist men and women in Sri Lanka. Persons riding busses in Sri Lanka will have noticed many people rising up from their seats upon seeing a *bodhi* tree, or a temple, or a Buddha statue by the road. They are not making a prayer. They do so to indicate or mark their respect for a great teacher, a human being. I am a Buddhist by birth. I do not follow the tough path of the monks, but whenever I pass by this road to which the *pirivena* is adjacent, I feel like rising up. The main reason which propels me to rise up when I see this *pirivena* is because of one significant person, to whom our venerable reverend referred, namely the late Venerable Ratmalanē Dhammārama Nāyaka Thera. He is important for us Sri Lankans and to students of humanities because of his significant contributions to Sanskrit and Oriental Studies. Sri Lanka, a reputed center for Sanskrit learning, was home to two people in particular who have contributed significantly in securing scholarly renown for this country. One is King Kumāradāsa, who lived centuries ago. He was said to have been a colleague of Kālidāsa as both belonged to the same group of eminent Sanskrit poets. The other one was Venerable Dhammārama Nāyaka Thera.

Kālidāsa is to us like Shakespeare is to Westerners. He wrote many poems, epics and dramas. Among his works, one book, *Raghuvaṃsa*, is extolled as his best. It is related to the story of the *Rāmāyaṇa*. A similar work, *Jānakīharaṇa*, was written in Sri Lanka by Kumāradāsa. He renamed Kālidāsa's story and infused it with a lot of aesthetic qualities. The title of the work, *Jānakīharaṇa,* contains Jānakī, another name for Sītā, the wife of Rama, and Haraṇa meaning 'abduction.' *Jānakīharaṇa* is significant because it is a large epic written by a Sri Lankan poet. At the time, literary critics, when referring to these two texts, compared them to each other even though they were, for a number of reasons, so incompatible. Unfortunately, Kumāradāsa's text has been completely lost.

The most noteworthy literary tradition in Sri Lanka is the writing of commentaries, etymological studies, and textual analyses. It fell upon the shoulders of the Venerable Dhammārama Nāyaka Thera to reconstruct the lost text of Kumāradāsa. He took hold of the commentary, with the Sanskrit word and the Sinhala word equivalents, and set about his reconstruction with no trace of meter, no hint as to the format of the significant cantos. He was able to reconstruct the entire text of approximately fifteen cantos. Some time after his reconstruction, the original text was found in a public library in Chennai (Madras). It is said that there was not even a syllabic discrepancy between Venerable Dhammārama's reconstruction and the original. Venerable Dharmārama's version is the one that has been handed down to us now. This was a magnificent accomplishment in Oriental learning. It alone was sufficient to raise this *pirivena* to a highly reputable academic, educational, cultural center. This *pirivena* also provides an excellent context for considering the theme of this chapter.

III

BUDDHIST TEMPLE WORSHIP

We turn now to consider Buddhist temple worship. The Theravāda tradition of Sri Lanka goes back twenty-three centuries. This tradition, which was transmitted by Arahant Mahinda, with the famous set theory question given to king Devānampiyatissa, was continued by the theras of the Mahāvihāra, the "Great Monastic Dwelling" in Anurādhapura. The Mahāvihāra *bhikkhus* have been very nicely described by Venerable Buddhaghosa, who was the leading commentator on Pali works. He refers to them as: *Sallekhiye no sulabhūpamehi, mahāvihārassa dhajūpamehi*. *Sallekhiya* is a quality which I do not think we could ever develop in this life because it is so difficult—it amounts to the erasing of all mental defilements. One cannot find any similes or analogies or comparisons to adequately describe these monks. *Mahāvihārassa dhajūpamehi*, means that they are like the banners of the Mahāvihāra. This tradition has been preserved through the ages by these venerable monks who continue to represent it. How this happens is a mystery. Many have tried to find out how this has taken place, but it remains a mystery for most people. All this is as "I have heard," *evaṃ me sutaṃ*.

Sri Lankan Buddhists can be classified into two categories: those who are Buddhists by conviction, and those who are Buddhists by convention. The conventional Buddhists I refer to as *sammutibauddha*. Those who are Buddhist by principle I refer to as *paṭipattibauddha*. I myself, along with most Sri Lankans, am a Buddhist by convention.

Those who live as conventional Buddhists have certain linkages, certain factors which bind them together as a community. The most important single factor is that they speak the Sinhala language as their mother tongue. These Buddhists, when they behave as Buddhists—not merely as Sinhala people, because as Sinhala people we have all kinds of classifications; we have caste and so many other patterns for social differentiations—only two categories emerge, as, for example in a sermon hall: the clergy and the laity. There is no other distinction or difference. But these venerable monks will be on a higher seat. Why is this practiced? It is because they are a significant, wonderful symbol. They symbolize the *ariyasaṅgha*.

That brings us to another dichotomy which is found recorded in the Buddhist tradition. That is, people are divided into two types: one is called *ariya*, and the other is called its negative, *anariya*. *Ariya* means "noble," a nobility that does not come from birth, nor from social status, nor from education. That nobility comes from the erasure of all mental defilements which are: *lobha*, "craving," *dosa*, "ill-will," and *moha*, "delusion." All of us are subject to these mental defilements. One may analyze them, ramify them, sub-classify them, it makes no difference. They are still there. That is why we have wars. War is the classic example of the manifestation of these defilements. *Ariya* means a person who has wiped out all those mental blackouts.

There are four related stages, which lead to the erasure of, or separation from the mental defilements. Those stages are called *magga-phala* with the final climax, Nibbāna. *Magga* is the "path" and *phala* is the "result." There are four such *maggas*: *sotāpanna*, which is translated as "stream entry." I think it can also be re-etymologized as "one who enters the doctrine having heard it." "Heard it" does not refer merely to audition. Hearing here means understanding, fully entering the path, having understood it. The second is *sakadāgāmi*, one who will return once as far as rebirth is concerned. The next is *anāgāmi*, one who never returns. And then there are Arahants, the saints. This state is achievable in this very life. What is important is to recognize that one has these mental defilements and that one has to overcome them.

We have, then, two dichotomous pairs: the *ariya* and *anariya* dichotomy, and the laity and clergy dichotomy.

I would like to provide an outline for what we, as laity, do at the temple. I would not want to call these activities "rituals" because these activities are not rituals, as I understand them. One might refer to these as "practices." I will refer to these as "Buddhist temple worship." One might consider what the temple complex is. First is the *āvāsa*, which means "a small residence."

I deliberately use the Pali words to refer to these since it is the language we use at the temple when observing these practices, and not Sinhala. An *āvāsa* can be of different dimensions, where one has necessarily a Buddhist monk, but may not have all the other components comprising a Buddhist temple.

A *pansala* is literally translated "temple," a Buddhist temple. There are three major types: *rajamahāvihāra, purāṇavihāra,* and ordinary *vihāra*. The *rajamahāvihāras* are the loftiest ones designated by royal titles and go back in time for several centuries. *Purāṇavihāras* are also very ancient (*purāṇa*) temples, but the royal connection is not quite clear. Ordinary temples are those other than these two types.

There are also three major sects of monks in Sri Lanka: Siamese sect (*Siyam nikāya*), Amarapura sect (*Amarapura nikāya*) and the Rāmañña sect (*Rāmañña nikāya*). The *rajamahāvihāras* and most of the *purāṇavihāras* belong to the Siamese sect. They form the major monastic sect in this country. *Pirivenas*, which term we have already used, are basically educational institutes, although they are located within the temple premises.

One might wonder how these dwelling places, temples, and educational institutes gain their support. These are generally maintained by the laity. In the really rural setting, villagers continually support the temple. In the temple there may be a board of donors called *dāyakasabhā*. They look after the needs of the monks. Asking why they look to the needs of the monks is an important question, especially when one considers it from a so-called objective, material viewpoint. Why should we support them? The most important thing about the monks, in the ideal sense, is that they do not expect anything for the services they perform. They provide all their services to us, whatever we require, irrespective of the time of day. If one taps at the monastery door, a monk will come out and ask what the problem is. If he can help, he will. I think the close bond with the laity is there and that is very important. The monk is the best teacher of the laity. Some people call him the best friend as well. One could also call him the best well-wisher.

Although temples are primarily places for religious practices or observances, they also function as centers for education. This is a part of Sri Lankan culture. The monks perform many essential services besides this too. When a child is born, he or she has to be named. This naming is a complex process. One must consult an astrologer. He will specify which letters and syllabic units should make up the name. To get this information, a poor farmer or laborer must go to the temple. Most monks are not only knowledgeable in Sanskrit, Pali, Prakrit, and Sinhala, but are also versed in astrology and Ayurvedic medicine. They practice these as social services. A lay person requesting the service of a monk will bring with him a handful or sheaf of betel. It has no monetary value, but it has a cultural value. This is presented to the monk when one requests something of him. The monk, if asked what name is appropriate for a newborn, will proceed to check the horoscope and determine the auspicious letters and syllables for the name. As a result, in our culture if one addresses a senior by their first name it is considered an insult. You might, over a period of time, address your professor in the United States by his or her first name. If you do that here you will be grossly misunderstood.

In Sri Lanka children are not sent to school right away. They are first introduced to the written language by a monk, who will do it so willingly and with a great deal of well-wishing. So it is with the monk that a child begins his or her education.

Where is a poor person to seek help if he or she is a drunkard, a domestic abuser in the family or have problems with one's family? He or she cannot go to a psychiatrist or other professional practitioner. A poor person in difficulty goes to a Buddhist temple. A monk will always be willing to listen to someone talking about difficulties in life. With soothing words, he will pacify the troubled person such that he or she can go home comforted. I know of many people who were drunkards who later gave up their drinking, primarily because of the instruction of Buddhist temple monks. Of course, to be able to do this, a monk has to be educated, virtuous, and exemplary.

Most importantly, a temple is a place where the doors are never closed. The *dhammasāla*, the sermon hall, is open to anybody. If someone has no place to go he or she will go to the temple seeking help and solace. If someone's wife drives him from home, he will go to the temple. Indeed I have witnessed things like this happening in villages. This reflects the significance of the bond between laymen and monks in the village setting. Now, let us discuss the *pansala* and its components. This is at least the way I look at the temple. Others may view it differently. I think the *pansala* represents three significant things for Sri Lankans—the Buddha, the Dhamma and the Saṅgha.

The Buddha is represented by *ti-dhātu*. *Ti* means "three" and *dhātu* means the "supportive element," or the "essence." There is no easy translation for this word in English.[49] The Buddha is also represented by *sārīrika dhātu*, which are bodily relics that are enshrined in a *cetiya*. There is also the *pāribhogika dhātu*, things which the Buddha is said to have used in his lifetime, the best example of which is the *bodhi* tree. There is the *uddesika dhātu*, a symbol, such as the *pratimā* (Sinhala: *piḷima*) the image of the Buddha. All of these represent one jewel of the triple gem: the Buddha.

The next gem is Dhamma. I was trying to find how Dhamma is represented in a *pirivena* and *pansala*. Is it to be found in books? Is it in the monks? The monks do preach Dhamma, but is the Dhamma in them or is it only in books? It is only in two places that I could find the Dhamma. One is the *pot-guḷa*, a library for religious texts in the traditional ideal temple.

I have tried to find out exactly how the Dhamma is represented in Buddhist temples. Perhaps Dhamma is represented in the quiet emptiness. Second, Dhamma is present in the chanting that is heard and also in the lives of the monks, which is inferred. Dhamma is not limited in this way to the monks. Laymen also can recite Dhamma and, of course, seek to live it. Laymen learn to recite Pali passages and do so when paying reverence to the Buddha and also in personal daily religious practices. A passage

---

[49] See Kevin Trainor, *The Relics of the Buddha: a study of the cult of relic veneration in the Theravāda Buddhist Tradition of Sri Lanka*, New York: Columbia University, 1990.

recited when we offer incense and lite camphor to the Buddha is
as follows:

> I venerate the Buddha who has the fragrant
> body and face [or mouth]. I offer to him
> manifold fragrances [or incense]. Then with
> the lamp and the brilliance of lit camphor, I
> venerate the Buddha who is the light of the
> three worlds and who is the one who dispels
> darkness.

Laymen often recite a *sutta*, a "discourse." There are
actually three main discourses which we memorize. One is the
Karaṇīyametta Sutta,[50] the discourse on "loving-kindness."
It is all about loving-kindness—how we expand our thoughts
of kindness, first to oneself and then to the whole world, to
everybody. When this is done, one may bless oneself, that is, one
thinks about the truthfulness of what one has just recited with
conviction, and similarly one blesses others with that truthfulness:
"By these truthful words, let there be forever happiness for me.
Let there be auspiciousness for me. Let all diseases be dispelled."
This is a kind of meditation which calms one's mind.

Merit transfer, *puññānumodana*, is a very important rite
for lay Buddhists. Whatever religious practice one does, one is
expected to transfer the resultant merit to everybody, including
gods, spirits, all living beings. A "god" for a Sri Lankan Buddhist
is not to be considered equivalent to the Christian or any other
notion of God. These gods are beings which inhabit another
realm. The one who performs good deeds transfers the merit to
the gods with the wish, "Let all gods feel happy or rejoice." This

---

[50] See, for example, the *Metta Sutta* in *Sutta-nipāta*, edited by Dines Andersen
and Helmer Smith, Oxford: Published for the Pali Text Society by Geoffrey
Cumberlege, 1948, vv. 143 ff., with an English translation in *Woven Cadences
of Early Buddhists*, translated by E. M. Hare, London: The Sacred Books of the
Buddhists, by Geoffrey Cumberlege, 1947, vv. 143 ff. See, further, *The Khuddaka-
Pāṭha together with its commentary Paramatthajotikā I*, edited by Helmer Smith,
London: Published for the Pali Text Society by Luzac & Company, Ltd., 1959,
pp, 8-9, with an English translation in *The Minor Readings*, translated by Bhikkhu
Ñāṇamoli, London: Published for the Pali Text Society by Luzac & Company,
Ltd., 1960, pp. 10-11, and note the commentary's discussion in *Paramatthajotikā
I*, pp. 231 ff., with its English translation in *Minor Readings*, pp. 265 ff.

rejoicing, *anumodanā*, can be transferred freely to someone else. Or, others may indirectly participate in the good deeds of another. If one is incapable of performing meritorious actions because one is financially bankrupt or lacks education, one can still appreciate by receiving happiness or joy in the meritorious acts of another. That is a kind of *anumodanā* actually, a kind of mental balance which is considered very important to be developed by Buddhists. One thinking of one's dead relatives when doing something merit-worthy would transfer merit by articulating the statement '*idaṃ me ñātinaṃ hotu-sukhitā hontu ñātayo*' "Let this pass over to my dead relatives. May the dead relatives be happy."

One often sees Buddhists traveling to various sites of religious significance in Sri Lanka. They often go to *Kataragama* where there is a shrine for god Kataragama/Skanda. One may wonder whether they are being Buddhists when they engage in performing ceremonies and accompanying rituals to a god.

It must be noted here that a Buddhist at the shrine of Kataragama is not the same person qualitatively as he is within the precincts of a Buddhist *vihāra*. Whatever one does as a Buddhist at the *vihāra* is kept distinct by the *patthanā* "wish," which ties one to another world. It binds one and all one's actions, forming a connection up to *nibbāna*. When one goes to a Hindu shrine such as Kataragama it is a practical purpose that is achieved. What one does there has no after-life connection. So, whatever has an after-life connection in the Buddhist way of thinking makes one a Buddhist. One is defined as a Buddhist by the *puññakamma* not by any other *kamma*. The *patthanā* one makes after performing a *puññakamma* is as follows: "Let me not get hereafter any association, any contact with the (spiritually) ignorant. May I obtain association with good people until I reach final emancipation." So, *puññakamma* always has emancipation as its target, whereas going to a shrine of a god/deity has a practical, this-worldly purpose. These two are quite distinct from my perspective.

The Nibbāna-attainment, *nibbānapatti,* is also connected to the "*ti-bodhi*" concept. *Ti* means "three," *bodhi* means "realization." According to the Theravāda tradition, Nibbāna can be realized through one of these paths: a *sammāsambodhi*, a fully enlightened one, a representative of which is Gautama Buddha; a *paccekabodhi*, which is translated as "private Buddha" or individual Buddha (of which there have been many); or through *arahattabodhi*, reaching emancipation, being a saint. If one listens to the Dhamma from a *sammāsambodha*, one will develop one's mind to the point where one reaches emancipation. In Sri Lanka, however, a normal aspiration of the Buddhists is to reach Nibbāna through *arahattabodhi*, through listening to someone preach. We await a Buddha coming in the future, *Metteya* or *Maitrī*.

Another activity performed in the *pansala* is meditation, *bhāvanā*. Some people do and some people do not practice meditation. There are different kinds of meditation. In Buddhism the essence of meditation, as I perceive it, is to be fully conscious/aware of what one does. When walking, one is to be conscious that one is walking. When breathing, one is to be conscious that one is breathing. Speaking and breathing are two activities that are taken for granted and considered natural (and hence done without much conscious attention) for human beings. We only start to pay attention to speaking when we fail to understand something said, or when we learn a foreign language. We seldom pay attention to our own mother tongue. We never focus on our normal activity of breathing unless we have some problem with it.

In Buddhism, consciousness of both speaking and breathing is to be cultivated. The proper use of language that is to be cultivated is specified under the significant notion of *sammāvāca* 'right speech.' In the practice of meditation, breathing has been cultivated to its ultimate limits.

When we do meditation as a religious practice at an initial level it does not involve such extensive concentration. Normally, we concentrate on wishing well for everyone, as follows: "Those who are suffering, let them be free from suffering. Those who are in fear, let them be free from fear. Those who are in grief, let them be free from grief. Let all beings be free from suffering, fear and grief." Then we say three times *"sabbe sattā sukhitā hontu"*— "Let all beings be happy." Following this, one develops self-love. This is not love for the self but kindness or love for oneself with detachment. Then one tries to develop this externally for others. This is one version of what is called *mettābhāvanā*. One continues, "Let me be free from envy, or ill-will." "Let me be free from harm." "Let me conduct myself happily." One extends these feelings to one's teachers and parents. "Let them be free from ill-will. Let them be free from harm. Let them conduct themselves happily. Let them be free from grief."

When all this is completed within the precincts of the *vihāra*, we visit the Saṅgha, which is the last item in routine temple worship. *Abhivādanā*, 'veneration,' is done to the members of the Saṅgha in order of seniority, which is determined by the number of rain (*vassa*) retreats which a monk has observed. Such a monk is considered senior in a relative sense to the others. Then one goes to the other *theras* and then the junior monks. One venerates or salutes them. Then the monks articulate a kind of benediction, a literal version of which is as follows: "For the person who is in the habit or nature of respecting people, for the person who always looks after the elderly, four supportive factors increase: 'longevity,' 'body complexion,' 'happiness,' and 'energy.'" This is concluded by making the following wish: "As a result of this merit may you achieve longevity, the fortune of good health, the fortune of heavenly bliss, and finally the fortune of Nibbāna, emancipation." And when the layman/lay devotee takes leave, the monk will say *sukhī hotu* "May you be happy." These are some of the overt features of Sri Lankan Buddhist temple religious practice.

CHAPTER XVII

LAY BUDDHIST RITUALS

C. Witanachchi

Professor C. Witanachchi, Professor of Pali and Buddhist Studies emeritus of Peradeniya University, introduces Lay Buddhist rituals or practices with a helpful threefold classification: those primarily concerned with favorable results in this world (lokiya), those oriented to favorable results after death, and concluding briefly with practices leading to Nibbāna, freedom.

In this presentation of Buddhist rituals, I will focus on Sri Lanka, rather than on other countries in which the Theravāda tradition flourishes. By "ritual," I mean rituals broadly in the sense of religious practices. I usually use the term "ritual" to describe ceremonies performed with the intention of securing the blessings or aid of some higher external power. Here, however, I will take the broader use of the term, as is done by some scholars, with reference to all religious practices, including practices such as meditation, which I do not like to call a ritual.

Theravāda Buddhists claim to possess the pristine teachings of the Buddha in their Pali scriptures. They always try to describe themselves as people practicing this pristine form of Buddhism. However, though the basic doctrines accepted by Theravāda Buddhists are derived from the scriptures, many of their practices date back to the commentarial tradition. The Theravāda commentaries were, for the most part, translated into Pali from Sinhala in Sri Lanka in and around the 5th century. It is quite possible that some of the ritual practices were developed in this country based on interpretations of practices originating in India. Various other sources might have contributed to the development of these practices. In brief, much was added to the Theravāda Buddhist tradition during the commentarial period and afterwards. So when we carefully examine the Pali scriptures and consider the practices prevalent today we find that there is quite a wide gap. But still, for all, these practices have in some form a basis in the Pali scriptures.

In spite of a long period of development, Theravāda Buddhist rituals are quite simple when compared to some of the Mahāyāna and Tantrayāna rituals. When we examine the scriptures we find a very profound philosophy, but the religious practice prescribed in them is quite simple, almost devoid of any elaborate rituals or ceremonies. A simple verse taken from the *Dhammapada* (stanza 183) would perhaps indicate how simple this practice could be in early Buddhism:

> Refraining from all that is detrimental,
> The attainment of what is wholesome,
> The purification of one's mind:
> This is the instruction of Awakened Ones[51]

One realizes that no elaborate form of ritual or ceremony is necessary to practice this type of religion.

In fact, there are some people today who do not like calling Buddhism a religion. They just like to call it "Dhamma." Some people say that the evolution of what is called Buddhism has come at the neglect of Dhamma, the pristine teachings of the Buddha. But this type of simple practice cannot be maintained for a long period without any protective form of organization, that is, without guardians or custodians of this religion, of this philosophy. And once such an organization is in place, there are various institutions, ceremonies, and practices which accompany it.

These custodians want some sort of identity in society. They prefer not to imitate everything that other people do. They want to show that they are different from others. Naturally, in

---

[51] Stanza 183, of *The Dhammapada* translated by Carter and Mahinda.

a country like India where there has been a very old form of religion, the Vedic religion, which dates back several millennia, even antedating the time of the Buddha, numerous ritual practices developed. In such a society, no religion could survive without acceding to at least some of the ritual practices already in place. Buddhists had to devise means to attract more and more followers into their religion, especially because the Buddhist Saṅgha could not have survived without the support of lay people. A lay society needed various forms of rituals because the laity were not ready to be followers of just a simple form of a difficult philosophy. They wanted something to go along with this philosophical teaching so that these rituals could act as a social expression of their religious teachings.

Over the centuries various rituals and ceremonies evolved. When we come to Sri Lanka we can find considerable differences between what is recorded in the Pali scriptures and what is going on around us today. This is as Professor Richard Gombrich has noted;[52] the precept might be one thing and the practice quite different.

For convenience, I divide lay Buddhist practices into three categories. In our Theravāda Buddhism in Sri Lanka, it is the tradition to describe religious practices as leading to three forms of happiness. In our classical Sinhala poetry this is sometimes called *tivagasäpa*. *Ti* means three; *vaga* means type; *säpa* means happiness: three types of happiness. I have not found a Pali equivalent for this. The three types of happiness are: (1) *lokiya*: happiness here in this world (happiness in this life), (2) samsaric: happiness after death (in one's next life and lives to come), and (3) nibbanic happiness. These are the three forms of happiness at which all forms of Buddhist practices aim. Very often, in their sermons, Buddhist monks instruct people to act in such a way as to derive these forms of happiness. These three types are not always mutually exclusive. There may be a lot of overlap between them. Nevertheless, for convenience, we can consider them in light of these three categories.

---

[52] Richard Gombrich, *Precept and Practice*, London: Oxford University Press, 1971.

I

LOKIYA: HAPPINESS IN THIS LIFE

Most Buddhists think that when they begin some important activity in their life in the world today (*lokiya*)—maybe a wedding, or maybe they have constructed a new house, or maybe they are starting some kind of industry or business, or maybe a child is going to sit an exam, or something like that—blessings with the religion is a necessity. Or even when they go out in the morning to their jobs, or school children before they go to school, they think that they must do something to bring some form of blessing. This is called *mangala*, "blessing." In many houses there are small shrines with a small Buddha statue or a picture of the Buddha, where they sometimes light an oil lamp and burn some incense sticks and offer some flowers. In the evening they may offer flowers and also some cool drinks or tea. Before the mid-day meal they will offer some food at this shrine. But before going out in the morning, many people would like to at least just bow down with their palms clasped together, called an *añjali*. Some people will even recite the three refuges, or the three gems, and also the precepts, and in reciting recommit themselves to observing the precepts. They might not have the time to recite all the stanzas that they normally would want to recite. School children would bow down at these shrines and also bow at the feet of their parents before going out.

Similarly, when Buddhists go along the road, for instance, if they pass the Temple of the Tooth in Kandy, they would stop there and salute the tooth relic in the temple. On my way here today I saw two women standing by the Queen's Hotel doing this, at some distance from the Temple and the tooth relic. Upon passing the Gätembe temple by the University of Peradeniya, on their way in the direction of Colombo, many people stop and put a coin in the till. Of course that is not for the Buddha but for the guardian deity. This rather simple ritual act can be elaborated for more important occasions.

In Sri Lanka, one of the most popular rituals is to feed the Saṅgha just before mid-day. Important activities in life may start with a ceremony like this. The laity invite a group of monks to their house. And, ceremonially, sometime with beating drums, the monks arrive with a casket of relics to represent the Buddha. Before entering the house the laity wash the feet of the monks and lay a cloth for the monks to walk on. This type of ritual dates from the time of the Buddha. Actually, on one occasion, the Buddha is recorded as prohibiting the monks from walking on cloth laid down for them. But, subsequently, there was a demand from the people in the sense that by doing these acts the laity sought blessings. This was brought to the attention of the Buddha who allowed that this could be done, but done only after washing the feet of the monks.

Then alms are offered to the monks. Along with food some useful articles are also given: a towel, a robe, maybe a fan, or a set of the "eight requisites," which include the three robes, belt, a bowl, a razor, needle and thread, and a water strainer. These eight are the minimum possessions that a monk should have. Unless a monk possesses these eight requisites, he is not given the higher ordination. The monks, after partaking of the meal, bless the laity who provided them with their material needs and one monk delivers a short sermon to enhance the joy they receive from their good act. They also invoke the blessings of the Triple-gem, the Buddha, Dhamma and the Saṅgha and also the blessings of gods on the laity. At the end of this ceremony, merit is transferred to the gods as guardians because the gods also need merit. Buddhists think that most gods do not get much opportunity to acquire merit. The dead also, if they need merit from the living, expect their living relatives to transfer merit to them. This is done at the end of any important religious ceremony, especially after an alms giving ceremony.

Another important ceremony is the recital of *paritta*, which means "protection," as Professor Lily de Silva has discussed in her talk, "On *Pirit*," which is the Sinhala form derived from the Pali word *paritta*. During the time of the Buddha, as today, people believed that there were various supernatural forces in the world, both personal and impersonal. These could be either evil or beneficial. *Parittas* are used to reap the benefit of the benevolent forces, and to protect against the malicious ones. The benevolent gods are believed by the Buddhists to be followers of the Buddha himself. When the *parittas* are recited it is believed that these gods like to come and listen. When they do, the evil forces recede to the background. The gods can thereby protect the people. Also, because they are pleased, having listened to the *parittas*, the gods could remain in the vicinity even after the recitation is over.

Certain discourses of the Buddha, selected from the Pali scriptures, are put together and now form a book (the *Piruvānāpota* in Sinhala), composed before the 12th century. Discourses from this collection are recited by the monks. Sometimes monks are invited to a house to recite these discourses for a whole night. This is done especially on the occasion of a house-warming of a newly built house, or perhaps when someone is ill, or for warding off dangers and calamities of life. At the beginning of the *paritta* ceremony, monks are invited ceremonially by reciting three verses which give the purpose: to ward off all calamities, to bring forth all prosperity, for the destruction of all fear, all disease and all sorrow. For these purposes, the request made to the monks follows, "Please recite the auspicious *paritta*." This is the formal invitation. Throughout the night, the monks recite from the book of *paritta*.

There is also the practice of beating drums, referred to in Sinhala as *magulbera* (P. *mangalabheri*), "auspicious drum." Drumming is not done at just any time. Drums are used on very important occasions. At the beginning of a very auspicious occasion, drumming is performed. *Magulbera* is never used at a funeral. On that occasion a different form of drumming is done in which the rhythm is different. The drumming at a *paritta* ceremony or other auspicious occasions is done as homage to the Buddhas and gods. Actually, it has to be done thrice, as a rhythmic beat repeated for the Buddha and the gods. An important dimension of Buddhist rituals is not only paying homage to the Buddha, Dhamma, and Saṅgha, but gods are also invited because we believe that there are certain forces in the world which are beneficent as well as evil forces. So at the beginning of a *paritta* ceremony, gods are invited to come and listen. They are also thought to be followers of the Buddha and they also like to listen to the *paritta*. When powerful gods come, the evil spirits cannot continue to be present.

We recall how a pot of water is used in the *paritta* ceremony,: how a three-stranded thread, which is connected to that pot of water, is held by the monks, connected to the *paritta* book, and to the casket of relics representing the Buddha, is passed around to all present, binding the group together. That binding represents the Buddha, Dhamma, and Saṅgha, the three gems, or the three refuges. At the end of the ceremony, in the morning after an all night *paritta* ceremony, water from this pot is distributed among the people as holy water and people believe that by drinking it or by putting it on the forehead and head it can ward off evil. They also take pieces of the thread used in the ceremony and tie it on their right wrist.

Today there is a popular ritual called *bodhipūja*, offerings made to the bodhi tree. This practice dates from ancient times but during recent times it has become popularized. Perhaps the re-emphasizing of this practice has been influenced to some degree by church music and Christian ritual. This has become very popular because they are not only using Pali verses but a lot of Sinhala verses in this type of *bodhipūja*. People do this not so much for merit but for blessings here in this world. A certain guardian deity is associated with the bodhi tree. The bodhi tree in Anurādhapura is supposed to be guarded by this deity. Here the Hindu deity guarding the bodhi tree is called Viṣṇu, but in Anurādhapura he is called "the Black God," (*Kaludēvatā Bandāra*). I have a feeling that he is none other than the blue lotus colored god Uppalavaṇṇa to whom, as recorded in the *Mahāvaṃsa*, Sakka (Skt. Śakra), the king of gods, handed over the guardianship of Sri Lanka upon the arrival of the first group of Sinhala settlers. The Buddha, it is said, asked Sakka to guard this country. So Sakka came here and tied the *paritta* threads around the wrists of all the immigrants and handed over all of them to the Blue Lotus Colored god, whom I think is *Kaludēvatā Bandāra*, the Black God, who later became the guardian of the bodhi tree in Anurādhapura.

At a temple people will go around the bodhi tree circling with their right hand towards the center. This practice of circumambulating, keeping the right hand towards the center in the direction of the object of worship, is also a very old custom in India. It is a way of showing honor. Some people say that this is a pattern of behavior based on the clockwise movement of the sun. To go in the opposite direction is considered inauspicious.

Let me now give an example of veneration expressed by Buddhists of Sri Lanka—a practice that has its primary focus on results in this very life. This is not primarily veneration of the Buddha, the Dhamma, and Saṅgha, but of Arahants. When we laid the foundations for a Buddhist temple at the University of Peradeniya, in order to raise money we sold images of the Arahant Sīvalī. He was a disciple of the Buddha and it is said that wherever he went he was never wanting in receiving alms. That is why he is pictured as seated with his hand in the alms bowl. He is having his meal. It is said, in legendary history, that whenever the Buddha went to difficult regions on his tours, he would take Arahant Sīvalī with him because one would never miss a meal if one goes with Sīvalī.

Some time since then, and I do not know whether this began in Sri Lanka or Burma or elsewhere, a *mantra*, a mystical formula or secret verse, was devised for Sīvalī. A *paritta* also related to Sīvalī also was developed, although it was not part of the classical book of *parittas*, the *Book of Protection*. Many Pali verses taken from here and there and the legendary history of this figure taken from the commentaries and elsewhere were put together to form this *paritta*. By the figure of Sīvalī, one reads,

> Homage to the great Arahant named Sīvalī Who
> is a recipient of all forms of benefits. By his
> power may all prosperity be yours.

Today, many people buy this figure and take it home to be kept hung on a wall. It is a very popular practice.

This worship of Arahants in Sri Lanka may have started in relatively recent times, perhaps during the British colonial period when we had very close relations with Burma. Burma, at that time was also a colony of the British Empire. Lots of things were transmitted back and forth between Sri Lanka and Burma at that time. It is possible that the custom of Arahant worship was brought here from Burma for we do not have evidence for such a practice from ancient Sri Lanka. In Sri Lankan Buddhist homes there are pictures of the Arahant Sīvalī with the legend printed in Sinhala, English, and Burmese—not in Thai. We know at least that the custom was present in Burma at one time. The recitation of the Pali verse that I translated is used as a *mantra*.

Mantras are not limited to Pali verses, although the sense of protection afforded by Pali verses is very widespread in Sri Lanka. Often a *mantra* is inscribed with a diagram on a copper strip which is then empowered with a Pali *paritta*, placed in a small case and tied around one's neck or wrist. Some are empowered with the recitation of a *paritta* 108 times, an auspicious number.

Parittas of and for protection are not limited to lay practices. Even monks meditating in forests are given *parittas* for their protection. There are some *parittas* which were composed in Burma for this very purpose. In some of the *suttas*, the Buddha himself is supposed to have given such *parittas* to monks meditating in the forest. Being alone in a deep forest, surrounded by wild animals, forms of fear could come into one's mind. The *Mettasutta*, the *sutta* on loving-kindness (*mettā*), is a case in point.[53] The early *Mettasutta* does not mention this, but the commentary on this *sutta* provides an introduction which says that this *sutta* was recited by the Buddha for the benefit of a group of monks meditating in a forest. They used to sit at the foot of trees. There were tree spirits in the trees. When the monks sat at the foot of the trees, these spirits found it difficult to stay at the top of the trees. They had from time to time to get down from the trees. These spirits were walking about with their children and in order to frighten the monks away, they assumed horrible forms. The monks could not meditate in this situation. At the end of the rainy season, the monks went to the Buddha and they told him of their experiences. The Buddha told them to practice *mettā* and gave them the *sutta*. This is according to the introduction of the commentary, which is repeated today. There are many *suttas* like this which are used as *parittas* today, which, according to tradition, were initially given not primarily to lay people but to meditating monks. The monks also came from the same

---

[53] See references noted above, note 46.

background as the lay people. The monks had the same fears and beliefs as the lay people had. Merely by becoming Buddhist monks they did not all at once become Arahants. They had to get on. There are, of course, other ways of getting around fears. The Buddha himself, before he attained Buddhahood, went to places where unusual phenomena occurred and observed the situation to try to understand it. This is how he got rid of the fears that came to his mind. But not everyone could do that then, or can do it today. They need religious activities like the ones we have briefly discussed.

II

SAMSARIC: HAPPINESS AFTER DEATH

Happiness in the next life, our samsaric category, is certainly an important dimension in Buddhist rituals. The most important factor is the merit one gains from doing good deeds. With whatever good deeds one does with a heart or mind devoid of greed, hatred, and delusion, one gains good merit. And that will be helpful in one's future life—maybe in this life, but especially in the next life for one to be reborn in a good or happy place so that one can continue one's good works.

Especially with regard to this aspect of doing good works with a clear mind and heart we have the activities related to *poya* day observances. *Poya* is an observance performed by the laity with the intention of gaining merit. It is traditionally undertaken on the full moon day, the new moon day and the two quarter moon days, as has been discussed by others. Currently, however, of these four only the full moon day is celebrated regularly. On *poya* days Buddhists are expected to observe the eight precepts instead of the usual five, which are observed in normal, routine life. One of the five precepts is changed. Whereas in normal life a person is expected to have a clean life devoid of sexual misconduct, on this special day, one takes the precept of abstaining from all forms of sexual activity. In addition to this there is a precept by which one promises to abstain from using flowers, scents, or anointing one's body and attending shows, theaters, dancing, etc. Then one abstains from taking solid food after the meal taken just before mid-day. And one also abstains from using very comfortable and high chairs and beds. On the full moon *poya* day, these additional precepts are observed.

People go to the temple on the *poya* day very early in the morning, especially on very important *poya* days, such as the Vesak full moon day in May[54] and Poson full moon day in June.[55] Some people relinquish the eight precepts and take over the five precepts again in the evening and return home. Often, in villages and in famous temples, like the Temple of the Tooth here in Kandy, elderly people stay on through the afternoon and stay the night, reading or listening to a person who can read a book, and meditating. Then in the morning they relinquish the eight precepts and take up the five again and return home. All of this is done not so much to gain merit in this life but as a sort of training for one's attainment of the realization of Nibbāna one day, or when observing the precepts they say, "For this day I follow the footsteps of the way of life of an Arahant," indicating the goal they wish to reach one day.

At the temple, also, the laity performs *pūjas* to the Buddha, Dhamma, and Saṅgha. The three shrines that symbolize the Buddha are especially venerated: (1) the relic mound (P. *thūpa*, Skt. *stūpa*) in which relics of the Buddha are enshrined; (2) articles used by the Buddha—today the only thing that is found in Sri Lanka is the bodhi tree at Anurādhapura, said to be descended from the bodhi tree at Bodhgaya in India—(3) the Buddha statue representing the physical likeness of the Buddha. People offer flowers, incense, oil lamps, and at the proper time, they offer food and drinks. Even drumming is considered a form of offering, and flags, sometimes, are used, especially in decorating the bodhi tree. Of course, "bodhi" is not the name of a tree. It means "Buddhahood," and because the Buddha attained Buddhahood at the foot of a certain tree, that kind of tree has come to be known as a bodhi tree.

Through these activities, people expect to gain merit because they think that when they do these acts, their hearts or

---

[54] Vesak commemorates the birth, enlightenment and *parinibbāna* of the Buddha.

[55] Poson commemorates the coming of *Buddhadhamma* to Sri Lanka.

minds are pure. Doing these things with a pure heart, as homage to the Buddha, Dhamma, and Saṅgha who are regarded as their spiritual guides, the laity gains merit. And this merit can be of good stead in the life to come, to be reborn in a happy place so that they can continue their respective religious practices that they have been doing here. This would suggest that people would want to be reborn in a place where there is the practice of *Buddhadhamma*.

Attending upon one's elders and the sick is also thought to bring one a great deal of merit. If a person knows the Dhamma and explains it to others he or she gains merit in this fashion. At the same time, one gains merit just by listening to Dhamma. By acquiring merit one can help to ensure rebirth in a happy place. On the other hand, if one performs evil acts—if one speaks evil words or entertains evil thoughts—one will commit *pāpa*, sin through which one could be reborn in an unhappy place in which one will have to suffer for the unwholesome acts one has committed.

There are a variety of rituals undertaken with the hope of accruing benefits in the next life. However, it is said that by performing these rituals one also develops certain good characteristics in one's present life. By being charitable, although one may gain some merit thereby furthering one's likelihood of being born in a heavenly world, at the same time this act works to help one overcome one's greed. When one honors the Buddha or the Saṅgha, one is honoring someone who really should be honored. By that one may acquire certain good qualities oneself. The good qualities which one acquires in one's life will not be erased at death, but will be carried across to one's next life. Buddhists believe that very talented children acquired these abilities from their past lives. And when they see an intelligent person they would say, "Now this is a person who has acquired his merit during his past life." A Buddha, for instance, is not made in just one lifetime. It is believed that the one whom we call a Buddha is the final outcome of a process extending over hundreds of births. Through these lifetimes a future Buddha acquires an immense amount of merit and builds up his personal qualities to the highest level. They realize that ultimately these rituals could help one in eventually achieving Nibbāna. If one has acquired much merit, one will have a better chance of leading a happy next-life, which is one in which a spiritually rich life may be more easily pursued.

People believe that the dead can be reborn among gods, among human beings, among animals, and in the hells. There is also a place called the *peta* world, the world of ghosts. Actually, in the early Pali scriptures it is not called *peta*-world but *pettivisaya*; *petti* is derived from *pitṛ*, meaning "father," coming from the Vedic notion of the *pitṛ*, the fathers, one's ancestors. Buddhists have made this into a sort of half-way house between good and bad places of rebirth.

Among the departed, there are some who need help from their erstwhile living human relatives. Because of this, this uncertainty of life, all people like to do some religious services on behalf of the dead. The most important act in this context is feeding the monks. Whatever merit that one gains thereby is dedicated to the dead. We believe that if the dead need this merit, they will be waiting for it. They will be watching from somewhere, they will even come to one's house, it is said, standing outside and waiting for their living relatives to give them something. Such beings can benefit from this type of setting because they can rejoice in the good work performed by people here and then gain merit themselves. According to this belief, such merit will bring the departed immediate relief—immediate relief not from that birth, as such, but from the suffering they undergo there. They would get food, clothing, etc., for that life. Sometimes they are even portrayed as transformed into almost gods by this merit. This religious activity, then, is also for the benefit of the dead too, not just for the people who are performing it here.

III

NIBBANIC HAPPINESS

The third objective is for the supreme bliss of Nibbāna. I have not gone into this very much because for that one has to discipline oneself morally (*sīla*), seek purification of one's heart through mediation (*samādhi*) and with a peaceful mind one has to look at the world and oneself to realize the actual nature of the world, to understand what the reality is. That is wisdom (*paññā*). When one realizes this wisdom, then one is free. It is really freedom through wisdom. Not many people today, of course, know or try to gain this freedom in this life. They always wish for this freedom in a future life. That is why they want to have merit, so that they can have a good life after death. Maybe they will enjoy that life also and then after some births they would like to be free. Of course that is the wish of most Buddhists.

CHAPTER XVIII

RITUAL AND MEDITATION—CONTRAST OR CONVERGENCE

C. Witanachchi

Taking the two strands of religious practices on the scene among Theravāda Buddhists of Sri Lanka, Professor Witanachchi draws a distinction between rituals that are designed for particular ends, usually involving the activities of some other personal power through the mediation of a priest or an officiant, and meditation, which is immediate in one's awareness and has little to do with mysterious procedures in securing results. There are practices, however, that have developed that can be characterized as rituals which contribute to mental composure that can lead to mental concentration.

In this chapter I would like to consider ritual and meditation in the Theravāda Buddhist tradition of Sri Lanka and whether there is contrast or convergence in these modes of religious practice. Buddhists seek liberation—liberation from *dukkha*. The path to liberation from *dukkha* is Dhamma, customarily formulated as the "Noble Eightfold Path." This path consists of three main segments: moral discipline (*sīla*), concentration (*samādhi*) and wisdom (*paññā*). Moral discipline concerns our behavior in word and deed. Concentration has to do with mental cultivation (*bhāvanā*, literally means "to make become"). Our minds normally are in an uncultivated state. We usually allow the mind to run rampant. Through education, we are in a certain way trying to cultivate the mind in a certain direction. In Buddhism, too, this cultivation of the mind takes a very important place.

As a preliminary step to this cultivation of the mind, one first disciplines one's words and deeds. Disciplining one's words and deeds means getting rid of one's evil or negative speech and action. These things are harmful to oneself and harmful to others. If one speaks falsehoods, this will not only hurt others but ultimately oneself as well. The same is true of negative actions or deeds. From the foundation of being disciplined in speech and action, one goes on to disciplining the mind. From this point, one goes on to cultivate wisdom (*paññā*)—one may begin to turn the mind to understand the reality of the world.

What is going on in the world? What is happening to one's own self and other beings? This is what one tries to understand through this cultivation. This idea is expressed in a number of places in the Buddhist texts. For instance, in one place it is said a wise man, establishing himself in *sīla*, cultivates the mind and wisdom. These are from one of the two stanzas on which the whole of the book called *Visuddhimagga*—"Path to Purity"—is written. The book was written in the fifth century by the famous Theravāda commentator, Buddhaghosa.[56] This path to liberation through purification has to be cultivated throughout life by a person who intends to win his or her final liberation. At each moment of life one cannot let it go saying "I will do it today" and then stop, promising to take it up again next week, or on a Sunday, or on a *poya* day, or a Sabbath day—one cannot do that. It has to be done every moment of life. In every action, wherever one walks on the road, whether eating or reading, at every moment one has to cultivate this path. One has to be aware of it. This awareness (*sati*) is the most important part of Buddhist religious life.

But what is ritual? One does not perform rituals every day. One performs a ritual only when required, on particular days of the week or the month. If one is ill, for instance, one performs some ritual. If one wants some favor from somebody, if one

---

[56] For bibliographical reference to the Pali text and an English translation of this important work, see above, note 8.

wants to achieve some mundane purpose, one performs particular rituals. For each purpose there is a separate ritual. There are also specific rituals used to address a particular god, or to tap some unknown power for one's personal benefit. These things are not done every day in life—only when they are needed. These rituals (I am using the term narrowly to refer primarily to what most people consider religious rituals) involve some deity or supernatural power: a person, a deity, or some impersonal power. Normally, anthropologists say that in religion there is an appeal to some personal power, and with magic, the practitioner tries to tap some impersonal power found at large in the universe.

In both religion and magic, one tries through ritual to secure the favor of some supernatural power or to tap into some sort of energy or power extant in the universe for one's benefit or for the benefit of society. The performers of a religious ritual or magic do not always know the precise relationship between what they are doing, the ritual or act, and the intended result. There is no logical connection between them. One cannot understand it. There is something non-rational in that. There are certain formulae which are to be repeated, certain *pūjas* which are to be performed, and we are told that when they are performed certain results come. There is a mystery in that. In Christianity, one speaks of the "mysteries of Christ." In ritual, one always has this dimension. Someone is also needed to mediate between that power and oneself. One needs a priest.

With meditation, these things are not present. There is a much more direct connection between performance and result. What one is asked to do in meditation is to be aware of what is going on within oneself, in one's own mind. First, of course, one starts with one's bodily acts, with one's breathing. One could begin with one's walking, to know that one is walking. When one is speaking, one knows that one is speaking. When one is eating, one knows that one is eating. Anything that one does, one does that with awareness. At every point, awareness is very important. When one comes to the *satipaṭṭhāna*, the foundations of mindfulness, there are four subjects: first the body, then sensations, then the mind, and then what are called *dhammas*, that is, the practice of the path as one progresses step by step until one comes to the final liberation, Nibbāna. Every point of the path one does with awareness. Therefore, there is no mystery in that.

In meditation, the most important stage in development is always to be aware of what is happening in one's life. If, for instance, a thought of anger comes, one knows that there is anger. Should some form of sensual desire arise, one knows that it is there. To be always aware, therefore, is a very important factor in meditation.

In ritual, such awareness is not required. One does something in a certain manner because it is said that one should do it in that way. Through one's performance one expects some results. One need not know the sequence, how this happened, the logical or causal relations and all that. It is not necessary. And there is someone to perform the ritual, to mediate for one, limiting personal involvement even more. Contrastingly, in meditation, the person who teaches is merely an instructor. The Buddha himself was a teacher. He says "the *Tathāgatas* are teachers." A Christian priest told me that in Christianity, it is said that Christ is the priest of God. The Buddha never says that. The notion of teacher in contrast to that of mediator highlights the difference in the degree of personal involvement between ritual and meditation.

However, if you take the context of North India in the 6th century B.C., where and when the Buddha lived, there was a long tradition of ritualistic religion. There was a precedent of hundreds of years of Vedic rituals, as well as a tradition of ritual worship among non-Aryan tribal people. It was from these people that Buddha recruited his disciples. It was not easy for these people to wean themselves away completely from this ritualistic tradition all at once. Also, as with any society, not all the people are of the same temperament. So, different methods were required to lead these people to the correct path.

Sometimes the Buddha is called a person who can read the mental characteristics of a person, and in doing so knows the solution to prescribe—he knows the path for a particular person, knows how he or she should go about attaining his or her salvation. On different occasions, the Buddha prescribed different methods to his disciples. One disciple may be asked to go to a forest and meditate. To another the Buddha would say, "No, don't go to the forest. The forest meditation is not suitable for you. You stay in the monastery." Sometimes in the *suttas* the question arises as to whether the level of difficulty involved in meditating in forests and in other such remote conditions is too difficult for the average practitioner. It is a very difficult thing to be away from society. Forests can bring terror and fear to the mind. In addition, the beliefs of a practitioner brought from his or her background—their beliefs in various gods, god-like beings and other supernatural powers—disturb them. The Buddha answers those who doubt their ability to withdraw themselves from society: he says if a person does not have greed, hatred, delusion and such other negative emotions, there is no problem for him or her to live in forests. No terror and fear will come to them. It is only because they have these negative qualities that fear and terror arise in their minds. The Buddha professes, "I know very well that I don't have this. I have confidence. When I see that I do not have these qualities in me, in my mind, I have the fullest confidence that I can stay in the forest hermitage."

This shows that some people cannot live in forest hermitages. Therefore, it became necessary to prescribe some methods in which these people would try to strengthen themselves through some form of outside aid. In Buddhism it is always said that one should depend upon oneself. "Make yourself your own lord, do not go for outside help." Rely always on the Dhamma and one's own self. Dhamma is the only refuge one should take. When individuals start their meditation, teachers will first ask that they observe the five precepts, if they are of the laity. One thinks, "I have now taken upon myself this precept of not injuring any living being, or not taking what is not given," and so forth. Then the student is asked to concentrate on this for a while. "Now I have these *sīlas* in me." It is said that when one goes on concentrating like that, reflecting on one's own virtues, a joy arises in one's mind. That joy leads to happiness. Then when one is happy in mind, one's body becomes calm. And when one's body is calm like this, one experiences an ease (*sukha*) in oneself. When one is at ease, then one's mind becomes concentrated. In one *sutta* addressed to monks, it is said,

> In whatever monk, who was covetous,
> covetousness is got rid of; who was malevolent,
> malevolence of mind is got rid of; who was
> wrathful, wrath is got rid of; who was grudging,
> grudging is got rid of; who was hypocritical,
> hypocrisy is got rid of; who was spiteful, spite
> is got rid of; who was jealous, jealousy is got
> rid of; who was stingy, stinginess is got rid of;
> who was treacherous, treachery is got rid of;
> who was crafty, craftiness is got rid of; who
> was of evil desire, evil desire is got rid of; who
> was of wrong view, wrong view is got rid of.
> I, monks, say that if he follows the practice
> fitting for recluses there is a getting rid of those
> stains in recluses, defects in recluses, faults
> in recluses, occasion for the sorrowful states
> of what is to be experienced in a bad borne.
> He beholds the self purified of all these evil,
> unskilled states. He beholds the self freed.
> When he beholds the self purified of all these
> evil, unskilled states, when he beholds the
> self freed, delight [or joy] is born. Rapture [or
> happiness] is born from delight. When he is
> in rapture, the body is impassible [or calm].
> When the body is impassible, he experiences
> joy [*sukha*, or ease]. Being joyful, the mind is
> concentrated.

Here one is really relying on one's own virtue. I think the Buddha himself wanted his disciples to rely on themselves and not to rely on outside help in meditation. But it is possible that not every person can do this. Maybe, some of them cannot find their own virtues or they do not have confidence in themselves. They want to go to some outside person to gain confidence or rather to bring about the joy which would gradually lead to concentration of the mind. Who is the best person, in the context of Buddhism, to whom the disciples would go for this, because there is no reliance on a deity or any other power? They had their teacher in whom they had the greatest confidence as a teacher: the Buddha. The Buddha was known as having all of these admirable qualities. The disciples had confidence in his enlightenment. They were always asked to go to him if they had any problem.

But if the Buddha was far away, for instance, one would not be able to ask him a question directly. There are legends recalling times when a disciple was in difficulty, and from a far off place the Buddha would see. He would project a light from his mind, from his body, to the disciple. In this manner the Buddha would appear before the troubled disciple and explain things to him. You know, even today, there is the famous teacher, Sai Baba, in South India. There are people even in Sri Lanka, even Buddhists, learned, educated people, who think that lots of miracles do happen. When they pray, they hope that various things will materialize. I remember the case of a university lecturer who, having some problems, went to Sai Baba and who says that he is alive now because of Sai Baba. This man says that when he was praying, certain medicines appeared in a silver casket. He says he still has this casket with him. I do not know, but he believes that. So 2,500 years ago, this kind of thing could happen. Lots of people did believe. Even today, people still believe that when one mentions the name of the Buddha, when one has confidence in him, various things may happen. So this process starts with confidence in a teacher but then it goes a step further to what we could call something miraculous, something mysterious.

One finds in the texts the subject of reflections on the virtues of the Buddha being prescribed to some disciples. When one starts meditating, one is asked to reflect on the virtues of the Buddha. Of course one gets a list of these virtues very often in the texts. At first these virtues were not meant as aids in meditation. It is said that as the fame of the Buddha spread throughout the country, people would seek him out for spiritual guidance. But then, and this could be from texts added later to the canon, we find portions which recount the Buddha asking his disciples to reflect on these virtues. Perhaps this was to give them more confidence, more moral courage through devotion and faith. And it is said that, when one goes on reflecting upon these virtues, joy arises in one's mind. As I said earlier, this joy in turn puts the mind at ease and aids in concentration. It is also said that when one reflects on the virtues of the Buddha, no thoughts of greed, hatred, or delusion will come to mind. One will be free from those thoughts because one is concentrating on the virtues of the Buddha.

One can see how concentrating on the Buddha may improve clarity of mind better than concentrating on some other thing. Imagine concentrating on one's own body in a *satipaṭṭhāna* way. Then there is some distraction; either one feels lazy or bored, or some bodily pain or the like arises. One is disturbed. Or there could be an outside disturbance. Then one is asked to think of some pleasant object for a while, move one's mind from the former subject of meditation and think of a pleasant object. The commentaries say this pleasant object could be something like the Buddha. When one thinks of the Buddha, or a pleasant object, then again one finds that joy arises and the process starts again. One then comes to concentration. One is asked, then, not to go on concentrating on that object any more. Now one has reached what one wanted to achieve. One was initially distracted and disturbed; now one has brought back the composure of the mind. Then one is asked to return to one's former object of meditation. So it is for this, therefore, that the pleasant object—Buddha, Dhamma, Saṅgha, whatever it might be—is brought in.

If one goes around Sri Lanka today, the most common ritual that one will find is for ordinary people to go to the temple or the monastery with some flowers, incense, coconut oil, or maybe candles. In the past, when entering the premises there was a vessel of water to wash one's feet - now of course everyone wears shoes so there is no need. The flowers are cleaned and fresh water is sprinkled on them. People then go to the Buddha—the statue, the *stūpa* or the bodhi tree. The altar is washed, and those beautiful flowers are placed in the presence of the Buddha as those who come say "I honor you" or "I offer these to you." This is a form of honoring the Buddha. Lamps are lit and incense is burnt. Having created this atmosphere, people will gather to repeat the verses, giving the virtues of the Buddha. It is really a reflection on the virtues of the Buddha. Reflections on the Dhamma and the Saṅgha, of course, follow.

Therefore, in actual fact, this sort of what we call "rituals," not in the sense of religious rituals mentioned earlier, are an aid for these people to concentrate their minds. It is for this that these rituals were started. There is nowhere in the Buddhist texts where the Buddha has ever prescribed anything like that—no mention at all. It is said that just before his passing away, when his closest disciples asked him about funeral arrangements and so forth, he is supposed to have said, in effect, "Well, the lay people will look after that." The monks are not asked to do anything about that. Then the Buddha was asked what to do with relics, the ashes and all that. He said that in the case of a Buddha, or a Paccekabuddha, or an Arahant, or a great universal monarch, one can honor them with a *stūpa*, wherein the relics are enshrined. Why? When a devoted person sees the *stūpa*, at once the virtues of the Buddha come to his or her mind. Through that a joy is born in his or her mind. And, gradually, again it leads to concentration. It is for this purpose, therefore, that these rituals were first started. Even today, the people would, very often with flowers in hand, before they place the flowers on an altar, go around the *stūpa*, chanting verses giving the virtues of the Buddha, Dhamma, and the Saṅgha. Reciting the virtues of the Buddha, Dhamma, and Saṅgha is a very important part of performing any religious observance. This is the connection between rituals and meditation. Rituals were at first meant to help provide this connection, an aid to concentration.

This does not mean that all of the rituals found in Sri Lanka and other Buddhist countries today are really meant for meditation alone, as aids to meditation. There are some rituals which really take the shape of religious rituals. Now people have come to associate the Buddha, the Dhamma—especially these two—and the Saṅgha, not really the monks who are living today but what is called the "eightfold noble community of disciples" (those who have progressed on the path to Nibbāna, *ariyasaṅgha*) with certain rituals. The Buddha, Dhamma, and Saṅgha, in this sense, have come to be associated with some powers in the world. The Buddha, though no more, has left some power in the world. This power and the power of the Dhamma and the original

Saṅgha, though no more, are believed to abide for the benefit of the world. Through some of the rituals one can turn these powers in one's favor. That belief is present, although it is not in agreement with original Buddhist texts. And lay people believe in *devas*, especially *devas* who are regarded as guardians of the religion. One performs *pūjas* to these in order to get their favor.

In these rituals, really, there is an aspect of what is called the non-rational. For instance, if one sees the Kandy *perahera* (festival of the tooth relic), or one of the *peraheras* in Colombo, one cannot do any meditation while watching that. Of course it is possible that some form of devotion arises in one's mind when observing that. In the past, when the *perahera* of the Temple of the Tooth in Kandy passes by, the people who are watching it would shout *sādhu*, *sādhu*, with great devotion. Perhaps such devotion is not present in this way any more. It is possible that even such rituals could bring an aspect of devotion to awareness.

In the *paritta* ceremony, about which we have spoken, there are also some of the *suttas* delivered by the Buddha which are chanted with the hope of gaining the favor of gods and also the favor of the Buddha and the Dhamma for one's benefit. There one could see a ritual in the real sense of a religious ritual. In it one does not know how it works for one's benefit. Therefore one could see a non-rational dimension in it. But again, when one listens to a *paritta*, it is possible that one could concentrate one's thoughts, at least for a while. Some actually claim that they can do it while listening to a *paritta* chanting. Others, of course, get these ceremonies performed as a mere ritual, for they expect benefits to come by the mere performance. Some would, therefore, not even listen to the *paritta* being recited. They allow monks to chant while they themselves carry on, having tea, chatting with one another and chewing betel. In this case, it is merely a religious ritual being conducted. Through this chanting of *paritta*, such people think, some benefits accrue in a mysterious manner.

In the proper sense of the word, as rituals are understood in Buddhism, they were started as an aid to some people who could not rely on their own virtues and personal ability. They could make use of the ritual to begin to concentrate their thoughts and from then to direct their minds to the understanding of reality.

Questions and Responses

Q: Is it the case that a monk, who takes refuge in himself, who has self-confidence, and enters a forest to meditate, is a purer form of a Buddhist than a monk who lives in a monastery?

C. Witanachchi: I don't think it is necessary to enter a forest hermitage. What I think one should do is to make a forest hermitage wherever one lives. If one can live in a monastery and do the meditation, there is no harm. It is a matter of a mode of assistance. If one goes to a forest hermitage, one is cut off from the disturbances of normal society. Therefore one has a conducive surroundings there. One does not become a better monk by merely living in a forest. Sometimes a person living in a forest could "live in society" while living in a forest, with all the related disturbances going on in the mind; thinking of what happened in the monastery, politics, and all these things. What is the use of going to the forest in such a situation?

Q: Is whether to go to the forest or remain in a monastery a choice of the monk? Does that choice reflect an opinion about a monk's service to others?

CW: Yes, that view is sometimes expressed. I don't think that is really a Buddhist idea. According to the tradition, even today, when a monk requests that he be admitted to the order of monks, says, "Sir, please accept this robe and admit me to the Order so that I might put a complete end to *dukkha*." That is the purpose for which a person becomes a monk. Service to others is only a part of that while putting an end to *dukkha* is the main task. If one does not discipline oneself and try to find one's own liberation, then one is not a real monk. The Buddha said that first one has to free oneself and then try to serve others. The Buddha said to the first sixty disciples whom he sent out to the world to preach, "You are free from all bonds, now go and give the message to others."

Even a person who tries to train himself or herself without doing anything actively to serve others serves by being an example to others. I can remember a forest monk, when someone raised a similar question, replying, "Do you see that light post outside the window? It doesn't run about, but it sheds light all around it." By disciplining oneself, one can serve others without doing any thing else. That does not mean that one should refrain from serving others, of course.

Q: I have a question that raises an issue of the relationship between an individual and community. Does a monk see himself as an individual first or as part of a community?

CW: I think he has both orientations. If one takes the Saṅgha itself, the community of monks, a monk has his independence. He has to try to perfect himself as an individual. At the same time he has a role to play as a member of the Order. And the Order, the community of monks, has a certain hold on that individual, always. So that the community of monks has to act in such a way as to lead him to the correct path, to keep him from going astray, and to do so through various regulations and punishments, and so forth. Both dimensions are present. For the Buddhist Saṅgha today, in the Sri Lankan context, most of our monks seem to be more worried about the community than the individual.

Q: Would it be different between the ascetic monk and the cause-service monk?

CW: Yes, if you call the cause-service monks the monks living in the village monasteries, they would be more interested in community work, issues confronting the nation, and even politics. Monks in forest hermitages would be different; they would be more balanced between being in a community in a forest hermitage while developing themselves.

CHAPTER XIX

ON MEDITATION: QUESTIONS AND RESPONSES

Venerable Amarasiri with Venerable Dhammasara

at Parama Dhamma Cetiya, Mt. Lavinia, Sri Lanka

Two learned monks engage eager students in a conversation about meditation, which extends to issues related to the Theravāda Buddhist tradition, to the process of realization, even to interreligious understanding. Questions arise from all angles: are there any guarantees? What about the notion of impermanence, notions of the self? Can one carry meditative concentration into the every day world? And there are others. Our patient monks respond thoughtfully and Venerable Amarasiri leads a brief session of meditation, starting, appropriately, from the present moment.

Let us take this occasion to discuss, generally, some issues that you students from abroad might have regarding your studies of the Theravāda Buddhist tradition of Sri Lanka or the practice of meditation.

Question: Is the truth, which the Buddha unveiled for people in Dhamma, realized only by monks or can anyone realize the truth?

Response: What the Buddha realized during his lifetime he taught to the people. What he taught has now been preserved in books. At the beginning, the teaching was passed on orally. Later it was all recorded in Sri Lanka. And we have a good record of all the teachings in Sri Lanka. These teachings, originally recorded in Pali, now have been translated into many languages. The same set of discourses is now available throughout the world. This very reliable record has been with us for nearly 2,000 years. The Pali Text Society in England publishes all the texts. That is all the doctrine. Many commentaries on the discourses were written later on. Originally, Dhamma, as taught by the Buddha, is recorded there in the books.

But the way of practice differs in various countries with various masters, who have adopted various methods. What development one can achieve, and the purposes for achieving it, depends upon the characteristics of the people. For example, for Westerners, who are very busy, one seeks only the calming down of the mind. One is satisfied with that. But there are others who seek spiritual attainments, which we call "the path and fruit"—stages of mental development. This is a very advanced level which requires much more practice requiring that one live and practice separately from the people, in the monastery or in the forest.

Q: In order to understand the truths of the Buddha, is becoming a monk a prerequisite?

R: No, no, it is not necessary. Any layman can understand. Most of the people who attained enlightenment, even during the Buddha's time, were laymen. Busy people are not able to concentrate, being busy about other things—family life and all that. But in our case, we have nothing, nothing to worry about, no belongings. So we can devote our entire time to the practice, especially on meditation. Any layman can practice, of course.

Q: When one meditates, it is said that one's mind should be calm. Is that calmness itself insight or a prelude to a state in which one realizes truth?

R: The main purpose of meditation is to realize understanding. But one cannot learn the truth or reality without getting the mind calm. So calmness of mind is very necessary. That is why we have a certain kind of meditation called "serenity meditation," or "tranquility meditation." We practice that first in order to calm down and subdue the hindrances which disturb the mind. There are five hindrances which have to be calmed down by a particular type of meditation, with concentration on the breathing, or the postures, and so forth. There are over forty types of meditation meant for various characters and for various stages. One can practice any one of them and get the result of calming down the mind so that one will be fit to realize the truth.

There are three stages through which one progresses in calming the mind. The first we call the morality stage. People must lead a good life in order to get the mind quiet. It is only when the mind is quiet that it can be developed further. Concentration is the second stage. Only when concentration has been adequately developed can one realize the truth. The stage in which one finally does this we call the wisdom stage (*paññā*). We need morality, the stage of concentration, and the wisdom stage. The final aim is wisdom.

Wisdom is nothing but understanding reality. One can start by concentrating on a very simple subject—body postures or even the breathing—and learn the truth of reality. That is only a medium. Once one gains the power of concentration, the mind becomes more efficient to learn things. It is important, as one studies Buddhism, to practice meditation, at least to some extent.

Q: We have read of the Four Paths, Four Fruits, and Nibbāna—The ninefold world-transcending Dhamma (*navavidhalokuttaradhamma*). Would you discuss this?

R: Yes, you mean the different stages of development. There are ten fetters, or *samyojanas*, as they are called in Pali, which have to be eradicated. In the first stage, one eradicates three of them completely. The first of these fetters is self-notion (*sakkāyadiṭṭhi*). The second is skeptical doubt. The third is reliance on rituals and methods following other teachers. Once those fetters are eliminated one becomes a stream-enterer—a *sotāpanna*—which is in two stages: the path and its fruit. The second stage refers to a person who will be reborn only once (*sakadāgamin*). In this stage two fetters are suppressed but not eradicated completely. When one comes to the third stage, which is called *anāgāmin*, or the stage of a non-returner, the lower five fetters are eradicated completely. In the final stage, which we call the stage of an Arahant, the stage of complete enlightenment, the other five fetters are completely eradicated. This is how one reads the stages of development. The first stage is very important, because when one becomes a stream-enterer (*sotāpanna*), one would not be committing any unwholesome act which would lead one down to a birth lower than a human birth.

There are thirty-one planes of existence, the Buddha taught. There are four forms of living: animals, ghosts, titans, and hell. These four stages are below the human level. There people cannot do any wholesome deeds. Their mind is so weak that they cannot escape from their level of living. They will be suffering during the period of their lives in those four levels. Then there is the human level where everyone can clearly think through matters. Where Dhamma is available, they can think things through and they can progress.

When one becomes a stream-enterer, one will realize it and one will never do an unwholesome act which would lead one to hell or any lower birth. It is a guarantee that one will progress in the path. A *sotāpanna* person will be born to this world a maximum of seven times: some seven, maximum, others five, four, three, and so forth. It depends upon the mental development of that person.

Q: What guarantees that one will progress?

R: Knowing reality, especially.

Q: So, does that experience guarantee it?

R: One has to understand this. Each of us will have to question for ourselves: "Why are we here?" and "What is this that we possess?" So, now if I ask, "Who are you?", what would you answer?

Student I am James.

R: One's name is only a concept. One will have to know what really one is. That is what we call truth—knowing reality. Now, if I ask again, "Who are you?", what would you answer?

Student I would say that I am talking to you. I would say that I am in space and time.

R: It appears that one finds it hard to accept the concept. One is a conditioned material subject—conditioned with the matter and mind both. That is the shortest definition of a human being that we can give. Both the body and the mind are conditioned. "Conditioned" means always changing. One must realize that everything is changing constantly in this world. This is so for both matter and mind.

Student Okay, is reality knowing what experience is?

R: The shortest method of knowing this is by analyzing one's body as comprised of four material things: hardness, liquidity, heat, and movement of air. All these elements are changing all the time. We can turn to the *Abhidhamma* and study how this is happening. When these four elements are conditioned, or combined, there are four other conditions which arise as a result. We have a color, a smell, then we have a taste and we have nutrition. The four material qualities and the four others—color, smell, taste, and nutrition—are called the eight things which appear naturally. Everything in the world is formed of this octad: they are the smallest "atoms" or particles that we can define in Buddhism. Everything is changing all the time. This agrees with the most recent scientific theories. Everything is changing: the body and the mind. This is the first thing that one has to realize. If one does some meditation, one can recognize this.

Q: I think I understand this idea that everything is changing all the time. One can build the strongest building that has ever been constructed but someday it will be dust. One might not be able to see this happen in one's lifetime but gradual changes ensure that it will be so. Is this on target?

R: Yes. These are the characteristics which we realize in meditation. We realize that everything is changing, therefore it is suffering and, as a result, there is no personal entity there. These are called the three characteristics of nature (*tilakkhaṇas*). Everything is changing all the time. If it is changing, it is suffering. If it is changing and if it is suffering, one cannot call it "self." There is nothing called "self" there. These characteristics have to be realized in meditation. One can read it in books, but one cannot get it in books.

Q: I think you are referring to the immediate self, what one might call the "ego." Is this what we have to transcend? Once we transcend this are we liberated? Is it then that we have freedom?

R: No. Perhaps one thinks that there is an ego because one does not see the reality of it. The ego is an assumption.

One seeks to find out why we are born as human beings. It is due to ignorance and craving. Due to ignorance we have been accumulating both good and bad consequences of action (*kamma*). Every action has a result. So the main source of *kamma* is the four organs that we have. We see with the eyes. Whatever we see, either we like it or dislike it. Liking is craving. Disliking is repulsion. Both are *kamma*. If one knows the reality of it one will neither like it nor dislike it. One understands it. If one understands that this is something that is not real, that is always changing, then one is saved. One knows the reality of it. So in every action, if we can follow this method, we see the truth of life. So Buddhism is nothing but the realization of truth like that. The method is given. We have to follow this method. With hearing, one develops either liking or disliking. With seeing and tasting, it is the same. Everywhere we have to analyze the situation. For example, we ask, "What is this?" It is something that is changing, something that is conditioned. There is nothing either to like or dislike. Then one will be neutral. When there is no craving, ignorance is destroyed. It is because of ignorance that there is either liking or disliking. Craving or desire is the force that carries one from one birth to another through *saṃsāra*. As long as the force of desire is there, one will be reborn again. What we call enlightenment is not to be born again, which is the final realization.

Q: Did the Buddha discuss reincarnation?

R: Reincarnation is not what the Buddha originally taught. It is the Tibetan method. There are various variations of it. When

Buddhism went to Tibet, it got absorbed with the Tibetan methods. They think of reincarnation. Here, in our Theravāda Buddhism, we do not exactly say it is reincarnation. We just say another birth. The Chinese method is different from that. Different cultures have gotten involved in this and so we have methods in different countries. The Theravāda method is the same in all the Theravāda countries.

Q: How can one take the concentration attained in meditation into the everyday world? Is that concentration compatible with life in the world? How can we relate what happens to us in meditation to living life well in society?

R: The mind of ordinary people is constantly pursuing various sights, sounds and tastes. In this way the mind is always diffused and bending in the direction of several things. We have to get the mind at one point, at one thing at a time. That is what we seek to develop. One gets to one-pointedness of the mind by taking up an object and thinking about that. If it is breathing, we observe just the breath entering and coming out. Observe that point only. This can be easily experienced by doing the walking meditation. If one does the walking meditation for ten minutes, one can realize this.

Further, ordinary laymen are very busy with their lay life. They are not often in position to think clearly. When one tries to concentrate on something, memories arise. One has past memories and one thinks also about what will happen tomorrow. These are the things that will disturb the mind. So it's difficult to get a good picture of what one is concentrating on as long as the mind goes to the past and to the future. One can live for only one moment—the present moment. This is what we do in meditation. We think only of the present moment and there develop concentration by just observing what is happening now, at the moment. We can develop our everyday concentration by doing some practical exercises in meditation.

Q: Would an example of concentration developed in meditation, *bhāvanā*, be one in which a person is doing math, really concentrating right there on that math problem and not thinking of the past or of the future.

R: Yes, there also one has a certain sort of training. Even that can happen, but one cannot realize the reality of life in that activity. That is the difference.

Q: What does "another birth" mean to a Theravāda Buddhist? You mentioned that "reincarnation" would not apply in the Theravāda case. What is the perpetuation of *sasāra* called?

R: One will have to understand what birth is. Birth is just a conditioning of form and mind. It comes as a result of craving for worldly things. The force of craving is stored in the mind. That is what is called *kamma*, which is a very important force there. It is due to ignorance that we have stored up this craving. As long as the power of craving is there, one will be born again. These are essential factors in right understanding, the first dimension of the eightfold path. Under right understanding, we have to understand *kamma*.

Q: Between death and birth, is anything transferred besides craving?

R: We have to analyze it in this manner: We must first ask, "What is this birth that we presently have?" We have life. "What happens at death?" "What is keeping this body intact?" It is the mind that keeps the body intact. At death the mind gets separated from the body and the material portion of the body decays. As long as the force of desire is present at death, it takes place in another moment, a new birth. A new birth is the force of *kamma* joining with the material things from the father and the mother. These three have to become combined: the father's form, and the mother's, and the force of the mind with craving or desire. This combination is what we call conception. Once the conception occurs, the material dimension starts developing.

Q: Can we speak of that force of the mind as a stream of consciousness?

R: What we call consciousness is just a momentary thing. When one is sitting, one knows that one is sitting. My hand is like this and I know that the hand is like this. That is consciousness, is it not? As I change the position of my hand, what happened to the former thought about my hand? It was only momentary. That is why we say consciousness is not stationary—it changes constantly. This can be noted by doing the walking meditation.

Q: If all mind states are momentary, what guarantees that a stream-enterer will retain his or her realizations upon rebirth? What ensures that he or she will reach Nibbāna?

R: We have action and reaction, which we call *paṭiccasamuppāda*—"dependent origination." Every action has a reaction—that is the life process. There are causes for one's birth, there are causes for one's living, there are causes for one's dying and there are causes for one's attaining another birth. It is a continuing process. The force of that process is ignorance. This is what we are fighting against: ignorance. When one realizes reality, one knows that this is how it is going on. When one understands that, one can stop it. That is the method.

Q: Do we contemplate or think about the origin of existence, where we came from?

R: There is no thinking. One is aware. That is what we develop. We are only aware—not thinking. If one takes up breathing as a form of meditation, one is only watching the breath going in and coming out, only awareness is there. It is awareness of the present moment; what is happening now. With the breath, for instance, one is aware that now the breath is entering the nostrils, and now it is coming out.

Q: But for you as a Buddhist monk, where is the beginning point of existence?

R: Day to day? I don't get the question. One could say that ignorance, *avijjā*, is at the beginning.

Q: How do Buddhists, such as yourself, respond to the people who believe in Jesus Christ?

R: Anybody can believe anything because Buddhism is not a religion. It is a method of realizing the truth. It is a way of living, of developing one's inner qualities, of developing character. Therefore it can survive anywhere in the world, be it with Christians, Muslims or Hindus, all other faiths because we take all persons as human beings. People are a combination of matter and of mind. So we are all the same. When we analyze the situation that way, there is no difference among us: no racial difference, no linguistic difference.

Q: But as a Buddhist, what do you think about the teachings of Jesus Christ?

R: Well, the Buddha met so many sages and learned individuals of his time. He had nothing to say about any of them. He met certain people who came to question him, to argue with him, and he defeated their arguments. That was all. He had no remark about other religious people. I, personally, have not read much about Christianity but as far as I know, if any teacher teaches good qualities for human beings and if those qualities can develop the quality of humankind, then that is a good religion. We as Buddhists only take it up to that point. However, the Christian doctrine of deliverance is something quite opposed to our method. In Buddhism, we realize something after learning, after questioning, after arguing. But in other religions it is just by faith. Buddhism is not a religion based on faith, and we have no belief in an almighty God. Buddhism teaches that man alone is capable of either saving himself or confining himself to misery—individuals are responsible for their own deliverance or downfall.

Q: What about "stream-entering, *paññā*-arising"—the *lokuttarapaññā*; can one cause this world-transcending wisdom to arise? Can one make it happen?

R: No, one cannot make it happen. It comes about as a result of the procedure. When one comes to the *magga* path, one develops certain insight-knowledges. It is as a result of these insight-knowledges that one can pass out of the mundane sphere into the super-mundane. It is a realization that takes place. So once one realizes a particular stage of the path and fruits, one knows "Now I have come to that stage." The meditator can realize that. He has possessed those insight knowledges. The meditation methods are formulated in such a way that one can realize everything. Through analyzing, and observing, one sees the truth. Realization of this is not founded on belief. If one does exercises in meditation, such as walking meditation, there is a great deal that one can realize. So those realizations are called wisdom or *paññā*. If one realizes the truth of anything; that is wisdom, *paññā*.

Q: If one realizes what experience is, is there anything beyond that to realize?

R: Yes. Say, one realizes "What am I?" "What is this?" "How did this come about?" "What is going to happen?" All of these are realizations. One will know the process. Oh, this is a process that came as a result of this or that. And this is the process that is going on now. And in the future, it will all develop that way. One knows the process. That is where dependent origination comes in. It comes like this, it stays like this, it moves like this. One knows also the end. It becomes very clear. Clear understanding arises, nothing but understanding; understanding and realizing.

[At this point, Venerable Amarasiri kindly led the visiting students in a brief session of meditation.]

We start from the beginning, from the present moment. Now, what are we doing? You are all seated. Now you think of the body. Think of the body as seated. Do not take what is seated as "me." It is a material body that is sitting. That is what is called the *rūpa*, the "form." What is thinking about the body? The mind—that is a separate entity. Now, the body is sitting, the mind knows. Now, say you want to stand. The mind sends a message, "I want to stand." The air and the matter in the body react to that message. Now it has started, "I want to get up." Now one observes what is going on. Now the "I-element moves" and one just mindfully gets up from this seat and comes to the standing position mindfully. You are aware of the present position. If you want to get up, what do you do? Now you feel the weight of the body but in order to stand you have to change that position. Now you realize that you are shifting the weight to the two hands. That is the mechanism of it. Now the body is moving. The weight now goes to the legs. One realizes now that the whole weight of the body is resting on the two legs. Supposing you move to one side; now you realize that this portion of the body has become hard and tight and another part of the body has become light. What is the reason for this? It is a change of the elements. Of the elements, there is hardness (earth), which is hard and has weight. In the water element there is also weight. The other two elements, fire or heat, and air, do not have weight. What happens when one moves to one side is that the earth element and the water element have accumulated here. Air and heat have accumulated in the other area of the body, and consequently it has become light.

Now stand up. Now you feel the full weight of the body on these legs. Move a little to the side such that your weight is balanced between both legs. If you move a little further, now the weight is localized here and it has become light. You can see that [air] is this thing that makes you walk. All the poses are different stages of material configuration. This is what you should now realize, for this moment is a result of change. Suppose you just stand from there, doing it knowingly as I did. You just keep the hand like this and drop the other hand like this. This, as we have gone through it, is the method of body contemplation. One attempts to find out what is happening, first by focusing the mind on the tips of the fingers. The mind can be focused on each and every finger separately, or upon the whole hand. Simply observe what is going on. What do you feel? What do you realize there?

Some of you will realize the weight, I am sure. It is the mind doing the knowing, but the weight is there in the form. Look for something else there, too. You can see there is something like a process going on. Do you observe that? There is some vibration. The matter is always changing. That is what we call *anicca*, "impermanence." One can observe that. There is even impermanenceatthetipsofthefingers.Bydevelopingconcentration through meditation one can realize this. A realization attained by focusing on one thing can be applied to all the sensations in the body. That is what we call *vedanānupassana*—contemplation of feeling. There are four types of meditation or *satipaṭṭhānas*:

kāyānupassana, "body contemplation"; *vedanānupassana,* "contemplation on feelings"; *cittānupassana,* "concentration on thoughts"; *dhammānupassana,* "concentration on objects or phenomena." Each is a different method of observing reality. By realizing that all is changing all the time, one realizes that this is not satisfactory, that it is suffering. Why suffering? Because one cannot make it continue. We want to continue it as it is. But all the pleasures are temporary. One would like to continue the pleasures, which is a form of craving. There is no power by which one can make the continuation of pleasures to occur. That is the reality of things. If it is changing, it is suffering. If it is changing and suffering, there is no soul. There is no substantiality in all of this. That is what we have to realize. That is why we have renounced. There is nothing substantial in this body. All the pleasures are temporary.

CHAPTER XX

ON MEDITATION

Godwin Samanaratna

The late Godwin Samanaratna worked in several libraries before taking a position, four decades ago, at the Senanayake Library in Kandy. After his mother died, and upon his completing his duties to her, a small meditation shelter was built for him near Nilambe, not far from Kandy. It was not long after retiring to that location that men and women from Sri Lanka and abroad came to him for guidance in meditation, which he gave ever gently and untiringly. He also introduced meditation to patients in the Kandy Municipal Hospital and developed a curriculum for hyperactive children, while being regularly active in programs for the poor and less fortunate. In this brief chapter, we learn about the internationally known Meditation Center in Nilambe, about the important practice of freeing ourselves from the suffering we cause ourselves by coming to understand what is going on in our bodies and minds.

I would like to say something about the Meditation Center at Nilambe and also to say a few words briefly about meditation. This Center was founded in the early 1980s by a group of lay Buddhists who felt the need for a lay meditation center. This is the first and was for over a decade the only lay meditation center in Sri Lanka. And as you can guess, the whole thrust, the whole emphasis here is in trying to integrate meditation with daily life.

Over the years monks have come here to practice meditation and, on occasion, to teach. In the beginning we had mostly Western visitors, but I am happy to say that from around 1989 we have had more Sri Lankan guests, for whom we have developed special programs. We presently have one such program. We have teachers who teach Buddhism in schools who come here for meditation for two weeks. That is sponsored by the government. They have to pay for it, and they are on what is called duty leave. Most of them, though they teach Buddhism, have never meditated before. We have also special programs for Sri Lankans on full-moon days, which are very important holidays for Buddhists. I am also pleased to say that non-Buddhists have come here for meditation, and that we have organized special programs for them as well. In fact, I did a weekend workshop with a Quaker on a very interesting theme, "Peace Through Stillness." We also try to do social welfare work. We have two projects in the Kandy hospital, in the Peradeniya hospital, where we try to help poor patients who are unable to pay their accounts and we try to meet with them to meditate with them. Ideally, we are trying to incorporate contemplation and social action.

I will quickly go over our daily schedule to provide a clearer idea of what happens at the Center. The day begins at 4:45 when the gong sounds to wake up the meditators. From 5:00 to 6:00 there is group meditation; from 6:30 to 7:30 there is yoga; after which we have breakfast. Following breakfast we do what we call working meditation. The idea of working meditation is doing some work—helping in the garden, cleaning the toilets, helping the cooks in the kitchen—with a meditative mind to see how far one can work as not something different from meditation, to see how far one can be one with whatever one is doing. Then from 9:30 to 11:00, there is another session of meditation. From 11:00 to 12:00 there is what is called "individual and outdoor meditation."

The idea of individual and outdoor meditation is to help us see that we need to learn to meditate alone and we need to learn to meditate in groups. Another aspect of individual meditation is to see how one relates to oneself. Generally speaking, when we are alone with ourselves, without doing anything, it is possible that we may feel bored and lonely with ourselves. Sometimes we do not seem to enjoy our company with ourselves. This is a very interesting and important area to explore. Is it rather that we would want to escape from such state? But to work through such state somehow is the ideal. A phrase that I use often is "be a most valuable assistant, be self-contained in yourself." Solitude is a very important dimension in human experience. Another aspect of individual and outdoor meditation is learning what is called "developing a sensitivity to the surroundings," learning to relate to nature. I encourage meditators to experience, explore, to discover for oneself in the context of our individual and outdoor meditation.

At noon there is lunch, after which there is a period of rest until 1:30. From 1:30 to 2:30 there is individual meditation. From 2:30 to 4:00 there is another session of group meditation. From 4:30 to 5:30 is yoga, and from 5:30 to 6:30 one is on one's own at a beautiful time of day. Usually we have beautiful sunsets; each day there is a variation. At 6:30 there is devotional chanting in Pali, and after chanting there is sitting meditation. Then there is a break for a snack when we offer a drink that is called soy-coffee, a drink made from soybeans. Following this we have a group discussion. Finally, we end the day with meditation and lights out at 9:30 or 10:00. When you go to sleep early, you can wake up early. Our living conditions are extremely simple, primitive and rustic. We depend on candles. There are no beds here. There are not many chairs. Here again one makes an effort to see all of this in the context of one's life.

Turning to the matter of meditation, let me say that meditation is an attempt to understand by ourselves how our mind and body work and through that experience to free ourselves from the suffering that we ourselves create. So, one has to see meditation in the context of the four noble truths, which are an important aspect of the Buddha's teaching; to mold the mind, to shape the mind and to keep awareness. One very important aspect in meditation is developing what is called awareness, mindfulness, and alertness. There is a particular technique which enables one to develop this sense of alertness. The technique is very simple, where one allows one's body to breathe naturally and to be conscious of what is happening mechanically, to learn to be aware of it. After a few minutes of trying this, one can explore one's experiences.

At this point Godwin Samanaratna kindly led the students in meditation.

To catch the movement of the moment, read very slowly the words that follow, pausing for a moment or two after each phrase.

——————— ❖ ———————

Please close your eyes. Please become aware of your body, become aware of the different parts of your body. Become conscious of different sensations. As you do that, try to feel faintly, gently, softly your body. Feel your posture, your spine. Let go of the thought and bring your attention back to the breath. Now, just feel what it is to sit in this posture—with your spine erect, quite relaxed, with your knees bent. Feel the different sensations, different movements. Just feel what it is to sit—completely feel. Now, just allow the body to feel naturally and focus your attention, your awareness on these things. You are aware when the body is here; you are aware when the body is there; having your complete attention. When thoughts arise, learn to let go of them, gently, and bring your attention back to your breath, being in the present, in the here and the now. It is natural that you may experience discomfort. Learn not to resist it. Be alert and awake from moment to moment.

Please open your eyes, and when you change your posture please try to do it with awareness, observing the intention. Now, let us go over what happened and try to understand.

——————— ❖ ———————

Student: I had a real bad pain in my back and I couldn't really focus on my breathing because of the pain in my back. I was thinking about that.

Student: I just felt as if I was starting to come forward. I did not realize that I was dreaming. I was just falling forward. Also, I kind of released my pain by letting my foot fall asleep and then my body just kind of went limp.

Student: I had a problem with concentration but after a while I really felt aware of my body. I felt that I was a third person and at that point I was in no pain. But then my mind was wandering and I had to try very hard just to concentrate on breathing.

Student: I had a memory surface from when I was very young. I don't think it was something that I've thought about, yet it was very familiar to me. It was something that I've been aware of but have not really recognized that the source might have been this memory of a particular event.

Student: I felt a disorientation of my arms. My right hand was where my left was. I felt like they were switched.

Student: After a while, even though my thoughts were still jumping around, when I tried to focus on my breathing, the thoughts would drift away again. After a while I felt very detached from my body, very separate from it. I could still feel my hands touching but somehow I felt very apart from them.

Student: As I was listening to the wind moving in the trees and the birds and the things going on around I sort of thought about how different each successive moment was and how sometimes I heard the birds and sometimes I didn't, and sometimes I heard the leaves of a tree blowing in the wind in a certain way, and sometimes I didn't. It was just the way that things sort of came and entered my awareness and changed and went.

Student: At first I felt very dizzy and that I was drifting sideways. Then I kept trying to get my spine straight—it felt like my spine was playing little tricks on me. I finally readjusted my feet after which I was able finally to calm down just a little bit and to still my thoughts. Towards the end I was really getting more into it, the few thoughts that arose I could quickly detach from. But it was very difficult.

Godwin Samanaratna: I will try to offer some comments based on what has been shared. The first area is the physical aspect. You reported having unpleasant sensations to varying degrees. Ordinarily in our lives when we feel such sensations, we try to get rid of them. Why? Because they are uncomfortable. We are conditioned to react to pain in that way. But by doing so, we never learn about pain. We never make an effort to explore pain; we never make an effort to understand what it is. So, one very important aspect of meditation is to do just that, to understand, to explore, to discover. When you have physical pain, what I suggest is that you do not try to focus on the breathing because it becomes a distraction. We try to focus on breathing and then we are distracted by the discomfort. I often tell meditators that they have enough distractions in life. They do not need to let meditation become a series of distractions. I suggest that you focus your attention on that physical pain, to focus awareness on that sensation of pain. And when you try to do this, you may make very important and interesting discoveries. What are the possible discoveries you may make? One is the awareness that there is this physical discomfort and the way you live with it, with anxiety, with resistance, with dislike, with impatience. So you may realize that in a way the problem is mostly how you respond to it, how you relate to it. Ideally, what is being attempted in relation to the physical aspect is not to get rid of pain. In the Buddhist texts, even with the Buddha and enlightened ones, people were not without pain. The difference is the way they related to that. What we are attempting to do is to see how far we can relate to that physical pain without suffering as a consequence: learning to be gentle, learning to allow that pain.

Another profound experience you may have had while trying to explore, which is related to Buddhism, is that you might have something like a dream—that while the difficult pain is there, you may develop a sense of detachment. You may have an experience where you might realize that the difficult pain is there but there is no sense of ownership. As someone has said, "My pain becomes their pain."

Another experiment I would like to suggest is to consider when you have a pain to see how far you can live in the present with that pain; forgetting that you have had that pain in the past and not anticipating—just being with that pain from moment to moment. Now a question arises. Meditation means not to be unkind to the body. Does it mean that the most successful meditator is a person who endures the most pain? Meditation is learning to have the balance for avoiding two extremes. One extreme is pampering our body. We are conditioned to pamper our body, so immediately when we have pain we try to get rid of it. The other extreme is being unfriendly to the body, actively seeking discomfort. In meditation we learn to achieve a balance by avoiding these two extremes. In practical terms this means working with the physical pain, and then when the pain is unbearable, to change the posture. Keep aware.

There were some observations about what can be described as the body image changing. This is a very interesting area because I have been hearing numerous reports of this. The experience of the body image also arises when you have the experience as if the body is moving. In actual fact, the body is not moving. It might be of interest that one person mentioned some time ago that she was becoming a frog. There have been meditators who have told me that they have experienced what is described as out-of-the-body experiences. So what is attempted in meditation in this regard is to see how far you can become aware of this without necessarily becoming anxious, or if you are anxious just to know that you are anxious—just learn to be aware of the state of mind. You are to try to simply note what is happening and to allow whatever is happening to the body to happen.

And then there are experiences in relation to thought. This is very interesting; the content of thought, the structure of thought. Someday I would like to explore this more.

III

IN SRI LANKA

Already centuries old by the time Julius Caesar decided to cross the Rubicon, this remarkable island civilization has been the site of splendid accomplishments and stunning failures that have been a part of the human experience. Of paramount importance has been the role of Sinhala men and women in launching and sustaining the Theravāda Buddhist tradition (with assistance from Myanmar [Burma] and Siam [Thailand] during a period of decline), which today is known around the world. At the same time the intercultural and religiously plural dynamics operating in this resplendent isle give pause for sober analyses.

CHAPTER XXI

THE ARRIVAL OF THE SAṄGHA

Mahinda Palihawadana

Again we find ourselves in the capable hands of Professor Palihawadana who launches us into our more sustained consideration of the arrival and development of the Saṅgha in Sri Lanka, and does so with perceptive eyes on the past and, as it were, with his feet firmly planted in the present. Historical development includes the development of the understanding of history, and Professor Palihawadana, in his review, brilliantly discloses the appearance of a political ideology.

The subject I have chosen for this chapter is "The Arrival of the Saṅgha." "Saṅgha," as we have seen, refers to the community of Buddhist monks. Since about seventy percent of the population of Sri Lanka call themselves Buddhists, the country is regarded as a Buddhist country. The question before us is "When did it all start?" It all started as a result of the great missionary activity of an Indian emperor called Aśoka. Aśoka ruled most of India after having conquered it. At a certain stage of his career he got tired of this business of conquering. There came over him a complete change and he now set upon another kind of conquest: *dharmavijaya*, a righteous (*dharma*) conquest (*vijaya*). It seems preferable to continue to keep the term *dharma* (P. *dhamma*) as it is, untranslated. *Dharma* signifies all that is really different from mundane existence, that which is more than mundane existence. Aśoka embarked on this conquest of *dharma*, that is, a spiritual conquest, perhaps, a spiritual victory, a spiritual achievement.

In the process of this conquest, he shared his ideas with the people of India in an ably unique way. He gave expression to his sentiments of kindness, compassion, transcendence, in rock edicts. In various parts of India, his message was transcribed on rocks and left for all people to see for all time. In one of these many rock edicts, rock edict number 13, he says that he is no longer interested in the military conquest of territory but in *dharma* conquest. One thing that he meant by this is that he wanted the message of *dharma* to be spread far and wide. In this process he says that he sent emissaries to the north, to the northwest, and to the south. He specifically mentions Sri Lanka by the old term Tambapanni. From this we know that he did something to bring the message of *dharma* to Sri Lanka.

The story of this enterprise of Aśoka is given in greater detail in the old historical chronicles of Sri Lanka. The Saṅgha of Sri Lanka maintained, from very old times, a chronicle of the history of the Buddhist tradition called the *Mahāvaṃsa*, the Great (*mahā*) lineage (*vaṃsa*). It is the story of Buddhist Sri Lanka. Evidently the Saṅgha had a tradition of remembering the important events in the country, especially those events that are related to its Buddhist heritage. In this *Mahāvaṃsa* is given a lengthy account of how Aśoka sent a mission to Sri Lanka, a mission whose purpose was to make Sri Lanka Buddhist. According to this story, it was the son of Aśoka, who was called Mahinda, who came with four elder monks (*theras*) to the capital city of Anurādhapura. Close to this city he met the ruling monarch, Devānampiyatissa, who was out on a hunting expedition.

Together with Mahinda, there were thus five elders, or five *theras*. This is a significant number because according to the tradition in the Saṅgha, to admit a man into the Saṅgha and to make him a full member of the Saṅgha, a minimum of five other monks is required. By the fact that five monks were coming it is obvious that they were out to confer higher ordination in Sri Lanka. When a man becomes a Buddhist monk, there is first entry to the order which is followed a few years later, after he has completed certain studies, by the higher ordination, which makes one a full member of the Saṅgha. One really becomes a monk, or *bhikkhu*, with the higher ordination.

Here is the mission coming from the great emperor Aśoka to the small island of Sri Lanka and a little knowledge of politics would tell us that that would have appeared a very important event to the monarch of Sri Lanka, and indeed it was. From the way the story is narrated it becomes obvious that everything was favorable to conversion. First of all the mission is from the great emperor. Second, Mahinda was able to communicate with the people of Sri Lanka in Sinhala, the language of Sri Lanka at the time. How could this have happened? We are fortunate in having both in India and in Sri Lanka lithic records, inscriptions on rocks, dating from the third century B.C., and when we compare inscriptions in Sri Lanka and in India at that time we see that the language is remarkably similar. How could that happen in two widely separate places, perhaps as much as over 2,000 miles? That is because the Sri Lankans who were living around Anurādhapura were, themselves, people who had come from India and spoke a language of Indian origin. In the course of the two or three centuries that had intervened since their arrival in Sri Lanka the language had not undergone so much change that a visitor from India had to learn it afresh. If a visitor spoke the way he or she spoke in India, he or she would still be understood. There might have been a need to make only a few changes. So, again, that is the second factor, that Mahinda and the monks were able to converse in Sinhala. Third, it has been assumed that there were no strong previous religious commitments, in other words, some kind of organized religion was probably not being observed in Sri Lanka. This is only a supposition. Another way of putting the same fact, one could say that the way Mahinda presented the *dharma* probably did not call for a radical alteration of earlier religious culture. The more I think about it the more it seems that this is the way it really happened. There were earlier religious observances and beliefs on the scene when Mahinda communicated the *Buddhadharma*. He did it in such a way that no great change of the religious observances seemed to be called for. Things were propitious for conversion.

Aśoka was a disillusioned earthly conqueror. In his military campaign in the southeast of India, he is supposed to have caused the death of 100,000 people. This completely shattered him. But, having been a successful emperor, he still carried with him the concept of conquest, *vijaya*. He said the only true conquest is the conquest by *dharma*. Then again as a successful ruler, he brought the notion of administration into *dharma*. He was unique in this respect. In an administration you would have a finance secretary, a foreign secretary, a defense secretary and all that. He appointed secretaries for *dharma*, officials who were to see that people lived a righteous life. That is something absolutely unique in the history of religions. When Aśoka sent his missions, he was still acting very much like a king. If one compares this with what the Buddha did, however, one sees a striking difference.

It is interesting to note the achievements of Mahinda. (1) First, the king, Tissa, is converted. (2) Second, the king donates the choicest land in the capital of Anurādhapura to the Saṅgha. Here was built the Mahāvihāra, the Great Monastery, which was to become the home of orthodoxy for nearly a millennium in Sri Lanka. (3) Third, two members of the king's family, his nephew and one of his queens, choose to become members of the Buddhist Saṅgha. The Buddhist Saṅgha is supposed to follow a certain code of conduct, a discipline, *vinaya*, which consists of statements of what should and should not be done. The *vinaya* is the code of rules and regulations by which the Saṅgha is bound. If one wants to speak of a "good monk," the people in Sri Lanka would say he follows the *vinaya* scrupulously. In the *vinaya*, there are certain observances or rites that are regularly, periodically, to be performed. (4) Fourth, objects of worship are brought down from India. For example, the bowl which the Buddha used was brought to Sri Lanka and also a sapling of the Bodhi tree under which the Buddha attained enlightenment was implanted here. It is still here and receives great veneration in Anurādhapura. (5) Next, temples, or *vihāras*, are constructed. And today in almost every Sinhala village there is a *dāgoba* (P. *cetiya*) in which relics of the Buddha or of the great saints of Buddhism are enshrined. This, too, is an object of worship. It is a tangible sign of the presence of faith. Then, (6) finally, Mahinda also translated into Sinhala the commentaries of the canonical texts, so that he initiated literacy. That is an impressive list of achievements in a few years. It was tantamount to the arrival of a whole new culture with all its institutions and instruments of communication.

Why instruments of communication? To answer this question one must know how the Buddhist Saṅgha performed. First the Saṅgha is very literate. Here we have, by Mahinda, the commentaries translated into Sinhala—books. Then the Buddhist monks, the Saṅgha, have as their duty and their custom to explain *Dhamma* (Skt. *Dharma*) to lay people, to preach (Sinhala: *baṇa*). There are also religious rites for the worshipers: there is the *dāgoba*, there are the relics, there is the *bo* tree, so there is worship and religious rites. These monasteries (*vihāras*) that were built were the centers of literacy, religious art and culture.

As I indicated above, the Mahāvihāra in Anurādhapura remained for a very long time the center of Theravāda orthodoxy in Sri Lanka. And when the capital shifted from Anurādhapura its successor institutions, the other monasteries, or *vihāras*, claimed direct descent from it, so that later on when missions were sent to Myanmar (Burma) they spoke of the traditions of the Mahāvihāra being taken. That is the first important point that I want to emphasize, that the coming of the Saṅgha under the missionary program of Aśoka is the arrival of a whole new culture. Second, the conversion of the king Devānampiyatissa and the people of Sri Lanka had far reaching consequences to the entire subsequent history of the country even down to this day. Not only was it a cultural conversion but also it had enormous political significance.

Apparently both the monks and the monarch wanted the event to be also an act of establishing an institution. For example, when the king offered a pleasure park for the Saṅgha he asked "Now is the dispensation established in Sri Lanka?" Mahinda replied "It would be established." He did not say, "It is established." Later on, every fortnight the monks would assemble and announce to themselves whether there was any breach on their part of the *vinaya* discipline, a kind of confession, and this could be done only in a sacred area (*sīmā*, "a limit") which is set apart for that ceremonially in a particular way. There cannot be a proper Saṅgha without a *sīmā*, a sacred area. So when the sacred area was delimited for *vinaya* rites, again the king asked

"Is the dispensation established?" And Mahinda replies, "Well, it is established but it has not taken deep root." And he says, "It is only when a son born of Sri Lankan parents becomes a monk and studies the *vinaya* and recites the *vinaya* that the dispensation is firmly established." That is the final requirement according to Mahinda. Therefore it is evident that they desired a deeply rooted establishment basically of the Saṅgha. That is the reason for saying that the mission of Aśoka is basically an establishment of the Saṅgha in Sri Lanka.

From then on the Saṅgha had a massive role to play in Sri Lankan history. It became the depository of tradition, both religious and historical, of learning and culture. In the historical records that the Saṅgha maintained in the temples it must have been the custom to hand over from generation to generation the chief events of the time. In those days, learning was by memorizing and important things were handed to posterity by verses learned by heart. So there is a body of stanzas written in Pali, probably, and taught by teacher to pupil. These verses were not only concerned with religion but also with events in the country, mainly in what way the king of that period helped the religion.

In the historical record the Saṅgha maintained, pains were taken to portray Sri Lanka and the Sinhala people as having a mission to fulfill. That is very interesting. What is this mission? It was the mission of perpetuating the teaching of the Buddha. There is a passage from the *Mahāvaṃsa* which begins with a record of how the Sinhala people came to Sri Lanka. This is the story of a band of 700 people from India, headed by a man called Vijaya. He was a kind of "tough guy," really, as the story indicates. He with his followers, having been banished from his father's kingdom, were put on ships to go wherever the winds took them. He landed in Sri Lanka, according to the *Mahāvaṃsa*, and that is considered the beginning of the Sinhala race. Vijaya's landing is supposed to have happened on the day that the Buddha lay dying in India—just on that day, according to the *Mahāvaṃsa*. There is a very interesting passage in the chronicle which relates that just as Vijaya landed in Sri Lanka and as the Buddha was lying in his deathbed, the Buddha knew that Vijaya had come to

Sri Lanka. The Buddha calls the king of the gods, Sakka, and, following the translation by Wilhelm Geiger, said, "Vijaya, son of king Sīnhabāhu, is come to Laṅkā from the country of Lāḷa [India], together with seven hundred followers. In Laṅkā, O lord of gods, will my religion [*sāsana*] be established, therefore carefully protect him with his followers and Laṅkā."[57] In other words, the Chronicle describes a mission to the Sinhala people. The Chronicle continues to say that the lord of the gods asked another god ("to the god who is in colour like the lotus," i.e., Viṣṇu) to be the protector or guardian of the country. The Buddha, according to the Chronicle, has foreseen that Sri Lanka would be a place where Buddhism would be protected with a particular great god to be the guardian of the country.

This is what I would call the establishment of an ideology. If you examine the notion of an ideology you will find that it is sometimes defined as a body of concepts given to justify a certain social and political arrangement—a view underlying a specific way of life. An ideology will always justify how a group originated. It will assign a particular role to that group and it will establish a way of life which that group will live. Obviously, when the *Mahāvaṃsa* said that the Buddha himself has declared that Sri Lanka will be the repository of the *Buddhadhamma* and the Sinhala people will be the ones who look after *Buddhadhamma*, the Chronicle says that Sri Lanka will forever remain a land of Buddhists, a land where the Buddhist way of life will be followed, a land where the Saṅgha will have an important place, a significant and dominant place in the social structure. Its politics cannot depart from the ideas of the Buddha. Therefore, obviously, though unconsciously, the *Mahāvaṃsa* provides an ideology for the Sinhala people.

These events, the Buddha foreseeing Vijaya coming to Sri Lanka, and so forth, could not have occurred in the strict sense of the term. But the narration of these events, one must understand, is the expression, or the wish, the desire, the strong will of the Mahāvihāra Saṅgha to keep Sri Lanka a Buddhist

---

[57] *The Mahāvaṃsa or The Great Chronicle of Ceylon*, translated by Wilhelm Geiger, Colombo: Published by the Ceylon Government Information Department, 1960, p. 55.

country. Obviously that is a matter of far-reaching significance if two thousand and three hundred years ago an ideology had been established, and if also there was a wish to follow that ideology, there would come times when difficulties would arise and we have to see how those things were handled. Actually, if one examines the history of Sri Lanka one will find that the kings of the country and the people went along with this ideology. There are some important examples of this.

In the second century B.C., about a little more than one hundred years after the events we are describing, a war took place between the Sinhala king Duṭṭhagāmaṇu, whom Sinhala people regard as their national hero, and a Tamil king called Aḷāra. The Tamils, the other major race of the country today, also arrived in Sri Lanka, particularly in the north of the island, for trade purposes and made establishments. We really do not know the time scale. In time a Tamil king ruled the northern part of the country. There was a conflict between the Sinhalas and the Tamils, the first of a long line of conflicts. In this, the Sinhala forces led by Duṭṭhagāmaṇu had to contend against a strong Tamil force and he had to rally the Sinhala people behind him. Evidently there was no will for war at the time. How did he rally the people? His rallying cry was not for kingdom but for Buddhism. He was fighting not for the glories of kingship but in order to protect Buddhism. So you see clearly, that could rally the people. That shows that the Saṅgha had succeeded in establishing that ideology. There are scores and scores of such examples.

In the twelfth century a certain king said in an inscription, "Non-Buddhists, like the Cōḷas, (Chola: a Tamil imperial house in South India who invaded Sri Lanka) have no right to Lanka's throne." In the thirteenth century, a popular Sinhala work says that the residence of people of other beliefs in Sri Lanka will be temporary, only for a short time. If any one of them rules Lanka for some time, it goes on, the Buddha's power will not allow that rule to be established. In the eighteenth century, the main temple of Kandy, the capital at that time, in the central part of the country, sent a document on Sinhala law to the Dutch governor, who was ruling the maritime provinces. In this letter, the prelate of Kandy said the first rule is that the Sri Lankan king should not embrace any religion other than Buddhism. So we see that only a Buddhist has the right to be king in Sri Lanka and that Sinhala people have always to fight for Buddhism. That kind of attitude became solidified and strongly established. This could happen only because the Saṅgha had a dominant position in Sinhala society.

CHAPTER XXII

THE FUSION OF IDEOLOGIES

Mahinda Palihawadana

Building upon his previous talk, Professor Palihawadana broadens the scope of his consideration of ideology to refer also to a world view that includes unseen powers, and he is joined by Professor Wijayawardhana to discuss methods of dealing with these powers. Professor Palihawadana proceeds to discus astrology to complete his introductory survey of ideologies into which the Theravāda tradition entered in Sri Lanka, forming a cultural fusion. By leading us to see the merging of foundations of the secular government, methods of controlling unseen forces, and the authority of the Saṅgha, Professor Palihawadana summarizes informatively and succinctly much that we have considered in the previous chapters and provides an integrated comprehensive perspective.

In the previous chapter I discussed the coming of the Saṅgha and the establishment of a political ideology in Sri Lanka. In this chapter I want to turn to another aspect of the matter which ensues from the previous chapter, namely the fusion of ideologies in which I will be referring to aspects of the ideologies with pre-Buddhistic roots. I use the word ideology to refer to a body of concepts and beliefs which justifies and sustains the way of life of a group. Looked at from this point of view, we will find that the way of life of the Sri Lankan Buddhist is a kind of spectrum with many bands. In the previous chapter I focused attention on what I thought is the most important band, namely the political ideology which the Saṅgha worked out successfully for the Sinhala people; that is, the king shall be Buddhist. He shall protect the dispensation. And the justifying myth was that the Buddha on his deathbed saw Sri Lanka as the place where the faith would flourish, and that he entrusted Sri Lanka to the gods.

That will, however, not give us a complete picture of the way of life of the Sinhalas. So we move now to the other aspects. The Saṅgha had a well-organized system of communication and instruction through which Buddhist ideas and values were broadcast among the masses of the people. These Buddhist monks were the custodians of the people's literary education. In fact, the temple was also the school at that early time and instruction not infrequently included several secular subjects as well. One could say that the monastic order with its network of village temples was, next to the secular authority, that is, next to the king, the single most influential group in Buddhist countries like Sri Lanka.

However, it would not be correct to say that the ideology of these societies was inspired solely by Buddhism. It is not so difficult to see what sort of ideology existed in these communities from time immemorial. This ideology, which existed from most ancient times, is one that pictured the world as being peopled by numerous unseen powers including departed ancestors and planetary and astral divinities, that is, gods related to the stars and planets, and also all kinds of demonic forces, or demons, to put it plainly. They were either benevolent or malevolent towards people and towards their property and enterprises. This was the dominant belief.

To succeed in such a world of unseen powers, one had to know the art of coexisting with these beings, either appeasing them or coercing them or frightening them, as the case may be, or driving them away to safe distances, exorcizing them. One had always to have magical strength to cope with such a world. To gain such strength or otherwise to deal with these beings there were special ways and also specially trained or gifted persons, special mediators, through whom one communicated with these powers.

There are specialists to deal with these unseen powers. The planetary deities are called *grahaiyō*, and gods, *deviyō*. Demons are *yakku*. And the departed ancestors are called *pretayō*. There are several specialists in these matters called *mädurō*. For the *yakku* we have *kaṭadi*; for *deviyō* we have a person called *kapurala*. For *pretayō*, we have the *kaṭadi* to work with them. There would be some regional variations. Another very important person is the astrologist, who is called *nakṣetrakāra*.

Their method of dealing with these unseen powers is radically different from the way that Buddhist monks deal with the problems of human beings. As indicated, it is a question of gaining magical strength and satisfying these forces or frightening them or driving them away.

[*The following paragraphs are a composit of a series of comments made by Professors Palihawadana and Wijayawardhana in discussing various ceremonies.*]

There are exorcism ceremonies in which demons are dealt with. These ceremonies are organized by an *ädura* (the plural is *ädurō*), a specialist who knows how to handle these demons.

Sometimes benevolent demons are propitiated at the conclusion of a harvest and the ritual specialist dances, in full costume, the role of this demon swinging from a structure that is to represent a tree. In this same post-harvest ceremony, a malevolent demon, "black demon," *kaluyakka* is propitiated. He is known for causing trouble to young ladies. He is propitiated, also, when one who is ill does not respond favorably to treatment.

Often ceremonies are held when there is an illness in the home and a treatment has been given, which did not succeed. The family and friends would then decide that it must have been the result of a demon possessing the patient. So a ceremony would be held. The *ädura* would be consulted and he would recommend particular preparations be made in this or that way for a ceremony. When the preparations are ready, he, himself, would come to stage a ceremony, probably a night-long ceremony. Everyone, thereafter, would be satisfied that the demon has been appeased or that he has been driven away. Regularly a dancer will be dressed to represent a demon.

There are ceremonies when astral gods are involved. A person could fall ill due to some malevolent influence of some astral gods. The astrologist decides which ceremony is to be done. Clay images are made following special guidelines for preparation. They are carefully painted and thrown into water immediately following the ceremony. Plantain stalks are utilized to make structures at the ceremony compound or area.

There is a sequence in an all-night ceremony called the "lime-cutting ceremony," which usually comes in early dawn toward the end of the ceremony. The tool used to cut the areca nut in preparing betel to be chewed is used to cut the lime, which is placed at the major joints of the body of a person who is deemed to be possessed. This propitiation of the evil demons is accompanied with dancing. Dancers in this ceremony whirl a burning torch made with four balls of fire tied onto a circular frame. In this particular dance it is twirled it in a dexterous way—it is very beautiful to see. So this ceremony is connected with propitiation of evil demons and there is a lot of dancing going with it.

Fire walking is widespread. It is preceded by a ceremonial procession. Many fire walks are connected with the god Kataragama. Persons go into trance as a part of this ceremony. There is a special site in the south of Sri Lanka related in a special way with the god Kataragama, who is supposed to be presiding over the shrine there. Kataragama, also called Skanda or Murugam, is considered to be the son of the great god Śiva. Actually, as Professor Karunatillake has mentioned, Kataragama is the designation for a shrine, although basically a Hindu shrine, which is frequented by Hindus and Buddhists, and even some Christians. Although one might speak of a division between Hindus and Buddhists, Hinduism and Buddhism, there is cultural interpenetration. Kataragama is a very fine example of Hindu-Buddhist, Tamil-Sinhala cultural interpenetration. Buddhists go there in large numbers. An interesting point is that the shrine at Kataragama is managed by Sinhalas and thousands of Hindu worshipers from Sri Lanka and India come to worship the god

Kataragama there. *Kapurala* is a Sinhala word for a person who is presiding at a temple devoted to a god. Regularly a conch is blown at the beginning of this fire-walking ceremony. To prepare for this ceremony, one would begin burning logs all through the night so that by early morning, about 4:00 a.m., the fire pit would become glowing coals and would be ready for walking. The people who wish to take part in the fire-walking would go to a nearby river to bathe as a form of ritual purification. Following their ritual bath, they would engage in invocations to the god Kataragama and then they would return to the *devali*, the shrine proper. They would then walk through the charcoal, spread out about ten feet wide and about thirty to forty feet in length. One estimate has it that the temperature of a charcoal fire for a fire-walk is in the region of 1,370 degrees Fahrenheit. The temperature of the coals is so very intense that it makes it difficult to photograph well the actual ceremony because the mechanism for determining lense aperture tends to go awry except in the most technically advanced cameras. Numerous persons walk through the coals in such a ceremony.

[*Professor Palihawadana resumes*] The astrologer would, in certain instances, have nothing to do with what we have talked about. However, he is, in other settings, an enormously important man in a Sinhala village because there is a pervasive belief in astrology and there is nothing of any importance that is done without consulting astrology. It is an amazing thing. In the early Buddhist texts the Buddha has quite categorically stated that the stars have nothing to do with human destiny. He has asked, "What can the stars do?" But when we look at the Buddhist society that is Sri Lanka, we find that everybody has conveniently forgotten all of that. Why? There is a fusion of ideologies. The Buddhist monks did not really interfere with this. In point of fact, modern Buddhist monks themselves adhere to it and there are many Buddhist monks who are astrologers, that is, casting horoscopes and the like.

Every child, as soon as he or she is born, is taken by his or her parents to the astrologer. The parents give the time of birth and ask for a horoscope. Invariably this is done. And all through life, whenever there are important events in life—whether it is marriage or entering a new profession or going abroad, or starting a business—the astrologer is consulted. One of an astrologer's main tasks is to find good or auspicious times for undertaking such activities.

A rather important specialist in the village setup is the *vedamahatmaya,* "Mr. Doctor." He is the doctor, really, but not a Western-trained doctor of medicine. In our villages there is an ancient tradition of herbal medicine called *ayurveda,* which is also found in India and Nepal and other places affected by Indian culture. This person is a practitioner of a different kind because magic is not necessarily involved in his activities. *Ayurveda* has a certain magical aspect in this sense: there are the humors— phlegm, bile, wind—which, if they go out of balance, one becomes ill. The medicine prescribed is to restore the balance. And the medicine usually takes the form of herbal preparations administered to the patient. This form of medicine is known to be effective in some cases and it is said that there are no side effects. Some people prefer this form of medication precisely because there are no side effects. Not much continuing research is being done in *ayurveda* medicine in Sri Lanka. There is some interest in this procedure these days and some of the medications are being exported to Australia and to European countries. The ayurvedic doctors have something to do with magic in this sense: when they examine a patient they would give prescribed medicines but also sometimes they would say that the patient get something done with the help of one of the other specialists. So his work would fuse with one of these other practices. In the old days, this used to be the case, but now it is not necessarily so. Insofar as the other ceremonies have something to do with illness, having had an ayurvedic treatment first, the relatives might subsequently decide to have a ceremony performed even though the ayurvedic specialist might not recommend it.

It was to some degree to a society having such ideologies that Buddhism came. In contrast to these ideologies, Buddhism appealed to other instincts, to a different strand of the fabric of human consciousness. It succeeded in making conversions, but I would say not total conversion. The Sangha preached the message of the Buddha and it was widely accepted. The Sangha soon gained a social status above that of these practitioners of secular and medical skills. The greatest success of the Saṅgha was in establishing among these peoples a system of values of a higher order. Basically, this enjoined the people not to kill, not to steal, not to lie, not to violate family morals, and not to use intoxicants. These are the five precepts. Over and above this the religious communication of the Saṅgha attempted to inculcate many other values: to be kind and gentle to living beings, to value religious wisdom, to spurn noise and disturbance, to be uncompetitive, and most of all not to hanker after a great lot of things.

It was not a case of Buddhism dominating the entire cultural scene. In fact, it, in the sense of an organized religion, too, had to make important adjustments in the face of the perennial ideology. We might understand the result of this as a cultural fusion in which the Buddha and the Saṅgha were assigned the role of a countervailing spiritual power in the midst of the countless other powers, benevolent and malevolent. In the many rituals of appeasement and banishment the power of the Buddha was often invoked. This is a notion not found in the early Buddhist texts. Special Buddhistic rites also appeared that were designed to confer well-being to human beings. The development of the institutional Buddhist heritage and the practices of controlling, appeasing and banishing the unseen powers and forces indicate a fusion of ideologies in Sri Lanka.

It is important for us to note the theoretical aspect of accommodating other rites in the gambit of Buddhist practice. The religious rites of the Buddhist temple were based on a Buddhist psychological theory. While these rites were basically acts of piety and worship there was a theoretical requirement for their true fulfillment and that was that these rites should be performed not just outwardly but inwardly, "in the spirit," thus strengthening the potentiality of the participant's mind to turn away from greed, hatred, and ignorance. If a flower is offered before an image, the inward performance was the contemplation of the flower's fragility and brevity of life. So the rite is at the same time a kind of meditation, to reflect on impermanence. Now this theory of interiorizing the worthy act—that is, while physically doing it one is inwardly thinking of its meaning, significance—had wide-

ranging applications and far-reaching effects. It interpreted all
acts of charity and mercy as religious acts, and not merely as rites
done at religious shrines, because such religious acts strengthen
one's potentiality for wholesomeness.

The absence of greed, hatred, and ignorance becomes
strengthened. Popularly, however, these rites had a somewhat
different meaning also. The religious or the worthy act, in the
popular view, is a means of gathering strength in the face of the
unseen forces and powers of the universe, as we have noted.
Like any material goodness, it could be shared with others. Thus
one could appease an importunate spirit by giving him or her
religious merit that one had gathered in the course of one's life.
Professor Wijayawardhana, in "Buddhist Beliefs and Practices,"
and Professor Witanachchi, in "Lay Buddhist Rituals," have
indicated the practice of the transference of merit, the good
religious deed and its effect on one could also be shared with
others. That is a popular view. Similarly, while the Buddhistic
interpretation of the uncharitable and the socially harmful act, the
violation of the moral code, was that it strengthened the doer's
propensity to greed, hatred, and confusedness, by the wider
ideological interpretation, that is, the popular interpretation, the
social interpretation, it was a means to loss of strength in dealing
with the powers of the world. That is a kind of unconscious and
unarticulated theory.

In this system the physician, the builder, the maker of
things, the farmer, the craftsman, the artisan, all of them worked
in cooperation with the various ceremonial priests. The Buddhist
monks and all the others concurred in the common ideology
while each practiced his obvious special and technical skill.
For example, the indigenous, ayurvedic doctor, had mastered a
theory and practice over a number of years. While he diagnosed
and treated illnesses in terms of the theory of *ayurveda*, he often
would encourage the patients to take appropriate measures to
appease the planets or gods and to keep the evil powers away. We
see that in this ideological setting certain aspects of the Buddhist
teachings are used without taking its core agenda too seriously.
Thus, the thrust of the Buddha's message was that the mind
should be clear of its confusion. Now there is not much emphasis

given to what he said about this. Instead, these other practices are emphasized. Thus notions of the *saṃsāra-karma* constellation, the round of rebirths (*samsāra*) and the action (*karma*) that leads to this, are not taken in the way they were suggested or propounded, but are taken in an exaggerated way. Buddhism grants that there are other planes of existence, but does not suggest that men and women are at the mercy of beings that inhabit those planes. The Buddhist meaning of the worthy act is that it lifts the moral tone of consciousness. But in the popular ideology it almost becomes a means of gathering occult strength.

The notion of *karma* is developed in an unexpected way. It is held that astrological forces operate in such a way that the results of one's own past deeds are realized. For *karma* to be meaningful one does not have to think of other forces. *Karma* means that one's mind is affected in a certain way and when one carries that mind it has its own consequences. For example, if one's conduct has been such as to enlarge understanding then one has a mind which is wiser. To that extent, what one has done has changed one and therefore one is coping with the world in a better way. That is the basic meaning of *karma*. If one says that astrological forces, the influence of planets, also operate in such a way that one's own *karma* is realized, that is something different from the early meaning. This development amounts to a deterministic interpretation of *karma* in that it minimizes or ignores the effects of present decisions and unforeseen circumstances. Besides, the Buddha denied the notion of planetary influences.

This does not mean that there was a general loss of understanding since there is also considerable evidence of the sophisticated interpretation of the teachings. Also we cannot forget the fact that this popular ideology did not challenge the value system of Buddhism. In fact, the ideology pays its own supreme compliment to Buddhism by taking the Buddha as the spiritual power to whom all other powers were subservient. In the ceremonies dealing with demons and gods which we have briefly discussed, always the beginning is by worship of the Buddha, and Dhamma and Saṅgha. And when one asks the demon to get away from the place or from the patient, one always says "By the power of the Buddha I ask you to go away." That is an example of how two ideologies are fused.

Now, this social and ideological situation prevailed well into the modern period. In it we can see three main functional groups: (1) the secular authorities, the king, or the government, (2) the unseen powers that influenced day-to-day operations—the activities which deal with food-gathering, building one's house, attending to one's health and so forth—and (3) the spiritual authority, the Saṅgha, which was in charge of all religious educational activities.

CHAPTER XXIII

THE PROPENSITY TO VIOLENCE

Mahinda Palihawadana

*With the critical eye of a disciplined academic, the
sensitivity of a poet, the analytical skill of a surgeon,
and with the loyalty of a son of Sri Lanka, Professor
Palihawadana, with great care, unravels for us sources
of a terrible human proclivity with which we are all
familiar. He turns our attention to the ethnic conflict
between Sinhalas and Tamils, noting its political
history but also a quiet and steady process of multilevel
cultural interpenetration. He then points out the inherent
inadequacy of what he calls "measurement from ego-
sense," by which one measures all things—people and
things—from the perspective of one's own self and one's
own group. We have placed before us a response to the
question "Is there then hope for the mind besieged?"
And that response, one might gratefully acknowledge,
lies in the cultivation of awareness.*

Sometime about the year 1971 – 1972, I spent a sabbatical
year in the United States. At that time when I said I came
from Sri Lanka I could often see the hearer trying to figure out
exactly how that was. Most people ignore the information I give
and assume from my appearance that anyway I was from some
part of India. There were also other reactions. For example, as
when someone rather cleverly remarked, "Ceylon. Ah, yes, that
island in the Mediterranean." It looks as if all this has changed.
I am not sure, but it seems so. If it has happened so, it is not any

miraculous change in geography or geopolitics that makes Sri Lanka better known in the world today. The publicity Sri Lanka has received is not a reward earned for its twenty-five centuries of religion and culture, but for black weeks, months, and years of violence and unusual cruelty; a time when cruelty prevailed over culture. Cruelty above culture: let us always remember this in our discussion because the propensity for violence seems, at least to me, to be deeper than the veneer of culture with which every society parades at better times. What is important is to see this hidden dark side which fouls the affairs of humankind more starkly than the cheery side can brighten the same affairs.

Let me say right away that these events are an example of what could happen anywhere in the world today. There may be many kinds of violence: through the bow and arrow or through rockets and machine guns, but the basics of the situation are similar. It is those basics that matter. So let us ask what kind of mind these events reflect. I think that would be a proper approach to our subject because there is a dangerous trend in this age of rivalry and confrontation of great industrial powers who are interested in every corner of the globe. Because of that, everyone is concerned with the military and political issues in which these powers are embroiled. This makes our attention dangerously selective, whether it is in Sri Lanka or whether it is in Lebanon, or Iraq. The kind of thing that happens and the kind of public reaction to what happens all serve as a kind of mirror of the besieged mind, the mind that makes our turbulent times, the mind that seems to be fast losing its capacity to see things in a clear and simple way. And so it is becoming incapable of coping with the pressures issuing from within itself like from a wellspring of enormous destructive power.

Sri Lanka, lying barely twenty miles to the south of India at its closest point, is an Island of twenty-five thousand square miles. It is a multi-racial, multi-religious and predominantly bi-lingual country. The population is a little more than twenty million of whom very nearly 75% are Sinhalas. Sri Lanka Tamils constitute about 5%. Tamils of recent Indian origin are about 4%. Unlike the Indian Tamils who work on the tea estates in the central and south-central hills, the Sri Lanka Tamils are those whose forbears have been residents on the island from very early times. About 60% of the Sri Lanka Tamils are concentrated in six of the island's twenty-four districts, which lie in the northern and eastern coastal belt. Together the two groups of Tamils amount to nearly 10% of the population. Forty percent of them live among the Sinhalas and other racial groups in the south, west, northwest and central hills. The third largest ethnic group is the Muslim Moors who number about 7% of the population. With the Muslim Malays and the Burghers, the Eurasians, the little island has six distinct ethnic groups professing four faiths, that is, Buddhist, Hindu, Muslim and Christian. And there are two languages: Sinhala and Tamil. These two languages belong to different linguistic groups. Sinhala belongs to the Indo-aryan group of the Indo-European languages and Tamil is the most important member of the Indian Dravidian family of languages. The predominant Tamil districts of the island lie in close proximity to the south Indian state of Tamil Nadu, the heartland of Tamil civilization, with a population of about sixty-two million people.

When one reads the history of Sri Lanka, about two thousand three hundred years of which is fairly well attested through literary and lithic records, one is at once struck by the recurring feature of Sinhala-Tamil clashes. While Sinhala-speaking people arrived in Sri Lanka from the west and east of India around the middle of the sixth century B.C., at least so it is supposed, the first Tamils appeared in north Sri Lanka as traders arriving by ship around two hundred B.C., barely a generation after the most significant event in the history of the Sinhalas, namely, their conversion to Buddhism during the time of emperor Aśoka.

In the next forty years, following the arrival of the Tamils, that is, between 200 and 160 B.C., we see the Tamil chiefs capturing power in the kingdom. A bitter conflict emerges which ends in the first military encounter about 160 B.C. between Sinhala and Tamil kings. The protagonist is Duṭṭhagāmaṇu, a person whom the Sinhala tradition elevates to the front rank of its heroes. Since Aḷāra, the Tamil king who was regarded by both friend and foe as the epitome of royal justice, was in no sense an oppressor, the rallying cry of the Sinhala king was "Not for kingdom but for Buddhism." And in this he was actively supported by the Buddhist monks, the Saṅgha. And this seems to have remained a recurrent theme in the conflicts between the Sinhala kings and the Tamils. The Sinhalas were easily persuaded that Buddhism was endangered when Tamil power expanded. The most pious of the Buddhists, to whose religious culture violence should be distinctly abhorrent, rarely found it easy to repudiate this judgment. One should have expected for it to have been perceived that Buddhism is really endangered when its teachings are not followed. It was perhaps such perception that made Duṭṭhagāmaṇu conscience-stricken after his military successes, when it dawned on him that he flagrantly violated the first and basic precept in Buddhism—the precept not to kill—by the enormous carnage that he caused in his wars.

The Buddhist chronicle, which is written in Pali as we have noted, says, in talking about the war, that the tank in the neighborhood of the battlefield had its water turned red with the blood of the Tamil soldiers. There must have been terrific carnage. When Duṭṭhagāmaṇu was so conscience-stricken, he was assured by a leader of the Saṅgha that no fault would attach to him as those whom he put to death are not followers of the faith and therefore do not count. There is a tragic-comic statement that he killed only one-and-a-half human beings: "one" being the man who had taken refuge in the Buddha, Dhamma and the Saṅgha, and "the half" being the other man who had observed only the five precepts. Here we have the well-attested "us and them" dichotomy that racialism breeds, according to which those who are not of us are really less than human.

The political history of Sri Lanka teems with references to this kind of conflict. Once every few centuries a Tamil chief, mostly coming as an invader from the Tamil homeland in neighboring south India, would oust the occupant of the throne of Anurādhapura, the ancient Sinhala capital, and initiate a campaign of southward expansion. This is resisted by a Sinhala prince or a general until the kingdom is regained. We have instances of Tamil invasion, occupancy of the throne, and ensuing struggles with the Sinhalas in periods such as the second century B.C., the fifth century after Christ, and then in a series of invasions and conflicts between the seventh and ninth centuries.

This latter period was a period of rivalry for supremacy in south India among the Tamil royal houses of the Cōḷas and Pāṇḍyas. The kings of Sri Lanka not infrequently had a hand in these political struggles and their policy usually was to support the rivals of the dominant power in order to protect their own interests. In brief, they attempted to maintain a balance of power in south India. In the course of these struggles, Sri Lanka was repeatedly attacked by south Indian forces and the northern part of the island was frequently occupied by these invading forces. There were a few occasions when the kings of Sri Lanka attempted to cross the Palk Strait, the narrow strait that separates the two countries, and invade south India, again in the course of balance-of-power struggles. They would try to establish a prince of their own choice on the throne of Madurai or some comparable place.

The bitterest political rivalry between the Sinhala and Tamil kingdoms was during the period of Cōḷa imperial power in India in the 10th and 11th centuries. Epigraphical evidence shows that the Cōḷa kings of this period often claim to have annexed Eelam to their empire. Now "Eelam" is the word that the modern Tamil separatist guerillas are also using for that part of Sri Lanka that they want to carve out as a separate state. But in the olden days, Eelam really meant the entirety of the country. So that when the Cōḷa emperors claimed to have annexed Eelam it means that they thought that the entire country was part of the empire.

The real Cōḷa conquest of Sri Lanka began under a king called Raja Raja I, the architect of Cōḷa imperial policy. He pursued a maritime policy to extend the commerce of his country and convert the Bay of Bengal into a Cōḷa lake. The possession of Sri Lanka was no longer a buttress to his continental empire but an integral part of building up Cōḷa sea power. One of the early documents of Raja Raja I claims that he conquered Eelam. His invasion of Sri Lanka in 992 resulted in the fall and final destruction of Anurādhapura, which had been the capital of Sri Lanka for over one thousand years, and in the Cōḷa conquest of the northern part of the island, which was now organized as a Cōḷa province. Some of his inscriptions in Tamil Nadu say that regular supplies from villages in Sri Lanka were brought to the great temple of Tanjavur as a form of taxes. It was in the reign of his successor, Rajendra I, that the wider aims of Cōḷa maritime policy were unfolded. In 1017, a fresh Cōḷa expedition undertook the final conquest of Sri Lanka. One of the copper plates of Rajendra describes that he conquered the king of Sri Lanka with a fierce army and seized his territory, his crown, his queen and her crown, his daughter and all his wealth. The victorious Cōḷa general finally captured the Sri Lankan monarch himself and took him to India. Says the veteran south Indian historian N. Shastri, "Great must have been the damage that Sri Lanka sustained on the occasion," and in support he quotes the ancient chronicle of Sri Lanka. This is what the chronicle says about that war, "In all Sri Lanka, breaking open all relic chambers, (meaning the *stūpas*) they carried away many costly images of gold etc. And while they destroyed here and there all the monasteries, like blood-sucking demons, they took all the treasures of Lanka for themselves." I am referring to this passage from the ancient chronicle, but recall that I said earlier that the king Duṭṭhagāmaṇu turned the color of the water in the Anurādhapura tank red. Here one finds what was done by the Cōḷa king who invaded Sri Lanka. So both sides have been equally guilty. It took a bitter and prolonged campaign by the Sinhala king Vijayabāhu I, whom some authorities regard as the most intrepid fighter in the line of Sinhala kings, to recover control of the island from Cōḷa power about the year 1070. Thus the Cōḷa occupation of Sri Lanka lasted for 77 years at that time.

Now this pattern of events in the relations between south Indian powers and Sri Lanka—namely invasion, occupation, repulse, re-invasion—went on unabated until all south Asia was violently shaken by the arrival of the Arabs and the Portuguese. In the course of these Tamil invasions not only the garrisons and trading outposts of the Tamil powers stationed in the wake of the invasions but also the importation of mercenary soldiers by Sinhala kings from south India led to the growth of a large Tamil population particularly in the portions of the island closest to India and stretching down from there west and east along the seacoast.

This Tamil community with its own Sri Lankan characteristics has a fascinating history with its antecedents going as far back as to the third century B.C., as I have mentioned. When not caught up in the turmoil ensuing from the Indian invasions, this community usually formed the northern province of one or another principality governed by a Sinhala king, that is, it formed a part of the Sinhala kingdom. But, from the middle of the 13th century, except for a brief period of about twenty years, the Sinhala kings were not able to exercise suzerainty over the traditional areas of these Sri Lankan Tamils. So until its conquest by the Portuguese in 1620, Jaffna formed an independent kingdom in a much-divided Sri Lanka governed by Tamilian rulers for well over 250 years.

There is something that must be noted at this point, lest I give the wrong impression. In spite of the continuing presence of conflict in Sinhala and Tamil relations, there was also a process of intermixture and cultural interpenetration at all times and at all levels. Chauvinistic attitudes are not evident except when they erupt into violent conflicts. Intermarriage of Sinhala royalty and aristocracy with the nobles of south India, especially the Pāṇḍyas, went on all the while, particularly from about the 11th century onwards. So far did this process go that when the last Sinhala king, Narendrasinghe, died in 1739, the throne passed to his chief queen's brother, Kirthi Sri Rajasingha, whose family originally hailed from Madurai in south India. Actually, he was Dravidian and not a Sinhala. The family enthusiastically supported this family of Dravidian kings who enthusiastically supported the cause of Buddhism and blended with the Sinhala background with remarkable ease.

Apart from the royalty, the Sinhala and Tamils in general are also highly intermixed, both ethnically and also in religion and culture. Forms of Buddhist worship show the influence of Hindu worship. And the domestic ritual practices of Sinhalas also show marked Hindu influence. From the 10th century onwards, the Sinhala language was highly affected by Sanskrit, the theological language of the Hindu Tamils. Documents show that Buddhist institutes of learning taught both Sanskrit and Tamil. The deep-seated nature of the Hindu influence on the Sinhalas can best be seen in the observance of cult practices relating to a large number of gods—Skandha, Viṣṇu, Pattini, Gaṇapati, Sarasvatī,

Kataragama—common to both Sinhalas and the Tamils. In fact, the typical Buddhist temple is not complete without shrines to some well-known Hindu gods.

The colonial powers who invaded Sri Lanka in three waves since 1505 eventually captured control of the entire seacoast around the island. These maritime provinces were put under a single governor of Sri Lanka. The maritime provinces of Sri Lanka which the British took over from the Dutch, in 1798, constituted such a unified administration. The last independent Sri Lankan kingdom surrendered to the British in 1815. In 1948, the British relinquished their authority over Sri Lanka, ceding power to a legislature having jurisdiction over the entire island, thus restoring the *status quo ante* which obtained in the maritime provinces since the subjugation of the northern Tamil kingdom in 1620 by the Portuguese. That is to say, in 1620 the Portuguese had a unified administration of the seacoast as one single maritime province. So this ceding of sovereignty to a legislature having jurisdiction over the entire island was done regardless of whether there were two or three kingdoms before 1620.

During the course of the British administration, which lasted for one and a half centuries, the Tamil population was augmented by laborers brought from south India to work the tea estates. Nearly one million of them still remain in Sri Lanka, forming a strikingly separate band in the ethnic spectrum of the country. Both in politics and in social structure, they are distinct from the older Sri Lankan Tamil community. They are among the most deprived groups in the population. In contrast the northern Tamils had considerably widespread benefits of modern schooling under colonial rule. In consequence, it is often argued that the Sri Lankan Tamils occupy a disproportionate privileged position in the professions and in the civil service.

I have been trying to give some salient facts in this brief historical sketch that have a bearing on the present state of human relationships in Sri Lanka. Generation after generation, by word of mouth Sri Lankans have heard of these facts. One reads them in today's publications and other media presentations. Thus, there arises an historical awareness of what happened or what is supposed to have happened in earlier times. What is supposed to have happened supplies the rallying myths to the ideology of the racist's mind, which necessarily thrives on the notion of a return to the heroic age. The knowledge of historical facts is poured into a mind already conditioned—we might better say, programmed— to identify itself with a particular group, be it caste, race, class, or creed. One always tends, as a result of this, to think of oneself in terms like "I am a Sinhala," or "I am a Tamil." This social condition is inescapable. From childhood, day in and day out, one hears references to Sinhala culture, Sinhala food, Sinhala customs, Sinhala pride, Sinhala greatness, Sinhala power, the land of the Sinhalas and so on and so forth. It is the same with the Tamils. One would hear of Tamil greatness, Tamil power, pride, etc.

Nowhere in the world is a child made to realize that he is a human being among human beings. It is always the case of Sinhala or Tamil, Asian or European, white or black, upper class or middle class, and so on. This conditioning which breeds the unconscious habit of identifying with a particular group leads one to think always in terms of "us" and "them." It is to the mind that is so conditioned that society feeds the historical facts. Historical events are themselves the result of actions of people so conditioned. So, even a supposedly academic presentation of, for example, political history or dynastic history, will tend to be teeming with racial and other divisive terminology. Academic presentations of history, if one reads them carefully, are particularly full of the unconscious bias on the part of the writer, bias resulting from habits of identity. So we are always programmed to see history in "us" and "them" terms: the glory that was ours, the heroism we exhibited, our hero or our force, our warriors triumphed over them, and so on.

This is what I call "measurement from ego-sense." Such would be a proper Buddhist analysis of this phenomenon. When intellectuals equipped with this measurement of ego-sense analyze the social situation, they are led quite unawares to indulge in what I call "the statistics of perversity," statistics produced by the mind that is programmed to think in terms of "us" and "them." Such statistics are predominantly concerned with how many we are in contrast to how many they are, how much we have in contrast with how much they have, and so on. Indulgence in this exercise leads to the rousing and strengthening of elemental fears, suspicion and retaliatory urges, on the one hand, and, on the other, triumphalist hopes and visions. Thus are begotten thoughts like "Let us have it as in the days of Duṭṭhagāmaṇu," which probably racialist Sinhalas would like to say. Or "Let's have it as in the days of the Cōḷa empire," which probably a similarly minded Tamil would like to say. "This is our land, we have no other place"—a normal cry of the Sinhalas. "They are out to exterminate us"—which is how the Tamils feel. And also, "Our jobs are being taken away;" "Our children cannot enter University."

The mind which is habitually led to think in these terms sees discrimination not only where it is but also where it is not, and dangers where they are not. A mind so programmed is not aware of its own conditioning or of its illusory hopes and suspicions for which facts and statistics serve as a trigger. Thus its very social education makes the mind *ignorant* of what it ought to know best, namely itself. In the Buddha's teaching it is *this* ignorance that is at the root of our ill. This ignorance, the mind's ignorance of itself, is the positive fact of having the mind filled with the conditioning of which it itself is not aware and not the negative fact of not having access to information. It is this conditioned mind—conditioned class-wise, race-wise, group-wise—that is easily led to visceral and orgiastic reactions every now and again when confronted with situations which it measures from its deep-seated ego-sense. It is the mind which gets persuaded by the statistics of perversity which it churns out or which are churned out for it by minds even more beleaguered.

This is how I would understand what happened in Sri Lanka in the aftermath of the political freedom from the British Empire. The events from 1948, the years of independence, if seen in a clear and simple way will show us that the entirety of this catastrophic escalation of tragedy is due to the mind's inability for critical awareness, inability to liberate itself from the habits imposed by its conditioning. Whether we are Tamil or Sinhalas, or Marxists or Capitalists, we are all caught in the traps of the conditioned mind whose every reaction springs from its suicidal ego-sense, whose identification with divisive groupings are a reflection of its fear to stand alone.

Since one section of the protagonists in the racial disturbances in Sri Lanka are at least nominally Buddhists, it would be appropriate to see what is the Buddhist teaching on the mind going berserk, which is essentially what happens in this situation. The Buddha has often spoken of the mind's propensities—the word used in the Pali texts is *anusaya*—that is the aggressive propensity, the libidinal and possessive propensity, sustained by the habitual tendency of unawareness, the inclination not to see clearly. Now this, the inclination not to see clearly, is ultimately what sustains violence. It is what makes us victims of our own myths, such as the myth of our heroic age, the myths that spring from and at the same time sustain the "us and them syndrome." It is as if there is a flaw in the very texture of the mind, perhaps born of the necessities of primitive life, which habituates it to store up memories of past experiences, the necessary as well as the unnecessary. We build a store of memories from past experiences of pleasure and pain. This store is a stock of references, a residual cloud which tends to intervene in every present perception. It is this storehouse, this stock of memories of past perceptions unconsciously held, which is the source of the ego, the motor that powers the "us and them syndrome:" my race, my religion, my people, our homeland, how we ruled, how they were kept at bay—all of this springs from the ego-sense. Like a motor whose mobile power is seen only when switched on, the propensities are sources of enormous power seen only when they erupt in action. Again this phenomenon is described in the Buddhist books and the word used is *pariyuṭṭhāna*. For the propensities, the Buddha used the word *anusaya,* and for the propensities when they erupt in action the word used is *pariyuṭṭhāna*. So the phenomenon was very well known by him. Human propensities, when they so erupt, have catastrophic infective power. The frenzied man arouses frenzied others. This is the frenzy of the mob, but it is basically individual frenzy multiplied. The source is the ego with its hidden destructive propensities. We can see acts of racist mobs as a vicious circle born of a conflict of suspicions and fears. Due to the notion of the "us and them syndrome" the fears of one group lead to certain acts that give rise to fears of another group and this leads to actions which further fuel the fears of the other group. It goes round and round. Such would be a Buddhist understanding of the notions and emotions behind the "us and them syndrome" and the mob violence that it tends to create. It is possible to see the events of post-independence Sri Lanka in light of this understanding.

Independence came in 1948, and the old elites remained in their positions of power and influence for quite some time. Notions of the "us and them syndrome" surfaced soon enough. I think the whole complex development can be grasped in a few simple terms without going into detail. First comes the Buddhist complaint. There is first independence and the old civil service, trained in the English schools and so on, remaining in power— "We are so many but we have got only so much. The balance must be restored." The "them" in this complaint are the Catholics and the elite from the English schools. They monopolized the privileges. The response is to make Sinhala the official language. This, in turn, opens the door to Tamil suspicions. This is what they would say: "This is a move to edge us out. Their language is forced down our throats." This leads to the Tamil call: "Give us autonomy or a separate federalist state."

Now comes the next round of Sinhala fears. "They want to team up with their Indian kith and kin." When the Tamils asked for a separate state or for federal status for the Tamil provinces, the Sinhala fear was that the Tamils of northern Sri Lanka would team up with the Tamils of India. "We will be swallowed up." This is the Sinhala fear leading to the wave of anger and suspicion on the Tamil side. "We can never get anything from them. We must set up our own state." The Tamils thought that it was a reasonable thing to ask.

Visions on the part of the Sinhalas of what Dutthagāmanu did and of the glories of the Cōla days, on the part of the Tamils, undoubtedly played their part. The tiger of the Cōla crest is resuscitated, whether deliberately or unconsciously, by the Tamil Tigers, and the banner of Tamil nationalism is raised aloft. A tense situation rapidly escalated leading to outbursts of orgiastic violence and human tragedy on a scale that can never be conveyed in a presentation like this.

There were outbursts of violence in 1958, 1977, and again in 1980, and since, with Tamils in Sinhala areas and Sinhalas in Tamil areas being the targets of attacks. In the north, guerillas fighting for a separate state also took a large number of lives, conducted state bank robberies, destroyed state property and attacked police stations. In a surprise attack on July 23, 1983, a party of armed police personnel was ambushed and thirteen men were killed. Then, in the south, homicidal maniacs started reenacting scenes of a medieval witch hunt. Their method defies description. Hundreds of lives were lost in this barbaric frenzy. Thousands of homes were broken down and burned and property worth millions was destroyed.

But not all minds were equally frenzied. There was also the capacity for mercy. That part of the story would be best told in the words of a victim of Sinhala violence. This story will show you, in a vivid way, not only the nature of some of what happened but also a few of the undoubtedly redeeming features which unfortunately would not have received any media attention. This is a description given by a Tamil person about what happened to him.

On Monday, July 25, the day began for me like any other day. My Sinhala friend who normally looks in each evening came in to tell me that he was not feeling well and therefore not going to office. "What about the killing of the thirteen soldiers?" I asked him. He said that there had been some minor troubles near Colombo the previous night but did not think anything serious would happen. He told me that the particular group of houses we were in were safest because the Tamils lived among the Sinhalas. Mine is a sprawling housing complex. There is a large mango tree behind the first row of houses. And it is here that most of the young men congregate for their evening chats. They were chatting that day, too, and there was nothing unusual about it.

Soon a vehicle stopped and a few people got out. This appeared to fire the quiet-looking youngsters to action. And normally quiet-spoken, well-behaved, mild-mannered young men went on a spree of destruction never to be imagined. Doors were smashed open, house fittings destroyed and fridges, washing machines, record players, radios and electric cookers were thrown into big bonfires that came up in front of all the blocks. The very boys who call out to me on weekdays as I was on my way to office, "Morning Uncle," unkindly smashed the doors of my house, ransacked it and carried some of my things away and burned the rest. With meticulous care the houses of Tamils were broken into and the goods and valuables smashed and burned or looted. Where were the Tamils when this destruction and mayhem took place? They were, of course, with their Sinhala neighbors.

When my friend sent his wife and his sister to see what was happening to me, I had gone into the house of my immediate neighbor. The two of them went away satisfied that my family and I were safe. But as the mob approached, my neighbor's attitude changed. He was worried about the loud voices saying that Sinhala houses harboring Tamils would be attacked. "What can I do? You must go now." he said. The mob was now in a frenzy and drawing closer. In desperation, and giving up all thought of life, eight of us got out of the neighbor's house and ran.

With my family, I got to the side of the road. I asked them to wait there until I came. It was about 7:00 p.m. I knocked on the door of my Sinhala friend. He opened the door and looked aghast as if he had seen an apparition. "Why? What happened? Weren't you with your next-door neighbor?" he asked. Before talking any further he asked me to come in and close the door. When I told him that my family was out on the road, he asked me to bring them right in. My friend and his wife came up and told me something which kindled my eternal faith in the Sinhala people. He said whatever happened to them for keeping us in their house, they would keep us. I never saw my children and the kids so terrified as on that night when frequent threats were heard that attacks on houses harboring Tamils were imminent. My friend's neighbors decided to take turns throughout the night of July 25 just to protect me and my family. When the threats were direct, my friend and his wife stood their ground and said we would not be thrown out by the mob. "If you are to go, we go too." they maintained.

I am telling this to the world outside because there are thousands like me who are living today because their Sinhala friends protected them. I may have lost everything I owned in my life. I may not recover any of them, nor do I crave them. But because of the humaneness of my friend and his family, and the manner in which they risked their lives to look after us, hope has been kindled in us that there is a future for us in Sri Lanka, undivided, and united together with the Sinhalas.

Now that is what this man said.

As you see, the capacity for mercy was there but it was not strong enough to prevent the eruptions of the propensities to violence. It was silent and powerless where the propensity to violence was articulate and wreaking great destruction. Events make us wonder whether even the minds that have the capacity for mercy are not caught in the "us and them" mentality. For it was the presence of a pervasive climate of racism that in the first place made the atrocities possible. Unless there is a general atmosphere of racism this could not have happened. And indeed it was there. Is there then hope for the mind besieged? Hope may not be entertained as long as we do not wish to see the reality of the violence that lurks within us, as long as we argue that we are not vicious, it is the other fellow who is vicious, as long as we are content to be unaware of how we think in terms of "us and them" everywhere and at all times. But one can be honest to oneself. In deep awareness we can face the realities of the beleaguered mind. In awareness, new forces come into being and into play. Hope can be entertained. Peace is possible but only at the price of eternal vigilance, not at the movements of our supposed adversaries but at the operation of our own minds trapped in propensities to violence and to possessiveness.

CHAPTER XXIV

BUDDHISM AND THE SCIENTIFIC ENTERPRISE

Mahinda Palihawadana

Professor Palihawadana raises the question of the relation of Buddhist teachings and the developing body of scientific knowledge ever advancing into Sinhala society yet without seriously disrupting the complex strands forming the comprehensive ideology of the people. We can now see those strands clearly: karma (kamma), saṃsāra, the presence of unseen forces and powers. They have generally continued into the contemporary scene as has the Buddhist teachings. However, people in the scientific community, as well as those in the Buddhist community, both demonstrate a motivational concern with understanding how things have come to be.

Most Westerners, it seems to me, have the notion that technology was unknown to Eastern countries. I think one has to take that with a grain of salt. In Sri Lanka, especially, there was technology, especially in dealing with the river waters of the country. They constructed a sophisticated system of irrigation. Arnold Toynbee, in his *A Study of History,* has a special section dealing with the Sri Lankan *tour de force* of conquering the dry zone of the island for agriculture by constructing irrigation canals on a colossal scale, and in his words, "to compel the . . . highlands to give water and life and wealth to the plains which nature had contempt to lie fast and desolate." Actually, for some of the irrigation canals something was done that is considered a marvel to most modern engineers. For example, for the first 17

317

miles of one canal the gradient was a steady 6 inches every mile.
Now in recent times, when constructing the Mahaveli irrigation
scheme, some French engineers said that a particular spot was
an ideal spot for a particular construction like a sluice, and right
there at that site there was a sluice constructed about 800 years
or so ago. They constructed the new one a few yards away so the
archaeological remains of the former could be seen. There was
a technology, one that I call a humanistic technology because it
involved no pollution. This kind of irrigation flourished in certain
areas of India and elsewhere in Asia. In the eighth century, a
Sri Lankan engineer was invited to Kashmir for some irrigation
work.

Now regarding the enterprise of science. Since Westerners
brought the modern scientific enterprise to Asia, its story, that
is the story of science in Asia, is intimately bound up with
the story of colonialism. In the wake of colonialism came
the Christian missionaries. That is a rather tragic story. One
of the first priorities of the missionary agenda was to set up
schools to teach the scriptures, on the one hand, and to facilitate
colonial administration, on the other. They needed people who
could read and write and add and subtract and also who knew
a little bit of Portuguese or Dutch or English. The colonial
administrators recognized and supported these schools started
by the missionaries. They also set up government schools. The
long process that this venture in Western education set in motion
finally laid the infrastructure for the introduction of scientific
information and also took away from the Buddhist Saṅgha the
exclusive privilege it had enjoyed in the field of education.

Well into the early decades of the twentieth century, what
came from the West was, with some exceptions, not so much a
great lot of advanced scientific knowledge as various kinds of
finished goods and Western-inspired attitudes which were adopted
by the men and women who were converted to Christianity or
who were educated in colonial schools or in some other way
beholden to colonial authorities. Gradually, other things arrived:
the commercial setup, the agencies, the technicians, the engineers,
and so on. At first these trained persons were Europeans but later
they were trained on the native soil. One of the main changes in

the social setup that resulted from these developments is, along with the new political forces, a bureaucracy trained in the new Dutch and English schools that replaced the old order of secular authorities. And, in the post-independence developments, after 1948, the missionaries also lost their privileges as the Saṅgha had lost its privileges before in the field of education. The schools generally became secular in character.

Today, with a few exceptions, the schools are secular. Although religious instruction occupies an important part in the curriculum, that is, in schools religious instruction is compulsory—Buddhist children are to be instructed in Buddhism, Hindus in their religion, and so forth—the content of education, however, has been changing. The Asian school has taken on an increasingly modern character. The new emphases attract the most gifted students to medicine, engineering, computer science, management studies and the like. In the old setup it was likely that a considerable percentage of the talented students would have been attracted to religious or allied studies. A fair number from among them would have become members of the Saṅgha. Others, in the old setup, would have joined the more intellectual of the old secular occupations, such as becoming an ayurvedic or astrological specialist. In the old setup the brilliant students would have joined one of them. No longer is this so.

The most striking change is to be seen in the secular occupations and partly, also, in the Saṅgha. To take an example, the farmer today relies less on the plough and fertility rites than on the tractor and chemical fertilizers. The plough and fertility rites are still there, but not on the same scale as in the old days. The cleverer and more prestigious physicians are the product of a Western-style medical school rather than the herbal doctors. The ayurvedic medical system is still very popular, but prestige attaches to the Western doctor. And the brilliant young man who becomes the monk is an increasingly rare phenomenon. Does this mean that the Saṅgha is respected less? No, the Saṅgha still remains a powerful influence among the people. But that the erosion of its social prestige has taken place is undeniable. If this is not directly the result of science, it is certainly the result of other changes brought about by developments for which science has been responsible. How science has affected the religious quality of Buddhist communities is a difficult question. Some things are obvious. More than science itself, more than its methodology, its logic, or its inner nature, it is the new lifestyles that scientific achievements have generated that seem to run counter to the spirit and the value system of Buddhists. This may be because there is as yet only a comparatively small scientific community in our countries or it may be because what we still have is a fairly unsophisticated level of development in this regard, compared to industrialized countries of the West.

In any case, up to now, it is the creeping materialism of the new lifestyles that has been cutting into both the visible cultural fabric and also the intangible spiritual content of Buddhist religiosity. So far as the popular ideology in a Buddhist country like Sri Lanka is concerned, the ideology that is a fusion of Buddhist and pre-Buddhist and non-Buddhist practices, there are no distinct signs of retreat in the face of modern science. Those popular practices are still present. Perhaps there is some erosion, but they are still there. The popular ideology supported and coexisted with the feudal, hierarchical social structure in the past. Feudalism was breaking down very slowly in Sri Lanka. Today, that structure has collapsed. But the ideology remains. We have seen how the ideology extracted a few given themes from the Buddhist teachings, especially the ideas about *saṃsāra* and *karma*. These themes were useful to the ideology, to buttress its basic idea—the pervasive presence of unseen beings and forces in the universe.

Scientific materialism and Marxism would explain the universe in quite different ways. So the ideology can have nothing in common with either Marxism or scientific materialism. Where science succeeds in achieving results convincingly, for example in agriculture with the application of fertilizers and in medicine when one gives an injection and there is an immediate and visible result, the magical operations derived from the ideology fall into disuse. But the ideology is pervasive and it lives on in many spheres of life where uncertainties always exist. In spite of the fact that much can be controlled, there is also much that cannot be controlled in nature. The best evidence of the enduring nature of the old ideas is the massive popularity of astrology in spite of all that human science and all that astronomy have been doing to discredit the claims of astrology. Astrological theory is based on many mathematical calculations made hundreds of years ago. Those predictions and those calculations were a high achievement of those times, but modern astronomy does not quite agree with them. Astronomy affirms that the whole structure of astrology is founded on a false premise. But in spite of all that, astrology is tremendously popular. Nothing, up to now, has been able to dislodge it.

This ideology ignores the philosophical and psychological core of the Buddhist teaching. Although this is so, the core of the Buddhist teaching certainly affected the life of the community. The value system was accepted and followed as far as possible, human weaknesses notwithstanding. Also, in the various rites, the Buddha, Dhamma and Saṅgha were accorded a prime place.

What has been the relation of this understanding of Buddhist teaching and values and the advancing body of scientific knowledge? It is a noteworthy fact that there has been little controversy between Buddhism and science. One reason for this is that as of now we are having only comparatively simple scientific establishments. Two other factors are also worthy of our attention. First the Buddhist monk, who is the classical interpreter of Buddhism, has no mediatory role assigned to him. He is not a mediator between people and other forces. His role is basically that of an instructor. If new explanations of nature are proposed, as obviously science does, and if such explanations appear to be clothed in a strange idiom, that is, the scientific idiom, this does not necessarily matter to the monk unless it can be shown that they affect the core of the Buddha's teaching. For example, if it were thought the earth was at the center and the sun went around the earth and later it became clear that the sun was the center and the earth revolved around the sun, this would not make any difference to the Buddhist monk because a heliocentric universe is not a necessary part of the Buddhist explanation.

The core of the Buddhist teachings is about how to handle existential suffering—the first truth is *dukkha*. Now that, of course, still cannot be challenged, not in Sri Lanka. Those

Buddhist teachings have not been affected by science. Science obviously has not banished man's discontents. Nor can science convincingly prove that the agenda proposed by the Buddha will not work. The agenda was how to deal with the existential predicament and essentially it dealt with understanding that predicament and to be aware of the constant working of the inner propensities, to put it all very briefly. We cannot say that science has destroyed the foundations of that. That is one reason why there is no quarrel between science and Buddhism.

The other reason is that a considerable number of people, both in the scientific community and in the Buddhist community, have been impressed by the critical aspect of Buddhism, whatever is the ultimate value that this aspect has in the Buddhist teaching. It is widely known that the Buddha emphasized that one must be critical. There are many examples of this. For example, in one discourse, the Buddha speaks of himself and says that what he says is to be taken after examination. There are many places where he says that one must find out, must discover something for oneself and is not to take it on authority. This is the theme of the *Kalāmasutta*,[58] in which, when the Buddha arrived in a village called Kalāma, the people came to him and said that all kinds of religious teachers are saying many things; one is saying this and another is saying that. What are we to do? And the Buddha basically said, "Use your critical faculty. Do not take it on their word." And that admonition applies to the Buddha and his teaching as well. This emphasis on taking a critical view has impressed some people.

Whatever may be the ultimate value of this attitude, it must be more than the mere act of being critical. Just being critical, though it is an important, is not everything. If people in Sri Lanka had been critical of these myths of Vijaya—of the founding of the race, and all that, of the Buddha asking a god to look after the island because Buddhism would be there, which I mentioned in the talk, "The Arrival of the Saṅgha,"—they would have discovered the discrepancy between all that and the Buddha's own

---

[58]   Professor Premasiri has also drawn our attention to this *sutta* in his talk, "The Place of Ethics and Morality in Buddhist Thought."

teachings, and would have discovered that these are additions. So the critical aspect is important, but it is not enough, because what really matters is a deep awareness not only of these things but also of what is happening to oneself, what is going on constantly in oneself.

There is a common denominator between Buddhism and science, and also Marxism, which is another a critical system. And this common denominator has led several recent Buddhist scholars to treat science and Marxism quite seriously. In fact, in Buddhist studies, in the 1950s and 1960s, this was very evident. In the Buddhist community there was a definite response to scientific thought as well as to modern political thought, and a certain amount of reexamination of the roots of the Buddhist tradition to see how far they agreed with science and how far they agreed with political analyses like Marxism.

We have seen that Buddhism places strong emphasis on the understanding of the existential state of humankind. The words often used in this context are "as it is," or "as it has come to be"—one must understand the situation as it has come to be, as it exists, as it is (*yathābhūtaṃ* is the Pali word). There is no need to suppose that such understanding is necessary only in the case of the inner life, though this is primary. The primary emphasis is that one must understand the situation as it is, *yathābhūtaṃ*, of the human mind. We can extend it; anything that enlarges understanding can be considered as desirable from the Buddhist point of view. Buddhism also uses the formula of "conditioned genesis," or "dependent origination" (*paṭiccasamuppāda*), that is, to understand a thing you must understand its conditions. For example, what causes sorrow? It is said that when craving or ignorance exists, there is sorrow; craving or ignorance not existing, sorrow will not come into being. That is the basic formula, things become understood when one understands the conditions on which these things are contingent.

This basic approach agrees with science and therefore Buddhism creates a climate that is favorable to the scientific enterprise.

CHAPTER XXV

SINHALA BUDDHIST LITERATURE

G. D. Wijayawardhana

Professor Wijayawardhana presents this subject in the context of his own Buddhist awareness and the importance of Sinhala Buddhist literature for the religious life of Buddhists. Although considerably older, extant Sinhala literary sources can be dated as early as the 10th century, before an abbey was founded at the site of what has come to be known as Westminster Abbey, and this impressive, but not widely known, literary heritage has continued to flourish today. One finds in this literature beautiful devotional poetry, historical narrative, imaginative appreciation of the beauty of Sri Lanka, expository tales of Buddhist stories of old, accounts of human foibles and also much that adorns our humanity.

I would like to turn our attention to the Sinhala Buddhist literary tradition and to approach this subject as a practicing lay Buddhist, indicating the important place Buddhist literature occupies in the religious life of the average layman in Sri Lanka, which is widely known for its Theravāda Buddhist tradition, and, as of late, for its violence, which is unforgivable.

There are two major languages spoken in Sri Lanka: Sinhala and Tamil. Since almost all Buddhists are Sinhala speakers, we are, therefore, concerned with the Sinhala language and literature in this chapter.

"Who is a Buddhist?" In our traditional way of thinking, a Buddhist is a person who has gone for refuge in the Three Jewels (Skt. *triratna*): the Buddha, Dhamma, and the Saṅgha—the threefold refuge. A Buddhist is a person who has gone for refuge or advice and help in the threefold jewels. In our traditional way of thinking we are expected to pay our respects to the Buddha, Dhamma, and Saṅgha, to pay homage to them, to go to them in our hours of need, to pay our respects, to worship them, and make our offerings to them. We always have a lot of devotion (Skt. *bhakti*) towards the three, and a lot of faith (Skt. *śraddhā*) in them. These qualities of faith and devotion play a very important role in the Buddhist way of life.

One of the most important temples in Sri Lanka is the Kelaniya Temple just outside Colombo. This temple is an important center for pilgrimage, especially on significant Buddhist holidays. There one sees the Buddha image, the Bodhi tree, the *caitya* or *stūpa*, and all other constituent items of a Buddhist temple. We pay homage to the Buddha, who is no longer existent, by worshiping at his image, offering flowers, and by offering flowers to the *caitya*, which we believe to be the repository for some of his bodily relics. We also worship him by worshiping at the Bodhi tree, which is the tree under which he sat and became enlightened. We focus all our sense of respect to these objects because we can no longer worship the Buddha himself.

When we go to the temple, we worship the Saṅgha. We are expected to pay homage to the monks who perpetuate tradition, and have continuously done so for more than two thousand years by bringing the teachings of the Buddha down to us. In our view, they symbolize the very presence of the religion itself. So the Saṅgha deserves a special place of veneration. We pay our respects to them, we worship at their feet, and sit at their feet, and listen to their sermons.

So, the Buddha and the Saṅgha are there in one form or another for us to pay our respects. But how do we pay our respects to the Dhamma, the doctrine, the message the Buddha has passed down to us? Dhamma is no longer there in concrete or visible form, but only abstractly. The words of the Buddha that have been passed down to us for centuries are not the object of worship in the same way as are the Buddha and the Saṅgha. How can we pay our respects to Dhamma? We do this in the form of literature. The Dhamma is given a tangible form in the literature, in the various Buddhist texts that have come down to us over the centuries. We treat this corpus of literature with great respect because by doing so we are paying our respects to the teachings themselves which are at the foundation of Buddhism. So, in the eyes of the ordinary layman, the corpus of literature containing the teachings is indeed an object of worship because it symbolizes the teachings of the Buddha and it is there in some tangible form in the books for us to worship and to pay our respects.

Visiting a temple in Sri Lanka, one will always see the library (Sinhala: *potgula*), the collection of mostly palm leaf manuscripts which contain the teachings of the Buddha, housed in a place of special honor, perhaps in an upstairs room. The books are kept and exhibited in a respectful way, and the devotees, when they go to the temple, offer flowers and burnt incense and light an oil lamp. In that way they pay their respects to the collection of books, which in turn symbolizes the great respect they pay to the Dhamma. For us, this literature signifies the second of the chief jewels of the Buddhist heritage, the jewel of the Dhamma.

The Buddhist literary tradition in Sri Lanka has a very long history. Actually, the first extant Sinhala literary work comes down to us from the 10th century A.D. at the time when the kingdom was in Anurādhapura, our first seat of royalty, after the coming of the Sinhala Buddhist tradition. From the tenth century this literary tradition continued for a period of about ten centuries up to about the 19th century, when the kingdom was in Kandy. The Kandyan period was the last stage in the classical period.

Of course, the tradition was much older. Even though the books are not available now, we have ample evidence that there was lively literary activity when many books were written much earlier than the 10th century, perhaps as early as the 4th century. This literary activity probably goes back to the time when Buddhism was brought to Sri Lanka by Mahinda in the centuries prior to the Christian era. All in all, it is a long history. This literature was considered Dhamma personified, one of the Three Jewels.

For instance, there are occasions recorded in history when kings venerated the major Sinhala literary works. These works were carried in processions and treated with great veneration. There is also a tradition of enshrining the literary works in *stūpas* and such places purely for the sake of veneration, so people could pay homage to the texts as they would to the Buddha himself. Particularly in the Anurādhapura period, we know of many instances where the Dhamma itself was enshrined, written on copper plate and gold plate so that people could pay homage to those texts as they would pay homage to any other bodily relics of the Buddha. The texts were enshrined not so much to be taken out at a later date and to be read and checked as to whether they were authentic. They were enshrined purely as objects of veneration.

Our historical records abound with instances where kings have been patronizing the writing of books and manuscripts. The kings had the notion that they must extend this patronage for the perpetuation of Dhamma by means of writing it. Even today, the writing of Dhamma books, books containing Dhamma, is thought to be a great act of merit. Especially in the village temples, people having the financial means will employ scribes to commit Dhamma texts to writing, and in that way they would consider themselves to be earning merit by contributing to the perpetuation of Dhamma. People sometimes spend a lot of money to get these books written. Continuing this same tradition, it is considered a great act of merit to get these books printed and distributed to people on special occasions, especially around Vesak time. In this way, Dhamma can reach a vast number of people. This gift of Dhamma, *Dhammadāna*, is supposed to be the highest of all gifts, as it is written in the *Dhammapada*, "the gift of Dhamma excels all gifts." The highest gift of Dhamma would be to preach Dhamma. When a monk preaches Dhamma, he performs that supreme act of giving. The laymen, who are not in a position to preach Dhamma themselves, who are not learned enough nor conversant enough with Dhamma, consider publishing and distributing Dhamma to be equally meritorious. This way they, too, take part in making Dhamma available to many people.

Furthermore, reading the Dhamma texts is an act of merit, particularly on a full-moon *poya* day when the devotees gather at the temple and sit down to observe the eight precepts while meditating or listening to a sermon of a monk. When there is some free time, one of them will take out one of these classical literary works and read aloud to the others. This is considered to be a great act of merit, the reading of such a book aloud to an audience. Listening to the books being read aloud is meritorious as well.

One sees how much the literary element is entwined with the religious lives of the people as well as with the day-to-day life of Sinhala Buddhists. To cite an example: on a solemn and sorrowful occasion when a person dies and a funeral is held in a house, in order to provide some form of mental pacification, it is customary to read certain religious texts, for example, the *Vessantarajātakaya*,[59] the Buddhist birth story containing the life of the Buddha in his birth as Vessantara, when he performed the act of giving away his own children. This story, which is very poignant and emotional, is available as a poem. The relatives who gather on such an occasion would listen to this story read aloud by someone who is well versed in the language. Listening to this story helps people to come to terms with this death and the associated emotions by reflecting on the impermanence of life and this particular death as being a natural process, which is in this case nevertheless a sad event.

Of course, if there is any auspicious event in the house, like a wedding or upon moving, there is the *paritta* ceremony, the chanting of Buddhist *suttas* to bring about good fortune. This is another example of the corpus of Buddhist literature, in this case of particular *suttas* of the Pali canon, bringing about good fortune to an event. Thus, in daily life, in important events concerning life, literature plays an important part. It is so entwined in the lives of the people that one cannot think of a religious event

---

[59] For an English translation from the Pali text [not the Sinhala] of this story, see *The Jātaka or Stories of the Buddha's Former Births*, translated by H. T. Francis, Prof. E. B. Cowell, editor, London: Published for the Pali Text Society by Luac & Company, Ltd., 1969, V. 246 ff.

where literature does not play an active role. And this has been the situation over the centuries and even today.

One of the reasons that literature occupies such an important place in the religious life of Buddhists is that Buddhism, as it is represented in the Pali canon, is a way of life which appeals to the intellect, which is lean in its emotional or devotional content. The literature fills in this emotional gap, because the literature, particularly the Sinhala Buddhist literature, mainly deals with the life of the Buddha, episodes from his past births as a Bodhisatta and his last birth when he became a Buddha. In this way, the aim of the literature is to generate devotion and *bhakti* and to generate feelings of devotion and faith toward the Buddha, Dhamma, and the Saṅgha. I think, in the case of the Sinhala Buddhist tradition, it is this literature that adds emotional aspects to the more sober analyses of Buddhist thought.

The Sinhala Buddhist literary tradition deals mostly with the life of the Buddha and the stories of his past births in a way that helps people in their quest for a good life, for an ideal religious life of righteous living. The literature plays a very important role in fashioning the Buddhist ideal of the good life, of exemplary living. The most popular book in Sinhala Buddhist literature is the *Jātakapota*, the book of the past lives of the Buddha, how he performed meritorious acts and accumulated enough merit to become the Buddha himself at a later date. This particular book has great and broad appeal to Sinhala Buddhists, mainly because it provides a model for good living.

Sinhala Buddhist literature, by way of providing many engaging examples, offers guidance for Buddhists on how to live a virtuous life as a layman. By way of generating devotion and faith, and by setting examples of good living, the literature has come to acquire much importance in the life of Sinhala Buddhists of Sri Lanka.

CHAPTER XXVI

SINHALA BUDDHIST LITERATURE

QUESTIONS AND RESPONSES

with G.D. Wijayawardhana

Having briefly introduced the important role of Sinhala Buddhist Literature, Professor Wijayawardhana responds to broad ranging questions that show both how relatively uninformed his hearers were about the significance of this literary corpus for understanding dimensions of an impressive cumulative religious tradition and also their obvious interest in learning more.

Question: You were making the point about Sinhala Buddhist literature that it helps people to enhance their devotion and faith. How does this emotional response toward the Buddha arise without one becoming attached in a way that is not conducive to attaining a state of detachment which seems to be one's goal?

GW: Today, it is the general disposition that attaining emancipation is not possible. The primary focus is on what one can do to accumulate good deeds and to acquire merit so that, at a future state, one would be able to attain Nibbāna.

I don't think that in the mind of the average layman there is the ideal of attaining Nibbāna. There might be a set of monks who live a very religious life, particularly in hermitages, who have little contact with the outside world, and who are leading lives of meditation and reclusiveness. Perhaps, in the minds of these monks, the idea of attaining Nibbāna is present. Generally, the lay community in Sri Lanka would not consider it within their power to reach this stage. They generally believe that we are in the last stage in the dispensation of the Buddha of our era. What we are to do now is to lead a life of good deeds to accumulate merit so that at a future date, in a future birth, we can reach that state. I don't think that this stands in the way of the laity having a feeling of devotion and faith. I don't think the question of attachment arises.

Q: Were illustrations ever a part of the classical Sinhala Buddhist literature?

GW: There were no illustrations at all. Just the text was there. Sometimes a cover was illustrated with pictures from the Buddha's life, but it was never considered a part of the text.

Q: When were the *Jātaka* tales brought together?

GW: They were first written in Pali stanzas and then stories were woven with the stanzas and compiled by around the fifth century A.D. possibly by Buddhaghosa, the famous commentator. Of course, the stories are much older. They have existed in the form of folk tales in various traditions of India and were given a Buddhist appearance by altering them into a form of a *jātaka* tale. So the stories themselves are quite old. They were compiled in Pali in an orderly form around the fifth century A.D. The Sinhala translation, to which I referred, is of a much later date, around the fourteenth century A.D.

Q: Do the monks use the texts more as an example of how to live the good life rather than as an object to which to pay homage?

GW: Yes. The monks use these texts a great deal in their preaching. A monk, when preaching a sermon, may take a story from one of these texts and then expound on that story and draw a moral. In daily preaching the monks will often draw from these texts.

Q: You indicated that the literature served to fill an emotional gap during life crises, so that the people could alleviate the feeling of loss. What other parts of the Buddhist tradition in Sri Lanka today also serve to fill that gap, to alleviate feelings of loss and confusion?

GW: The reading of the *Vessantarajātakaya* in a house where a death has taken place is the most common example I can cite. Most people will read Dhamma in their times of need. Reading the texts is a form of meditation. One reads them and meditates on the teaching. This serves to calm one down in an emotional situation.

Q: Did literature ever function as a bridge to increase the acceptance of the teaching, to make it easier for the lay person to understand some more difficult teaching?

GW: There are a good number of lessons incorporated in the tales, whose purpose is primarily to explain the difficult doctrine. An example is a work called the *Dharmapradīpikā*, which means a "Lamp for the Doctrine." There are a number of books whose purpose is to explain Dhamma. Of course, these texts are more intellectual and not for the ordinary layman. The tales are more popular and better known.

Q: Are the stories of the Arahants frequently told?

GW: Yes, the Arahants are like chief disciples. Many texts have stories dealing with them, so they are incorporated into the teaching. These stories serve as an example of the good life.

Q: The first day we were here, we visited a temple and they had glass cases filled with books. It was indicated that many of them weren't published for everyone to read, they were just kept there. I was wondering if it is common for there to be texts in temples that haven't been put there to read, or is this individual to each temple, they are not shared.

GW: The practice is for each individual temple to have the main texts written on palm leaves. With the coming of printing, the texts became distributed widely. It is very unlikely that an important text is not copied. The majority of Buddhist works have come out now in print. Even after the practice of printing these texts appeared, copying them by hand on palm leaves continued to be seen as an act of merit. It is a difficult job.

Q: Are there palm-leaf texts that are considered minor works that could be variations on traditions that are less well known?

GW: No, if there are palm-leaf manuscripts that have not been subsequently printed it is unlikely that they are very old, probably dating only from the 18th or 19th centuries or later. I do not think that there are any unpublished or unprinted significant works dating beyond that period. Of course, there are palm-leaf manuscripts on ayurvedic medicine, astrology, things like that. There could be a wide range of subjects.

Q: Is memorization of the texts encouraged among the laity or is this not an issue? Is this important?

GW: Not now. At one time, the texts were handed down purely through memory. It is not considered important now.

Q: Has there ever been a tradition where people were trained to memorize the tales, and sent from village to village to tell those tales?

GW: Yes. At one time, it was the only way. Before the tradition of writing came into being, not everyone was able to read or write; only a few could read in each village. A literate person would be responsible for reading the texts to others. This then was a combination of oral and written traditions. When I was a child I remember people gathering in the temple and listening, even as recent as fifty years ago.

Q: You mentioned that in times of need, people would read the texts for comfort and to help with their concentration. As literature that represented Dhamma, could it have a power to help them?

GW: No, I don't think such a belief, that the texts had some spiritual power, exists.

Perhaps in reference to the Buddha, but not the Dhamma. I do not think people would believe the texts in themselves would possess any supernatural power.

Q: Has Sinhala literature changed over the years, has it taken different forms?

GW: Oh yes. The classical literature I mentioned was written prior to the 19th century.

Even now, religious texts continue to be written on religion and religious methods. There is a wide variety of literature, as with the Western world. Now there are Sinhala works of secular literature, such as short stories.

Q: You mentioned both the intellectual and emotional content of Sinhala Buddhist literature and seemed to stress the emotional dimension. Would there be an equivalent intellectual dimension?

GW: The role the canonical teachings play is complicated because it is somewhat removed from the layman. Although the Pali canon has been translated into Sinhala, the average layman would not have much to do with the Pali original. He or she would be moved by hearing the Sinhala translation. He would then apply it in a creative way.

Q: Was there ancient secular literature?

GW: Yes, there was. But very few were written down, perhaps ten percent. The vast majority was religious. Some of the secular works were poetry. There were books on medicine, astrology and so on, but very few.

Q: In many other religious traditions there exists a mythological literary tradition about creation, but it does not seem like that is true in the Theravāda Buddhist case.

GW: The Buddha himself faced this question of creation and said that it was extraneous to salvation, so why should we worry about creation. Of course, once again, drawing from the Hindu religious culture, Sinhala literature has texts dealing with this question. They are not authentically "Buddha's words," or *buddhavacana*, but they come from the inspiration of others. What the texts do, sometimes, is make a teaching authentic, claiming the words come from the Buddha. Actually, the Buddha never went into the question of creation. Most ideas have been drawn from the Hindu tradition and have been incorporated into Buddhist works. There are many ideas drawn from the Hindu mythology, beliefs, and so on, and they are incorporated into Sinhala Buddhist literature. Mythical stories about divinities have crept into these books and they exist, as it were, side by side with Hindu religious literature. Sometimes Hindu influence has exerted considerable force, particularly as one can see in the architectural features at Polonnaruva.

Q: Is there a tradition of poetry which is native to the island of Sri Lanka, like *haiku* in Japan?

GW: Yes, we have a very rich corpus of folk poetry which has grown from the Sinhala people, most of which is not written down but is handed down in oral form. The goal is to have it in print so more people can have access to it. Once again, the tradition, as with all aspects of our culture, came from India at many points in our history. It is not something which is totally independent of other influences. In this way it is unlike Japan. There has been a mutual influence between the island and India.

Q: In the Western Christian traditions, there has been a criticism as to the actual authorship of the New Testament epistles. Some letters attributed to Paul as the author were not written by Paul but by his followers. Has there been any textual criticism in the Buddhist tradition with regard to authorship, and whether the teachings recorded are actually from the Buddha or from his immediate disciples, or even later?

GW: Most of it is believed to be Buddha's own teachings, but of course there are certain *suttas* which are recognized to have been incorporated later and were not really spoken by the Buddha. In effect, though, they have been given the status of being words from Buddha himself. Particularly in the *Vinaya*, things have been added on at various points in time. The main texts of the *tipiṭaka* are believed to be the words of the Buddha himself. The tradition is that the venerable Ānanda, an attendant of the Buddha, was the one who listened to all of these sermons and had them in his memory. He would then recite the *suttas* and they were memorized by others and eventually were put in writing. They are the words of Ānanda who announced, *evaṃ me sutaṃ*, "thus it was heard by me." The major texts are generally believed to be the words of the Buddha himself.

Q: I have noticed in listening to the host families and others we have had speak to us, there seems to be a way of making analogies and teaching by example. Does this play a part in teaching a child what he or she needs to know?

GW: In teaching, stories play a very important role. Morals are brought out by parables and stories. Stories of the Buddha would be narrated for the sake of their moral example and content. In the teaching process I think that the examples in the parables and stories do play a leading role.

Q: I have noticed that many Sinhalas, when speaking English, will say "He is having a test," or something like that. Is there no passive tense?

GW: In spoken Sinhala there is no passive voice. However, we do have the passive voice in the written form of Sinhala. In Sinhala, there is a marked difference between the spoken and the written language. When the passive meaning is intended in the spoken language, it is conveyed in various ways, but there is no straightforward passive voice as such.

Q: Why? How did the written language come to be different?

GW: It is an interesting question, but quite difficult to explain. The written language, which has all the features of any language, was modeled on the Sanskrit and Pali grammars. The spoken language, if one takes the grammatical aspect, is a very simplified version of the written. For example, the written language is faithful to number: singular and plural. The spoken does not conjugate for number. The same verb is used for singular and plural. There are many simplifications in the spoken language. I do not know if Tamil and other languages played a role. Some scholars suggest there might be a Tamil influence. I am not sure.

Q: What language family is Sinhala?

GW: Sinhala belongs to the Indo-Aryan family. In that way, Sinhala is a sister language to Hindi, Bengali, which are languages spoken in the north of India. Grammatically and structurally Sinhala belongs to the Indo-Aryan group, derived from Sanskrit through Pali. In its vocabulary, particularly as it is spoken now, one can find quite a large proportion of

Tamil words because of the coexistence of the languages. There have been recent additions from Portuguese, Dutch, and English. Basically the structure is Indo-Aryan.

Q: In Japanese there is a definite masculine and feminine language. Does something like this exist in Sinhala? Is there a language that women would use that is different from the language that men would use?

GW: No, they all speak the same language. There are certain Indian languages which do have some added differences. In Sinhala it is all the same.

Q: This is a question from curiosity. I was talking to a man the other day on the street and when asked to tell a story, he ended up telling about his life. Is there much of an awareness of stories or fiction?

GW: I am surprised that he did not launch into a story. They are a part of our life.

Books abound with stories. The story image is very strong in the literary life of the Sinhala people. There are various characters in the folk literature, like pranksters, and other stock characters, and of the learned man who has no practical understanding of life.

One such engaging character is Andarē. Andarē is supposed to have been a court jester in the Kandyan kingdom. I do not know how much of this is really authentic, so many things have grown up around this figure. One day, it seems, he went to the palace to find that sugar had been left out to dry because it had gotten damp. Andarē asked someone what it was. In order to prevent Andarē from doing any mischief, they said it was some sand out to dry. Andarē could see that it was not sand but sugar and that these people were putting him off by lying. So he went home. On the second day, this was repeated; again they were drying this sugar. He had his son to come crying, saying that someone was dying in the family. On the third day, the same thing happened, the sugar was out drying, and he was again told it was sand. Then the son came running to him in the palace and said Father, so and so has died in the house, you are urgently summoned. He then pretended to be thoroughly grief-stricken and he said, "It is all sand in my mouth." (This is a Sinhala idiom, meaning there is nothing to eat, that one has no desire to live.) He started rolling about on the sugar and shouting, "it is all sand in my mouth" because this person has died in my house, in the meantime Andarē was eating as much sugar as he could. This was all a ruse to get the sugar.

This is an example of the stories that have grown about his practical jokes. On another occasion, a queen was very interested in this stuff called *goraka*, a fruit whose rind is so sour that we add only a little bit of it to our curry to give it flavor. The queen wanted some of this stuff, and since it was not available in the palace, she went to Andarē and asked him to get her some *goraka*. Andarē said he would bring some on the following day. In the villages, when one takes some of this stuff one ties it up in a neat bundle, like wrapping it up in coconut leaves and tying it in a bundle. This is called a *mula*, a lump or neat parcel. *Mula* has another meaning; it also means the "root" of a tree. Andarē went to the palace and reported to the queen that he had brought a *mula* of this fruit. When the queen came out and saw none of this fruit but only the root of a tree in one corner of the compound, she asked Andarē where was the *goraka* that she had asked him to bring. He pointed to the root and said that there is the *mula*. So, he was making a play on the two meanings of the word. She was deceived by this root.

Q: Is there a tradition of study of the interpretation of the texts and a value in intellectual pursuits?

GW: Certainly, yes. In the traditional temple education there is always encouragement to have intellectual discussion on philosophical points, like *karma*, or whatever. The *Abhidhamma* literature takes up problems in philosophy and deals with them from various points of view. It is not so much the concern of the people, but it is there for the intellectuals, especially the Buddhist monks, expounders of the doctrine. During part of the temple education, one is encouraged to read these books and enter discussions.

Q: It seems that astrology plays a very significant role in the lives of Sinhala Buddhists, more so in the older generations. Is the part of Sinhala literature that addresses astrology insignificant, yet part of Buddhist life?

GW: This is a very interesting phenomenon. We do believe a lot in astrology. When we begin something that is important, or undertake to do something that is significant, we try to pick a good, auspicious time; for example, the time for lighting the house and preparing the food in the New Year observances. In special ceremonies, especially wedding ceremonies, the astrological component is very important.

However, strangely enough, I do not think it has much to do with religion. As Buddhists, we take part in various observances, but astrology is not in the mainstream. It is apart from religion yet we believe in it and practice it. The two coexist. *Pirit* chanting has nothing to do with astrology. One can chant at any time. Supposing one starts building a house. Before the building commences one selects a suitable time and asks the monks to chant, and this would be something in the way of invoking a blessing. If one has chanting when the auspicious corner foundation stone is laid, it is considered positive, but it is not necessary to chant *pirit* when one lays that stone. It is something one does depending on one's belief. The two things coexist but are different. Without the *pirit* ceremony, one can consult a horoscope, and vice versa.

The same is true for the concept of demons and evil spirits which bring evil to you. People have a strong belief that there is a set of evil spirits or demons who can cause harm. There are many folk methods for getting rid of the threats of those spirits or demons. Some people go to specialists other than monks to get rid of evil spirits. Buddhism and these beliefs and practices exist side by side. These practices regarding evil spirits or demons do not receive any authority from the Buddhist tradition. It simply is this way. It is a very interesting situation here in Sri Lanka. So many religious beliefs exist side by side and still no contradiction is seen.

CHAPTER XXVII

HISTORICAL AND CULTURAL BACKGROUND OF ANURĀDHAPURA AND POLONNARUVA

A. B. Dissanayaka

Professor A. B. Dissanayaka, of the Department of Sinhala at the University of Colombo, a leading expert on the topic of his talk, situates us in space and time and demonstrates how ancient sites remain of interest to persons today because of the continuity of the Buddhist tradition in Sri Lanka. Websites containing stock pictures of both Anurādhapura and Polonnaruva are readily available and might be consulted to supplement Professor Dissanayaka's brief presentation.

Anurādhapura, situated on the bank of a river called *Malwattu-oya* in the North Central province of Sri Lanka, is considered the most important historical and cultural city in ancient Sri Lanka. The ancient city of Anurādhapura is of triple importance to us, with three reasons for its significance in our history, especially in our cultural history. First, Anurādhapura is important as the first historic capital in Sri Lanka. Second, it is important because it was the capital of Sri Lanka for the longest period. Third, it is important as the most sacred and holy ancient capital of Sri Lanka.

Anurādhapura was the first historic capital of Sri Lanka. According to our Sri Lankan chronicles, the *Mahāvaṃsa*[60]

---

[60] *The Mahāvaṃsa*, edited by Wilhelm Geiger, London: Published for the Pali Text Society by Luzac & Company, Ltd., 1958, with an English translation in *The Mahāvaṃsa or the Great Chronicle of Ceylon*, by Wilhelm Geiger, Colombo: Published by the Ceylon Government Information Department, 1960.

and the *Dipavaṃsa*,[61] both written in Pali, our historical era commences around the sixth century B.C. It is said that the first immigrants were from north India. We call them Aryans. Aryans came in search of new settlements. At first they colonized the coastal areas on the northern part of Sri Lanka, and gradually they moved into the interior. In this process small settlements were established, and then villages formed. Anurādhapura, "the city of Anurādha," originally called Anurādhagrāma, "village of Anurādha," was one of these small villages. In the fourth century, B.C., Anuradhagrāma, the village of Anurādha, was declared the first capital of Sri Lanka by the Sinhala king Pandukabhāya.

In the third century, B.C., Buddhism was introduced to Sri Lanka from India. This introduction was historically and culturally very significant. Since then all the kings, who were themselves Buddhists, patronized Buddhism. They built many things in Anurādhapura: *stūpas*, temples, monasteries, all for the welfare of the *Buddhasāsana*, or Buddhism, and of the monks. These ruins are spread widely in Anurādhapura, some of which are not excavated and are covered by jungle. Anurādhadapura is very important as the first historical capital of Sri Lanka.

Second, Anurādhapura is important because it was the capital for the longest period of Sri Lanka's history. In our past, we have had several historical capitals: Anurādhapura, Polonnaruva, Dambadeniya, Kurunegala, Gampola, Kotte, and Kandy. Of them, Anurādhapura was the capital for about one thousand and four hundred years, being established as such in the fourth century B.C. and lasting until the early eleventh century A.D. But other capitals lasted only fifty years, or a hundred years or two centuries only.

Third, Anurādhapura is important because it is the most holy and sacred ancient city of Sri Lanka. Of all the ruins and sites remaining in Anurādhapura, there are eight in particular that are considered especially holy, the "eight holy sites," *aṭamasthāna*, in Sinhala. And of all these eight sites, the first

---

[61] *The Chronicle of the Island of Ceylon or the Dipavaṃsa*, edited with an Introduction by Bimala Churn Law, Maharagama, Ceylon [Sri Lanka, *The Ceylon Historical Journal*, Vol. VII - July 1957 to April 1958, nos. 1-4, with an English translation in *ibid.*, pp. 129 ff.

to be visited by pilgrims is the Bodhi tree, which grew from a branch brought from the original Bodhi tree in Bodhgāya under which the Buddha attained enlightenment. The Bodhi tree, called in English a pipal tree, in Anurādhapura is the oldest historically documented tree in Sri Lanka, if not in the world. It is about two thousand three hundred years old. That tree is the most holy object of worship in Anurādhapura. The other holy sites are *stūpas* such as Thūpārāma, Ruvanveli, Mirisaveti, Abhāyagiri, Laṅkārāma, Jētavāna and the Isurumuniya temple. Thūpārama is the oldest *stūpa* in Sri Lanka, constructed in the third century B.C., by king Devānampiyatissa. This was at the early period of the presence of Buddhism in Sri Lanka. This *stūpa* is architecturally significant in that normally a *stūpa* would have a square base, while this one has a circular or round base. Also of significance are the circular rings of pillars originally meant to support a dome shaped roof over the *stūpa*. In Sinhala, we refer to this type of *stūpa* as *Vatadāgē*, meaning "round relic house."

The Ruvanveli *stūpa*, one of the biggest *stūpas* in Anurādhapura, was, according to the *Mahāvaṃsa*, originally constructed entirely of bricks in the second century, B.C., by king Duṭṭhagāmaṇu. This *stūpa* was in ruins in the last century and has been renovated and painted in white. Daily, pilgrims arrive there to pay homage, to observe *sil*, the precepts, while clad in white clothes. Around the terrace of the *stūpa* is a row of elephants made of bricks, mortar, and masonry giving the impression that the *stūpa* is being supported by elephants. Every year, there are many pilgrims from all over Sri Lanka, from India, Myanmar (Burma), Siam (Thailand) and other Asian countries coming to Anuradhapura, especially during the month of June on the full moon day, which we call *Poson Pōya*, which commemorates the coming of Arahant Mahinda, the son of the great king Aśoka of India, to Sri Lanka and the introduction of *Buddhadhamma* in Sri Lanka.

There is a site about seven or eight miles eastward from Anurādhapura that is important historically and culturally, namely, Mihintalē. An isolated, hilly site full of ruins of monasteries, *stūpas*, hospitals, in the middle of a flat plain, Mihintalē marks the spot where Mahinda, in the third century, B.C., spoke with the king of Sri Lanka, Devānampiyatissa, and first taught *Buddhadhamma* to him. It is the most important pilgrimage site, especially during *Poson Poya*, and many people go there to pay their respects and offer homage. At the foot of this hilly site is a small museum housing many objects recovered from the ruins of the area. There are also the ruins of a hospital complex originally constructed for the monks. According to Fa Hien, a Chinese traveling monk who came to Sri Lanka in the fifth century, A.D., there had been about three thousand Buddhist monks in this particular Mihintalē area.

Polonnaruva, the second ancient capital of Sri Lanka, is also situated in the northern part of the country, in the North Central province. After the fall of the ancient capital city, Anurādhapura, Polonnaruva became more and more important from the point of view of administration. Anurādhapura was attacked by a force from the south Indian Cōla kingdom sometime in the early eleventh century. After this invasion, Anurādhapura was under the administration of these south Indian rulers for about fifty years. While the Cōlas were ruling in Sri Lanka, many Sinhala princes set about to organize military forces. Tamil kings ruled Sri Lanka for about fifty years. During that time, Polonnaruva was their center of administration. One of these leading Sinhala princes was Vijayabāhu. He amassed an army and fought with the Cōla rulers, declaring himself to be king of Sri Lanka and established, in 1070, his capital in Polonnaruva. Since then, until 1215, Polonnaruva was the capital of Sri Lanka. During this period of about one hundred and fifty years, there were several Buddhist kings. Three kings were important for their accomplishments in agriculture and for the welfare of Buddhism: Vijayabāhu, the founder, Parakramabāhu I, who ruled for about fifty years, and Nissankamalla. These three kings erected many Buddhist temples and monasteries during their reigns. Actually the kings of the Polonnaruva period tried their level best to imitate the glory of the Anurādhapura period. For instance, when one considers such carvings as moonstones or guardstones one notes a lot of similarity. The artists of Polonnaruva imitated or copied what had been there during the Anurādhapura period.

One of the important Buddhist sites at Polonnaruva is the Galvihāra, the "stone temple," where one finds four very high-quality sculptures of the Buddha—one reclining, two seated, and one standing—created from a long, natural rock. Another significant site is the Tivankapilimagē, a very large image house built of bricks. There are many paintings on the walls of this shrine dating from about the twelfth century. Most of the paintings depict *Jātaka* stories, legendary stories of the previous births of the Buddha, and also various incidents from the life of the Buddha. In 1215 A.D., due to another South Indian invasion, the Polonnaruva period came to an end.

When we compare these two ancient cities, certain differences become apparent. At Anurādhapura, one notes that monuments and important sites are scattered all over a large area. It is a very complex area probably because Anurādhapura lasted for such a long time. But at Polonnaruva, about ninety percent of the monuments are located on an almost straight line going from north to south. There is another difference also. In Anurādhapura, more stone was used in construction than bricks—for monuments, monasteries, and other buildings. But when it comes to Polonnaruva, bricks were used for construction much more than stone. At Anurādhapura, the sculptures of moonstones and guardstones, of Buddhas and Bodhisatvas, are refined with some grace and simplicity. Possibly this was due to Theravāda notions of simplicity. There is not this refinement in Polonnaruva. One discerns some crudeness in the sculptures and carvings. Perhaps the artists of the Polonnaruva period tried too much to copy, to imitate what was created previously during the Anurādhapura period.

APPENDIX I

IN THE MONASTIC LIFE

Even today, men of Sri Lanka have been responding to the invitation of the Buddha, "Come bhikkhu," and they have continued to enter the monastic order, the Saṅgha. In this capacity, these men have served as teachers, counselors, exemplars, and friends. They have sought freedom from the bonds of an unresponsive self-oriented life and have discovered an ever fresh receptivity of others and the world around them, whether in a local temple or forest hermitage.

On Becoming a *Bhikkhu*

*Venerable Paññāsīha Mahānāyaka Thera
of the Mahāragāma Bhikkhu Training Centre*

(with Venerable Dhammavihāri, interpreter)

*The late Venerable Paññāsīha Mahānāyaka Thera, a
highly regarded senior bhikkhu in Sri Lanka, formerly
head of the well-respected Mahāragāma Bhikkhu
Training Centre, speaks about the procedures leading
to one becoming a fully ordained bhikkhu, and the
educational program of training to become a teacher and
counselor. This important training center is also a very
popular place at which many people choose to spend
poya days. We are grateful to Venerable Dhammavihāri
for serving as the interpreter for this informative talk.*

When we consider a young person desirous of entering the order to become a monk, we speak of it as "a divine vision," which is an ability to see into the minds of others. They are examined and screened, with regard to their ambition, to their quality, temperament, moods and so forth. When young persons are accepted after careful scrutiny and scanning, as it were, they are called novitiates (*sāmaṇera*) and are put through a preliminary course of training in various items, including training at the material, physical, and environmental levels, as well as the spiritual training. Then when they reach their twentieth birthday, they are tested again for graduation, or what we call a higher ordination (*upasampadā*), to gain senior status in the order. After this higher ordination, like a good medical student who graduates as a doctor, there is further training as an apprentice, working under the tutelage of a more senior monk. In this stage of training, in order to become qualified for the task of preaching to the public, one learns from a senior what to teach, how to teach, and how to conduct oneself in public. This is called "the five years of dependence upon the teacher." It is a period of compulsory dependence. One cannot leave the teacher for a minimum of five years, by which time the *bhikkhu* has shown himself competent and with the confidence to go into society and communicate his message without faltering and without defecting.

This period of probation may be extended a year or more, at the discretion of the tutor, if the pupil does not show full confidence and ability to manage by himself. What is important to note here is that it is better to undergo this training before undertaking missionary and other activity in the world outside. The graduation is a public ceremony. There is an assembly of the whole congregation of monks, and it is announced to the congregation that this pupil has completed his period of probation and that the tutor is confident that he is qualified. At this time the bond of apprenticeship is released in a public manner. When the community of monks, the Saṅgha, accept his credentials, the ability of this man to teach and guide others is established now on his ability to teach and guide himself.

The concern and the seriousness with which we look upon this aspect of training our monks is because a monk at some stage has to become a counselor, one who gives counsel to the lay community. So we take care that he is amply qualified and tested for his competence to do this. To counsel and to guide people is no easy task; anyone who does so should possess vision, maturity and responsibility. A monk must avoid hastily coming to conclusions because, to become a leader of the community and to be a counselor, it means putting people on the right track and not misleading them on the path of Dhamma. Threfore, right from the Buddha's time on, we have taken as a very serioud undertaking this responsibility of teaching others.

One can draw a parallel from the secular world, from the world of laymen, whether it be in the field of teaching, or in the practice of medicine, or in the legal profession—every apprentice has to go through a period of training; teacher training, residency, board approval, and so forth. An apprenticeship is very vital to the full growth of a trainee, and this was envisaged and understood by the Buddha as far back as 2,500 years ago. He did not want to put out into the world people lacking in competence to do the work assigned to them. This system of training has come down to us through these centuries because we are inheritors of a tradition. But during certain times, both good and bad, there has been decadence and deterioration and the work has not been done up to required standards. We are fully aware of this and that is why today, at this institution, I have undertaken to revive the ancient training method and put it right wherever it has gone wrong, and restart the work of *bhikkhu* training or training of young monks.

Our basic structure here is, as I mentioned earlier, to train young monks as novices. They are first admitted to the order and the elementary, preliminary routine is followed. Then, when they show competence, they move to the higher grade of *upasampadā* when they are ordained as a full-fledged monks, *bhikkhus*. Thereafter, when the complete their period of dependence on a teacher, they begin their service as teachers to others and as counselors to people in the affairs of the world. There is training for a dual role: one is counseling others for higher, transcendental achievements, within this life and beyond; and the other is to counsel people on down-to-earth problems. This is possible only when a monk has gone through his full training both as a novice and as a full-fledged monk.

The academic life of the trainees is a ten year program right from the initiation onwards. First we give them basic training in learning the languages required for Buddhist studies. Thereafter we also prepare the candidates for their public examinations—not ordinary public educational exams—but they are government-sponsored examinations for the use of the monks. It is a course of training called a *Prachīna Pundit* degree or Oriental degree. In working through three stages: primary, intermediate, and final, they have learned a fair amount of the teachings—the Dhamma and the discipline—which become part of their lives. And that degree, the *Prachīna Pundit*, is now recognized by the state as equal to a B.A. degree, so that one can branch off at that point to any postgraduate studies.

Our system here is self-contained because once we take students as trainees or undergraduates we do not wish to send them outside. To maintain the homogeneity of our concept of education, right from the first stages up to the graduation, we give all of our courses and guidance internally. We have seen that when the young *bhikkhus* get mixed up in secular education there is a risk of them sometimes drifting in that direction and getting degrees that are only of secular interest, unrelated to the internal monastic training. So we are careful to see that during this entire period of nine or ten years they get all the courses of training from within. After they have achieved the equal to the B.A., then we ally ourselves with the postgraduate institutes that are now available here in the country. Some of our trainees have gone on to do graduate research degrees and have done the government exams of the M.A., and M. Phil., and some of them are registered to do the Ph.D. degree.

Although the monk's education is defined within certain boundaries, it is not narrowly confined. We give the option to the *bhikku* students to sit for certain examinations conducted by outside bodies—those that can conform with our thinking. So if a monk is interested in graduating in two or three different areas of interest, it is possible for him to do so. He can prepare himself for various types of examinations. They can choose their own areas of study, such as the *Suttas*, the *Vinaya*, or the *Abhidhamma*—which is the area of philosophical studies in Buddhism—and other specializations within the program of studies. And there are monks here who have done all three courses. When all three are put together, it makes a complete set and the monk becomes a master of the *tipiṭaka*, "the three baskets" of the canonical literature.

In addition to what we call the academic study, we also recognize the need to respond to the needs of the people of Sri Lanka, that is, to their need to receive guidance with regard to the Dhamma. That need is fulfilled by training young monks to preach, to deliver sermons, to instruct people, in order that dissemination of the Dhamma, or the teaching of the Buddha, will be achieved. To that end, this form of instruction is also part of our major curriculum.

There is a pattern of observing the Buddha's day in our culture. The tradition was to observe four days of the lunar month as religious days—the four quarters of the moon: the new moon, the waxing half-moon, the full moon, and the waning half-moon. At these phases of the moon cycle, it was recorded that Buddhists went to the Buddhist temples to spend the day in prayer and worship and learning. These are referred to as the *poya* days, four times a month, where lay people would observe *sīla* and refrain from day-to-day activities. This observance enabled the people to cut themselves off from the humdrum of day-to-day living, to have some leisure in their life—leisure combined with religious pursuits.

But as time passed, people became more engaged in worldly activities so that today the practice has developed, even in Sri Lanka, to observe only the full-moon day as the *poya* day—the day to go to the temple, to spend some time in meditation, in worship, in reading. On the *poya* of "the full-moon day," there are 3,000 to 5,000 people who come here to these premises to observe this day in prayer and worship. The whole place is full, it is like a campus teeming with people of all ages.

There is one area for juniors, one for the youth, another for the elders. These three areas are separated out with blocks of buildings, as it were, and different programs maintained for each group. Although there are from 3,000 to 5,000 visitors every regular full-moon day, occasionally, as in the month of May, the Buddha's birthday, the day of his enlightenment, and of his final *parinibbāna,* which we call *Vesak,* we have as many as about 15,000 people coming out.

At these occasions there is a kind of collective work, a communion, when all people participate in religious activity together, and the activities range from acts of piety to acts of intellectual achievement and meditative experiences. They spend time meditating and listening to Dhamma, and have the emotional satisfaction of worship and prayer. Gatherings of this size are not possible in every monastery, because they do not have the facilities. But over the years we have been able to welcome these people—the children under 14 or so, the youths, and the adults and elders—in three different arenas. The programs offered are tailored to cater to the intellectual and physical ability of each group. There is a very carefully regulated system of religious instruction and training on these days of the full moon at this institution, the Mahāragāma Bhikkhu Training Centre.

Starting from the year 1886, over a century ago, throughout Sri Lanka they started a system whereby Dhamma was taught in the temples in something like "Sunday schools." We have as many as 3,000 students turning up every Sunday in this institution to learn the Dhamma as a separate discipline in addition to what they were learning in the schools. In total, there are about 1,400,000 students learning the Dhamma in Sri Lanka.

Another area of religious activity for the lay people in Sri Lanka is the observance of a practice when a death occurs in a family. Within seven days we have a funeral service to pray, as it were, for the repose of the dead. A monk delivers a sermon dealing with the question of death and what it means in life; how one should live and how one should die. At the end of this service, there is a ritual of transference of merit, that is, wishing well for the dead person in case he or she needed support from the living so that his or her journey beyond may be facilitated—a kind of booster from here. Temples in Sri Lanka do this regularly. Since we here are organized as a community of monks, we have been able to offer this service better and in a more organized way than elsewhere.

When the Buddha was living it was customary for him to stay in a retreat for about three months during the rainy season. For the other nine months, more or less, he went out from village to village, from town to town, meeting people, discussing their problems and personally counseling them in order to turn them from a bad life to a good one. We also do the same today. Operating from here as headquarters, we move to different areas. Often three or four of us go off with the Nāyaka Thera into colonization schemes at some distance where they do not have the facilities for learning the Dhamma. We spend three or four days out in the field with each one of us delivering as much as six sermons a day, going from home to home, from school to school, from village to village, carrying the message of the Buddha, how bad people can become good people, and the good can become better.

We do this out of a deep awareness that, as monks, we are not wage earners; we do not have our own wherewithal. We depend on others for our existence, for our food and our clothing. So we feel indebted to the public-at-large and seek to give back to them as we have received from them. In the spirit of gratitude we go out on our way to preach to the people, to give them something that will make them happy and better. That is how this goes in a sort of circle of giving. We receive something from them and we give back to them something much more valuable, much more rewarding.

This place is run by an organized body of lay people who do the funding and routine work, and we have started our branch institutions on the same basis. We have established similar major institutions in Mātara, in Kandy, and in Kurunegala, and also in distant places like Anurādhapura and Trincomalee.

About a half-century ago, the Buddhist world was, in a sense, spread out in different parts: here in Sir Lanka, there in India, in Southeast Asia, in China, Japan, Korea. But in 1950 the late Professor Gunapala Malalasekera had a vision of a World Fellowship of Buddhists to link together these different countries of the East and India and Southeast Asia. So the World Fellowship of Buddhists was established in celebration of the 2,500th anniversary of the Buddha's birth. The Buddha's Jayanti, about 1955, brought the whole Buddhist world together, linking up Buddhists in China, Japan, Korea, India and this country, and the countries of Southeast Asia, Myanmar (Burma), and Laos, Siam (Thailand) and so on. And we also have been able now to link up with Buddhist centers in the Western world, both in Europe and in the United States, and also in Australia.

We are able to produce from one center information received from any other part of the world. We have been able to establish, in keeping with the purpose of the founders here, a Buddhist center which can collect data, file it, and keep it available. We have been able to produce *The World Buddhist Dictionary*, now in its second reprint, providing information on all these places. We should be able to produce a center on an international level. The land has been donated and the plans are afoot to create a big center on Bauddhalokamawatha, in Colombo, where, through the modern techniques of computers and other direct communication methods, more information will be readily available for all to consult.

A Conversation at Gätembē

with Venerable Pollamurē Sorata Thera

Venerable Pollamurē Sorata Thera, who was at the time head of a very respected temple at Gätembē near the entrance of Peradeniya University, and who now has retired from that position to head the Elagolla Meditation Center, talks about his own experiences in living a monastic life in a quest for freedom from attachments and attainment of a peaceful mind. One readily sees how the advice and guidance of this kind bhikkhu-counselor has been highly valued by men and women in Sri Lanka and elsewhere.

We have this opportunity to discuss what might be of interest to students from abroad about the daily routine, day-to-day activities, in a temple or, if you prefer, the life history of a monk. I will not present a formal talk on this occasion, keeping it open for informal discussion.

Question: When someone enters the Order, what goals for his life does he have in mind? Is attaining Nibbāna a goal? Is teaching the Dhamma a goal?

Sorata Thera: The main purpose for entering the Order is to practice for Nibbāna. That is the main goal. In present-day Sri Lanka, small children may enter the Order because their parents tell them, if you would like to join the Order, we would appreciate it. By that event, even the parents gain some merit. That is the popular opinion. Further, the children themselves often like very much to be free of the household life.

In my own case, before I entered the order I lived in a village in a remote area of Sri Lanka. In early childhood, this idea had come to me that I would be a monk. I wanted to join the Order and live in a temple. Gradually, with that idea in mind I decided to be interviewed by the chief priest at a temple and to seek his advice. Some of the poorest parents in Sri Lanka like very much to give their sons to the temple, for two reasons: to gain merit, and to get a good education. The poorest people sometimes do not get the chance to receive a good education because they just do not have the necessary funds and facilities. When a child enters the Order, all the community helps the child to receive a good education.

The subjects studied are especially Sinhala, Pali, Sanskrit, Buddhism, and sometimes English. Science is also a subject. Another dimension is the development of spiritual education. That means the practice of meditation and to know how to live a life of discipline. When these two dimensions are connected, the normal educational subjects and the spiritual education, there might arise a perfect person for society.

Q: When children enter the Order, do they consider this to be a lifetime commitment, or do many, after they have received an education, leave?

ST: Some monks, after receiving their education, if they prefer to continue living as a bhikkhu, then certainly they can continue. This is my experience. I am over fifty years old. I have set aside the idea of giving up my monkhood so that I can serve the people. This is a life very free from numerous problems. I do not have any household problems, you see. I am free from all those troubles. So I can serve – I can spend my whole time in service to the people. Therefore, I prefer this monkhood.

But some monks, because of their lack of understanding, think, since they have come into the Order from childhood, that they cannot understand the lay society. They do not have the experience of lay society. So, actually, they think of lay society as possessing some special things, some luxurious things. In this context, they think, "I am suffering in this way." "I can go back home and have a good household life."

They might prefer that way. It is not prohibited, actually, for someone to go home. Even regarding myself, if I want to disrobe, I am allowed to disrobe. In Buddhism there is freedom. If someone prefers to be a monk, then he is allowed to enter this way of life. For the lay person, living in a household presents no problem for practicing Buddhism. If someone wants to attain Nibbāna, the highest goal, if he strives for that in an energetic way, he can. Even the lay person can attain that goal, Nibbāna. If we can see the arising of bad thoughts, if we can set aside all bad thoughts from our minds, then we become free from suffering. You yourself can practice this. It is no problem. Without attachment and without hate, you can set aside all those bad thoughts, and when you do this you can become free, you can find peace of mind.

Q: How does renunciation contribute to an enhanced meaning of life, a deeper meaning of life?

ST: Renunciation means to set aside our attachments to worldly things. There are many things that make up necessities for life, for example houses and such things that we have to use. But we can use all those things without attachment. Say, for instance, if I want to use this tape recorder, I can use it without attachment. If I am attached to it, then there is a problem. I can use it, take care of it, but without attachment. So, I can use things with peace of mind. In the same way, renunciation means to set aside our attachment to worldly things and worldly desires. We can use those things, but without attachment.

This temple is considered a big temple, when compared to Sri Lankan temples. But we do not have any attachment to this temple. We just use it. It is not my temple. It is a temple in which I live. This is not our temple. It is a temple where we live. We use it.

In your case, the setting might be different but the issue is the same. You might have a girlfriend or a boyfriend. You say, "This is my girlfriend," or "This is my boyfriend." What do you mean by "my?" It is attachment. When another person talks with your girlfriend or boyfriend, or when another goes to see a film or something, sitting by your girlfriend or boyfriend, what happens? Hatred and anger arise. Hatred and anger arise because of that attachment. Therefore renunciation is very important for achieving peace of mind.

Q: I have a question related to what you were just speaking about. I read a small booklet called "A Happy Married Life" and it said, within the Buddhist framework, that one of the obligations between wife and husband is fidelity. How can you expect fidelity or maintain fidelity and achieve non-attachment?

ST: That is a very nice question, actually. Now, in household life the problem arises because of one main reason: attachment, more and more attachment. That is extreme attachment. We must, to some extent, have this relationship but not with attachment. When a wife and husband live together, the problem arises, sometimes, when they do not have mutual understanding. For instance, the husband may think that he needs to experience new things. The wife also might have similar ideas. But if he cannot control his mind, then he may go further and further to find newer and different things to experience. Therefore, they both must have some discipline, their own personal discipline, with understanding.

In Buddhism there are five precepts for the lay society, the *pañcasīlas*. There, the third one, regards sexual discipline. The Buddha does not prohibit the sexual life for the lay people. But he says that there must be some limits there. Otherwise, you may suffer a lot. Therefore, in the household life the most important thing is to have mutual understanding.

If I have a girlfriend, say, I must understand that my girlfriend also likes to see someone else's beautiful face, or to smile at others. If I were to find her smiling at another boy, and if I hate this, that is my fault because I do not have proper understanding of my girlfriend, or my wife as the case may be. I must have understanding. But I can advise her, look after her, not to let her go further. This mutual understanding is very important. Also, attachment leads to confusing relationships.

Q: You used the example of a tape recorder with regard to attachment and becoming non-attached. Does that mean that it could be possible for a *bhikkhu* to live in society in a way that is, on the surface, not different from a lay person? Therefore, what would be the distinction between the lay life and the life of a *bhikkhu*? What is the difference between a lay person who tries to lead a non-attached life and a *bhikkhu*?

ST: The Buddha says that if we have some wealth or the like, we should protect it, but not become too greatly attached to it. If I say, "I am using this pen," I should use it and I should take care of it, but attachment is something else. The problem arises because of attachment. If I have a television set in my room, then if I am attached to it and something happens to it, I will tend to suffer a lot because I have too much attachment. I do not have a final, real understanding of the television set because the television set is not a permanent thing. It is also breakable. So I might try my best to take care of it to some extent. If something happens to it, I have to accept it. Now, we say, "It is my body. I like very much to feed my body for years and years, hundreds or thousands of years, and I try to protect it." But if something happens to my body, I should accept that as nature.

Attachment means that there is some ignorance, because we think if everything in the world is permanent, we should become attached to those things. We think ourselves to be permanent things. Naturally, however, the purpose of this world is not to maintain permanence. Everything is changing. We should understand the nature of things. And if we understand that impermanence is the real nature of the world, why are we attached to things? Take even this body, for instance. I shall leave this body and go someday when I die. What happens to my body? I have to leave it here. So, I am not attached to this body. Therefore, we should think in that way for the entire world, for all the things in the world. Then we have no need to become attached to those things, only to protect them and use them for our day-to-day needs. That is the way we seek to live.

Q: I have a question about meditation. It seems there might be two types. One type of meditation strives to develop *samādhi*, pure concentration, and the other type tries to develop insights, *paññā*, into various teachings of Dhamma. The second, the insights into teachings of Dhamma, seems more advanced. Do you think it is at all fruitful to engage in meditation of the second type without first being skillful in meditation of the first type?

ST: What do you prefer as the meditation object? Mindfulness or reading or something? How do you begin that meditation? Respiration?

Student Reply: Yes, mindfulness of breathing. Would that be developing *samādhi*? I find it easier simply to think about the teachings, trying to figure them out in my head.

ST: One thing to do when we start to meditate is to find a proper teacher. Without the proper guidance, we cannot do this practice. Therefore, you may have a lot of books about meditation, but you cannot meditate with the book. We need to find a meditation master. He may give you a proper object to meditate on, then you can meditate according to his guidance and in discussions with him. Then you may develop the *samādhi* and the *paññā*. Otherwise you will develop neither *samādhi* nor *paññā*, only knowledge. *Paññā* means real understanding. Knowledge means *ñāna*, gaining some knowledge through books and by listening. That is not real *paññā*.

Therefore, if someone wants to meditate, he or she must have proper guidance and, little by little, step by step – not by a sudden leap – you can gain peace of mind. Nibbāna is not a sudden leap. It is a gradual course, little by little, little by little. Therefore people say meditation is not easy. That is true, but you can do it if you undertake the practice; you must have determination.

Q: If you do not have the opportunity for proper guidance, what would you suggest?

ST: That is a wonderful question, actually. You will find proper guidance in the United States. There are meditation centers there. Also, to meditate, it is not necessary to be a Buddhist. That is a wonderful thing. Meditation is to calm down the mind, to understand the mind, the thoughts. We, ourselves, when we meditate with our Buddhist groups, we say, "Set aside the idea of Buddha." "Concentrate on breathing." If you think about the Buddha, then you meditate on Buddha, not on respiration. Therefore, it is not necessary to be a Buddhist. You can continue with your religious beliefs, but to gain peace of mind you need to find an experienced teacher with good advice and continue.

Q: In the lay life, there seems to be support for people who have problems. If someone is feeling distressed or someone is hurt, your family is there, or your friends can help or comfort you. In the Saṅgha, is there support for one another, a sense of having people to turn to or having other *bhikkhus* to help you along the way?

ST: We actually do not help others with money or other things. But everybody likes to have a peaceful mind. That is our aim. Even in getting an education, traveling from country to country, we do so to gain a peaceful mind. So, as monks, we can guide people to find peace of mind. We can help to do this through meditation. That is one way. Another way is seen when lay people have household problems. They come to our center and they talk with us personally. We try our best to give the proper advice. A very important quality in the household life is to have patience. Another is to understand each other, understanding between husband and wife, and even between the children and parents. One thing I understand, myself, is if someone has a problem, if he or she finds a person who can release that problem or transfer that problem, a person who listens to that problem, he sort of relaxes the problem, relieves the problem because here he has handed over that problem temporarily to the responsible person. Likewise, we monks also act like that responsible person. We accept all those problems. We are not keeping those problems in our minds. We are throwing them away. But we accept those problems from our friends. And they find release.

There is also support among *bhikkhus*, one *bhikkhu* toward another. Even our brother monks have problems. They have some mental problems sometimes. I find sometimes a brother monk thinks, "Why am I failing in this way? I have to set aside my goals and go for counsel." Sometimes he thinks and thinks and thinks, and is greatly troubled with a lot of suffering. So, we understand sometimes there is such a situation and we are open to have discussions in the hope that there might be a solution.

Q: Would you say that going forth and leaving the lay life is not really leaving people behind, is not leaving life with other people behind, because there is still a sense of community within the Saṅgha?

ST: In my own experience, most monks disrobe because of two or three reasons. One reason is the need to help their parents. Sometimes when parents have only one son, if he comes into the Order, then after growing old the parents do not find someone to help them. So the monks disrobe and help their parents. Even in the monkhood we can help according to our rules. It is especially mentioned that you can help your parents even if you are a monk, you can go begging alms and you can give to your parents in this way. But sometimes monks disrobe because of the needs of their parents.

Another reason is that sometimes monks find problems in the temple with the helpers. If a monk is not clever enough to satisfy the helpers, if he does not have a lot of experience, sometimes the people do not care very much about the monk. If something happens in that way, sometimes they will disrobe and return to society. Very few of them, because of thinking about sensual pleasure, disrobe. Less than one percent, after thinking about the pleasures of the outside life, disrobe.

Q: In considering *paṭiccasamuppāda*, I understand that the initial step can lead from ignorance to karmic formation, that ignorance is the root cause of it. How exactly does ignorance cause karmic formation?

ST: It is very good that you raised this question. This is actually a common question. Most Westerners tend to ask the same question. You know, *paṭiccasamuppāda* is represented as a circle. In a circle, how can you find a beginning? If you are dealing with a list, as a list, the compiler puts something first. So you could ask, why did the compiler put something first in the list? You may ask this question, why do you find "A" at the beginning of the alphabet? It is difficult to give a succinct answer. This question about "first" in *paṭiccasamuppāda* is the same. But, we should say, rather, because *paṭiccasamuppāda* is presented as a circle, there is no beginning. In *paṭiccasamuppāda*, ignorance, *avijja*, appears and one might think it is first on the list, with "old age, sickness, and death," *jātijāramaraṇa*, last. But because of "old age, sickness, and death," ignorance arises. And so it goes in a circle. My understanding is that ignorance comes first only in the sense of making a list. If you want to make a new list, you can put another one there. But the idea of a circle re-circling is important.

Q: Often people say that when persons enter the Order they are leaving the world. Is this the best way to understand what is going on?

ST: When we practice properly the discipline of a monk, we come to understand how the world works. We develop our minds to understand nature. We are not departing from the world. We are in the world, but with understanding. If we can stay in the world with understanding, there is no separating. We cannot go away from the world. It is not necessary that we go away from "the house." We should live in the house with understanding. That is very important. If I think the house is a troublesome place, full of problems, I may go to another place, but there will be problems there. Then I think I have to go to another place. There also will be problems. Therefore, wandering here and there to find peace is mad, actually. To understand oneself internally and to understand the external world is very important. This is what we are seeking in meditation. If we do not have the ability to understand our minds, we will not get beyond ignorance. We seek to understand ourselves first, our thoughts. Then we can understand the whole world. That is why the Buddha says that if you understand yourself, then you understand everything. If we can clear up this ignorance with real understanding, then the whole world is a very special place in which to live. Therefore, being a monk is not jumping from the house or fleeing from life. We become monks in order to understand. Being a monk helps us to get that understanding relatively quickly. Life as a monk is like the life of a bird, being free.

Q: With regard to our discussion about non-attachment, what is the place for emotion in the *Buddhadhamma*? For instance, a person might pass away and one feels sad about that. Is that emotion of sadness considered attachment?

ST: Yes. In Buddhism there are emotions, surely. There are good and bad emotions. Good emotions are those like loving kindness, like *saddhā*, which means the "energetic and purified mind." Those good emotions do not produce bad effects. But if you produce bad emotions, like anger and jealousy, then you will be producing bad results. Buddhism always encourages us to produce good thoughts and emotions and to minimize bad thoughts and emotions in our daily life.

Q: What distinguishes a good emotion from a bad emotion?

ST: We address this issue in terms of *puñña* and *pāpa*. *Puñña* are those activities that promote well-being for oneself and for others. *Pāpa* is just the opposite. Our discussion is good for you and for me, too. I'm also gaining something from our discussion because I am producing pleasant thoughts in my mind. In a sense, I am expressing kindness to you. So, what we are doing is *puñña*. The opposite is *pāpa*. For instance, if I started to scold you or to speak harshly to you or to say bad words here, then you and I would both suffer.

Q: How do these two ideas, *puñña* and *pāpa*, fit in with the goal of eliminating all *kamma*?

ST: Two important terms are related to your question: *puñña* and *kusala*, which you no doubt know. *Puñña* refers to a power that is produced by some good action. That power we call meritorious power. Those merits we can use in this life and throughout samsaric life; this life and the next, and so forth. We can use those merits for our welfare and the welfare of others. In that same act there is another power which we call *kusala*. *Kusala* means "skills." What skills? They are those that reduce defilements from our minds. Say, for instance, if I give *dāna* or alms to a monk, I may offer that to him with loving kindness. At the same time, I reduce my craving for this food. I offer it. This is my food, but I offer it without craving. This is *kusala*. Then again, because of that giving, that is another power to help me for my next life. That is called *puñña*. The two powers can be produced with one act. *Puñña* is helpful to continue in samsaric life, that is *kamma*. *Kusala* is important to minimize and to cut off samsaric life. So, *puñña* and *kusala* and the two powers involved can be produced with one act.

Q: How do those persons who enter the Order and choose to go into a forest hermitage play a role in the lives of the laity?

ST: Some monks prefer going to a hermitage. They hope to find peace of mind more quickly. Living in a village, we do have time to meditate, but it is limited. Some plan on returning to a village setting after finishing a successful period of meditation. In this way they make a decision to enter a hermitage setting. A great deal depends on their getting good guidance. With good guidance, they might be quite successful in doing this. If they do not get good guidance, they may spend their whole life in a jungle hermitage without successful results.

In my understanding, if we understand Dhamma it is not necessary to go to the jungle to meditate. Even in a home we can find a quiet place where we can meditate to try to understand Dhamma. Some people come here to this temple and to this hall to meditate. At the beginning they often say that this hall is not suitable for meditation because all the time there are the sounds of vehicle traffic with continuing honking of horns and screeching of breaks. But after one or two weeks, they realize themselves that this is the most important place to meditate because we can live right here in society and meditate with an understanding of the nature of this society. We can't stop these vehicles. We can't change that. Right now, we are having our discussion right here.

There is no problem with the sounds of the vehicles. This is real understanding.

So, if someone can meditate and understand and realize the reality of the world together with helping others, that is, according to my view, more important than gaining individual purification. Our life will not last long. If you are kind enough to serve people and at the same time serve yourself, then that is the *bodhisattva* ideal. If I think I may come to serve people after realization myself, then perhaps it may happen. But perhaps it may not; then I will never get a chance to serve people. Therefore, I prefer this way. That is the guidance of my monkhood.

APPENDIX II

IN FORMS OF SERVICE

Two brilliantly inspirational organizations have taken root in Sri Lanka: Marga Institute and Sarvodaya. Although Marga is best interpreted as grounded in the noble humanistic rational and intellectual pursuits, it has turned with commitment to the service of humanity and, although as an organization it does not identify itself with any one particular religious tradition, Buddhists, Hindus, Muslims, Christians, and Humanists have worked together for decades and have done so consistently for others. Although Sarvodaya, also, has not become aligned with any one religious tradition, its motivational spirit is more akin to Buddhist principles of "giving of self and of labor," for the uplift of all men and women, starting with those of us who need it most pressingly.

The presentations and discussions which follow were held at Marga Institute, Colombo, Sri Lanka, on May 25, 1992 and at Sarvodaya on the following day. References to events then current have not been altered in an attempt to represent the present-day situation in Sri Lanka. The presentations are unique in providing a reliable historical survey of the time and in representing well the continuity of Marga's contributions arising from thorough and effective development studies, and of Sarvodaya's vision of providing uplift for all.

For information on Marga Institute today, see its website:
www.margasrilanka.org,
and for Sarvodaya, see its website:
www.sarvodaya.org.

DIMENSIONS OF DEVELOPMENT IN SRI LANKA
A WELCOMING INTRODUCTION TO MARGA INSTITUTE

Victor Gunawardene

Marga Institute is committed to enhancing human development in Sri Lanka, and through an understanding of the Institute's disciplined intellectual inquiry and on-the-ground thorough analysis one can learn effective processes for doing the same elsewhere. Mr. Victor Gunawardene, a spokesperson for Marga Institute, sketches the scope of involvement and motivation of this impressive group of men and women in Sri Lanka.

On behalf of Marga Institute, let me welcome all of you. It is a pleasure to receive another group of students from Colgate University. Let me begin by briefly commenting on Marga Institute. The Marga Institute was established in 1972, as a private, nonprofit, multi-disciplinary center for development research, both within Sri Lanka as well as within the greater region. The focus of our studies has been on development issues, particularly those that arose immediately after the development decade, which began in 1960. We also have the advantage of being an independent institute which can look objectively and critically at the work of the government, of the state, as well as the work done in the private sector. For that reason, over the years, government, as well as funding agencies overseas, and non-governmental organizations too, have come to Marga Institute (1) to review governmental programs at the macro- and micro-levels, and (2) to ask Marga Institute to commission studies related to development. For instance, in 1987, the Asian Development Bank commissioned Marga Institute to make a study of what it called the "Strategy for the Accelerated Development of the Southern Province."

The southern province was the area in which the southern insurgency arose, first in 1971, and then again, beginning in 1987-1989. It was, in a sense, the area of a revolution, in the southern part of the country, similar to the insurgency in the north and east. So, the Asian Development Bank thought that through an accelerated strategy for the development of the southern province perhaps some of the problems pertaining to unemployment could be dealt with by the state. We did that study for the bank and the bank commended it and gave it to the state. That program was implemented in the southern province and beyond. It has been chosen as a model for development in other provinces also, particularly with the implementation of what is called the 13th amendment to the constitution, which provides for devolution of the administration in the provinces. We normally have nine provinces, but in the north and the east two provinces have been merged temporarily, so we curently have a total of eight provinces. These have administrative units and also units of development. This illustrates of the impact of the research studies that Marga has done.

Since the environment is a matter of much concern, a study has been commissioned by a United Nations (UN) agency, namely the "Study for the Sustainable Development in Relation to Environment Policies." That study was also commended and action was organized jointly by the Central Environmental Authority of Sri Lanka and Marga Institute. That, too, has been used by the government as a model for development studies.

Here, as in your country, there is now a requirement that before a major development project can be undertaken, there must be a preliminary assessment of the environmental impact. This is another dimension of development, careful studies for which, in our region, we are fortunate that the Asian Development Bank has entrusted to us.

The World Bank commissioned another study which would investigate the linkage between education and employment. Unemployment is a very serious problem in this country. In

1977, over 20% of the workforce was unemployed. Currently [in 1992] it is about 14%. There is both unemployment and underemployment. Here the World Bank wanted us to look at the whole structure, the spectrum of education and employment, and see how we could contribute to the linkage between the world of education and the world of employment; what shortcomings there are in the system(s); how we can best improve the skills and aptitudes of those in the educational sector and suit them better for the world of work and employment, both in the state and private sectors.

We at Marga Institute are also engaged in micro-level planning, namely, the whole process of change agents. What kind of catalyst do we require in the rural sector to bring about change, to bring about adaptation? Mrs. Myrtle Perera is in charge of our "Women and Development" program. This is a program that covers a broad spectrum of studies. Her focus has been, in particular, the contribution of women to development: income generation, in terms of knowledge, aptitude, attitudes, etc., as well as covering child studies.

Then we have social studies. We have been looking in particular, for the last few years, at the problem of aging. This again is a world-wide issue and our population is now making the transition from a predominantly young population to a population that is aging. Culturally, you might say that we are perhaps more suited than those in the West to deal with the problem of aging because we have the concept of extended family and have cultural attitudes which equip us, in a way, to deal with this problem.

Nevertheless, there are very serious economic problems, and other problems peculiar to each sector: the urban sector, the rural sector, and so on. We have done some studies sponsored by the United Nations Economic and Social Commission for Asia and the Pacific (ESCAP). We have also done a series of studies on the problem of migration. We have quite a number of people, perhaps a few hundred thousand, who go as migrants to West Asia in different capacities: some as unskilled workers, some as field workers. They make a sizeable contribution to the economy in terms of remittances. Those remittances, besides helping the state's exchequer, also help the individual families to upgrade their quality of housing, their lifestyle, to provide for the education for their children, and so on.

We also have had a program of regional cooperation which brings together a collective of scholars in the South Asian region. This program was initiated in 1978. It is called the Committee for Studies for Cooperation and Development in South Asia. In that network we have Jawaharlal Nehru University, in Delhi, the Pakistani Institute of Development Studies, the Tribhuvan University in Nepal, the Bangladesh Institute of Development Studies, and the Maldives. This collective has made an important contribution which the South Asian Association for Regional Cooperation (SAARC) has acknowledged as having been vital to the whole SAARC program. There are sixteen subject areas in the SAARC program. There is also, besides a regional dimension, an international dimension. The focus has been on South Asia since 1978, and with the creation of SAARC, increasingly we have looked at some of the issues and problems that have come up within the SAARC program as well as outside. In doing this, we have had some linkages: first with the Friedrich Naumann Stiftung in Germany and, currently, with the Frederick Ebert Stiftung, also of Germany. Likewise we have had other linkages. We have a program called "Development Information Network for South Asia" (DEVINSA). Here we have had the support of the Industrial Engineering Research Conference in Canada.

In brief, the DEVINSA program seeks to collect, collate, and annotate unpublished literature—theses, various other studies, and so on—done by scholars in the South Asian region. We have a monthly bibliography, abstracts, and an annual bibliography. This program has been in existence for five years. Marga is the focal point, linking the libraries in different universities and countries. They send related material which is edited and then we send it back. We also have a data bank. We have a statistical and a computer services unit. One collects data related to development studies; the other is storage and retrieval. We also do various statistical services pertaining to the different projects we do.

Some time ago we had a science and technology division, which was, during its short span of existence, able to make a contribution in the sphere of science and technology to village-level development. Although that science and technology division has closed down, we still have field studies. We have an experimental farm about 53 miles north of Colombo where we do work on multi-cropping, inter-cropping, animal husbandry, that is, dairy farming, poultry keeping, and aqua-culture. Besides growing a variety of vegetables we also grow a variety of fruits and flowers. The purpose of this 48-acre farm is to serve as an experiment in agricultural techniques and inputs to optimize the productivity of that plot of land. It also serves as a demonstration plot for the region. To some extent we have succeeded, in that we have trained people from the villages and they in turn have adopted these methods on the land where they live and also where they are now employed, some of them in the public sector. We produce milk, yogurt, eggs and so on, which are sold locally. Some of the produce is brought here and the members of the Institute avail themselves of that facility because it is available for below market prices. We have been affected by drought, on the one hand, and by heavy rain, on the other. This farm is located in what is called the "intermediate zone" where the rainfall is scarce for a considerable period of the year, and when it does rain, it pours, and it is subject to flooding. So, we have to contend with the vagaries of the weather. Nevertheless, we have made some progress.

Besides those broad areas of study, one might ask, what is Marga? What does it stand for? What does its name mean? Its origin is Sanskrit, *mārga*. *Mārga* means "way," or "path." Our logo, at Marga, indicates the various paths to development. So, there is a pluralism of approach, and also a pluralism of outflow. We are multi-disciplinary. We have personnel of different ideologies. We have a free form here. Politically, we are nonpartisan, but because we are nonpartisan we have the advantage of offering this forum for public discussion. For instance, we have had a program under what is called the Law and Development Studies Division, where we have discussed controversial issues which are not easily discussed outside in the country-at-large. There is a division called the Political Studies and Intourist Services Division, and one of the studies undertaken was the study of violence in Sri Lanka, between 1970 and 1990.

Reference is there made to the insurgency of 1971, and the current incidents in the northern war. We looked at criminal violence, or what we call conventional crime, and we looked at political violence, including ethnic violence. We looked at the violence of state agencies, at the violence in educational institutions, and we looked at violence in the family. That study was undertaken with funds from the Norwegian Agency for Development Cooperation (NORAD).

We have a quarterly journal, *The Marga Journal*, which is the academic publication of the institution. We also have intramural publications. There is also the *Marga Newsletter*, published quarterly, which replaced the *Marga Magazine*, which was published monthly. We also have occasional publications, such as a Five-Year report.[62] The latest report was introduced in connection with our 20th anniversary which came in March, 1992. One of our publications was a book edited by your own Professor Carter.[63] Besides the work of the five divisions, we also have other activities which we undertake which may not be of a research kind, nevertheless they seek to carry forward the knowledge we gain from research.

For instance, there is "Communication for Peace and Reconciliation" (COMPAR).

Moreover, several of us, besides formal affiliation with Marga Institute, also belong to other organizations. Examples are: South Asia Partnership, or The Committee for Religion and Peace in Asia. Mr. Bogoda Premaratna, who has visited you at Colgate, is Secretary General of that. As you know, he is a distinguished educationist, a former principal of Royal College, and Director of the U. S. Educational Foundation. He is also a Buddhist scholar. He works very closely with the Marga Institute; in particular, he directed the study of education and employment linkages, and with the Committee for Religion and Peace in Asia.

---

[62] The web-site www.margasrilanka.org/publications.html provides current information on Marga publications

[63] *Religiousness in Sri Lanka*, edited by John Ross Carter, Colombo: Marga Institute, 1979. The translation committee of Marga Institute translated this work into Sinhala as *Śrī Laṅkāvē āgamikabhāvaya*, 1985..

Among the many other activities, we link, say, with the professional associations in Sri Lanka. There is an NGO link with the Organization of Professional Associations (OPANGO, for short). We try to carry forward the work of the professionals through the medium of non-governmental organizations, NGOs. Let me say a little about our structure. At the apex is the Governing Council (GC), which currently is composed of ten members drawn from the members of the institute. The Executive Vice Chairman is currently presenting a paper on South Asia as a dynamic partner in the whole issue of development. Our current Chairman, who is the former Secretary General of the United Nations Conference on Trade and Development (UNCTAD), is Dr. Gamini Corea. Besides these two members, there are others such as our Director of Administration, Mr. M. Mazzahim Mohideen.

So, we have the Governing Council at the apex. Then we have the Executive Committee of the Governing Council (GCED), just below it, which deals with the policy matters that arise from day-to-day. The next collegial body at this time is the Board of Management, which is composed of the directors of the divisions. Each of us is responsible for administrating the divisions as well as conducting research related to the projects.

We have a staff of about one hundred people, including a core research group of about thirty-five. The rest are field workers, administrative workers, support services, and so on. We are proud of our library. It is acknowledged as one of the best libraries in Sri Lanka for its range, and research studies. The library is now open to scholars from outside the institute. It is used not only by Sri Lankan scholars but by visiting scholars as well.

We do have Fellows—researchers who are affiliated for a short period with Marga Institute to carry out their research on some aspect of Sri Lankan studies, and they profit from access to our library. It is open only during office hours: weekdays, 8:30 a.m. to 4:30 p.m. We at Marga Institute are not a closed society. We are open—ideologically, intellectually, and also in terms of access to our facilities.

SARVODAYA

Cyril Fernando

In giving an overview of the fundamental principles and multiple practices of the Sarvodaya Shramadana Movement (founded by A. T. Ariyaratne, recipient of numerous awards, among which are the Mahatma Gandhi Peace Prize from India, the Niwano Peace Prize from Japan, the Hubert H. Humphrey Award from the United States), Mr. Cyril Fernando provides examples of the theme in the title of this internationally known movement: "Giving of Labor for the Uplift of All". The Questions and Responses section elaborates the scope of involvement if this movement grounded in the social ethics of the Theravāda Buddhist tradition.

Sarvodaya is one of the largest non-governmental organizations (NGOs) in the entire world and it is easily the largest in Sri Lanka. We are essentially a movement that works among the villagers. I am really sad to find visitors coming only here to the headquarters with the head office, and it all appears as just another part of the city. There are many buildings, comfortable seating accommodations, everyone seems to be well-dressed, and there are no apparent problems for the people. But, if you go to the villages, it becomes quite different. I compare these headquarters to the mast of a ship. When the ship arrives in the harbor, what you first see is the tallest thing, the mast. But if you go down below the deck, there is a huge part of the mast that is submerged, not visible to the eye. The Sarvodaya movement is like that. The real Sarvodaya is not here, but in the villages.[64]

---

[64] Current information on Sarvodaya can be found at www.sarvodaya.org.

Sri Lanka is essentially a country of villages. We have roughly a total of 23,000 villages in Sri Lanka, out of which the Sarvodaya movement is active in over 8,000 villages at the moment. So you see, we have encompassed more than one-third of the population in Sri Lanka by our movement. This does not mean that all of these 8,000 villages are full-fledged Sarvodaya villages. The fact is that there is some form of organization, some sort of activity, some sort of program going on in these villages, and the people are motivated. The total land area is a little bit bigger than West Virginia, 25,332 square miles.

Our movement is called Laṅka Jātika Sarvodaya Śramadāna Saṅghameya (LJSSS). There is a movement aspect as well as an association aspect. The movement is something that is moving all the time forward. The association is a legally accepted body. There are two things to be observed here, therefore, but most people who are members of the association are not necessarily members of the movement. There are members of the movement who have never even heard of the association, the Sarvodaya headquarters, because they are Sarvodaya people who have accepted this way of life and try to live thereby in the various villages. The president and founder of Sarvodaya is Dr. A. T. Ariyaratna, who has received awards from many nations. There are also directors who are heads of special projects: of finance, of development, of research, and important programs in the villages.

One important program is "Sarvodaya Economic Enterprise Development Services" (SEEDS). This is something that came up recently because we felt that we had to have our own income-enriching programs if the movement is going to be self-reliant, self-sufficient. Otherwise we had to be depending solely on outside resources. So, Sarvodaya started SEEDS, under which we launched production of many things, like metal work, printing, and numerous income-producing programs. Another important program operating on the village level is "Poverty Eradication and Empowerment of the Poor" (PEEP). Still another important program is "Early Childhood Development Program" (ECDP). We believe that children should be looked after even before they are born. When they are "found" in the mother's womb itself, we start treating them, treating the mother properly, with nutrition, rest and mental encouragement, all of which help the child.

We are also active in what we call "Sarvodaya Rural Technical Services" (SRTS), a program developing appropriate technology. We have our own people functioning as trainers or leaders and they help to develop and produce what the people require: medicine, tools, and water supplies. This technology is completely in the hands of girls. The people who train, plan and help build what is needed are girls, because in Sri Lanka the mothers in the villages are very much involved in the preparation of food and working in the kitchen. It is they who are really facing the problem of clean water which is a major concern. When things break down, the women cannot always count on the young men being able to repair it. The girls are trained in this technology and they know how to set things up and make repairs. We have many training programs in many areas. We also have other small industries, the building of bridges and culverts, and so forth.

We also have what is called the "5 R" program. This program was developed because of the very tragic circumstances that have taken place in Sri Lanka ever since 1980, with both the communal clashes in the north and violence of the youth in the south. This situation called for immediate relief activities. So, the "5 R"s stand for, first, Relief. The second "R" stands for Rehabilitation, which comes next. The third "R" is for Reconstruction. The fourth "R" is for Reconciliation, to bring about reconciliation between the conflicting groups. The final "R" is called Reawakening, to re-awake them as human beings in one human family. Each stands for an aspect of assistance offered to these troubled communities. It is a very important program, especially concentrated in the areas where assistance had to be rendered, namely in the north and the east, and certain parts of the south in Sri Lanka.

These are the five important programs coming under the movement that is conducted from here, all headed by the Executive Director. Apart from this, we have independent units. We have "Sarvodaya Suwasetha," for children who are handicapped, malnourished, destitute, orphans. This is apart from the early childhood development program, which is for normal children.

We also have Sarvodaya Women's Forum, an independent movement by the women themselves, where the mothers' groups and other women get together as a movement. We also have "Śantisena," the "peace brigade." This was started as relief services in case of unexpected calamities, like cyclones, drought, and so forth. People rush into the places where aid is required and provide it. This group was developed and slowly evolved into what is now called the Peace Brigade, Śantisena, or Peace Corps, if you will. It is widely organized, and there is a special unit headed by a special person who coordinates it. There is, apart from that, Sāmodaya, a unit that helps children or adults who are addicted to drugs and smoking, and other antisocial activities. They are taken note of, are brought closer, given affection, love, care and protection, and are being rehabilitated. This is an important program, highly praised by the government. People are very appreciative of this program.

We also have what is called the Sarvodaya Legal Aid Services. Some people in rural areas are very badly off when it comes to cases of litigation. They do not have the economic means to find lawyers to speak on their behalf. What Sarvodaya Legal Aid Services does is to help the people to resolve their conflicts or problems without resorting to the courts, to have them advised and guided through a settlement and to finish it before having it all develop into a major case.

Also we have what is called Sarvodaya Śramadāna International (SSI). SSI is the last unit. This is a very, very big organization. Along with the expansion of the movement, you can expect certain drawbacks, flaws, errors that might come up. We do not claim to be completely fault-free. There may be certain places where we fall short of our expectations. But, being mindful of these shortcomings and deficiencies, we strive at our best to bring about in Sri Lanka what we call the ideal awakened society. Sarvodaya's ideal is to avoid the two extremes as mentioned in Buddhism. Lord Buddha tried both: the extreme of luxury, and then he went to the other extreme of practicing all sorts of ascetical ways of living. The secret lay in between;

the middle path. What we want for people to do is to avoid the luxurious life, affluence, a lifestyle that is free of affluence and also free of want—no poverty, no affluence in society. This is our objective.

For that, Sarvodaya has devised a program called "Ten Basic-Human-Needs Satisfaction Program." This is the program that is implemented island-wide and in all sections. People have identified what their basic human needs are: they start with the environment, then water, then food, then clothing, then housing, then communication, then fuel, then education, then cultural and spiritual needs. These are the ten basic human needs. We are trying to satisfy these with our local resources.

Sri Lanka has been abundantly blessed by nature. I am sure you will have seen already how green the country is—I am not referring to the color of the political party currently ruling. It is a beautiful green island, full of verdant pastures, varying climates, fruitful seasons. We therefore believe that we have the potential within us and within our island to meet these needs if people cut down their greed and try to satisfy their need only. If you put ahead the greed of one person, all the resources of the entire world put together will not be able to meet that. But, if you work according to the need of the people, I am sure there are enough resources on the globe that, shared cooperatively, can yield a decent living for all human beings. This is what we are trying to achieve at Sarvodaya.

QUESTIONS AND RESPONSES

Q: When visiting Marga Institute, I asked if they were following any Buddhist economic development model. They said not particularly, not actually, other than trying to take a middle path between excess of materialism and excess of falling into total isolationism. From what you have said, it appears that self-sufficiency is the theme at Sarvodaya. Are you working with Buddhist models on this?

Cyril Fernando: Yes. I think that you hit the nail on the head when you said that we are striving toward self-sufficiency. Here, at Sarvodaya, what we are attempting is not so much self-sufficiency as self-reliance. Self-sufficiency will be a question if the people are divided in their objectives. For example, if what you think is sufficient for you is limitless, then there is no way of answering that by Sarvodaya. That is why we say first comes the Sarvodaya philosophy of a contented life following the middle path. Therefore, basically and essentially we had to base ourselves on the Buddhist economic principles. Lord Buddha, I think, is one of the greatest economists that the world has seen. In one of his *suttas*, I think the *Siṅgalovādasutta*, he has said, in effect, you consume one-fourth of what you produce; two-fourths, that is, one-half, you plow back into your own industry, you invest it; and the one-fourth remaining you save for future needs. It is beautiful economics.

Q: You mentioned the need to establish a middle path between affluence and want. Does that mean that eventually the goal would be complete equal distribution of wealth and property?

CF: No, we are not going to do that ourselves. To do that is using power from above. But we are basically appealing to the intellect of the human being. He or she is left free to do whatever he or she wants. The Buddha never said "Do not do it," he said, rather, "If you do this, that will happen, if you do that, this will happen." He never said "Do not do it," or "Do this." He said, "This is the path." We at Sarvodaya show the path and we try our best to be an example to the others by doing it ourselves. Preaching is not as important as practicing. Through practice we try to show the people that there is a middle path available which is very practicable. So we cannot, like lawgivers or commanders from above, say "Do not share your wealth with other people."

It is not an equal distribution. Suppose we have a family unit, and we have a portion of rice. To divide it equally would be unfair. The father, the breadwinner, laboring for the family, has to have a little larger share. If you try to give the same share to a child who is an infant, he or she would die of indigestion. You cannot have equal distribution. This equal distribution idea is something that people have generalized.

It is not *equal* distribution. We seek to satisfy the need according to the need.

The pyramids were constructed by slave labor. How did our Buddhist kings construct the enormous *stūpas* in Anurādhapura? There is a beautiful story recorded in the *Thupavaṃsa* about the Mahāstūpa constructed in Anurādhapura by Duṭṭhagāmaṇu in the first century B.C. The king said that there is no forced labor. Anyone can come and give their labor, their *śramadāna*. The king was wise enough to understand that the people also had their material needs. He ordered that four storehouses should be built at the four cardinal points of the *stūpa*. He had them filled with all the requirements, all the dry rations. The people were told that at the end of the day, when they had toiled and labored, they should go to the stores and take whatever they wanted for their daily needs and go and prepare them. What happened? It was a beautiful thing that he did. There was no need for people to rush. There was no competition. People thought that they donated their labor for a worthy cause. If we take more than is appropriate for what we have given, then we are cheating. If we take less than what we have contributed, then we are also losing. Therefore, we are to take according to our need. If there is anything in excess in the sense of our taking less so that there would be enough to go around, in order to meet the needs of all, let that be the merit for our next life. So there was no equal distribution of their dry rations. Take according to your need, that is all.

Q: Is population control a concern, and if so what program would it fall under?

CF: We are not going to preach, as it were, population control or birth control as such, because in our culture birth control is in-built. There is no need for us to stress all that anew. Recently a Buddhist monk was asked by a Westerner that since Sri Lanka is so poor economically, why don't you preach to the people the ways of birth control. The monk replied that we do not believe in birth control, we believe in self-control. You can drive the point home to the people in their own language that, for example, these are the results if you have a large family. We have family advisors. In our children services, we have workers, focusing on preschool children, going from house to house meeting parents, telling them the effects of having a large-size family. It is really in-built as it were. We don't need to have a special program for population control.

Q: Has the population increased?

CF: Oh yes, very much. What is common to all people is happening in Sri Lanka also.

Q: What are some of the concerns in your women's forum?

CF: Children's programs, environmental protection and conservation, hygiene, and the like. We do not have "women's lib" here, because in Sri Lanka's traditional culture we never had a need for it. Women have always been accepted as equals, or more than equals. Queens sat on our thrones. Sri Lanka was the first country to have a woman as prime minister. I have been asked whether it is true that our women are so neglected that they are not even allowed to come to the dining table to eat with the family. They could, of course, if they wanted to. There are no rules to say that they cannot. My mother never ate with us. She preferred to come and go. She ate last. It was her duty to see that everyone in the family ate. I feel that this illustrated that she was indeed the head of the house.

Q: I am going to be involved in the Peace Corps in Thailand in a few months. In your judgment, have any international programs failed to adjust to the needs of Sri Lanka?

CF: What we believe in Sarvodaya is to get the people of the villages to identify their needs. We have made mistakes in the beginning because of our zeal to share. For example, when we found that sanitary conditions in a village were so poor we felt they should be given toilets. Then upon follow-up to see how things went, they had to look for the key. We asked why they hadn't used it and they replied that they were waiting for their daughter's wedding, when the future son-in-law would come to open it first. People did not feel this to be a need. We asked another why he didn't use it, and he replied that we can use a toilet only if we have enough food to fill our stomachs.

No one initially asked these villagers what they needed. Planning should always be done with the participation of the villagers. Planning, implementation, organizing and follow-up should all have the people's participation.

Q: Is Sarvodaya sponsored by the government?

CF: Oh, never.

Q: Beyond sharing and giving, what are some other factors that your movement believes work?

CF: Personal development encompasses kindness, compassionate action to remove suffering, equanimity in doing good, living without being disturbed by what others say, by loss or gain. You remain a balanced person, unshaken by outside forces. From there we go on to focus on the co-principles of the community: sharing, pleasant language, constructive activity, and equality. These are the four principles people practice for constructive social behavior.

Q: Do all of Sarvodaya's activities focus on villages or is there work done in the cities as well?

CF: Sarvodaya is trying to help all the people. At the beginning we have personality awakening. This leads to family awakening. This leads to rural awakenings and then urban awakenings. They all lead or should lead to national awakening. And this should lead to universal awakening. It is a very idealistic, utopian scheme. But we have to start somewhere.

Q: How does Sarvodaya deal with people who are not Buddhists? How does it adjust its techniques to account for the different values? I am not saying that there will be conflicts, but there are differences.

CF: I think I might be a good example. When I was in the university, I was an active member of the Christian movement. I wanted to become a padre and convert all the people in Sri Lanka to Christianity. When I got out of the university, I entered Sarvodaya. I never found anything done by the Sarvodaya moment that was comparable to Christianity. There was more going on here than in Christianity. For example, there is a passage in the Bible that I have found that instructs you to practice loving-kindness to animals. St. Paul dreamed a vision about snakes and a voice came telling him to kill and eat them. This is an issue in Christianity that we do not have in Buddhism. People come to Sarvodaya, some remain faithful to their religious heritage, but all respect Buddhism.

Q: How close are you to reaching the goal of self-sufficiency?

CF: We have a long way to go.

Q: Do other countries use Sarvodaya as a model?

CF: Yes, there are over sixty countries that have started their own groups.

APPENDIX III

WITH APPRECIATIVE AND CONSTRUCTIVE APPRAISALS

Ambassadors are like walking hour glasses, funneling like apertures information contributing to enhanced understanding first in one direction and then in another as the demands of the occasion require of them, first to turn this way and then the next. Alert Ambassadors tend to be very busy people. Two United States Ambassadors made contributions that help to fill out the scope of this collection of talks providing a glimpse of the currents of more recent Sri Lankan history.

Appendix III, "With Appreciative and Constructive Appraisals," represents talks and discussions given and led by Ambassadors Marion Creekmore and Teresita C. Schaffer to the students conducting a one-month study tour, "Living in the Buddhist heritage in Sri Lanka." Ambassador Creekmore spoke on May 26, 1992, and Ambassador Schaffer spoke on May 30, 1995. Their insights and their candid yet sympathetically constructive observations would have been blurred and distorted were references then to current events altered in an attempt to reflect an apparently more recent contemporary setting.

SRI LANKA—A *VERY* INTERESTING COUNTRY

Marion Creekmore, U.S. Ambassador

I am delighted to be here. As you probably know, a diplomat's job is to promote good relations between countries and that is to make people happy with you, and so this morning I am late because I made two Sri Lankans very happy. They have beaten the whey out of me in tennis. I am delighted that you are here and I hope you find this month to be as exciting as I think you will.

This is a *very* interesting country. You will find diversity and enlightenment, and interests here that would be hard to find elsewhere in a place as small and as compact as Sri Lanka. It is about the size of West Virginia, but it takes a little bit longer to travel from here to there than it does in West Virginia.

I know that you are going to be spending a lot of time studying Buddhism and culture in Sri Lanka, so I thought, perhaps, you should have a sense of Sri Lanka's political and economic life and how it got to be the way it is, and that this would be a good background for you. I would then be happy to entertain any kind of question you may have.

Sri Lanka has now been independent since 1948, so it is a country with more than forty years of independence. It is one of the few developing countries in the world that has been a functioning democracy since the day of independence. As you know, from your studies of the colonial period and the post colonial period, that is really rather remarkable in itself. There have been a number of elections in which power has passed peacefully from one major party to another—something we take for granted in the United States but which is fairly rare in many parts of the world. This is a very important factor to keep in mind. You should also know, as you have probably studied but perhaps may not yet fully have grasped the significance, that this system of government, this democratic system of government, almost came to an end in 1988-1989—the period when there was a Sinhala insurrection in the south with the Janatha Vimukti Peramuna (JVP), "People's Liberation Front," and at the same time there was an insurrection by the "Liberation Tigers of Tamil Eelam" (LTTE) in the northeast. It just about brought this country into anarchy.

In August of 1989, Sri Lankans could not walk out on the streets of Colombo and feel safe. In August of 1989, posters went up saying that the hospitals would close, and for three weeks the hospitals were closed. If you were a patient in the hospital, it was tough. In August of 1989, if you were a Sri Lankan man or woman and you kissed your spouse goodbye in the morning, neither of you knew if you would come back that evening.

The JVP virtually paralyzed the government. Over the next several months, however, this insurrection was brutally suppressed by the government by countering terror with terror. It was tragic. There were tremendous human rights abuses, but the insurrection was ended. By the beginning or middle of 1990, it was clear that this insurrection was over and that the system of the country and the government would survive.

Shortly thereafter, however, by June of 1990, the conflict in the northeast, which had been quiescent in part because the government had been negotiating with the Tamil Tigers, entered a new hot phase when the Tigers declared war again and went actively into military warfare. This war goes on today. There is some hope, but not a great deal, that it will end fairly soon. Until this fighting ends, the country will not be able to get along its economic path the way it should. On the other hand, the basic threat to the institutions of the country and government are not the same as earlier even though the war goes on. The war is costing lives. The war is costing resources that need to be put elsewhere. But the war is really kind of "up there." Unless you have members of your family fighting in it, most Sri Lankans do not feel directly touched by it. This will probably go on for some time. There is some hope, I say, because there is a select committee of the parliament that is trying to frame an alternative to present to the people in the northeast that would work out the ethnic issue that has plagued this country since independence. If it succeeds, it will be the first time that the major Sinhala and other parties have unitedly presented a proposal for negotiation. It is not certain that this will succeed because there is no time in the independent history of Sri Lanka up until now when the major Sinhala parties have come together to offer a practical plan for dealing with the ethnic conflict in the north and east. Each time in the past, one party has offered a plan and the other has played political football and shot it down. The guilt is on all sides. The guilt is also on the Tamil side. There is plenty of guilt to go around. What this country needs is to solve that ethnic problem, because that is the only way it is going to get its act totally together and realize the vast potential that this little island has in terms of economic development. This place may not be a possible Singapore but it can certainly be a possible Malaysia. This will not happen until this country can deal with its political problems satisfactorily.

This brings me to economic considerations. In 1950, Sri Lanka had the third highest per capita income in all of Asia. Today, it has a per capita income of a little over $400, which means it can draw funds from the "International Development Association" (IDA), of the World Bank, which means it is one of the poorer countries in the world yet it has managed, because of a devotion of its people to health and education, to have some of the higher standards in the developing world. In fact, the literacy rate here is 87-90%. That compares to 36% in India. That compares favorably with many of the countries in the so-called developed world. Life expectancy here is over 70 years of age. That is right up there with the developed world. A highly educated citizenry, relatively low wage scales, people who live a long time—all this works because resources are directed in that direction. So Sri Lanka has the potential to take off economically.

Another thing that is quite favorable now is that this is a country that for thirty years tried the socialist economic model and it did not work. The shift to a market oriented economy was not done out of theoretical belief but out of practical experience that the other way just did not work. This country realized it long before Eastern Europe or the Soviet Union realized it. In fact they started on this economic policy in 1977 and the current government, which is an extension of the previous one, is pursuing it with a greater vigor. The great tragedy, economically, is that this country, which seemed to really be progressing in 1983, has spent the years 1983-1990 fighting insurrections. Consequently it has not been able to direct its full attention to its economic potential.

The current government's economic approach today, which despite its political rhetoric is supported in basic principles by the opposition party, is an economic policy that we could not have written better had we written it in Washington. It is a policy that is designed to encourage more activity by the private sector, to sell off the state enterprises that have consistently lost money, to encourage what the current government calls "people-ization," which simply means spreading the ownership of private corporations out to the citizenry through the stock market, and the concentration on areas where there is a competitive advantage.

You will meet people who will talk both pessimistically and optimistically about the economy's potential while you are here. I stand four-square on the optimistic side, in terms of potential. Whether that potential will be realized will depend on the next two to four years, and whether the right policies get implemented. One of the things about being a democracy, of course, is that you are going to find that there is a lot of politics played on every issue. That is part of the system. That is part of our system. We believe it is good because we believe that over the long haul, it all works. In the short haul, it sometimes causes problems. As this country moves toward provincial council elections next year, a new presidential election, probably in December of 1994, new parliamentary elections in 1995, all of the politics are going to get churned up with all of the economics, and exactly how fast and how far the country's economy will be able to advance remains to be seen.

This is a vibrant country, a country where a lot is happening politically, a lot is happening economically; a country with a rich, deep culture; a country whose recorded history goes back over 2000 years; a country where you can go from ruins that are dated about the time of Greece; where you can see the loveliest tea country in the world, and some of the finest beaches. This is a country that stands as the center of Buddhism, a great religion, a great philosophy, which I encourage you to delve deeply into. I think you are going to have a great time, and I wish you well.

Let me say in closing that I think you are in for a wonderful month. You will find Sri Lankan people, be they Sinhala, Muslim or Tamil, to be extremely intelligent, very personable, genuine, friendly. You will find this country to be something to remember for a long time. It has a way of drawing people back. I might tell you that in 1984, when I was living in New Delhi India, serving there in our embassy, I came here with my family for vacation, and all of us agreed that someday we had to come back to see this place again. You can imagine how delighted my wife and I were when we got this assignment. Our daughters, who are now married, have come with their husbands to visit. My only regret is that in about three to four months my tour is up. I am in the process of enjoying the last few months and weeks of what has been an absolutely fantastic and amazing tour, and I have thoroughly enjoyed it.

QUESTIONS AND RESPONSES

Q: What kind of organization do they have for military service?

Marion Creekmore: It is a voluntary service. They have no problem getting volunteers now because there is a very high percentage of unemployment. The current military establishment is in the neighborhood of 60-70,000 people. This compares to what was estimated to be between 3,000 and 10,000 in 1983, when the current phase of the ethnic problem in the northeast broke out. It was basically a "parade ground" military until 1983. Since that time, it has become a fighting force with all the problems in expanding from that small size to 60 or 70 thousand today. Back when the current phase of the war broke out in June, 1990, recruitment posters went up and the lines were enormous. It is basically a volunteer army. It has a professional leadership core. Most of the current leaders were trained in the West, most of them in Britain. The tradition here is that the military is subservient to civilian rule. There has only been one small attempt, back in the 1960s, of a few lower ranking military people trying to seize control of the government. This is not a country that has a tradition of the military seizing control. If you talk to any of the top military leaders, you come away absolutely convinced that they believe in civilian control.

Q: Are many of them women as well?

MC: It is basically a male army.

Q: What is India's involvement with the situation and how does the United States react to the conflicts?

MC: The official line is that we want peace and stability in this country, and we want good neighborly relations between our two countries. There is a strong belief here that in the early 1980s there was some official or unofficial Indian involvement in encouraging the Tigers. It is quite clear that there was some involvement by the southern Indian state of Tamil Nadu. There is a question about whether or not the central government in India was involved. You will hear all sorts of arguments and I am not going to go beyond saying that there are a lot of arguments out there.

In 1987, there was an agreement reached between India and Sri Lanka to try to work together to put down the whole dispute in the northeast. The Sri Lankans will correctly tell you that they were more or less forced into this agreement because the Sri Lankan army was moving fairly rapidly against the Tigers in the northeast and it looked like they might invade the city of Jaffna. Had they done so, there would have been tremendous civilian casualties. The Indians officially first did some food drops and then effectively said that Sri Lanka should not go into the city of Jaffna militarily. After a period, the then president J. R. Jayawardhene and the then Prime Minister Rajiv Gandhi reached the 1987 Accords by which the two countries agreed to work together to put down the problem.

The Indians miscalculated in the sense that they thought that they could tell the Tigers to lay down their weapons and the Tigers would do so. But the Tigers proved, as many terrorist groups prove, that they are their own masters. They will take help from wherever they can get it but they have certain definite goals and they will pursue those against all comers. So, within about three months the Indian troops that were brought in were fighting the Tigers and did so for about two years.

The current president, President Premadasa, insisted that the Indians withdraw their troops, which they did in March of 1990. They probably would have done so anyway because it was becoming politically not such a good thing in India to have troops in Sri Lanka, at the time. Whether the Sri Lankan president's attitude actually accelerated the withdrawal is an open question. But by his demanding that the Indian troops get out, the president stole some of the thunder of JVP insurrectionists in the south who were using Sinhala chauvinism as a flag to rally people to their support as they were trying to take over the government in that period that I mentioned, 1988-1989. Politically, it was a good move, I think, to take this line that the "Indians must get off of our soil." It created subsequent problems, because the Sri Lankan military did not fill in behind as the Indians left. There was, then, a vacuum created, and the Tigers moved very quickly into that in June of 1990. As a result, it took Sri Lankan military about a year to get back to the position, militarily, that the country was when the Indians pulled out.

So, when you talk about this issue, you have to look at it in terms both of military strategy in dealing with the Tigers, and also political strategy in dealing with the JVP. It is very tough to fight two insurrections simultaneously.

Q: In light of all the discussions about elections, what might be said about the legitimacy of the government?

MC: I am going to answer you in a roundabout way because a direct answer is a very live political question here today. You will be given every possible answer you can imagine.

In December of 1989, when the President was elected, and in February of 1990, when the parliament was elected—this was in the middle of all the violence we have been talking about—nevertheless, in December of 1989, 55% of the people eligible to vote went to the polls and voted. Compare this with the United States where about 35% vote. People went to the polls to vote even though they were threatened with their lives, and many people were killed, yet 55% still went out and voted. In normal times, 75-80% of the voters in this country would have gone on to vote. There is no doubt that a lot of people got killed, a lot of intimidation took place, and there was probably some ballot box stuffing. The real debate is did one party benefit more than another because of that situation, and that is what the presidential petition that Mrs. Bandaranaike, the leader of the opposition who was the defeated candidate in that election, circulated. Her position is that there was violence, therefore it was not a fair election. The current government's position, headed by Mr.Premadasa, who won the election, is that there was wide scale violence, but all parties suffered and, he would argue, that his party suffered even more than the opposition. So, it certainly was not a clean election, but it was probably—and this is a personal judgment—probably about as good an election that could have occurred at that time.

Whether that means that since things are now better there ought to be a new election or wait until the next election is something I will let the Sri Lankans work out. Obviously, Ariyaratne, who is a very impressive man, has some strong views on this issue. So do very many others, who disagree among themselves and whose supporters disagree also. I do not know what the final outcome will be of this case before the courts on the presidential petition. If Mrs. Bandaranaike wins, then there has to be an immediate presidential election. If she loses there does not have to be another presidential election until December, 1994.

You will be hearing a lot about when the next presidential election is going to be, particularly, as you know, there was an effort for impeachment made last August that failed. There are many people who would tell you that the president has to have an early election because he still has a lot of people in his party that he cannot trust. As you talk to people, you will tend to find that the people who want an early election are in the opposition. Talk to people in or supporting the ruling party, they will say that an election is not needed until 1994, and we have to make our economic reforms work. The president has the power to determine the date of the election as long as the presidential petition case does not go against him. If he loses that, then there has to be an immediate election.

This is a highly educated and highly politicized society, and everybody has strong political views on most of the national issues. You will find that out in the villages as well as in the cities. You can go into the villages in this country and people are sitting there, reading newspapers, listening to radios. They are much more interested about things that are going on than you will find in some small towns in the U.S. It is a very interesting place.

Q: I have heard that financial aid has been extended by the U.S. to Sri Lanka but it has never reached the populace, it is just being pocketed by parliament. Do you believe this is true, and if so, is anything being done?

MC: The answer is no, I do not believe it is true. In fact, I am positive that it is not because virtually all of our aid goes to pay people to teach skills. We do not just write checks. The World Bank and some of the other institutions and donors do that as a way of financing capital projects. Virtually, all of ours is to pay in many cases Americans who are here to establish markets, out in the Mahaveli Project area working with farmers to teach them how to grow commercial crops that can be sold, rather than paddy rice. We do bring in a good deal of PL480 wheat which comes to the flour mill up in Trincomalee where it is turned into flour. This is very closely monitored by our people. I feel quite confident because we are monitoring it very closely, that that is not a problem that we have in this country.

Q: I understand that some U.S. aid was given specifically for the Mahaveli Project and that some of the vehicles were found to be taken over by the military. Is there something to this?

MC: Back during the first six months of the new war, that is, from June, 1990—I use that date because the hostilities reopened after about a two 2 year hiatus—we had three or four of our vehicles in that area taken over by the military. As soon as we got word of this, we protested at the very highest levels, and we got all the vehicles back very quickly. We basically said that if we do not get those vehicles back, our aid ends. We are not providing vehicles for the military. There are some other people who did not get their vehicles back as quickly as we did. There are some vehicles that have been stolen by the LTTE as well. All of ours have been fully accounted for. When I came in, in late 1989, one of these things happened fairly quickly and we made a test case out of that incident. If anyone knows of any of our vehicles that are not currently in the right hands, please let me know, because I will move very quickly on the matter.

Q: How beneficial have the programs been here and what, in your thinking, would be the best for Sri Lanka ten years from now.

MC: What I think would be best is to form an economic development model somewhat similar to other countries, i.e., Malaysia, Thailand, Taiwan, and Singapore. I think Sri Lanka could double its per capita income in that period if it basically uses the market approach to economic development. I think this would increase not only the income of the citizenry but will provide the kinds of job opportunities that are absolutely essential to prevent another Sinhala insurrection in the south.

Let me turn your question slightly this way, and say that I am convinced that if the economic program does not work in the next five to seven years, there is going to be another insurrection in the south that will be worse than the one they have come out of. I am not alone on this. Major people in the government and also in the opposition agree with me.

One of the reasons that the market approach is basically now accepted across the political spectrum is because it is recognized that government enterprises cannot provide the kind of employment opportunities that are needed for people who are coming out of school systems with at least secondary educations and their aspirations for employment that result from that. The government employment sector that is not concerned about generating profits and having long-term sustained growth cannot produce the kinds of job that are needed. So, I think there is a real potential to do this, by this country really growing economically not only in the Colombo area but around the country. There is an even bet as to whether it will make it or not.

Q: Is it an increased market activity that will be brought in, or will it be restructured?

MC: Basically the restructuring is going on. This is a country that is staying within International Monetary Fund (IMF)—World Bank—guidelines. My prejudice is that despite the criticism that you hear from a number of developing countries and from some American academics about the World Bank Fund plan for economic development, I basically believe it is the right way to go. I come to you with this prejudice in mind. Sri Lanka has gone through the stabilization period. They are in the process of restructuring—selling off—state run enterprises that have been losing money for years. I think this is the right idea. They are opening the borders for foreign investment, foreign expertise—they are begging the outside world to come in, if they can bring in something the country needs, economically.

I think an open kind of economic system is the only way this small island country can make it economically and provide the kinds of job opportunity it is going to need to meet the aspirations of its people over time. That is why there is a program of industrializing, while also keeping a strong agricultural base, dealing with food processing, and heavy industry, trying to find ways or areas of competitive advantage. I think one of those areas is going to be in the electronics field: the assembling of various types of electronic equipment is I think one of the next stages that is going to come here. We are already seeing some of the light industries move out of Korea and elsewhere to come and locate here because the wage scale is cheaper here than in Korea. This is part of the normal expected economic development pattern. I would see a relatively sophisticated type of manufacturing base expanding here. They already have many things they do in rubber that is very good here. There is a $60,000,000 Australian investment in the free trade zone, making surgical gloves sold to Europe and the U.S. They have some of the best rubber in the world. That is the kind of thing where you take your comparative advantage and make it work for you. The clay for ceramics is very good here. Noritake will soon have its largest plant in the world here in Sri Lanka. There is another place called "Laklane" that produces high quality stuff that goes to Bloomingdales and comparable stores in Europe and Japan. That is the kind of thing that I think they need to do.

Q: In visiting Sarvodaya, we discussed procedures in determining what villagers need: does one ask or are projects to be imposed?

MC: I do not see a contradiction. I think you do both. I believe in the "bottom-up" development strategy of Sarvodaya. It is also the same theoretical basis that underlies Janasavaya, which is the President's program. I can go to both of those and sit down with you and show you elements that I think ought to be changed because I do not think they are working. But I agree with the notion of starting at the village and getting the villagers to work together for their own interest and produce things that will actually sell. One common problem in all of these schemes is that sometimes you are teaching people to produce what they can without knowing if there is a market of buyers. Without that, it will not work. I think both of those programs are worth pursuing. I must confess that I am saddened at times that they all do not work together, that there is more competition there than might need to be the case. Then again, there is a lot of competition in the United States, competition normally is a healthy thing.

Q: What is the administration's analysis on the Tamil situation in terms of policy?

MC: I think there are some legitimate grievances of the Tamil people that need to be rectified. I also think that some of the claims of the Tamils are really not legitimate. All of this goes back to a long period of history, and I think the worst thing to do, which too often happens here, is that the whole contrast is drawn as right or wrong. I think the Sinhalas have a lot that is right and a lot that is wrong on their side. I also think the Tamils have a lot that is right and wrong on their side. I do believe—and our government's policy supports this— this being a single country, that the territorial integrity and sovereignty of the country should remain. The Tamil Tigers' basic goal is to create a separate state, to carve out a portion, the lines of which are under debate. We basically are for a united Sri Lanka. We also are against the use of terrorist methods to achieve political goals, and I am fully aware of the debate around the world that one person's terrorist is another's freedom fighter and all of that, but I do not have any sympathy when people set off car bombs in the middle of a street where civilians are walking. I cannot rationalize that with any kind of political philosophy. So, I do not think that there is any doubt that the Tigers pursue terrorist methods. I do think there is some concern that there is not a real alternative out there to the thing the Tigers push for. I do not think that some of the Tamil people have that alternative. That is why I am very hopeful that the select committee will come up with something. Basically, we list the Tamil Tigers as a terrorist organization; this is official U.S. Government policy. I think you will find that more and more countries are doing that since it becomes pretty clear that they were involved in the assassination of Rajiv Gandhi.

Q: Do you see a possible balance with the Tamils?

MC: Part of the old problems are already being dealt with. Tamil is now regarded as one of the official languages. A lot of this goes back to 1956, when a piece of legislation was passed called "Sinhala Only," which basically was a way to make Sinhala the national language. It was to take the language of 70+ % of the population and say everyone had to speak it. Until that time, most Tamils spoke English and most Sinhalas spoke English and many spoke some of the other languages. This basically meant that for more than a generation you went to Tamil schools and learned everything in Tamil and to Sinhala schools and learned everything in Sinhala, and, if you were rich, you continued to go to English schools. What happened is that the ability to communicate got lost. More than a generation went through that process. The current policy supported by the opposition as well as the government was that there are two official languages, Sinhala and Tamil, and that English is a "link" language and that English should be taught as a means to link this country to the world of international commerce, which is essential. One can graduate and be the finest speaker in Sinhala in the world, but you will have a hard time getting a job with, say, IBM, or the Sri Lankan equivalent. I think it is great to encourage the study of Sinhala. It is a beautiful language; it has a very rich culture. However, this has to be done in addition to teaching people in this country to speak English. I am delighted that the government and the opposition are all putting strong efforts and emphasis today on the teaching of English around the country. I do not say that because our language is English, but it just happens that, at this stage in world history, English is the language you need if you want to develop economically.

OBSERVATIONS FOR UNDERGRADUATES IN A FASCINATING COUNTRY

Teresita C. Schaffer, U. S. Ambassador

I am delighted to have this opportunity to talk to you. As some of you may have heard, I've been away for two weeks and this is the first official engagement I have had since I've been back. The reason for my being away was perhaps appropriate; my son just graduated from college and my other son is a sophomore at Lewis and Clark. So I have a special feeling for undergraduates who come this far and who come to take a look at a fascinating country.

I have been here almost three years and I suppose you can say, by way of introduction to the scene in Sri Lanka, that I have now been up the roller coaster and down it again in terms of the political odyssey this country has gone through. I arrived in October of 1992. At that time Sri Lanka had pretty well come out of one of its two civil wars, the one against the Janatha Vimukti Peramuna (JVP), the ultra nationalist group that you may have heard of. It was a very bad three year period when that particular struggle was going on marked by tens of thousands of disappearances and terrible abuses of human rights, really, by everyone. The security forces everyone heard about; what was perhaps internationally not so well known were the abuses committed by the JVP The other civil war, I am afraid, is still with us; that is, the one involving the north and the east and, specifically, the Liberation Tigers of Tamil Eelam (LTTE). What I would like to do is talk just a little bit about the north and east problem as it is most commonly known here, about the political situation of the government, about what has happened in the human rights field and in economic policy, and, finally, about

what is in it for us, as the United States. What do I do all day?
What does our government care about here? What are we trying
to do about it?

To start with the north and east problem. Since you have
been studying Sri Lanka, I am sure you know that this is not a new
phenomenon, but it is not really an ancient quarrel either in the
same sense that, say, the Middle East problem has been going on
for a couple of thousand years. It is, in its present virulent form,
primarily a phenomenon of independent Sri Lanka and it got its
start pretty much right after independence when the governing
group declined to give citizenship to a large group of Tamils, the
so-called Indian Tamils, and set things off on the wrong foot.
But it certainly got a powerful push from the campaign of the
present president's father, Mr. S. W. R. D. Bandaranaike for "one
language." And, as someone quipped at the time, "One language,
two countries; two languages, one country." That proved to be
prophetic.

The present phase is an interesting one characterized at the
moment, I would say, by disappointed hopes. When Chandrika
Kumaratunga became prime minister last August, she came in
having campaigned on a peace platform. She took a big risk
in doing so. The conventional wisdom was that this would be
political suicide for any politician. She got herself elected and
she then got herself elected again as president in November. In
trying to put some policy behind her peace platform, she did start
a negotiating process with the Liberation Tigers of Tamil Eelam.

Now this certainly was not the first time that a Sri Lankan
government had attempted to negotiate a settlement. Through
the 1980s, governments did that at roughly two-year intervals;
'83, '85, '87, and then there was an extra year until 1990. Each
time the effort failed and, fundamentally—I am oversimplifying
a great deal—the reason for the failure was a combination of too
little, too late on the part of the government and, I would have to
say, a substantial measure of bad faith on the part of the LTTE. In
other words, nobody looked particularly good, if you look at their
history. This time the government started out with high hopes and
determined to make an appeal over the heads of the LTTE to the
Tamil population of Jaffna. The mood in this country was quite

extraordinary at the time. It is hard to remember that this was only a few months ago.

On April 19, 1995, as I am sure you know, the LTTE pulled out of the process and went back to the battlefield leaving us and, of course, Sri Lankans with the question, "Why?" You will get different answers to that question, and you should ask it because the answers you get are instructive. If you talk to opponents of the government, they will tell you that the effort was misguided and naive to begin with. You need to keep in mind, however, that the opponents of the government, in fact, supported the effort while it was going on. If you talk to people in the government, they will say it was LTTE bad faith. If you talk to Tamils who are not fully associated with the government, they will say the government did not deliver what it promised and therefore the LTTE could not believe them and, therefore, the government probably was not sincere.

My own answer has elements of all three responses but combines them a little differently. I believe that the LTTE was, at best, ambivalent about the peace negotiations to begin with. They were not sure they really wanted a deal. They wanted to try it out for size, and probably the deal they wanted was one that was completely incompatible with what the government could give. That means that the challenge of that round, which, unfortunately was not fully met, was to try to get them to change their minds. And evidently they did not. That I think is the fundamental reason that this process came a cropper as it did. There were other contributory reasons. I think that both sides failed to find a way effectively to communicate with each other. When you are talking about people who have had very little interaction, you cannot be sure that the message that you transmit is the one they receive. I think that systematically this has plagued both sides in these negotiations.

One could go through the published record of the talks which is very full—which may in itself have been a problem—and point to lots of things, lots of times when the style of each side grated on the other. But looking at all of those things that might contain the germ of lessons you might like to learn next time, I think the one that probably came closest to making the real difference was the tendency on the part of the government to promise more than it could deliver in a short time. This is not an easy problem to avoid when you consider that even in extremely well-established and well-organized governments there is sometimes a gap between what you say and what you do. But the fact is that in Sri Lanka they were operating in an environment in which that gap was going to be scrutinized and measured and interpreted in the most hostile way possible by a very suspicious adversary.

Now that that has happened, what next? Well, I think the reality is that the action is going to be primarily in the military sphere in the short term and, of course, you have been here almost a week and you have seen some evidence of that already. How does one get back to a negotiating process? That still is what, I think, the Sri Lankan people would like ultimately. It certainly is what their foreign friends would like. I cannot fully answer that question except to say that in the short term the partisans of a peaceful solution need to figure out in greater detail than I have just given you what they should do differently next time. They also need to figure out how one could structure a new effort that would look different enough from the old one to permit the participants to go into it without committing political suicide, and figure out how each side can determine whether the other one is really prepared to live with whatever deal they might reach in some hypothetical future negotiations. I would say at this point that the onus is primarily on the LTTE but certainly not exclusively so. That is quite an ambitious agenda when one considers the many failed negotiating efforts. But I think it is an effort that you cannot escape. Suppose tomorrow morning that the Sri Lankan army marched into Jaffna with no significant civilian casualties and established territorial control. This is not going to happen but suppose, for the sake of argument, it did. Even under those circumstances, they would still be left with the problem of writing a constitution that the people of this country would be prepared to live with. So, even a military victory cannot take the place of a political settlement.

What has been happening in the human rights field? This was a major item on the US's bi-lateral agenda with Sri Lanka for a good many years. This is an area where the new government has made a major difference. I mentioned that during the JVP period there were tens of thousands of disappearances. Disappearances had almost stopped as of a year ago. There had been a very significant change in the way the Sri Lankan authorities were conducting themselves, an improvement in discipline and a leadership that wanted to see that improvement in discipline continue. What happened after the installation of the new government was a step that a lot of people believed that no Sri Lankan government would dare take, and that is the beginnings of an accountability process, trying to find out in greater detail what happened during the worst of times in the human rights realm. That process has continued; slowly, but it has continued.

It is not clear where it is headed. The text book solution, if you will, from the point of view of the Western human rights community would be that it ought to end in prosecutions. I am not sure that that is a feasible solution, given the difficulty of putting together legal cases against people whose alleged offences took place that many years ago and in that kind of circumstance. I am not sure from that point of view that it is even a desirable solution. You cannot cure human rights violations by conducting trials that will not pass the "red face" test. And in any case, I am not sure that is where they are headed. I think you may, at the end of the day, assuming this process continues, get something more along the lines of a report, which at least provides some measure of information and therefore relief to the families of those who disappeared during this time and which goes some distance towards cauterizing the wounds of that period, not perhaps totally healing them but at least sealing off that period and permitting the country to get on with life. With these very big transformations in the human rights environment, that topic has slipped to a less prominent part of our bi-lateral dialogue, frankly because there is less to talk about. I mention it here because it has been one of the features of Sri Lankan life which has been well known overseas and I wanted you to have a sense of where I think things stand and where we, as a government, are putting this in the hierarchy of the things we deal with in Sri Lanka.

I promised to say a bit about the political situation of this government. Chandrika Kumaratunga was elected in the parliamentary election with, at least on paper, a wafer thin majority—one vote. Since then she has effectively expanded her parliamentary majority to include everybody except the principal opposition party, namely the United National Party (UNP). A number of those parties, first of all, represent minority communities through several Tamil parties and one Muslim party that are supporting the government legally or de facto. More significantly, several of them are not technically part of the governing coalition. That means that, although she has got a very solid working majority, if things go badly awry, there are a number of parties that are perfectly capable of jumping ship. At the moment, I do not think they have any interest in doing so and that, plus the very large victory she won in the presidential election in November, I think, put Mrs. Kumaratunga and the People's Alliance in a fairly strong position politically.

However, since the fighting resumed on April 19th they are clearly much more vulnerable than they had been before because the main policy they have been offering to the country does not seem to have worked, or, at a minimum, seems to be in a bad phase. And so you are going to see a greater degree of nervousness and stridency in the way the government talks about its main policy and in the way it describes its opponents. To American ears a lot of this is kind of jarring, but you have got to remember that politics is a blood sport in this country. People take their politics very seriously. On occasions when, in the American tradition, you normally make at least a pretense at some kind of bipartisanism, in this country that is not necessarily the case. You may go at your opponents hammer and tong, even if it looks like a kind of state ceremonial occasion. Coming from the tradition I come from, I find that unfortunate but that has been the practice here. So you will see a degree of nastiness, politically, which may—even coming against the background of today's Washington—seem a bit extreme.

Having said that, there have in practice been very wide areas of—consensus is probably too strong a word—at least a working agreement across the political spectrum. The first of these, interestingly enough, is economic policy, where the People's Alliance Government picked up a very large percentage of the open market policies that the UNP had pioneered and which they consider to have been their greatest success. This is partly changing times. The last time the Sri Lanka Freedom Party (SLFP) was in power, the fashion was much more towards State ownership of resources and controls and State management of large sectors of the economy. Those policies failed in country after country and, consequently, Chandrika Kumaratunga realized that that was not a viable basis for starting off her own government and she started it off in a quite different direction. But, as I said, in practice the opposition also went along with the government's peace initiatives while they were going on. They never associated themselves with them, never formally came out and endorsed them. But they held their peace, with a lot of individuals in the opposition quietly saying, "Well, this is a good thing. We should allow it to go forward. We shouldn't stand in the way." This is a wider degree of cooperation than most Sri Lankan governments have enjoyed. That degree of consensus is now up for grabs and, I think, you probably will not see any great changes during the time you are here. But further down the road, I think a lot depends on how successful or unsuccessful the military looks over the next couple of months. A lot depends on the extent to which Chandrika can recoup the initiative in the public relations area, in the public domain. If she goes back to being able to set the agenda, then I think she may be able to keep the opposition sort of neutral for a bit longer. In the normal course of events, after a government has been in power for a while it accumulates more reasons for people to be cross with it. So there is a kind of natural progression there. She can keep the national progression more in her favor if she is able to recoup the initiative both militarily and politically. And it is going to be harder for her, correspondingly, if she cannot.

To wind up briefly; what is the United States interested in here? What do I spend my time doing? Where are your tax dollars going? The three issues for us during most of my time here have been the war, human rights, and the economic relationship. I have talked about the war, but what the U.S. is interested in is encouraging a political settlement which keeps Sri Lanka as one country, but with dignity and protection for all minority communities. We came out with a very strong statement against the LTTE's decision to go back to the fighting. We have not sought a third-party or mediating role in this conflict. Up until now there has not really been a market for it. The present government is willing to use mediation in principle, at the right time, but does not believe that this is the right time. And the LTTE has blown hot and cold on the issue. So there has not really been anything there for us or for anybody else to try to do, playing a third-party role. We have been more in the posture of trying to encourage more creative thinking and policies that would support eventual move towards the peace process. In light of what has been happening in the past month and a half, like everybody else we are back at the drawing boards trying to figure out what might be the most useful ways to spend the next couple of months in order to prepare the groundwork for a possible resumption of a negotiating phase.

Human rights I have already spoken about. This was a major topic on our bi-lateral agenda. It is, fortunately, able to be a less prominent one now but is a continuing issue that the U.S. does watch in different countries in particular in countries where, as in Sri Lanka, there has been a history of problems.

As for the economic relationship: we have an aid program here. The amount of money involved has varied largely in proportion to the availability of food aid from the United States. This is partly a function of how much money Congress appropriates—and that is going down—and partly a function of how much we have available by way of surplus food, and how much of that is being absorbed by what you might call a catastrophe country, places where there is mass starvation. In addition to our food aid, we have quite a successful development assistance program here which has tried to encourage policies that will support economic growth. We have another cluster of projects that supports the environment, and a third that focuses on supporting democratic institutions and the groups that have been left out of Sri Lanka's economic progress in the past couple of decades.

This is an unusual country. Everybody can read. Infant mortality is more like southern Europe than it is like south Asia. Consequently the things which have been the mainstay of aid programs elsewhere in the region—family planning, basic field projects in agriculture, primary education—we do not do here because the Sri Lankans have already done it. So we have the luxury to focus on other things to make up for what the Sri Lankans historically have not done so well, which is to keep the productive sectors of the economy growing so that there will be more of that famous pie to distribute. We also have growing trade investment relations here—I dare say, not growing quite as fast as we would have hoped in view of the fact that the fighting has resumed. But basically this is a strong market. It is a country that is probably easier to do business in than, say, India. Most of the companies which are either selling major equipment here or trying to invest here have had an opportunity to become familiar with the place, and therefore do not over react when they hear that there are problems here again. They are able to access them, to figure out what parts of the country they are still willing to take the risks in, and to make this into a profitable venture, and, perhaps more importantly from a Sri Lankan point of view, one which creates a lot of jobs locally.

Well, you have got a treat in store for you. I gather you are going to see the cultural triangle and the many places which are so important to the Buddhist tradition here which you have been studying. I hope you have a wonderful time. I think you will.

GLOSSARY

Unless otherwise noted, all terms are in the Pali language and are presented below in the order of the English alphabet

Abhidhamma	the third portion, collection, "basket" of the canonical texts
ädura	Sinhala: a ceremonial specialist who knows the preparation for and proper execution of ritual ceremonies to control demons
akusala	that which is detrimental, not wholesome, as in *akusala-kamma*, detrimental action
akusalamūla	roots of the unwholesome, i.e., greed, hatred or ill-will, delusion or ignorance
amisadāna	a gift in kind
anāgāmi	the third path, one who never returns to this human realm as far as rebirth is concerned
anattā	no-soul, no self, that without soul, insubstantiality, one of the three characteristics of the world
anicca	Impermanence; lit., not permanent, one of the three characteristics of the world
anumodana	meritorious act is extended to others, happily, rejoicingly; lit., "being happy along with," often with special relevance to departed relatives
anusaya	the persistence of a dormant or latent disposition, tendency to detrimental moral action
Arahant	Worthy one; as a stage on the paths, this is considered the fourth of the four paths (*maggas*)
ayurvedic medicine	the form of medical knowledge based on the cumulative tradition of indigenous Indian and Sri Lanka medical practice

avāsa	a small residence of a monk but not necessarily forming a part of a temple complex
avijjā	not knowing, ignorance, unaware
avyākata	that which is unexplained, not defined, as in *avyākata-kamma*, action neither wholesome nor detrimental
āyatana	an immaterial sphere; there are four such states of consciousness in *samādhi*
bali	Sinhala: pl. of *baliya*, meaning image, picture, or figure representing spirits or deities forming a part of healing ceremonies in Sri Lanka
baṇa	Sinhala word for preaching, usually a sermon by a monk
bhāva	becoming, in dependent origination a psychological process of building up "I-consciousness"
bhāvanā	mental cultvation with reference to meditation
bhikkhu	a mendicant, a (Buddhist) monk, a member of the monastic order (Saṅgha)
bhikkhunī	the Pali word for nun, often mistakenly used to refer to women in Sri Lanka who observe the ten precepts, "ten-precept mother," *dasasīlmāṇiyō*
bodhisattva	Skt. *bodhisatta* in Pali; a being for enlightenment, one moving along the path of becoming a Buddha, in Theravāda with special reference to the Buddha in a former life
brāhmaṇas	classical Hindu texts having to do with ritual procedures
brahmavihāras	four sublime states of loving kindness, compassion, sympathetic joy, and equanimity
buddhadhamma	The truth about right living as taught and demonstrated by the Buddha and found to be salvifically supportive by men and women through their participating in the religious tradition that has developed from their response to this realization
buddhapūja	homage to the Buddha, offerings of food made in small quantities to the Buddha

buddhasāsana	originally "instruction of the Buddha," in time coming to suggest something akin to a Buddhist doctrinal system
caraṇa	behavior, when proper it leads to an "uncomplicated, inwardly rich life."
cetanā	will, volition, intention, that which provides motivation for action.
cetiya	a heaped up mound containing a supportive element of the Buddha: a bodily relic or an item used by the Buddha or an image of the Buddha, which forms a part of reverence of the Buddha in temple worship
dāgoba	Sinhala: a memorial mound containing the relics of the Buddha or a praiseworthy disciple, Pali, *thūpa*, Sanskrit, *stūpa*
dāna	giving, an act of giving
dhammadāna	the gift of Dhamma of which the highest gift would be preaching Dhamma
dhammā-dhipateyya	rule or sovereignty of Dhamma
dhammaladha	that which one has acquired or obtained by righteous living
dhamma-vinaya	the teachings and monastic regulations
dhammavitakka	analysis in light of Dhamma, righteous thought
dharmiṣṭa	that which is established on righteousness, contrasted with *adharmiṣṭa*
diṭṭhe-dhamma-vedanīya	that which is to be experienced in this existence
diṭṭhi	opinions, ideas, ideologies
dosa	hate, animosity
dukkha	misery, suffering, sorrow, unsatisfactoriness, awryness, dis-ease, disquiet, one of the three characteristics of the world
hoppers	Sinhala: a delightful Sri Lankan steamed food item made principally from rice flower pressed out into cupped pancakes

indrakīla	a primary or chief post, richily symbolic, used in the construction of a temporary pavilion for a pirit ceremony
indriya	refers to the senses—eyes, nose, etc.—indicating how they are "lords" dominating our perception
jātaka	a birth story, specifically, birth stories of the Buddha's former lives, 550 of which comprise a part of the Theravāda Buddhist canon
jhāna	trance, a state of consciousness, the first four states of *samādhi*
JVP	Janatha Vimukti Peramuna, "Peoples Liberation Front," designates a Sinhala insurgency in the 1980s
kamma	volitional action which carries consequences in this world and the next, Sanskrit and Sinhala *karma*
kapurala	Sinhala, a person who presides at a particular temple devoted to a deity.
kāya-kamma	physical volitional action
khandhā	the five categories or constituents constituting an individual, affected by clinging
kusala	that which is wholesome, as in *kusalakamma,* wholesome action or deed
kusalamūla	roots of the wholesome, i.e., absence of greed, of hatred or ill-will, of delusion or ignorance
lobha	greed, craving, intense desire
lokuttarapaññā	world-transcending wisdom, the arising of the genuinely transformative awareness
LTTE	"Liberation Tigers of Tamil Eelam," a movement seeking independence from the central government of Sri Lanka and the establishment of a separate state for men and women who are Tamil
magga	the term means "path," and is used in two senses: (1) as in the eightfold path, and (2) referring to four attainments: the first path (stream-attainer), the second path (once-returner), the third path (non-returner), and the fourth path (Arahant)
magga-phala	path (*magga*) and result, fruit (*phala*), with reference to the four paths and fruits

mahāpirit	Sinhala: "Great Pirit" or "Great Paritta" containing three suttas: the Gem Sutta (Ratana Sutta), the Sutta on Loving Kindness, (Metta Sutta) and the Sutta on Auspicious Blessings (Mangala Sutta)
Mahāvihāra	the Great (*mahā*) Monastic Dwelling (*vihāra*) of major historical significance in ancient Anurādhapura
maitrī	Sanskrit for *mettā*, representing for some a more comprehensive and focused relationship than Pali *mettā* (cf. Lily de Silva in chapter XIV)
maṇḍapa	a temporary pavilion within which monks sit and chant *paritta*
mano-kamma	mental action, action completed by the mind
mettā	sympathy, unlimited friendliness, loving kindness
moha	delusion, bewilderment, absence of proper understanding
nama-rūpa	lit., name and form, mental and physical constituents
NGO	Non-Governmental Organization
niccatā	the notion of permanence
nirodhasacca	the truth of cessation, the cessation of suffering
pañcasīla	five (*pañca*) precepts (*sīla*)
paññā	Sanskrit *prajñā,* insight, wisdom
pansala	Sinhala: "leaf hall," monastery, hermitage, temple
pāpa	bad, with reference to bad behavior, acts that are detrimental to oneself and to others, evil
parinibbāna	the final complete attainment of Nibbāna particularly with reference to the Buddha
paritta	carries the basic meaning of "to protect," and refers to a long standing and widely occuring Theravāda Buddhist ritual, in Sinhala *pirit*
pariyuṭṭhāna	designates a biased outburst, an eruption of propensities which, when it erupts, has catastrophic infective power
pasāda	being pleased, satisfied, akin to the being aware of a sense of "grace," Sanskrit, prasāda

paṭicca-samuppāda	dependent origination, causal co-production, a central teaching of the Buddha
paṭipattipūja	a reverential gift which is the following of moral principles
paṭivedha	an event of penetration into the highest, the dissolution of the mind's pollutants
pau	Sinhala: form of *pāpa,* bad, unwholesome deeds
perahera	a spectacular festival procession
pirit	Sinhala: for the Pali word *paritta,* with the basic meaning of "to protect," and refers to a long standing and widely occuring Theravāda Buddhist ritual
pirivena	for Sinhala classical form, *pirivēṇa,* a college of a monastery
prakrit	Sanskrit: a vernacular language with special reference to India
pūja	offering gifts with a reverential gesture, both externally in religious practice and internally
punabhāva	lit., "being" (*bhāva*) "again" (*puna*) the customary word for the English term "rebirth"
puñña	Sanskrit, *puṇya.* In Hindu usage refers primarily to practices in religious rituals to gain particular benefits. In Buddhist usage, refers to an enhancing quality of life arising from moral action, opposite of *pāpa,* what is bad
Ṛg Veda	Sanskrit: Rig Veda, ancient Hindu Sanskrit revealed scripture of poems honoring gods
rūpa	material form, as in the case of the body
saddhā	faith, interpreted in this volume as a quality of confidence expressed in the Buddha, Dhamma and the Saṅgha
sādhu	an utterance expressive of approval, akin to colloquial English "Yes!" in this sense
sakadāgāmi	one who will return to this human realm as far as rebirth is concerned
samādhi	lit., "bringing together," "heaping up," integrative concentration

samātha-bhāvanā	tranquility meditation, the form of meditaton leading to calm
sammāpaṭipadā	the correct path, the rightr path of moral living to overcome suffering
sammāsamādhi	right or proper concentration, one of the items of the eightfold path, compare *samatha-bhāvanā,* tranquility meditation
saṅkhāra	"formations," dynamic volitive, emotive contents of the mind, one of the most difficult terms in Buddhist teachings
saññā	the state at which the mind names, designates, that which is perceived
saññāvedayita-nirodha	refers to a fresh mind, when the mind is free of content arising from affective engagement with perceptions
saṃsāra	the whirl of repeated existence
sassatavāda	Eternalist teaching
sikkhā	religious learning, training in discipline involving also an inwardly enhanced life (*caraṇa*)
sīl	Sinhala: form of Pali *sīla*, precept
sīla	virtue, moral living, the orderly life, precept
sotāpanna	"stream entry," the first of the four paths
stūpa	Skt. a memorial mound containing the relics of the Buddha or a praiseworthy disciple, Pali *thūpa*
sugati	a favorable existence, usually considered a heavenly existence, one of a higher order than the human
sutta	a discourse in the Pali canon
Sutta Piṭaka	the portion of canonical scriptures containing discourses of the Buddha
taṅhā	"thirsting for," craving
tantrayāna	"the way of tantra," with reference to texts and ritual procedures consisting of spells and meditative descriptions of deities, used in rituals, representing a practice developed in India, moving to China, Tibet, and to some extent Japan

Tathāgata	an epithet of the Buddha, the one he most often used to refer to himself in the canonical texts, meaning "the one who has gone thus [who has attained that of which he has spoken]" and "the one who has come thus [who has come as former Buddhas have come]"
Theravāda	the school, teaching, position or way of the Elders, one of oldest and major Buddhist schools in the world today
ti-bodhi	"three realization," which refers to the realization of a perfectly enlightened one (*sammāsambodhi*), the realization of a private, solitary Buddha (*paccekabodhi*), and the realization of an Arahant, a perfected person (*arahattabodhi*). In Sri Lanka the more customary aspiration is to attain Nibbāna through becoming an Arahant, through *arahattabodhi*.
tilakkhaṇa	the three characteristics of the world, of all that can be perceived
tiratana	three gems, threefold gem, triple gem: the Buddha, Dhamma and Saṅgha
tisaraṇa	three refuges, threefold refuge, triple refuge: the Buddha, Dhamma and Saṅgha
triruvan saraṇayi	"may the refuge of the triple gem be on you," a Sinhala phrase very frequently used in Sri Lanka
ucchedavāda	anihilationist teaching, that death is the end and there is nothing more
udāna	a solemn utterance of an inspired thought, usually in metrical form
upādāna	grasping, clinging, "taking to oneself"
Upaniṣads	an important collection of scriptures in the Hindu tradition, reflection on issues of reality and containing the culmination of the Vedas
upasampadā	the second, higher ordination into the monastic order, the Saṅgha
uposatha	the day on which special religious activities are observed, Sinhala *poya*, based on the lunar calendar
vacī-kamma	verbal action, speaking

vedanā	feeling, the first reaction to a perceived impression
Vesak	Sinhala: the date on which the Buddha's birth, enlightenment, and final Nibbāna occurred, a special *poya* day widely celebrated in Sri Lanka
vijja	an awakened intelligence, awakened potentiality not based on previous knowledge, arising from an unobsructted mind
Vinaya	The portion of canonical scripture containing the rules and regulations for the monastic order, strictly monastic regulations
viññāna	consciousness, a general term for all that is mental
vipāka	effect, consequence of volitional action as in *kamma-vipāka*
vipassanā-bhāvanā	insight meditation, the form of meditation leading to insight-wisdom
Visuddhimagga	lit., "The Path of Purity," a monumental commentary of the Pali canon written in the 5th century in Sri Lanka by Buddhaghoa